Fair Cooperation

A New Paradigm for Cultural Diplomacy and Arts Management

P.I.E. Peter Lang

Bruxelles · Bern · Berlin · Frankfurt am Main · New York · Oxford · Wien

Annika HAMPEL

Fair Cooperation

A New Paradigm for Cultural Diplomacy and Arts Management

ENCATC Book Series
Cultural Management and Cultural Policy Education
Vol. 3

The European Commission support for the production of this publication does not constitute an endorsement of the contents which reflects the views only of the authors, and the Commission cannot be held responsible for any use which may be made of the information contained therein.

Translated from the German by Conor Heathcote.

Cover illustration: *"Overlapping communities" (vertical close-up)* (detail), © Nic McPhee, 8 janvier 2013, www.flickr.com.

This publication has been peer-reviewed.

1 avenue Maurice, B-1050 Bruxelles, Belgique
www.peterlang.com; brussels@peterlang.com

Printed in Germany

ISSN 2466-7137
ISBN 978-2-8076-0469-8
ePDF 978-2-8076-0470-4
ePUB 978-2-8076-0471-1
MOBI 978-2-8076-0472-8
DOI 10.3726/b11690
D/2017/5678/69

Information bibliographique publiée par « Die Deutsche Bibliothek »

« Die Deutsche Bibliothek » répertorie cette publication dans la « Deutsche National-bibliografie » ; les données bibliographiques détaillées sont disponibles sur le site <http://dnb.ddb.de>.

Find purpose, the means will follow.
Mahatma Gandhi

Table of Contents

Foreword by Professor Dr. Wolfgang Schneider

As a form of cultural expression for communities, the arts were international from the beginning. Paintings are shown in exhibitions all over the world, books are translated into many languages, and architecture is a global phenomenon. But what about cooperation between artists? What interests them in working together and how do they find common ground? What kind of frameworks do they need to work in? The Foreign Cultural Policy (FCP) of the Federal Republic of Germany is based on the exchange of artists: it encourages dialogue and enables cooperative production. The FCP, though, is in the first place an instrument of foreign policy, which permits us to ask the question: Which interests are behind its programs and projects? What does the FCP expect from artists and what do artists expect from the FCP? Theoretically, this all reads very impressively. The talk is of cooperation on equal terms, the equal rights of cultures, and the two-way nature of international relationships. But how are things in practice? How much cooperation is possible, how does one bring it onto an equal footing, and how sustainable is it?

Annika Hampel has taken as her object the study of the arts, cooperation, and cultural policy in order to find answers to the question of how cultural exchange can be successful, and which criteria need to be in place in order to make the processes of mutual understanding and cultural creation fruitful for both sides. In a long-term observation of projects at the Goethe Institutes of India, she investigated FCP support for cooperative cultural projects, interviewed participants in these projects, and formed her own impressions. Taking as her examples more or less successful works created together by German and Indian artists she asks critically: "Is the FCP intended to go out and persuade, or to receive and to listen? Are German interests alone directive, or are those of the partners also accounted for?" Working conditions and practices are placed under equal consideration as the required framework conditions for an international culture of cooperation. "Key to the conception of these cultural policy perspectives with regard to the practice of international intercultural cooperation are the experiences and insights of those who are cooperating." The author's empirical research is based on more than eighty interviews. Five case studies form the basis of her analysis and reflection. Annika Hampel understands her research on artistic cooperations as "a contribution to opening up their untapped potential use as part of a successful and effective foreign policy". It is her goal to close a gap in the field of current research and to consider the perspectives of the policy actors alongside those of the partner states in order to help implement the concrete aspirations of cultural policy in cultural practice.

Annika Hampel knows her area of work well, and has spent an extended period out in the field in various contexts. She is familiar with the FCP in practice, very well acquainted with the discourses of its operation, and has taken part in various ways in the theoretical debates surrounding it. She succeeds in capturing and strictly defining the terms of her subject for investigation. She makes use of the political and cultural sciences as well as sociology, and succeeds in concisely presenting elements that have a potential overarching significance. She refers, for example, to artistic cooperation as "a format of voluntary working together, with the goal of allowing something new to arise from the foundation of a common working process." She presents the characteristics of the FCP succinctly and intelligently, citing the relevant sources and allowing the most important scholars such as Lepenies, Kathe, and Schreiner, to present their case alongside decisive political figures such as Hamm-Brücher, Schwencke and Fischer. Selected texts, for example, from Lehmann, Lechner, and Mass, have also been used in order to allow the active agents of the FCP to relate their impressions. Annika Hampel's posture is clear from the beginning and she does not hold back, but contributes trenchantly to the discussion. The work of the Goethe-Institut is difficult to characterize – lying somewhere between representation and cultural exchange – but the heart of the author beats for the latter. She criticises self-promotion, cultural propaganda and export, demonstrating her position using the example of the "Year of Germany in India" (*Deutschlandjahre*, see Ch. 4.1) and advocating for the principles of the UNESCO Convention on Cultural Diversity. Here, cultural capital – following Bourdieu and Putnam – serves as a resource to be used for social inclusion and not – as is still the practice in cultural policy – to stabilize means of distinction. She posits "to reduce the focus on the cities and to democratize access to the arts, cultural activities must be decentralized and transported, for example, into the provinces of the country."

The author places great store in the contextualization of her research activities. Therefore, she dedicates herself to focusing on the cultural and cultural policy specificities of India. From her participation-based observations, she filters expert knowledge that could be of significance with regard to partnership-based cooperations. Her thoughts on the conditions necessary for the success of artistic cooperations go far beyond the relationship between rich and poor, and explore the distinction between rural and urban, as well as a range of other conditions, which vary, between the partners – such as the local level of support for the arts, professionalism, and cultural infrastructure. Even here, the difficulty of formulating a single cultural policy in a country with a five thousand year old culture, and a diverse plurality of ethnicities, religions, and languages, becomes apparent. This leads "to the question of which cultural policy, according to which theoretical framework, can and must be implemented practically, especially in light of the challenges facing the country in the form of an explosive population increase, environmental destruction, and violence – particularly against women and children".

The agenda of the Federal Foreign Office for German-Indian partnerships in the 21st Century speaks of a consensus that cultural cooperation should enable mutual understanding and assist in deepening the knowledge of both parties. Therefore, Germany has invested in bilateral relations from their side: supporting the Goethe-Institut at six locations and in four Goethe-Centre projects – enabling artists from Germany and India to work together. From her questions and observations, Annika Hampel produces some sobering findings. She observes a disparity between the political claims and their practical realisation – demonstrating on the basis of five observed cooperations what is actually required to build successful partnerships in the arts collaboratively. Her choice of projects is justifiable; their diversity offers insights across the spectrum of artistic practice. In essence, the statements she makes are based on the interviews with the participants. Almost 2000 sections of text were coded and categorized for their content with the help of a computer program. This made it possible to differentiate statements on individual aspects of cultural cooperation, weigh, and compile them. This gives rise to thirteen criteria: the development of the partnership, the basic conditions of the cooperation, contextual knowledge, intercultural competence, common language, the external guidance of the cooperation, context-oriented transfer, reciprocity in hosting the cooperation, the orientation of the process, the failures of the experiments, the continuity of the cooperations, the exchange of experience and, finally, "Fair Cooperation" – turning away from the hierarchisation of the partners, and pleading for a continuing debate on equality in terms of goals and support. She acknowledges that a relationship on equal terms between the partners is an ideal realised in only a few cases. Putting idealistic notions aside, Annika Hampel speaks of the "ambivalent relations" in cooperations between the 'Global North' and the 'Global South', and invokes the notion of fairness and fair play: an attitude she defines as being that of the greatest possible respect for one's partner.

"There is the central question of whether the donors can and will give up the role which has legitimized their existence until now. For them, it would mean changing, and placing their own powerful and controlling position and function into question." The thesis ends with a radical proposal for the restructuring of the current relationships within so-called partnership-based cooperations, which have been shown to be no longer defensible. The 'student-teacher' relationship should be repudiated, for example, through the equal division of art and management, including control of the budget. A diagram strikingly delineates an ideal model for the cooperation process with an impressively transparent approach. "The discourse on global cooperation, while acknowledging, respecting, and promoting cultural diversity, presents potential courses of action which would allow the exploitation of the underused potential of artistic cooperation." Annika Hampel is concerned with securing quality and sustainability. She makes it clear that the Goethe-Institut in India is, with its contemporary positioning, on the right way to fulfill the role of mentor for which she advocates, by enabling rich bilateral personal experiences and therefore making a valuable contribution to the further development of the discourse.

Annika Hampel achieves a resounding success and does the FCP a great service. Her insights will find their way into the socio-political debates of domestic cultural policy. Her scholarly approach is excellent and, in confining herself to essentials, she displays her competence. She knows how to use her knowledge: Her literature and sources are state of the art. Her formulations are accessible, her examples cleverly chosen and her evaluation precise. She acts deftly to position her large body of material – developing criteria and concrete recommended courses of action for cultural policy. "Partnership-based cooperation" in the FCP is now a defined term of cultural science. Although not all of the findings can be directly transferred without modification, there are now parameters which problematize the topic, and which can influence practice, and recast the artistic processes of international exchange. It is made clear that artists ought to maintain their decisive position in project management. Indeed, a consequence of the demands which cultural policy places upon them is that we must now begin to understand the artist as a 'cultural policy maker'.

Professor Dr. Wolfgang Schneider, 2014

Director of the Department of Cultural Policy at the University of Hildesheim

UNESCO-Chair in Cultural Policy for the Arts in Development

Acknowledgements

This research and the English translation of *Fair Cooperation* would not have been published without the support of a large number of organisations and individuals. I would like to take this opportunity to thank some of them.

In the first place, my thanks go to the interview partners in Germany and India who patiently answered my questions. Their trust and openness allowed me a comprehensive insight into their cooperations, and their great interest in my research opened many doors.

My heartfelt thanks go to my doctoral supervisor, Professor Dr. Wolfgang Schneider from the Department of Cultural Policy at the University of Hildesheim. His critical feedback and his encouragement were always equally a support and an impulse for improvement, and that support has continued even after the completion of my doctorate.

I would also like to sincerely thank the staff of the Goethe Institutes in New Delhi, Bangalore, and Mumbai – in particular Heiko Sievers, Christoph Bertrams, Robin Mallick, Maureen Gonsalves, Farah Batool and Sigrid Mund. They were always open to my questions and placed their own network at my disposal for the purposes of this study. The institute also partly funded my travel and accommodation within India, and the Goethe-Institut in New Delhi provided financial support for the translation of my research.

My thanks go to the European Network of Cultural Administration Training Center (ENCATC) – in particular the President Annick Schramme, and the Secretary general Giannalia Cogliandro Beyens – for their financial support for the English translation and publication of "Fair Cooperation".

My thanks also go to the German Academic Exchange Service (DAAD – *Deutscher Akademischer Austauschdienst*) who provided financial support for my second research trip to India.

Last but not least, I would like to expressly thank the translator of this publication, Conor Heathcote. Your humorous outlook on life, dear Conor, and your reassuring words kept me believing in our shared project.

Dr. Annika Hampel
Karlsruhe, June 2017

Note on the Text and Translation

The English version of *Fair Cooperation* is an abridged version of the German original. Many of the sources which Dr. Hampel is dealing with here are at present only available in German. While every effort has been made to use the official English versions of texts, names, and sources as far as they exist, original translations of their content have often had to be resorted to. The overwhelming majority of the quotations which appear in this document have been translated from the German along with the remainder of Dr. Hampel's text, where the original source material can be found.

Notations by the author have been added to some quotations in square brackets, and marked as such where necessary. The Annex to this dissertation is a separate document which has not been published for reasons of data protection. It can be requested from the author by interested parties by contacting: Annika.Hampel@gmail.com.

The views expressed throughout this book are not necessarily those of the translator.

Conor Heathcote

Cologne, June 2017

List of Abbreviations

AKP	Auswärtige Kulturpolitik der Bundesrepublik Deutschland (see FCP)
ATSA	ARThinkSouthAsia
Attakkalari	Attakkalari Centre for Movement Arts in Bangalore
CSCS	Centre for the Study of Culture and Society in Bangalore
CSR	Corporate Social Responsibility
DAAD	Deutscher Akademischer Austauschdienst (German Academic Exchange Service) in Bonn
DIG	Deutsch-Indische Gesellschaft e. V.
FCP	German Foreign Cultural (and Educational) Policy – i.e. the AKP
HKW	Haus der Kulturen der Welt in Berlin
I_	Interview partner
ICCR	Indian Council for Cultural Relations in New Delhi
IFAB	India Foundation for the Arts in Bangalore
ifa	Institut für Auslandsbeziehungen (Institute for Foreign Cultural Relations) in Stuttgart
Ig3D	India goes 3D
KHOJ	KHOJ International Artists' Association in New Delhi
KSB	Kulturstiftung des Bundes (Federal Cultural Foundation) in Halle (Saale)
MMB	Max Mueller Bhavan (the Goethe-Institut in India)
NSD	National School of Drama in New Delhi
PPP	Public Private Partnership
RAQS	RAQS Media Collective in New Delhi
Rs.	Indian rupees
ZCC	Zone Cultural Centre(s)

Art, Cooperation, Cultural Policy

An Introduction

> This is the time for groups and collectives to work together to pool their ideas and resources, share experiences, and build networks thus making every rupee work harder and longer for them. (Ghosh, 2013: n.p.)[1]

Globalisation increases the "complexity of social challenges" in a diverse and fragmented world (Holzberg, 2009: 41). To respond to global questions[2] there must be, in the opinion of contemporary scholars and politicians, an international cooperation towards collective processes of understanding and cultural creation, which takes a variety of perspectives into account (cf. e.g. Kettner, 2009: 241 f., German Federal Foreign Office, 2000: 4 f.). Indeed, such fundamental principles as the participation of previously uninvolved actors – above all those from civil society – in decision-making processes, as well as cross-cultural communication and cooperation in all areas have been declared indispensable across the scholarly literature (cf. Heinrichs/Kuhn/Newig, 2011, Sennett, 2012). In this sense, the growth of diversity can be seen as an opportunity: it demands and supports the intensification of cooperative and network-based activity, processes of exchange, dialogue, and development (cf. Deutsche UNESCO-Kommission e. V., 2005, Trunk, 2011: 9). At the same time, there are risks associated with the need for multinational cooperation. In the face of social and cultural differences, globalisation can also be felt to constitute "a threat to the individual identity" (Trunk, 2011: 8). This can lead to a reach for regional traditions, inherited cultural forms, and national values in order to better strengthen and give expression to cultural identities, eventually to the extent of countenancing conflict (cf. Bertelsmann Foundation 2006b: 2).[3]

In summary, the networks and interdependencies created between people around the world by globalisation are becoming more numerous, more intense, denser, and more complex (cf. Körber, 2006: 81, Meyns,

---

1 n.p. = no page.

2 For example, the financial and economic crises, environmental and climatic change, security policy, resource scarcity, and poverty.

3 On the opportunities and dangers of globalisation see Hoffmann (1996b: 275-284) and Kettner (2009: 241 ff.).

2010b: 48). However, the realities of life for the newly interconnected actors, including their individual cultural identities, interests, and life goals are highly diverse (cf. Kakar, 2006: 123). Globalisation is, therefore, a "new field of tension in international encounters" (Surana, 2009: 193). This tension is at the same time its source of potential. The reality will be assessed and interpreted by various actors. The challenge is, and will be, to acknowledge these varying interpretations, and to respect their contradictions. To this end, the German globalisation critic Harald Schumann wrote on the website of the Goethe-Institut of China in May 2011:

> Trapped in the struggle for their respective national majorities and/or interests, they fail to extend global cooperation to the lengths required [...]. With the growth of inequality, it will become ever more difficult to mobilise a political majority for the necessary reforms. If the current trends prevail, then globalisation will once again – as it already was once before, a hundred years ago – be shattered by its own contradictions and turn back on itself. Either humanity finds the way to global cooperation or the world will sink into decades of violent conflict which, in the long run, no state, and no nation, will be able to escape.[4]

1.1 Subject, Questions, and Objectives of the Study

In the process of globalisation, culture is often considered to be *per se* "a unifying, mediating, and supporting element". Its concern is with "entering in dialogue with one another, encountering, and getting to know one another on the same level in order to overcome prejudice, in a meeting which takes place on a peaceful basis, and as independently as possible of political dogma" (Goethe-Institut e. V., 2012d: 4)[5]. Culture is valued as the "foundation for stable international relationships" between Germany and its worldwide partners (German Bundestag, 2011: 4, cf. also Hamm-Brücher, 1980: 20). Pursuant to this aim, it is relied upon, or, as the Centre for Global Cooperation Research puts it, "reasonably expected to bring people together and to arrange for joint projects".[6]

Responding to the challenges posed by the worldwide networking of economic, social, cultural, and political activities, is supposed to be part of

4 Quoted from http://tinyurl.com/n2ahfa7 (Accessed: 28.12.2013). Cf. also Lee (2010: 6).

5 Cf. also Schreiner (2011: 27, 74 ff., 82 f., 124).

6 Quoted from http://tinyurl.com/qjdtvpl (Accessed: 19.10.2013). Cf. also I_73: 30 (I_number: number = Interviewpartner_Number of the interview: Number of the row of the transcribed interview). The Centre for Global Cooperation Research in Essen is a part of the Käte Hamburger-Kolleg *Politische Kulturen der Weltgesellschaft*, see the website of the institution at: http://www.gcr21.org (Accessed: 02.01.2014).

the responsibility of Germany's Foreign Cultural Policy (FCP),[7] amongst other initiatives. It is ascribed a central role in two respects:

On the one hand, culture is considered, alongside the social, political, ecological and economic dimensions, as a "precondition" – that is to say as a context, "field of intervention" (Gad, 2010: 96) and "motor" (Steinkamp, 2010: 14 f.) – of individual and social development processes (cf. UNESCO, 2005: Article 13, UNESCO, 1982: n.p.):[8]

> Art and culture give new perspectives and stimulate social processes; they influence human development significantly and encourage peaceful coexistence. (Lehmann in: Goethe-Institut e. V., 2012d: 4)

On the other hand, relationships within the FCP are described as a "cooperative partnership" and a "dialogue of equals", referring to relations between two or more "equal partners" (Goethe-Institut e. V., 1998: 206):

> We meet here in the expectation that an intercultural dialogue at eye level, particularly in the field of culture, is a learning, thinking and productive process from which both sides can draw benefit.[9]

This claim from a cultural mediator is surprising. What the FCP is and seeks to accomplish has wavered between different positions and goals for decades. Is it a cultural export designed to present a positive image of Germany to strengthen national economic and political interests and secure its power (cf. Schreiner, 2011: 273, Michels, 2001: 15), or is it the "two-way-street" of cultural exchange (AA,[10] 2003: 6) imagined by Joschka Fischer – German Foreign Minister from 1998 to 2005? To pose the question differently, is the FCP intended to go out and persuade, or to receive and to listen? Are German interests alone directive, or are those of the partners also accounted for? (cf. Ch. 2.2)

Cultural policy makers, as well as those working in the cultural institutions and federal ministries responsible for cultural relations automatically assert – without legitimacy or reflection – that the FCP represents a realisation of the ideals of a "dialogue of equals" and "cooperative partnership" (Lehmann, 2008a und 2008b, German Culture

---

7 For "Foreign Cultural Policy" read "Foreign Cultural and Education Policy". The FCP includes education policy through the promotion of cultural education. German: Auswärtige Kulturpolitik (AKP).

8 For a detailed description of the sphere of culture for development see Gad (2012b: 13 ff.) and Gould/Marsh (2004: 15). For the field of policy and practice of/for culture for development consult Ch. 2.2 and 3.2 of this study.

9 Quoted from http://tinyurl.com/qadnpsn (Accessed: 27.12.2013).

10 AA: '*Auswärtiges Amt*' – the German Federal Foreign Office.

Council,[11] 2012).[12] This claim is even more surprising, as the principle of "cooperative dialogue" is a difficult one to implement – a phenomenon the American sociologist Richard Sennett details scientifically in his monograph "Together: The Rituals, Pleasures, and Politics of Cooperation" (Sennett, 2012: 127, cf. also Ch. 2.1). Martin Kämpchen, an expert on German-Indian cultural relationships,[13] asks: "These are well-intentioned and indeed necessary terms, but are they realistic?" (Kämpchen, 2013a: 67) To answer this question, the premises, processes, and structures with which partnerships in the arts on an international level are realised must be known. However, the directly involved cultural practitioners[14] who implement international cooperation in artistic production and cultural mediation have at no point up to the present been, invited to, consulted, or involved in this cultural policy discourse.

It was conspicuous at the 57th Loccum Cultural Policy Colloquium[15] that although artistic cooperation was discussed by representatives from the cultural policy branch, the range of actors who actually implement the various forms of international artistic cooperation were unrepresented, as a survey undertaken by the conference leader Albert Drews revealed. At the tenth working consultation of the Federal Coalition for Cultural Diversity[16] by UNESCO on the 10th and 11th of May 2012 in Hildesheim, the participating guests explicitly stressed their lack of knowledge of the activities of the participants in the 'North/South' dialogue.[17] The aim, therefore, must be to explore the work conditions and practices of partnerships in the arts with the involvement of the artists and cultural intermediaries who are to finally realise and implement the

11 'Deutscher Kulturrat e. V.'

12 See also the website of the German Bundestag at: http://tinyurl.com/oug2kox (Accessed: 13.01.2014).

13 The website of Mr. Kämpchen can be found at: http://www.martin-kaempchen.com/ (Accessed: 07.07.2013).

14 Cultural practitioners are people who produce art, as well as persons who moderate, meditate and organise cultural and artistic production (cf. Zembylas, 2004: 272).

15 'Loccumer Kulturpolitisches Kolloquium'. The Evangelical Academy of Loccum established the Loccum Cultural Policy Colloquium in the 1970s and since then takes a considerable part in the broad social discourse on cultural policy in Germany (cf. Schwencke *et al.*, 2009: 135 f.). Their website can be found at: http://www.loccum.de/ (Accessed: 14.11.2013).

16 'Bundesweite Koalition für Kulturelle Vielfalt'.

17 UNESCO is the organisation of the United Nations for education, science, culture and communication. The organisation describes its role thus: "UNESCO's mission is to contribute to the building of a culture of peace, the eradication of poverty, sustainable development and intercultural dialogue through education, the sciences, culture, communication and information." (Quoted from http://tinyurl.com/mno4w92, Accessed: 13.01.2013).

goals and requirements of the FCP. The perspective of the stakeholders is indispensable. Without them, the FCP lacks any foundation. For this reason, "a conversation with the protagonists, and a dialogue with cultural creators in order to intensify [...] a cultural policy of the artists, is something to aspire towards" (Schneider, 2013c: 13 f.).

It is not until the reality has been grasped that it will be possible to set out the framework conditions for a realistic and achievable culture of international cooperation in the arts. The FCP, therefore, with its conceptual claim to apply the principles of cooperative partnership and undertake a dialogue of equals in its present delivery of policy, needs to be examined (cf. Schneider, 2012: 36 and Ch. 5).[18]

With regard to the objectives of this research paper, it is against this background that the following questions are posed to lead the investigation:

- How are the FCP's cooperative artistic projects currently realised?
- Upon which structures and processes are these cooperations based? What are the privileges, roles, and understandings that arise from these?
- What challenges exist in shaping international cooperation in the arts?
- Can the current state of global artistic cooperation be said to consist of partnerships and a dialogue of equals?
- Which framework conditions in terms of cultural policy are necessary in order to enable the realisation of genuinely cooperative partnerships in the future?

These questions are addressed in particular to the artistic cooperations between the 'Global North' and the 'Global South', which have been broadly supported since the beginning of the 21st Century. That is to say, respectively between the industrialised nations which are principally located in the northern hemisphere, and 'Developing Countries', or 'Emerging Markets', which are generally found in the southern.[19] The

---

18 In general, the international discourse offers a clearly idealistic claim which is in contrast to a far more modest reality. See also Kathe (2005: 30 f., 369, 441 f.). He describes the mismatch between the claims and reality of the FCP as "discrepancy theory".

19 Rather than 'Developing Country', 'Third World' or similar terms, 'Global North' and 'Global South' are employed in this study as neutral designations. The terms, are not precise, however, and are therefore marked accordingly. The 'Global North' comprises, for example, not the entire geographical North, but rather only the rich and industrialised areas. The 'Global South', on the other hand, designates the ca. 150 'Developing Countries'. Characteristic of countries of the 'Global South' are limited industrial development, debt, a high level of inequality and poverty, lower educational

research here refers as an example, to the German-Indian relationship[20] of on-going cooperation between actors in the arts.

As a step towards cooperative partnerships in the future, the perspectives of both the German and Indian partners have been included. Country-specific factors will be illustratively presented and taken into account in the course of the research paper. The recorded observations and recommendations are to apply within this specific and concrete paradigm.

The goal of this research, however, is to make the German-Indian experiences and insights useful as an example of the more general configuration of artistic cooperation between the – very different – partners of the 'Global North' and the 'Global South'. This first requires a correcting balance for the existing cultural-political characteristics and framework conditions of the partner countries concerned – e.g. with further research (cf. Ch. 7) – and a context-oriented transfer of these insights onto other 'North'-'South' cooperations (cf. Ch. 6.7, 7). Such a transfer appears to be possible on three grounds. Firstly, this study incorporates the experiences of German experts who have not cooperated exclusively with Indian partners, but also with actors, for example, from France, Great Britain, Italy, Iran, Venezuela, Côte d'Ivoire, etc., who report similarly about their joint work. The author spent a total of five months in 2007 accompanying cooperations between German and Ghanaian, as well as German and Bolivian artists, in addition to the German-Indian cooperations. Moreover, since 2012, she has taken part in debates on artistic cooperation along with actors from Europe, Asia and Africa. Within the limits described above, parallels and correlations are apparent in the structures and processes of cooperation, as well as the associated challenges. This is the case particularly with regard to partnerships with formerly colonized regions.

The goal of this qualitative study is to develop criteria for the future realisation of international partnerships of equals in intercultural artistic exchanges. Key to the conception of these cultural policy options with regard to the practice of international intercultural cooperation are the experiences and insights of those who are cooperating. Interviews with those involved in cooperations will give an understanding of how current cooperations are configured. This inventory and critical analysis of the current practice of cooperative partnerships in the FCP will be carried out through the presentation of five selected case studies. These serve

---

attainment and life expectancy, as well as an experience of colonisation, etc. (cf. http://tinyurl.com/ngsxdem, Accessed: 31.12.2013).

20 With regard to fairness and equality, the terms should be used equally. This is, however, irritating. With Indian interlocutors, however, the term 'Indo-German collaboration' was used consistently.

as comparisons of the differing conceptions and implementations of cooperation work taking place under various conditions.

This research project seeks to deepen our understanding of the possible actions and effects of "a cultural dialogue, afflicted with great expectations" (Maaß, 2009: 148). The research presented here interests itself with what has been regarded since the 1980s as the thorny question at the heart of the FCP, the relevance of which remains undiminished until today – 35 years later:

> What must ideal cultural relationships look like and how could they be realised? This remains, like any thorny question, unanswered, and left as the target of the endeavours of those responsible […]. It is the creative task that is demanded […] in the sphere of cultural relations […] of our generation and those to come. (Hamm-Brücher, 1980: 16)

1.2 The Research as it Stands

The present research paper aligns itself with the body of application-oriented cultural policy research in international comparison at the Department of Cultural Policy of the University of Hildesheim.[21] The object of this study are the "tasks and objectives" of cultural policy, as well as its "means and possibilities"[22] (Schneider, 2008a: 7). Studies of cultural policy seek, therefore, "to grasp and to describe the strategies of action and justification of the responsible cultural managers and politicians" (Fuchs, 2008: 89) and to integrate these strategies into the theory of the discipline (cf. Bauer, 2010: 2). The research in cultural policy at the Department of Cultural Policy at the University of Hildesheim seeks, in particular, to close the gap between the concrete requirements of cultural policy and their implementation in cultural practice. This is especially relevant with regard to the cooperations in cultural policy between partners from the 'Global North' and the 'Global South'.

This dissertation, while being located in the applied cultural sciences, and concerned with the FCP, follows an interdisciplinary approach "in response to the growing awareness of the multifaceted character of scientific problems" (Nünning, 2004: 294). A single scientific approach would be unable to deal with the practical nature of the research project. From this closeness of practice naturally follows the exchange and transferability of the findings and theories gained.

---

21 'Institut für Kulturpolitik der Universität Hildesheim'.

22 For example, in the forms of cultural policy frameworks, cultural management and cultural administration.

The basis of this investigation is formed by comprehensive literary research, primarily in the libraries of the Institute for Foreign Cultural Relations (*ifa*)[23] in Stuttgart on German-Indian cultural relations, and at the University of Cologne on the German FCP. The anthologies of Wolfgang Schneider (2008a) und Kurt-Jürgen Maaß (2009a) were used in order to grasp developments and tendencies, tasks, structures, institutions and actors in the German FCP.[24] The documents of the 57th Loccum Cultural Policy Colloquium, entitled "Foreign Cultural Policy: Current Challenges in a Changing World"[25] is another insightful source (cf. Drews, 2012).

Research on cultural policy remains small in scale despite the national and international discourses and debates on cultural policy since the 1970s (cf. Ch. 2.2), perhaps, as according to Höpel (2007: 15 f.), because the cultural science approach was dominant. Succinctly summarised, the current state of research on the FCP, with regard to its manifest lacunae can be described thus: In the main, it lacks an empirically founded and theoretically grounded analysis of the practice of cultural policy, such as, for example, with regard to its instruments or actors (cf. Bauer, 2009a: 127-148, Maaß, 2009a: 21, Maaß, 2009b: 32):

> Cultural studies research accompanying the practice of cultural policy opens manifold possibilities, but it so far lacks decisive theories, convincing designs to produce research, and the necessary 'gate opener' of research policy. In particular, considering the social and political expectations placed on politically sponsored cultural exchange, it would be desirable if empirical theories of action were to encourage this field to change for its own benefit. The interconnected theoretical, methodical and methodological points through which diverse processes of cultural mediation are viewed within the 'intercultural' disciplines and research contexts, offer generous perspectives for further research around German and international Foreign Cultural and Education Policy. (Bauer, 2010: 184, cf. also Schreiner, 2011: 26)

Further, there is a lack of research work to expose the underlying mechanisms of action comprehensibly. Furthermore, studies that focus on the FCP from a perspective other than the German have so far been rare, and the perspectives of the partner country or countries are poorly represented. Finally, there are also few comparative national studies reporting on the status quo of the various FCPs of countries in Asia, Africa,

---

23 'Institut für Auslandsbeziehungen'.

24 For a detailed documentation of the existing research literature on the German FCP, cf. Bauer (2010: 26-58).

25 Original German title: 'Außenkulturpolitik. Aktuelle Herausforderungen in einer Welt im Umbruch'.

and Latin America while the international comparison of the cultural policies of individual states is primarily limited to Western countries.[26]

This lacuna in the research must be gradually eliminated in the future in order to produce a legitimation of the FCP. In doing so, obtaining independent researchers would be an important goal. While the writers of the existing research literature are themselves involved in the practical implementation of the FCP, the achievement of an approximately objective or neutral stance acceptable to scholarship seems doubtful. The challenge of making a comprehensive study of the FCP is also a result of the wide and varied fields which it offers for research – those of the policy and practice of the FCP, with their many and varied themes, and their large number of actors (cf. Bauer, 2010: 6 f., 14, 58, 104).

This research work makes use of the aforementioned gaps in research on the FCP, in that it is based on an empirically founded investigation focused on India, taking into account its essential internal and external cultural policy features. The Indian actors in the cooperations are able to have their say on an equal footing with their German partners, and this paper seeks to develop a theory for the practice of international cooperation in the arts from both of these perspectives. It is a further tile in the mosaic of academic study of the initiatives, concepts, processes and structures of the FCP.

Research on cooperation is a young topic and field of research. Analysis of publications and scientific literature has shown that research into cooperation so far has taken place primarily in the areas of economics and business administration (cf. Zentes/Swoboda/Morschett, 2005: 8 f.),[27] especially within management and organisational theory. These investigations are highly heterogeneous by virtue of their varying contexts, methods of analysis, sources, and presentation of their results (cf. Holzberg, 2009: 14 ff.). "In addition to work devoted to foundation and development, there are a multitude of investigations into the successful conception and leadership of cooperations." (*ibid.*, 14) Accordingly, the focus of research is on the cooperation process. However, synthetic analysis of the effects of cooperation work, the implications of its environment, as well as the perceptions and attitudes of the actors involved, along with

---

26 For more detail about the state of research on the FCP described here see Düwell (2009: 61), Bauer (2009b: 423 ff.), *id.* (2010: 7 ff.), Roßkopf (2010: 25, 104 f.).

27 Zentes/Swoboda/Morschett (2005) have investigated both German and international journal publications from the period 1993-2005 for the frequency with which the theoretical basis, institutional form, success factors and value added in cooperations are analysed. For cooperation research in the field of business administration and public economy see, for example, Schuh/Friedli/Kurr (2005), Brauer (2010: 57-76), Rautenstrauch *et al.* (2003).

their relations with one another, is becoming increasingly common. All of these factors influence cooperation work significantly.[28]

Claus Leggewie, Leader of the Centre for Global Cooperation Research, noted in the workshop "Examples of Successful Cooperations (1) – Artistic Practice and Improvisation",[29] 21st-25th August 2012 at the *Ruhrtriennale* 2012-14, that scientific research on the foundation and development, design and leadership of cooperations in artistic and cultural practice are not available. He remarked that although cooperations determine artistic production and consumption to a certain extent, their realities, in particular their objectives and modes of operation remain unknown. His interdisciplinary research centre has therefore made it its task to analyse the possibilities of global cooperation by examining joint work in the subsystems of society such as politics, economics, and culture.

The philosopher, cultural, literary, and theatre scholar Kai van Eikels also spoke at the above event on the desire amongst organisational theorists to make the potential of cooperations in the performing arts useful in the field of commercial cooperations. Cooperations in the performing arts are already widely viewed in both politics and business as examples of best practice for interdisciplinary and international partnerships. This is because the product of this type of cooperation – the performance – is neither separable from the process of cooperation itself, nor reducible to its constituent parts, but depends on the contribution of all of the collaborators. In artistic cooperations, it is the process, and the group, which stands in the foreground, not the product or the individual performance (cf. Ch. 6.9). The agents of these cooperations in the arts, however, do not seem to be aware of their function as a role model, or the potential ascribed to their work:

> The dimension of artistic cooperation has been barely explored, since the possibilities of this type of project are at the moment underestimated by those responsible – who take neither the time nor the money to support cooperation projects between artists sustainably. Even if, in the meantime, deliberate efforts were made from the German side to enter into international cooperations, this dimension would still be little regarded. (Ittstein, 2009: 134)

---

28 Alongside cooperation research, there exists the systematic analysis of networks, which has established itself in recent years, beginning in the field of sociology (cf. Fangerau/Halling, 2009: 7, Hollstein/Straus, 2006). Its aim is the description of all of the actors involved in a thematic network, along with their relationships. All of the relevant relationships in this area are described and the relations of the actors with one another are categorised. The goal of this research paper however, is nevertheless, the exploration and investigation of selected cooperations (cf. Ch. 1.1).

29 Original German title: 'Beispiele gelingender Kooperation (1) – Künstlerische Praxis und Improvisation'.

This précis from Daniel Jan Ittstein, in his dissertation – completed in 2009 at the University of Passau – "Music as a Strategic Instrument of Foreign Cultural and Educational Policy"[30] – makes it clear that the current promotion and organisation of artistic cooperations is far from making the most of their potential and their usefulness. One reason for this is the above-mentioned non-existence of research into artistic cooperations within the FCP. The investigation of artistic cooperations is therefore a fundamental subject for research, and would be a contribution to opening up the untapped potential of these partnerships as part of a successful and effective foreign policy. It is even more necessary in light of the socio-political participation required in a globalized world, which demands in turn the intensification and growth of cooperative work (cf. Commission on Global Governance, 1995: 336 and Ch. 1).

The subject of this dissertation builds on the discussions of certain conferences that have taken place from 2012 onwards, which were directly or indirectly concerned with artistic cooperation. These included, for example, *Radius of Art: Creative Politicisation of the Public Space / Cultural Potential for Social Transformation*[31] – a conference held during February 2012 in Berlin by the Heinrich-Böll foundation, which showed the multitude and multiplicity of international cultural cooperations in the fields of culture and society, and which gave the first impulse for a global network of cultural cooperations.[32] The 57th *Loccum Cultural Policy Colloquium* debated artistic cooperation, in a workshop of the same name, which hosted cultural policy makers and cultural agents from around the world (cf. Hampel, 2012: 97-106). At the *2013 Theaterformen*[33] festival in Hannover, festival scholars from Europe, Asia and Africa spoke about their partnerships, in a colloquium on "Sense and Nonsense in International Cultural Cooperations".[34]

In addition, the author was acquainted with three documentary films on cooperation projects in the arts between partners from the 'Global North' and the 'Global South.[35] In 2007, the Goethe-Institut Portugal brought

---

30 (German title: Musik als strategisches Instrument Auswärtiger Kultur- und Bildungspolitik). Ittstein investigated cultural mediation in German-Indian partnerships, taking as his subject the German-Indian Festspiele of 1990. In doing so, he answered the question: What is the potential of music as a strategic instrument of the FCP in building German-Indian relations? (cf. http://tinyurl.com/l9bz9jt, Accessed: 02.01.2014)

31 'radius of art: Kreative Politisierung des öffentlichen Raums/Kulturelle Potentiale für soziale Transformation'.

32 Cf. http://tinyurl.com/k5td3yd (Accessed: 30.08.2012).

33 See http://tinyurl.com/m39x5hs (Accessed: 03.12.2013).

34 'Sinn und Unsinn internationaler Kulturkooperationen'.

35 Copies of all the documentaries are archived with the author.

to life a trilateral music project with the name *Lisboa-Maputo-Berlin*. The idea of the project was to find out if art migrated along with the artists who produce it: how the art of their places of origin enters into dialogue with that of the countries in which they perform. For this purpose, musicians living in Lisbon and originating from Portugal, Mozambique and Guinea-Bissau were invited to work together with Céline Rudolph – a singer and music professor from Berlin – in order to develop a program together incorporating the various musical styles of the artists. This process, as well as the following concert tour from Lisbon via Maputo, and Johannesburg to Berlin, was the principal subject of the documentary.[36]

In his documentary *Namibia Crossings – Spirits & Limits*, Peter Liechti describes how twelve musicians from Namibia, Zimbabwe, Russia and Switzerland "connect [...] their musical cultures" and "encounter [...] other music groups on their journey through Namibia".[37] "The journey [...] proves itself to be an experience of both artistic and human extremes for the Swiss initiators and all the participants."[38] It continues:

> The film [...] is actually a highly informative record of a failure. It reveals in an almost exemplary manner the naïveté of attempting to artificially create synergies. The badly healed past of Namibia is too complex – still bearing the scars of German colonialism; the practices of the local musicians are too different, its separation is too wide from [...] contemporary music, while the motives of the participants for the advancement of their own careers are too narcissistic.[39]

The third documentary on the German-Indian theatre partnership *Do I know U*? from the Theatre for Young Audience *Schnawwl*[40] (National Theatre Mannheim) and the Indian theatre *Ranga Shankara* in Bangalore, bearing the title *The seven voyages of Schnawwl & Ranga Shankara*, also finds a place in the presentation of the results of this investigation.

While the first documentary film from the Goethe-Institut uncritically depicts the cooperation between artists from countries of the 'Global South' – which were often the subject of colonisation – and the 'Global North', Peter Liechti's documentary is often more reminiscent of a feature film. The third film alone clearly shows the misunderstandings, conflicts and struggles of the participants with one another, which result from

36 For a detailed description of the project, see Grätz (2012b: 219-233) and the website of the Goethe-Institut at http://tinyurl.com/o3mjrc9 and http://tinyurl.com/opxdlkd (Both accessed: 31.12.2013).

37 Quoted from http://tinyurl.com/nb48am6 (Accessed: 31.12.2013).

38 Quoted from http://tinyurl.com/nvfbzc6 (Accessed: 31.12.2013).

39 *Ibid.*

40 'Kinder- und Jugendtheater Schnawwl in Mannheim'.

their linguistic, cultural and artistic differences, as well as the varying objectives with which they justify and establish their projects. Because of this complexity, documentary films dealing with cooperation work which seriously tackle and consider the challenges of international, and therefore intercultural, cooperation are rare.

1.3 The Structure of the Study

To begin with, in Chapter 2, the essential terms used by this research paper on artistic cooperation will be defined and placed in relation to one another. Cooperation as a form of participation will be coupled to the theory of social capital (cf. Ch. 2.3). In addition, the concepts and agendas that guide the German FCP with regard to international cooperations in the arts will be investigated. In this context, the role of the Goethe-Institut as a 'key actor' in German-Indian relations through the FCP will be identified and described.[41] Chapter 2 will serve as the theoretical basis of the following research.

Geographical, social, political and cultural environments exert an influence on cooperations in the arts. Chapter 3, therefore, is devoted in detail to localising the research topic in India, paying particular attention to an analysis of the country's 'cultural policy'. This chapter, as well as the one concerned with the Goethe-Institut in India, already contains results from original research.

Chapter 4 provides a short historical overview of German-Indian partnerships, with a focus on the arts, beginning with the cultural agreement between the countries in 1969, and leading up to the *Year of Germany in India*[42] from 2011 to 2013. It introduces the primary subject of the investigation – current cooperations between Germany and India in the arts.

The Year of Germany in India is the context for the majority of the cooperation projects between German and Indian actors explored in this work. The investigation of this foreign policy concept was described by

41 The definition of 'key actor': "key actors practice […] a substantial influence on the participation of other actors, they structure the participation in a space of tension between inclusion and exclusion. In general these key actors tend to be strongly networked, i.e. they have at their disposal a multiplicity of institutionally regulated and informal relationships to other actors." (German Federal Enterprise for International Cooperation [Deutsche Gesellschaft für Technische Zusammenarbeit], 2006: 12) Key functions of key actors are providing legitimacy and resources as well as building networks (cf. *ibid.*).

42 'Deutschlandjahr in Indien'.

the Goethe-Institut as a "desideratum".[43] The cultural policy critique of the Year of Germany in India will go into more detail on this specific format of German foreign policy. In conclusion, and as a further frame of reference for the research project, the German-Indian partnership will be considered from an intercultural perspective. This forms the basis for the discussion on the challenges of German-Indian cooperation work in Chapter 5.

Chapter 5 provides a focused presentation of the results of the research study, filtered from the statements of the interview partners using the project's scientific framework. This chapter is devoted to answering the question of how the aspirations of cultural policy are implemented in practice, if this is at all possible.

It will become clear in the course of the investigation that cooperation work is highly "conditional":

> The success of building networks [for example, in the form of cooperations – author] does not happen automatically. It is bound up with conditions.[44]

The current state of these conditions leaves clear room for development in German-Indian cultural cooperations. Chapter 6 seeks to draw out which cultural policy framework conditions are necessary in order for the culture of cooperation in the FCP to realise its aspirations to dialogue, partnership, and equal partnerships in the future. That is, to answer the question – how is it possible to draw nearer to this ideal conception of cooperation work? From these conclusions, a range of general cultural policy options for artistic cooperation with international partners will be formulated.

This study concludes in Chapter 7 with an outline of the ideal cooperation process. This chapter presents an overview of the social relevance of the results of the research, as well as of the areas that require future investigation and research.

---

[43] Quoted from Bruno Gross, Managing Director of the Goethe-Institut from 2011 to June 2017, at the 57th Loccum Cultural Policy Colloquium.

[44] Quoted from Kerstin Schulenburg at http://tinyurl.com/nbvx4ey (Accessed: 03.05.2013).

Artistic Cooperation and Cultural Diplomacy

Clarification of Terms

Chapter 2 lays the theoretical foundation of this investigation of artistic cooperations. What is the difference between Cooperations, Networks, Exchange, and Dialogue? In this chapter, the crucial terms used in this study will be defined and placed in relation to one another (cf. Ch. 2.1). Developments in the FCP will be presented using German government documents, as well as agendas and action plans from political and international organisations such as UNESCO. Detail will be provided on the most relevant and current concepts, with a focus on international cooperations in the arts under the FCP (cf. Ch. 2.2).[1] In conclusion, the sociological theory of social capital, which forms the basis of all cooperations, will be presented and coupled to this investigation (cf. Ch. 2.3).

2.1 Cooperation: Defining the Term

Cooperation is the central term of this study. The term cooperation describes: "working together, particularly in the areas of politics or economics."[2] Its synonyms include "partnership" and "collaboration".[3] The Indian interview partners preferred to speak of "collaboration". The author has therefore included this term in her conversations with them, however, as the word collaboration, particularly in German usage, can also be understood to encompass cooperation with an enemy power or occupying force against the interest of one's own country, she has not made use of it herself.

In parallel to the term cooperation itself, the terms network, dialogue, exchange, partnership, and co-production are frequently used to describe the broader process of cooperation (cf. Rautenstrauch *et al.*, 2003: 7).

---

1 For a documentation of all official government documents, sources, and archive materials with a central significance for foreign policy research, see Bauer (2010: 205 ff.).

2 According to Duden at: http://tinyurl.com/n7b6e2d (Accessed: 14.02.2014). For detail on the establishment of cooperations, see Sennett (2012: 35-64, 96-129, ix, 9 ff., 68 ff.). The history of cooperations will not be pursued further at this point, as it does not contribute further to the goals of the investigation.

3 According to Duden at: http://tinyurl.com/n7b6e2d (Accessed: 14.02.2014).

How these terms relate to the notion of cooperation itself will be made clear below.[4]

Research into international cooperation led the political scientist Robert Axelrod to publish *The Evolution of Cooperation* in 1984 (cf. Axelrod, 1987). This text served as the foundation for a great number of additional research papers on cooperation in the social, political, and legal sciences. In this book, Axelrod articulated the "game theory" of cooperation.[5] This theory is concerned with the decisions of cooperating individuals, whereby the actions of others influence the result that any particular individual wishes to achieve with his own actions. According to this model, the usefulness to both players is "[increased] in the course of ethical cooperations, when both players cooperate", while "unethical [cooperation] reduces it, although it can be of individual benefit in situations where the other player continues to give his friendly cooperation" (Barthel, 2010: 46).[6]

The usefulness or advantage referred to here leads us to the basic definition and nature of a cooperation. Literature from the field of cooperation research – principally in the science of business administration (cf. Ch. 1.2), defines cooperation as "the combined effect of the actions of two or more people" (Barthel, 2010: 45, cf. also Brauer, 2010: 61). Cooperation is a strategy, which unites efforts towards a common goal (cf. e.g. Fowler, 2012: 18), in order to fulfil this goal to greater degree than possible for individuals maintaining separate approaches, or to make its achievement possible at all (cf. Garcia dos Santos, 2011: 56). The basis of such a cooperation needs to be a cross-section of commonly held interests, goals, and motivations (cf. Nestvogel, 2009: 134, IFAB, 2004b: n.p., Brauer, 2010: 62). Individual goals can exist and be pursued in addition to these. However, the level of mutual acceptance and compatibility of these non-identical and non-congruent goals is decisive (cf. Holzberg, 2009: 71). A cooperation is successful when it achieves its goals and

4 A limited selection of authors have been called on to discursively expand on the terms and to find and fix a definition for the use of this study.

5 The game theory is one of several theories of cooperation. Further cooperations theories and strategies include the Core Competence Approach, Transaction-Cost Approach, Incentive-Contribution Theory, Rational Choice Theory, and the Resource or Resource Dependence Approach (cf. here e.g. Holzberg, 2009: 26 ff., Dizdar, 2008: 81 ff., Swobda, 2003: 47 ff.). Literature on the subject stresses that there are no discrete theories in existence to explain the creation of and functioning of relations within cooperations. The theories in existence are applicable, for example, to topics such as strategic alliances in business, and barely useable or useful for the analysis of artistic cooperations. For this reason, they will not be discussed in depth here, and our focus here will be on a sociological analysis of cooperations (cf. Sennett, 2011 and 2012).

6 For a detailed description of the game theory, see Swoboda (2003: 45 ff.). The prisoner's dilemma is a central component of this theory (cf. Axelrod, 1987: 7).

provides a use or advantage for the parties that enter into it (the so-called "Rational Choice Approach", cf. Sennett, 2012: 5).[7] Cooperations are not founded on altruism, or cultural moral ideals of a good coexistence: They are entered into because they allow parties to produce better results than through non-cooperative action (the so-called "Positive Sum Game", cf. Sennett, 2012: 72).

Alongside this goal orientation, additional important elements of cooperations include the voluntary nature of the decision to cooperate (cf. Hollstein/Straus, 2006: 103), as well as the broader (legal and economic) independence and autonomy of the partners.[8] Most cooperations are time-limited,[9] even though analysis has revealed that a lack of time on the part of the participants is a factor in the failure of networks and cooperations (cf. e.g. Sennett, 2012: 168 f. and Ch. 5.4.2).[10]

The India Foundation for the Arts (IFAB) in Bangalore has articulated several negative criteria for cooperations. According to their definition, a relationship is not a cooperation:

- When one partner is only involved in the project as an advisor, or source of resources.
- When workshops or courses are offered that bring together the experiences of a variety of people, but do not encourage horizontal interaction between them.
- When a cooperation project is devised by only one of the partners.
- When ideas, methods, and practices are not shared or exchanged between the partners (cf. IFAB, 2001: 19, *ibid.*, 2002b: n.p.).[11]

---

7 Sennett describes this as an "open-ended process", because the loss and gains of the respective partners only becomes evident in the course of their partnership. Gains do not have to be exclusively material. They can also consist, for example, of valuable information (cf. Sennett, 2012: 78). Success in cooperations is difficult to measure because of the immaterial and multidimensional nature of the goals of the cooperation. Furthermore, any success consists of success from an individual perspective, and that of the cooperation of a whole, based on a judgement of the satisfaction of all of those involved (cf. Holzberg, 2009: 57).

8 It will become clear when presenting the results of this present study (cf. Ch. 5) that the financial independence of a partner or several partners is seldom guaranteed – in particular when they come from the "Global South".

9 According to Rautenstrauch *et al.* (2003: 66), the main reason for this is mutual uncertainty and a lack of trust towards the partner.

10 Because a great number of cooperations arise in a very short space of time, the participants must be able to present their concerns in a focused way in order to clear these with one another (cf. Sennett, 2012: 17). The phenomenon is intensified by the fact that parties are frequently confronted with completely unknown actors.

11 See, for example, Ch. 5.1.

As already discussed, the success and life cycle of cooperations are dependent on their ability to achieve their goals, or provide results, as well as on the common and mutual usefulness that results from them. Since the parties to a cooperation are dependent on one another with regard to the achievement of their goals, developing trust between them has a vital role to play. This is a view supported by a great number of recent scholars (apart from Axelrod, who does not count trust and friendship amongst the important conditions for cooperation, cf. Axelrod, 1987: 164 ff.). These have found trust to be a foundational component of cooperative work (cf. Sennett, 2012: 150 ff., Barthel, 2010: 52, Ch. 5.4.2)[12] – a view also confirmed by the results of this study. Trust can be understood here as the assumption "that developments will take place according to expectations [...]. With regard to cooperations, this is accompanied by the additional expectations, that the future actions of partners will take place in the framework of certain shared values, will not lead to harm to the partner in the transaction, and will not create a risk. Values are universal standards or principles such as loyalty, fairness, readiness to help, reliability, honesty, responsibility, integrity, competence, consistency, and openness, which are regarded as desirable in the context of mutual coexistence" (Holzberg, 2009: 88).[13]

Without a basic consensus on core values (trust, fairness, etc.) and rules (of communication, of behaviour, etc.), it is seldom possible for a cooperative interpersonal relationship to arise (cf. e.g. Brauer, 2010: 62). At the same time, these various pillars of cooperative work – also described by Barthel as "ethical standards" (Barthel, 2010: 45), which are deserving of dialogue (cf. Sennett, 2012: 129), mutual respect (cf. Ch. 6.13), solidarity, and "open-ended, fluid processes" (Hoyle, 2012b: 38) – are normative standards against which cooperative processes are judged, and are much of the time politically developed.[14] Cooperations are "frequently a place of normative standards and idealistic description", according to Jütte (2006: 199).[15] This raises the question: Why is it not possible to implement these ideals and norms in reality?

The parties to a cooperation bring together their tangible and intangible resources,[16] share and exchange them, express themselves with reference

12 See also Rautenstrauch *et al.* (2003: 67, 81 f., 91 f.) and Holzberg (2009: 181). On trust and friendship as a basis for cooperation, see also Ch. 5 and 6.

13 The term "trust" has been extensively defined by the German sociologist Niklas Luhmann. See here e.g. Hollstein/Straus (2006: 237).

14 Innovation is another attribute frequently assigned to cooperations (cf. Srivatsan, 2002: 1, Steinkamp, 2013: 5).

15 See also Fowler (2012: 18), Sennett (2012: x).

16 Intangible resources include, for example, knowledge, competences, skills, experiences, and time.

to one another, and establish connections with each other, (the so-called "Resource Dependency Approach", cf. Lohmann, 2008: 314-337, Sennett, 2012: x),[17] in order to gain some benefit. Herein lies the oft-invoked 'Win-win situation' (cf. Rautenstrauch *et al.*, 2003: 81 f., Sennett, 2012: 72 ff., Petersen, 2010: 24 f.), whereby the norms of mutuality and equality between partners serves as a "relationship maxim" (cf. Axelrod, 1987: 170, Nestvogel, 2009: 134, Ch. 2.1 and 2.2),[18] also with regard to the partners' respective obligations and responsibilities.

However, the varying economic situation of the partners – or more bluntly, their differing level of capital (cf. Ch. 2.3) – presents the parties with the problem of power relations, inequality, and dependency (cf. Hoyle, 2012: 2, Dizdar, 2008: 64-158, Roberts, 2012: 33). This is because the unequal level of access to – above all material – resources that the participants are able to contribute is a source of power (cf. Sennett, 2012: 7 ff., 133, Ch. 5.9.1 and 7.13). Hierarchisation, as well as an inequality of power and control weaken cooperations and lead to their failure (cf. Sennett, 2012: 179). Cooperations are always accompanied by competition and rivalry (cf. *ibid.*: 5, 64 f., Holzberg, 2009: 43), for example, over resources or recognition. Indeed, a cooperation can also exclude actors: "We commonly associate the word 'inclusion' with cooperation [...]. [It] can exclude rather than include [...]." (Sennett, 2012: 147) Cooperations are therefore not *per se* positive, and can sometimes allow existing power groups to manifest themselves (cf. Ch. 2.3).

Mutual trust, as well as the structure and stability of a cooperation can be reinforced through institutions (cf. Holzberg, 2009: 79, Seubert, 2009: 267):[19]

> Institutional rules [...] have the task of 'deprobelmatizing' certain interactions which may be 'problematic' for the participants, in that they provide incentives, which occasion cooperative behaviours which are mutually beneficial (Axelrod, 1987: 197, see also *ibid.*: 117, 162, Ch. 6.6).

Institutions can help to establish structures, rules, and norms, which are binding for a cooperation. They are able to ensure that the interests of all of the parties are represented equally (cf. Hofstede *et al.*, 2010: 416 ff.). In the case of a conflict, they are able to act as a mediator in order to build consensus. As 'key actors', institutions have access to core competencies

---

17 Also Holzberg (2009: 72), Rautenstrauch *et al.* (2003: 81 f.).

18 See also Rautenstrauch *et al.* (2003: 6, 10) and Garcias dos Santos (2011: 56).

19 At the same time, a certain flexibility must be ensured in the adaptation to the dynamic and changing conditions of context and environment (cf. Holzberg, 2009: 77 ff., Zembylas, 2004: 100, Sennett, 2012: 71).

including legitimacy, resources, and networks (cf. Gesellschaft für Technische Zusammenarbeit, 2006: 12 and Ch. 2.2.1). Apart from this, simply thanks to their possession of real estate, institutions possess a long-term rootedness and stability that is often lacking in project-based cooperations (cf. Ch. 5.7), particularly where future cooperation is dependent on if and how the previous partnership 'worked' or not (cf. Axelrod, 1987: 205 and Ch. 6.11).

This description of the institutionalisation of cooperative work is, of course, an ideal. Sennett notes critically that institutions are thoroughly capable of promoting hierarchies on the basis of power relations, which they themselves generate by regulating access to power. Institutions can also be damaging for cooperations, for example, when they impose goals on participants (cf. Ch. 5.3), or when they attempt to cut down the complexity of cooperations (cf. Sennett, 2012: 29). However, by establishing rules, institutions can also ensure participation: "To enable participation, the organizer may establish tacit ground rules, the conventions and rituals for exchanges […]." (*ibid.*: 53) Frequent interactions and repetitions, often encourage more stable and sustainable cooperations, according to Sennett (cf. *ibid.*: 12 ff.). This frequency of interaction can be ensured through the institutionalisation of partnerships, according to Axelrod (cf. Axelrod, 1987: 162).

Cooperation is a style, that is, an arrangement of participation, which has become increasingly important since the 1980s due to structural changes, including above all the process of globalisation. In this context, cooperations are spoken of as an 'instrument of internationalization'. The potential of cooperations with regard to the goals of sustainable development was discovered in the 1990s. Participation in this sense means 'to have a part in' or also 'to work together'. Sociologically, participation means including individuals in processes of decision-making and intention forming. The grade or intensity of this participation is decisive,[20] but this is highly conditional – for example, on the level of training or knowledge resources (cf. Thermann, 2005: 44). Financial means are also a condition for participation. In order to take part, competence in content and method, social communication, and action are necessary.[21] Schönhuth provides a rule of thumb for determining the form of participation: "Who should take part with whom, when, in what, in what way, and to what

20 For more on the level and form of participation, see Thermann (2005: 35 ff.).

21 Competence in content and method – e.g. choosing and critically evaluating methods of participation according to situation and context; social communication – e.g. sensitivity to, and ability to engage with dialogue, conflict, and reflection; competence in action – e.g. to participate actively and decisively in the process.

purpose?"[22] The form and intensity of a cooperation can be examined in a variety of ways, for example, according to[23]:

Cooperation subject	Who are the actors in the cooperation?
Number of participants	2 partners (dyadic), 3-7 partners (small group), more than 7 partners (large group)
Opportunities for entry	Open/closed
Object of the cooperation	What should the cooperation 'produce'?
Cooperation level	Local, regional, national, international, global
Cooperation direction	Vertical, horizontal, diagonal
Cooperation length	Limited/unlimited timeframe
Cooperation form	Formal/institutional or free/informal

As the "leading metaphor of modernity" (cf. Fangerau/Halling, 2009: 7, 13), the term 'network' often appears in connection with cooperation. It is necessary to draw a line between these terms. Kerstin Schulenburg, an independent lecturer and consultant, provides a detailed explanation of the distinction between networks and cooperations. According to her definition, cooperations are less complex than networks for reasons including their lower number of legally independent actors in possession of a common goal, but no common concerns or ideals, who pursue these goals within the framework of a concrete project. Cooperations are elements, or stepping-stones within a network. According to Schulenberg, successful cooperations have a role to play in creating trust and confidence as steps in the process of network construction, which comes with its own meaningful cycle of expansion and contraction: "Successful cooperations project a motivating positive example, whose 'communications appeal' should not be underestimated."[24]

On the other hand, networks are a web of cooperations. They are a complex, decentralized construction, with a large number of legally independent actors with a common vision in relation to a specific topic, who develop a strategy and set operational goals in the form of projects and cooperations to be implemented by individual members of the network.

Schulenburg's definition provides the basis for the distinction drawn between the terms 'cooperation' and 'network' in this study. The term

22 Quoted from http://tinyurl.com/q5xoj2x (Accessed: 24.02.2014), see also Radtke (2011: 43), Nassehi (2006: 33).

23 Summary by the author based on an analysis of literature on cooperation research in business studies.

24 Quoted from http://tinyurl.com/oy8nl4r (Accessed: 21.02.2014).

'network' will not be used further in this investigation because this study is concerned in the first instance with cooperations in the arts, which in the long term may eventually lead to the establishment of a network.

The expression "cultural dialogue"[25] (cf. Schwencke *et al.*, 2009: 55, Radtke, 2011: 24 f.), which enjoys a variety of political usages – particularly in foreign policy with regard to engagement with differing cultures (cf. Goethe-Institut e. V., 2012b: 3, Auswärtiges Amt, s.a.) – consists of the idea of supporting international understanding and a peaceful way of coexisting (cf. Radtke, 2011: 24 f.)[26] where cultural diversity has led to misunderstanding and conflict (cf. *ibid.*: 19, 96). However, the use of dialogue as "a means for unity on basic values, and smoothing over power imbalances" (*ibid.*: 16),[27] is a "romantic longing for 're-communalisation' in a time of social disintegration and elevated insecurity" (*ibid.*: 37). In the final analysis, it merely contributes to inequality of power, because consensus demands that one culture must promote its values, premises, and dogmas until these are elevated to a position of absolute and universal validity. The partner in dialogue, ergo, must be ignored (cf. *ibid.*: 28, 96, Strohschneider, 2010: 99, Magdowski, 2012: 71).

For Radtke, conflicts must therefore be able to stand in the political space and in international relations, in order to prevent violence and the exercise of power (cf. Radtke, 2011: 138). Cultural dialogue is therefore a politically idealised term, which suggests a form of non-dominant communication in "the absence of shared basic values" (Brauer, 2010: 67, cf. also Pfannkuche, 2010: 33), "or even because the cultural expressions under discussion have from the beginning been subject to a hierarchical schema" (Surana, 2009: 28, cf. also Radtke, 2011: 16). From this premise it therefore follows, that cultural dialogue should not be allowed to be politicised (cf. Ch. 2.2):

> As far as I can see, this means that cultural dialogue is not in the first place an item for politics or diplomacy. They may be able to initiate dialogue, they may even profit from it. However, we should not allow our good intentions to blur these spheres. Particularly so that 'cultural dialogue' does not become reduced to the status of a label to cloak or conceals an interests-directed foreign policy. (Rau)[28]

---

25 German: *Dialog der Kulturen*. A distinction is not made between the terms 'cultural dialogue', 'dialogue between cultures', 'dialogue of cultures', 'intercultural dialogue', etc. (see here Sattler, 2007: 188, Terkessidis, 2010: 10, 131 ff., Tibi, 2001: 26 ff.). These distinctions do not contribute to this study or the clarification of its terms.

26 See also http://tinyurl.com/n4vdgmv (Accessed: 23.02.2014).

27 Radtke questions whether the ideas of equality of rights and power are not exclusively Western ones (cf. Radtke, 2011: 16). For discussion on this point, see Ch. 5.9.

28 Quoted from http://tinyurl.com/ku44nxr (Accessed: 23.02.2014).

"Cultural dialogue" – described by Johannes Rau, German President from 1999 to 2004 as a "categorical imperative" (Rau, 2002: n.p.) that cannot be given up (cf. Radtke, 2011: 29) – evokes 'forced dialogue' (cf. Ch. 5.4.3) from interlocutors from the 'Global North', and 'dialogue frustration' from their partners from the 'Global South'.[29] This is because the term is an "empty and dumb phrase, initiated and budgeted by policy", because "it remains unclear [...] if and how it can be achieved" (Radtke, 2011: 29, cf. also *ibid.*: 30, Kämpchen, 2013a: 67, Broder, 2006, n.p.).

The term 'cultural dialogue' is confusing because "cultures do not speak" (Radtke, 2011).[30] Dialogue can only be entered into by people – who have a variety of ethnic, cultural, religious, and linguistic origins. The result of this is that cultural characteristics cannot be set in stone. Cultural labels are relative, and can only describe the individual in a limited way. Sociology speaks of 'transnational identities', where several nations are expressed in an identity, or where an identity is composed of identifications with several nations[31] (cf. Kneidinger, 2013: 92-101, Deutsche UNESCO-Kommission e. V., 2010: 9 f., Sattler, 2007: 188). The term 'dialogue' can be defined with help from linguistics. Dialogue is a literary genre and form of speech. It is distinguished from other forms and media of linguistic communication such as monologue and dispute (cf. Radtke, 2011: 26). According to communications theory, the broad characteristics of a dialogue can be defined using the following basic conditions:

> There must be at least two interlocutors who are able to contribute several differing perspectives, which are all acknowledged and legitimate. A communication can be acknowledged as a dialogue when a relationship of

---

29 According to cultural actors at the 57th Loccum Cultural Policy Colloquium in February 2012. This dialogue-weariness presumably arose through the years of cultural dialogue: In 2001, the 'UNO International Year of Dialogues between Civilizations' was accompanied by a "Global Agenda for Dialogue among Civilizations" and a "Manifesto for a Dialogue among Civilizations" (Radtke, 2011: 17 f.). In 2008, the 'European Year of Intercultural Dialogue' received a budget of ten million euros (cf. Radtke, 2011: 18), and was followed in 2010 by the 'UNESCO International Year for the Rapprochement of Cultures'. Radtke speaks of a "whole dialogue industry" (Radtke, 2011: 22), because of calls for dialogue to take place everywhere and all the time, and for every goal and purpose.

30 See the title of Radtke's publication (2011). See also the Goethe-Institut interview with Olaf-Frank Radtke at http://tinyurl.com/mdsqtpt (Accessed: 23.02.2014) and Rau (2002b: n.p.).

31 The term 'nation' is also questionable, since it is only when cultures are provided with spatial, linguistic, or religious borders, that states, populations of a territory, societies, or communities become nations, "which we should use like a container to enclose a homogenous culture under one term" (Radtke, 2011: 45).

> exchange on equal terms takes place […] in which good will is evident on all sides, and which, above all, leads to an increase in understanding. (Radtke, 2011: 26)[32]

We can see that there are certain conditions that need to be fulfilled before an interaction can be described as a dialogue. According to this definition, the term 'dialogue' – even without the qualification 'on equal terms' – demands that the partners, their perspectives, and values, are given equal weight (see also Rau, 2002b: n.p.). Accordingly, meaningful dialogue consists of "[recognising] cultural differences to allow the establishment of new parameters, which make a productive interaction with one another possible, and not in order to find a synthesis, compromise, or common denominator" (Garcia dos Santos, 2011: 55).[33]

A dialogue that is based on symmetrical positions for its interlocutors, readiness to understand and cooperate, a common obligation to 'truthfulness', mutual recognition, and the will to a consensus, is "highly demanding". It is therefore relatively "unlikely" (Radtke, 2011: 9, see also Gross, 2012: 22 f., Strohschneider, 2010: 110), because it means that techniques and frameworks need to be in place to allow all of the participants to be able to contribute their perspective.

The ability to dialogue lies particularly in holding back or keeping silent, observing, and above all listening (cf. Lepenies, 1995: 62, Garcias dos Santos, 2011: 56, Sennett, 2012: 18). Listening means taking part in a discourse with a partner in order to learn to respect and understand their perspective, and to place one's own position in question and to engage in reflection (cf. Hoffmann, 1998: 24, Holzberg, 2009: 180, Sennett, 2012: 278),[34] without betraying one's own identity and position (cf. Tibi, 2001: 27, 33, IFAB, 2001: 18).[35]

In this sense, for its participants, dialogue means taking on the posture of a learner in the sense of Lepenies' 'Learning Community',[36] and acknowledging the opportunity to learn that this variety of perspectives allows (cf. e.g. Kämpchen, 2012: 14, Holzberg, 2009: 176, Rautenstrauch *et al.*, 2003: 36 f.):[37] "The success of a dialogue depends on the willingness

---

32 See also the definition of dialogue at http://tinyurl.com/pd8d278 (Accessed: 21.02.2014).

33 For in depth reading on cultural dialogue, see Rau (2002a) and Tschernokoshewa (2009).

34 Also labelled as cultural relativism (cf. Roßkopf, 2010: 46, 70).

35 See also Ittstein (2009: 148), Sennett (2012: 127), Hoffmann (1999: 187).

36 German: *Lerngesellschaft*. See also Schönhuth at http://tinyurl.com/lbojy8o (Accessed: 23.02.2014).

37 On dialogue as a process of learning, thinking, production and experience on an individual level and the level of interaction, see also the website of the Goethe-

of both sides to make changes."[38] The challenge of undertaking dialogue lies in the mutuality and reciprocity of the attitude and relationship between the partners. In particular, the Europeans have to free themselves from their Eurocentrism, allow competing value systems, and engage with other patterns of thought and behaviour in the cultural exchange, in order to be able to live out a partnership of equals (cf. Knopp, 2006: 117 f.). The real work in a dialogue begins, according to Knopp, when the partners have different basic values that they both view as being universal (cf. *ibid.*, Sennett, 2012: 6, Hoyle, 2012b: 38):

> [T]hen the process of cultural exchange becomes a creative search for commonalities among diverging perspectives. Only those projects that are based on such an attitude truly take the concept of dialogue seriously – and they can lead to the most profound success, when commonalities are indeed discovered after a period of genuine effort. (Knopp, 2006: 117 f.)

According to this quotation from Knopp, dialogue is meaningful in that it allows the discovery or development of something in common (see also Surana, 2009: 214, Rau, 2002: n.p., Tibi, 2001: 26) – for example, common goals, interests, or understanding of cooperation (cf. Sennett, 2012: n.p.) – in order to make working together possible (cf. Ch. 6.2).

In summary, according to the definition of this study, artistic cooperations are a form of working together voluntarily, with the goal of allowing something new to arise on the foundation of a shared working process. There are always at least two independent parties who are working together. Ideally, these are equal. However, this equality seldom exists, particularly between partners from the 'Global North' and the 'Global South' (see here Ch. 5.9.1).

Co-production is a step before cooperation. It is under the control of a leader, who enables and initiates the cultural creation – often on the basis of the financial means in their possession. This leader allows selected 'partners' to participate (cf. Roberts, 2012: 33), imposes their ideas and rules, and thus ensures for themselves a position "from which they can determine the nature of the whole working process" (Garcia dos Santos, 2011: 55, cf. Ch. 5.2, 5.9). In this case, it is not possible to speak of 'cooperation', because of the inequality between the partners, whereby one side supports, initiates, and transfers knowledge and expertise, while the other receives (cf. Garcia dos Santos, 2011: 55).

Institut at http://tinyurl.com/legjp94 and Schulenburg's website at http://tinyurl.com/q8axb7e (Both accessed: 22.02.2014).

38 Quoted from Schönhuth's cultural glossary at http://tinyurl.com/kdqzhug (Accessed: 23.02.2014).

According to Sennett, cooperation is a craft requiring diverse skills and preconditions (cf. Sennett, 2012; ix ff., 6, 63, 227). One of these skills – alongside the gift of empathy[39] – is being able to undertake dialogue (cf. *ibid.*: 6, 18 ff., 275). This encompasses the ability to listen well, behave tactfully, reach agreement, and deal with awkwardness. These skills, like intercultural competence, need to be encouraged so that parties in complex international cooperation are able to act. It is therefore a step in the wrong direction when representatives of the FCP and their sponsors speak of 'dialogue', unless they mean encouraging this faculty through training.

Networks cannot be equated with cooperations. On the contrary, cooperations – as Schulenburg shows – can help to lay the groundwork for the establishment of a network. These various projects ideally come together in the form of a network.

'Cultural exchange' does not mean the exchange of knowledge, experiences, skills, ideas, positions, perspectives, norms, or values (cf. Lepenies, 1995: n.p.), or the representation of culture in the narrow sense of art such as literature or visual art, which can be exchanged or loaned in the forms of concrete objects. It is a way for people from differing cultures to understand and learn more about one another. This exchange is a part of the cooperation process. It is the foundation upon which new things can be built (cf. Ch. 2.1).

Terms like "partnership" and "equal footing" stand for the equal treatment, and recognition of the equal value of the partners (and their cultures), for example, through a common project development and implementation process. Hoffman writes:

> Cooperation as partners means first of all including the partner in the whole scope of the shared project by listening to their needs and wishes. (Hoffmann, 1999: 192)

Clemens Spiess, who made an inventory of German-Indian cultural relations along with a number of recommendations, further states that the principle of partnership must also in the long term mean reaching an equal distribution of the financial costs of the project (cf. Spiess, 2009: 127 and Ch. 6.13). Just how rarely the maxims of partnership can actually be realised in the face of wildly differing conditions will become clear in Chapter 5.9 of this study. As Hamm-Brücher put it as far back as 1980:

---

39 Sennett distinguishes between sympathy and empathy. Both of these express mutual recognition, and create a connection. However, in one case, this connection is an "embrace", and in the other an "encounter". Sympathy overcomes differences through a process of identification completed in the imagination. Empathy follows the other party under their own conditions (cf. Sennett, 2012: 23, 127).

> Moreso than in industrial countries, our principles of partnership and openness are constantly put to the acid test in developing ones […]. (Hamm-Brücher, 1980: 32)

The theme of the equal rights and equal value of the cooperation partners to one another, as well as the attempt to realise them in practice can be seen running through the core of this investigation. Chapter 6.13 will present an alternative to these diffuse terms – 'fairness'. The aim here is to allow synergies to develop in the future, which understand the common implementation of differing ways of living as mutually supportive and leading to mutual development.

Ultimately, the success and interpretation of a cooperation depends on its participants, and their attitude, political, social, cultural, and economic context (cf. Sennett, 2012: 170, Holzberg, 2009: 31, I_42: 42, Ch. 3 and 6.3). Individual and shared expectations, goals, and interests are also important (cf. Lee, 2010: 8). As Ch. 5.1 will show, these can be very different from the German and Indian sides. However, this must in no way mean that they are irreconcilable (cf. Holzberg, 2009: 176). Decisive, rather, is that these requirements are openly discussed, and that they are accorded an equal right to exist (cf. Rautenstrauch *et al.*, 2003: 85). One of the competences of cooperative action is to identify, discuss, and negotiate differing points of view (cf. Ch. 6.2). This means establishing and designing individual cooperations where the partners are given a hearing, and respectfully allowed to think, speak, and act in their own way, and where the varied perspectives of the parties are accepted (cf. Garcias dos Santos, 2011: 56, Nestvogel, 2010: 139 f.).[40] Personal relationships and long-term contacts are essential in this process (cf. Schönfeld, 2012: 14, Ch. 6.11).

2.2 Cooperation: Demands of a Foreign Cultural Policy

The persons responsible for driving cultural policy, both internally as well as abroad, formulate content goals, define frameworks, and determine rights. They make resources, structures, and infrastructures available for the "actions of political and social actors in the broadly-defined field of artistic and aesthetic production and reception, as well as culturally creative activities (Wagner, 2009: 26, see also Höpel, 2007: 14). The goal of this is to allow creativity to unfold, and to enable art and culture in all its variety (cf. Deutsche UNESCO-Kommission e. V., 1998: 1).

---

40 See also Holzberg (2009: 180) and Surana (2009: 20 f.). The ability to compromise and resolve conflicts is also included in cooperative action.

The international cooperative work that this study investigates represents one iteration of the format and goals of the FCP. The policy is responsible for creating the (structural) preconditions for cooperations in the arts, and for making the required funds available for them to take place and unfold themselves.

The FCP is organised at a national level (cf. German Basic Law Article 32, Paragraph 1), and provides "for the support and teaching of the German language around the world, the presentation of the diverse German cultural landscape, exchanges with other cultures, and for the strengthening of Germany as a place of learning" (Schneider/Götzky, 2008: 51 f.). Responsibility for the FCP lies with the Federal Foreign Ministry. This means that the FCP is anchored in foreign policy, following its political goals and direction (cf. Schwencke *et al.*, 2009: 37 f., 112 f. and Ch. 2.2). This has the consequence that the arts are placed in danger of being made into a political instrument – for example, for diplomatic or economic interest (cf. Hoffmann, 1994: 21, *ibid.*, 1999: 186). However, according to Article 5, Paragraph 3 of the German Basic Law, the arts should be free in their context and expression. They should act autonomously. However the FCP is bound up a set of constantly changing interests determined by political, aesthetic, and narrative ambitions (cf. Schneider, 2012: 41, Morr, 2011: 7) whose goal is the furtherance and expansion of power (cf. Ch. 2.2). This situation is liable to lead to pressure on the freedom and diversity of the arts (cf. Schneider, 2011d: 13, 21, Knüsel, 2011: 70 ff.).

This study of international cooperation work is based on the term 'culture' in one specific, and one broad sense.[41] In a narrow sense, culture is understood as any form of creative activity in the forms of visual art, music, literature, film, radio, television, theatre, dance, architecture, and, to a limited extent, archaeology. Defined in a broader sense, the term culture encompasses:

> […] the whole complex of distinctive spiritual, material, intellectual and emotional features that characterize a society or social group. It includes not only the arts and letters, but also modes of life, the fundamental rights of the human being, value systems, traditions and beliefs […]. (UNESCO, 1982: 1)[42]

41 Cf. Schreiner (2011: 169 ff.), who determines that analysts of the FCP often work using both definitions.

42 A so-called "wider sense" of the term 'culture' was adopted at the *MONDIACULT UNESCO* world cultural conference in Mexico City in 1982, which had been developed because of the socio-political discussions of the 1970s in Germany. For detailed information on this broader definition, see Radtke (2011: 43 f.). For criticism of this approach – for example, with regard to the loss of identity or control, see, for

As a matter of internal policy, the FCP as a political field is concerned with the question of its own cultural identity. That is, what is to be understood and passed on under the definition of 'culture'? The FCP presents itself to the outside world through the construction and reproduction of cultural differences, serving this distinction (cf. Ch. 2.3). Ideally, however, this would not merely be a question of representation, but rather of the peaceful exchange of cultural identities while recognizing their inherent differences (cf. Schreiner, 2011: 83, 99, 113 ff., 168, 273). Here we can see the split between representation[43] and exchange, which has affected the FCP for decades. Should it produce propaganda and encourage sympathy or sustainable and long-term cultural dialogue (cf. Spiess, 2009: 19, Schreiner, 2011: 114 f.)? In order to understand this discrepancy, the development of the FCP and its goals since the 1950s needs to be assessed.[44] In conclusion, the decisive aspirational conceptions of the FCP with regard to international partnerships that can be deduced from these political and historical developments will be presented.

In the 1950s and 60s, as the FCP was still "methodically at the beginning", the contemporary discourse on its operation spoke of "cultural propaganda", "self-presentation", or "cultural export" (Kathe, 2005: 37). The goal was to improve Germany's image abroad in the wake of the Second World War (cf. Kusch/Beckmann, 2011: n.p.). This effort was focused on building sympathy and trust (cf. Bauer, 2010: 97). "The work of the FCP was focused on promoting the German language and economic relations, as well as on a cultural program focused on the classics." (Lehmann, 2011c: n.p.) The interests of the host countries were not significant. Although cultural exchange began to be discussed from the end of the 1960s, the concept of the cultural export model remained unchanged (cf. Kathe, 2005: 52).

Kathe pinpoints the FCP's first change of course in 1958, whereby its goals were modified to include "development assistance, educational support, and cultural exchange", especially in the "Third World" (*ibid.*: 50). The export of Western values and achievements played a decisive role in these processes, which were geared towards the creation of new economic partnerships. The culture of the host countries was not of interest: "There was still no space for altruism in development aid. It was still a source of satisfaction when one's own 'valuable' culture was the

example, Lau (2001: 46): "The broader definition of culture is tautological, since culture is always extending, even in the absence of an official definition."

43 For more on representation in the FCP, see Schreiner (2011: 260 ff., 270 f.).

44 For an in-depth history of the German FCP, see Düwell (2009: 61-111), Niklas (2005: 43 ff.), Singer (2003), Denscheilmann (2013: 65 ff.), Kathe (2005: 35-64), Bauer (2010: 4), Eisfeld (2004: 11 ff.), Hoffmann (1999: 186), Lau (2001: 41 ff.).

subject of wonder even in faraway Africa" (*ibid.*: 51). Kathe uses newspaper articles to illustrate how an ever-greater value was placed on support for development aid by the beginning of the 1970s, and how cultural institutions themselves "fell in line and began to present themselves as helpers of the Third World." (*ibid.*)

The change of government in 1969 saw the dissolution of the classic cultural program. Willy Brandt, Chancellor of Germany from 1969 to 1974, defined the FCP as a "third pillar" alongside diplomacy and economic policy (see Auswärtiges Amt, 1970: 185).[45] This, according to Lau, marks the point at which 'cultural exchange' with the world, and not systematic competition moved to the centre of cultural policy (cf. Lau, 2001: 42). Kathe gives the following overview of the political reforms of the 1970s:

> Political interest in the FCP grew distinctly from the beginning of the 70s; control from the Bundestag was increased, its connection with foreign policy was perfected and, for the first time, a worldwide presence was aimed at, in order to broaden the stage for German foreign policy as a whole in trade and diplomacy. (Kathe, 2005: 21)[46]

The topic of mutuality first seriously arose within the FCP in 1967 when the sociologist Richard M. Emge stated "the FCP needs to come into contact with reciprocity, otherwise those who are constantly 'receiving' will rapidly develop resentments towards the 'givers', who are usually more socially and culturally developed" (Emge, 1967: 125, 156, cf. Ch. 5). At the beginning of the 1970s, this train of thought developed into a discussion of the forms, content, and goals of the FCP (cf. Kathe, 2005: 57), which led – on the basis of the expanded definition of culture – to a conceptual widening of the tasks of the FCP (cf. Schwencke *et al.*, 2009: 37 f.). This expanded from the role of making a one-sided presentation of German art abroad to encompass dialogue and reciprocal exchange. "The principle of dialogue and cultural exchange became a hallmark of the FCP." (*ibid.*: 38) An intensification of relations with countries in the developing world played a central role in these encounters (cf. Lau, 2001: 4 f.). Because of this thematic expansion of the FCP, these contacts needed to "explode the academic and aesthetic frameworks that had been valid up to that point", according to Walter Scheel, German Foreign Minister from 1969 to 1974. Meanwhile, future

---

45 It was also described by Dahrendorf as the "supporting pillar of our foreign policy" (Auswärtiges Amt, 1970, Section 1.3).

46 Whether the FCP is in reality fundamental to foreign policy, or more akin to a decorative addition to security policy or an aesthetic form of trade promotion (cf. Bode, 2002: 149 f., Lehmann, 2011b: n.p.), is an on-going debate which it is not possible to follow here in detail.

cultural work was required to "stretch to cover all areas of international and social cooperation" (Scheel quoted in: Hoffmann, 2008: 170).

This was followed by the "sobering up" of the 1980s (Kathe, 2005: 52):

> It became increasingly difficult to offer Western modes of thought in many countries, which were ever more on the defensive against their increasing 'westernization'. There was even criticism from within the Goethe-Institut regarding the so-called partnership principle that was developed by Dahrendorf with regard to the Third World, arguing that this was precisely what was hindering development in these countries. (*ibid.*)

These conflicts were resolved when the Goethe-Institut developed guidelines "in future, to accept the conditions prevailing in the host country, and to be guided by them." (Kathe, 2005: 53):

> A 'reconditioning' towards Western and democratic values was not to be raised. [...] The 'cultural taboos' of the host country were to remain untouched, to avoid any more uncomfortable conflicts. (*ibid.*)

Kathe concludes in his analysis: "The idea of cooperation with third world countries was hereby conclusively made a think of the past." According to him, by the end of the 1980s "cultural development aid had shrink to a few individual projects." (*ibid.*) This was most probably also a consequence of the government of Helmut Kohl – Chancellor of Germany from 1982 to 1998 – that focused on linguistic instead of programmatic work, and placed a renewed emphasis on self-promotion and export orientation (cf. *ibid.*: 333, Bauer, 2010: 88 ff.).

In the mid-1990s, the German sociologist Wolf Lepenies formulated the culture of a "learning community" (Lepenies, 1996a: 48) in reaction to the continuing predominance of the cultural export approach. According to this "culture of learning" – as opposed to a "culture of instruction" – the ability of one's own culture to learn with regard to other cultures can lead to a qualitative cultural cooperation (Lepenies, 1996c: 200, see also Lau, 2001: 43, Bode, 2002: 153). Georg Lechner, who occupied leading positions in the Goethe-Institut abroad for forty years, twenty of which were spent in India, commented that the "reconfiguration from a teaching to a learning model [...] is only possible [...] through cooperation, and is not achievable with a quick fix" (Lechner, 2004: 296). In other words, international cooperation work is essential for Lepenies' "global learning community".[47]

[47] Quoted from http://tinyurl.com/n6re87n (Accessed: 20.01.2014).

In line with changing global relations, the foreign cultural policies of nation states are confronted with new challenges alongside the classic tasks of image promotion and trust building (cf. Körber, 2009: 185 ff., Schöfthaler, 2009: 322 ff.). The goals of the German FCP in the 21st Century are of a more integrated and preventative nature – for example, promoting national understanding, securing peace, as well as preventing crises and conflict (cf. e.g. Feilcke *et al.*, 2012).[48] As early as the mid-1990s, the German writer Hans Magnus Enzensberger defined the FCP as a "a 'dialogue-capable early warning system' in an intransparent, conflict-prone world, characterised at the same time by the unification of the global market as well as new forms of local particularism" (Lau, 2001: 43, see also Enzensberger, 1996: 36 ff., Hofmann, 1999: 186). Amongst the assumptions that lay behind these new tasks of the FCP – such as conflict prevention and crisis management – was that there existed a basis of shared universal values including, for example, human rights, freedom, and democracy (cf. Kakar, 2006: 125, UNESCO, 2005, Article 1, Tibi, 2001: 26).[49]

This activity portfolio gave the FCP a comprehensive social mission. Culture can help a society to engage critically with its own reality and its own self (cf. Fücks, 2012: n.p.): "It is in the art of a country where the central social questions are posed." (Goethe-Institut e. V., 2011a: 58) Alongside cultural workers – as translators and interpreters of realities – civil society actors should have a part in co-creating processes of social change, secured and made possible through cultural training (cf. Deutsche UNESCO-Kommission e. V., 1998, Ermert, 2011: 54).[50] Cultural policy, both foreign and domestic, is thereby also the 'social policy' that should enable, organise, and defend the arts (cf. Deutscher Bundestag, 2007b: n.p.). The 58th Cultural Policy Colloquium in Loccum in 2013 went further, and described it as 'future policy'. Nevertheless, several critical voices continued to warn:

> The relentless pushing for a social effect of artistic work is an attack on the concept of the autonomy of the arts through the simultaneous exploitation of its protected space. (Fücks, 2012: n.p.)

---

48 See also http://tinyurl.com/oug2kox (Accessed: 17.01.2014).

49 The recognition of basic values is as a rule attributed to all of the participants in a dialogue or cooperation, however this does not always reflect the reality (cf. Ch. 2, 4).

50 Cultural training can be understood as "the connection of training and cultural practice". Cultural training is "an active engagement with art and culture", as producer, practitioner, and recipient. "Cultural training should make people able to develop their personality, and to strengthen their social, creative, and communicative abilities." (Schwencke *et al.*, 2009: 92 f.) For more detail, see, for example, http://tinyurl.com/l2ksfdy (Accessed: 13.01.2014).

In addition to this comes the fact that this variety of tasks is not unproblematic – leading the marginal FCP to become unclear and overstretched. These goals and tasks can no longer be dealt with politically (cf. Maaß, 2005: 21, Schreiner, 2008: n.p.).

The goals of the FCP's portfolio outlined above should be reached through the employment to trust-building measures that acknowledge diversity, such as, intercultural dialogue, and international cooperation, (cf. Bauer, 2009a: 130 f.), especially since this expansion in the FCP's range of tasks, and the increased demands placed on it, require new partners (cf. Schneider, 2012: 35).[51] Accordingly, in the estimation of the German government, an equal exchange of partners and cultures play a central role in the FCP.[52] Following a historical analysis of the FCP throughout the previous three decades, Bauer summarises the central political model of the FCP at the beginning of the 21st Century as follows:

- The FCP is organised on the lines of a "cultural exchange through partnership", so that partner countries "give and receive at the same time", and the effects of the FCP can also influence German society.
- "Foreign cultural relations present an equal and mutual dialogue of German culture with other cultures."
- Because of the "mutuality in cultural relations the transfer of knowledge about other cultures and understanding for other cultures is supported, and should lead to a deeper understanding of one's own culture".
- Continuity, sustainability, and the long-term nature of relations are important (Bauer, 2010: 96 f.).

This mutual exchange between cultures as partners avoids the 'missionary conception' of the simple spread of Western ideas and ways of living to the countries of the 'Global South' (cf. Ch. 6.7). Differences are acknowledged in cultural encounters, and commonalities are built on (cf. Nestvogel, 2010: 139 f.). The implementation of the FCP should take place on the basis of this set of ideals (cf. Ch. 5.9).

Against this, stands the FCP as "mentality policy", which should indirectly influence "the posture and values" of the partner, and which reinforces the universalistic ambitions of individual cultures (Fuchs 2007: 115). With this intention, "cultural policy is absolutely not a harmless political field, but an important – perhaps even the decisive –

---

51 For an understanding of the FCP from the point of view of an intermediary organisation, see Ch. 2.2.1.

52 See http://tinyurl.com/oug2kox (Accessed: 16.03.2014).

means of power with regard to our social and political order" (Wagner, 2009: 453, cf. Ch. 2.3).

Political concepts define and legitimize a field of work. They offer theses and pathways for the realisation of practical action; they formulate goals in line with political ambitions. Below are presented the leading cultural policy concepts for international cooperation in the FCP on a national and international level:

In June 1970 the German-British sociologist, politician, publicist, and former Parliamentary Secretary in the German Foreign Office, Ralf Dahrendorf, laid out fifteen theses on international cultural, scientific, and social policy, which called for a reimagining of the FCP. In December 1970, these were approved by the Foreign Office as 'Guiding Principles for the Foreign Cultural Policy'[53] (cf. Lau, 2001: 41 f., Bauer, 2010: 74). Dahrendorf described the FCP as "an activation of knowledge, ideas, and energy in all social groups and all of the fields that serve the maintenance, and development of life, for the mutual benefit of the participating states" (Dahrendorf quoted in: Kathe, 2005: 58 f.).

According to these Guiding Principles, in the future the FCP "will engage with the cultural and civilizational problems of the present more intensively than before" (Auswärtiges Amt, 1970: 184). With this, the Guiding Principles lay down a broader definition of culture, which is to be confirmed on an international level in the 1982 UNESCO Mexico City Declaration (cf. Schwencke *et al.*, 2009: 38). The FCP should not exhaust itself in self-publicity and information transmission of a cultural 'one way street', as it did in the 1950s and 60s (cf. Kathe, 2005: 38), but should help to encourage understanding between nations: "The value of what we give depends on how much we are willing to accept. Openness to others is a principle of our foreign cultural policy." (Auswärtiges Amt, 1970: 185, see also Lechner, 2004: 238, Lau, 2001: 40) The FCP is accordingly a cooperation and cultural exchange (cf. Kathe, 2005: 59, 292) and part of "the dynamic process of change in our society, which shows the way forward towards the international cooperation of all social groups" (Auswärtiges Amt, 1970: 184).[54]

The Guiding Principles of 1970 influenced the Enquiry Commission established in the same year by the German Bundestag, which in 1975 published the "Report of the German Bundestag Enquiry Commission into Foreign Cultural Policy".[55] This Commission had the task of

---

[53] German: *Leitsätze für die Auswärtige Kulturpolitik.*

[54] For more detail on Dahrendorf's Guiding Principles, see Kathe (2005: 291 ff.), Hamm-Brücher (1980: 37 ff.), Lechner (2004: 237 ff.), Sartorius (1996: 87 ff.).

[55] German: *Bericht der Enquete-Kommission Auswärtige Kulturpolitik des Deutschen Bundestages.*

"developing recommendations for a future foreign cultural policy on the basis of an analysis of strategic goals, subject matter, organisation, and finance." (Bauer, 2010: 84)

The Commission's report states, "foreign cultural policy cannot continue to be limited to a one-sided cultural exportation. It needs to be open to relationships of cultural exchange and partnership-based cooperation" (Schneider, 2012: 36). This cooperation as partners is stressed explicitly in connection with so-called 'developing countries', and includes an "intensification and simplification of free cultural exchange and cooperation with Western industrial nations" (Bauer, 2010: 86). The expansion of cultural work through exchanges with 'developing countries' opened new fields of dialogue. The program offered was to depend on the appropriateness of the situation and needs in the host country. According to Bauer, the report of the Commission in 1975, and the position statements of the German government in 1976 and 1977 represent the high point of the reform phase of the FCP. The report put in place for the first time "a binding conception of principles, guidelines, goals and subjects for the foreign cultural policy of the federal German state" (*ibid.*: 89).

The approach developed by the Enquiry Commission was given a new depth in 1982 by the publication of the "Ten Theses on Cultural Encounter and Cooperation with Third World Countries",[56] under Hildegard Hamm-Brücher, Minister of State in the German Foreign Office. The principles formulated by her amount to an equal cultural exchange for the mutual strengthening of "intellectual wealth" and the "processes of responsible and independent development" (Hamm-Brücher/Auswärtiges Amt, 1982: 191 f.). These theses are an exhortation to, amongst other things, the "mutuality of cultural relations" and "the equal treatment of cultures" (*ibid.*). Instead of "one-sided presentation of one's own cultural achievements", giving and receiving in a way that respects and encourages the diversity of the cultures should be the goal (cf. *ibid.*: 191). The prerequisite for this is "mutual understanding and knowledge of one another" (*ibid.*: 194). Hamm-Brücher explains her concerns in the following way:

> If we do not make the 'foundation' of mutual trust broader and deeper – […] through the expansion of cultural relations […] – all these decades of political efforts could be in vain. (Hamm-Brücher, 1980: 20)

Following the change of government in 1998, the new Foreign Minister, Joschka Fischer, "attempted to make a sea-change in the foreign cultural policy" and to undertake "a revolution in this area of policy" (Wittek,

---

56 German: *Zehn Thesen zur kulturellen Begegnung und Zusammenarbeit mit Ländern der Dritten Welt.*

2006: 11). The '2000 Concept'[57] was "the first comprehensive program for cultural foreign policy since the attempts at reform in the 1970s, which reflected worldwide political, social, and economic developments", as Bauer quotes the Foreign Office (Bauer, 2010: 93, see also Maaß, 2009b: 26). The 2000 Concept is a complete strategic concept for the FCP. In it, the FCP is given a broadly social and foreign policy mission as an integral instrument of German foreign policy. Among its goals are the promotion of democracy, the establishment of human rights, securing peace, and preventing conflict, fighting hunger, and protecting resources (cf. Schwencke *et al.*, 2009: 38, Fischer, 2009: 196 f.). These goals are to be achieved through strategies including personal exchanges, and the use and development of media in international cooperation (cf. Maaß, 2009b: 26). The 2000 Concept lays an emphasis on a strengthened connection between the institutions and actors involved, and the inclusion of civil society. Exchanges are to take place according to the principle of the "two-way street" (Auswärtiges Amt, 2003: 6), and the concept sets out the decisive criteria for programmatic cultural work: artistic quality in terms of innovation and aesthetics, demand and social relevance in the partner country, and the sustainability of its effect (cf. Knopp, 2010b: 16 ff., Ch. 2.2.1, 2.2.2).

In 2011, the German Foreign Office published a re-conception of the FCP with the title "Foreign Cultural and Educational Policy in the Age of Globalisation. Winning Partners. Conveying Values. Representing Interests" (cf. Auswärtiges Amt, 2011).[58] According to the Foreign Office, "this concept determines the course of the Foreign Cultural and Educational Policy for the coming years."[59] According to the German Social Democratic Party (SPD), this new direction in the FCP under a Christian Democrat/Liberal government coalition represented a turn away from the previous values like dialogue, exchange and long-term partnerships, above all with so-called 'developing countries' (in: Deutscher Kulturrat e. V., 2013b: 25). The concept of 2011 "abandons the basic understanding of the FCEP as a holistic process of dialogue open to results" (Schmidt, 2012: 131). Art and culture were said to be now at the service of political and economic interest: the FCP was turned into a program of 'cultural diplomacy' with art and culture as its instruments, deprived of their freedom of action (cf. Die Linke in: Deutscher Kulturrat e. V., 2013b: 14, Ermert, 2011: 54). Instead, at the centre of this new concept are "efforts to elicit sympathy for Germany and to present a

57 German: *Konzeption 2000.*

58 German: *Auswärtige Kultur- und Bildungspolitik in Zeiten der Globalisierung. Partner gewinnen, Werte vermitteln, Interessen vertreten.*

59 Quoted from http://tinyurl.com/oug2kox (Accessed: 15.01.2014).

modern image of the country"[60] as well as to secure German influence in the world through 'nation branding'[61] and cultural export. The openness of the FCP declared at the beginning of the 1970s is lost. Schneider draws a parallel to the era of colonialism: "People should be 'won over' for our values and ideas. That means that partners should adopt the things that we have identified as correct." (Schneider, 2012: 38, cf. Ch. 5) In the eyes of renowned cultural politicians, the concept introduced a paradigm shift: "From a historical point of view, representation and propaganda step back into the foreground."[62] Before the Bundestag elections in autumn 2013, the German government answered this criticism, stating:

> [The concept stands – author] in continuity to the basic principles in force up to the present. Intercultural dialogue, the creation and maintenance of sustainable networks and long-term partnerships continue to be among its key elements.[63]

This statement does not appear to be particularly credible, since the new concept from 2011 places the format of the 'Years of Germany'[64] at the focus of its activities and financing. These programs are a continuation of the West German tradition of representation from the post-war decades, and have the aim of presenting a positive image of Germany through the media of art and culture. They can be classed as a publicity measure, which are indispensable in the light of globalisation and the shifting pattern of power in the world, particularly in the so-called 'BRICS' countries.[65] India

---

60 Quoted in: *ibid.*

61 A nation as a brand with a marketable 'image', cf. Maletzke (1996: 108).

62 Cf. Ronald Grätz, Secretary General of the Institut für Auslandsbeziehungen (Translated as "Institute for Foreign Cultural Relations", but generally referred to as "ifa") in Stuttgart, and Olaf Zimmerman, CEO of the Deutscher Kulturrat (German Cultural Council) in Berlin (in: Deutscher Kulturrat e. V., 2012: 17), as well as 'Die Linke' (in: Deutscher Kulturrat e. V., 2013b: 14). Attention should also be drawn here to the description given by Klaus Kinkel – German Foreign Minister from 1992 to 1998 – of the FCP: "[S]tate and industry must work closer together in the interest of actively securing territory in foreign cultural policy" (Quoted in: Günsche, 1997: n.p.).

63 Quoted from http://tinyurl.com/oug2kox (Accessed: 14.01.2014). On the focus of the FCP from 2013 to 2017 from a party political point of view, see Deutscher Kulturrat e. V. (2013b).

64 German: *Deutschlandjahre.*

65 I.e. Brazil, Russia, India, China, and South Africa. The collective term 'BRICS' was introduced in 2001 by the worldwide financial concern Goldman Sachs. The population of these countries represents half of the global population. For a description of the BRICS countries, see also Chakraborty (2013: 20) and in detail Steinhilber (2007: 72 ff.). One of the current debates surrounding this group of countries (as of November 2013) is offered by the *Bundeszentrale für politische Bildung* at http://

is the fifth country in which the Foreign Office implemented initiative took place; following Years of Germany in Japan, China, Kazakhstan and Vietnam. Russia followed India in 2012-13, and the Year of Germany in Brazil took place from May 2014 to May 2015 (cf. Meitzner, 2012: 127).

The stated goal of the Year of Germany in India, as well as all other Years of Germany, is to "present a multifaceted, innovative, and contemporary image of Germany abroad" and "thereby to strengthen the Federal Republic's position as a home of modern science and business." (*ifa*)[66] Germany offers its expertise as an "innovative and creative partner" (No Author, 2012g: n.p.), in order to attract new talent and open new markets (cf. I_45: 504, Wagner, 2005: 6, 17, Bauersachs, 2012: n.p.). Behind the extensive effort invested in the creation, maintenance, presentation, and promotion of a positive image of Germany abroad within the framework of the Year of Germany lies the idea that states should or have to market themselves through a process of nation branding (cf. Körber, 2009: 185 ff.).

The Year of Germany in India was planned and realised by four project bodies – the Foreign Office as financier with overall responsibility, the Asia-Pacific Committee of German Business[67] as representative of the relevant economic interests, the German Federal Ministry of Education and Research representing German academia, and the Goethe-Institut (cf. Ch. 2.2.1 and 2.2.2).[68] The Goethe-Institut developed the cultural program, which took over the role of "crowd puller" (I_69: 22), as well as taking out the internal project management of the initiative (cf. Bloch, 2010: n.p.). Georg Blume, *ZEIT* magazine correspondent in New Delhi, commented on the leading role of the cultural institute in the following terms:

> [The Goethe Institute's role as project leader of the Year of Germany in India – author] was not received well [...] by the participating concerns who, through their representatives like the German Asia-Pacific Business Council, had up until that point taken part in the Years of Germany as equal partners. (Blume, 2011: n.p.)

The Year of Germany in Brazil, for example, took place under the leadership of the Federal Association of German Industry e. V.[69], leading

---

tinyurl.com/kuv75sr (Accessed: 25.12.2013). For more on India's role in the BRICS community, see the articles by Tobias Debiel, Herbert Wulf and Siddarth Malavarapu (cf. Debiel/Wulf, 2013 and Malavarapu, 2013).

66 Quoted from http://tinyurl.com/k62ynoo (Accessed: 07.07.2013).

67 German: *Asien-Pazifik-Ausschuss der Deutschen Wirtschaft.*

68 See comprehensive information on the Years of Germany at http://tinyurl.com/mq68vzl (Accessed: 07.07.2013).

69 German: *Bundesverband der Deutschen Industrie e. V (BDI).*

to "more results, instead of creative Goethe Happenings" (Blume, 2011: n.p.). Alongside the project bodies are the sponsoring partners, including well-known German firms such as BASF, Bosch, Deutsche Bank, Allianz, and Siemens.

Whether "cultural export [...] is a thing of the past, and now mutual fertilisation" counts (Deutscher Kulturrat e. V., 2012: 12), or if mutuality is a thing of the past, and cultural export once again drives the shape of the FCP, will soon be seen during the tenure of the new Foreign Minister, Sigmar Gabriel from the SPD beginning in January 2017.

In order to settle the dispute between representation and exchange in the FCP, it should be acknowledged that it is not a question of 'either/or'. Representation work as well as cooperation need to have a role in the FCP. This investigation into artistic cooperations illustrates that representation has a role to play in order to allow potential cooperations partners to approach and get to know one another in terms of their work, artistic practice, personalities, and spheres of living and working (cf. Ch. 5.2, 6.1, 6.7, 7). This means that the representation of art and culture abroad should constitute an overture to exchange, in order to allow something new to take shape. In this sense, presentation is the basis of cooperation. However, following this step, a process of engagement needs to follow. This process is challenging (cf. e.g. Ch. 5.6), however it is the only way towards the necessary understanding in a globalised world (cf. Ch. 1.1).

On an international level, the conceptions and debates of UNESCO play a central role in shaping the FCP, and thereby for international cooperation in the arts. In 1966, the UN's "Declaration of Principles of International Cultural Co-operation"[70] expressed its support for cultural cooperations in every form, in order to enrich cultures through the spread of knowledge and the stimulation of talents (Article I and Article X), as well as an understanding of the life of the partner. This exchange should help to enable peaceful coexistence with one another (Article II). In this sense, it should be realistic for all people to be able to engage in cultural cooperation – that is, to take part in their creation (cf. Ch. 2.3) and share their knowledge and abilities (Article V, cf. Ch. 5.1) – to enable a reciprocal exchange to take place (Article VIII). In Article XI, the temporal scope of cultural cooperations from the point of view of the UN is made clear: "Cultural co-operation shall contribute to the establishment of stable, long-term relations between peoples [...]" (cf. Ch. 5.4.2 and 6.11).

In 2005, the UNESCO Convention on the Protection and Promotion of the Diversity of Cultural Expressions (CDCE) was concluded. This convention grew out of a diverse array of UNESCO culture conferences.

---

70 See http://tinyurl.com/k4gtze7 (Accessed: 17.01.2014).

The first of these was held in 1970 in Venice (cf. UNESCO, 1970a, UNESCO, 1970b). The second took place in Mexico City in 1982, and was responsible for adopting the Mexico City Declaration on Cultural Policy (cf. UNESCO, 1982). The third took place in Stockholm in 1998, and produced the Action Plan on Cultural Policy for Development entitled "The Power of Culture" (cf. Deutsche UNESCO-Kommission e. V., 1998). A range of additional UNESCO reports and declarations formed the remainder of the basis for the agreement. These included, for example, the report from the World Commission on Culture and Development, entitled "Our Creative Diversity" (cf. Deutsche UNESCO-Kommission e. V., 1995). The 2005 Convention was followed by additional papers including the UNESCO World Report from 2009 entitled "Investing in Cultural Diversity and Intercultural Dialogue", and the Action Point Plans for 2013 to 2016, headlined "Diversity. Cooperation. Action" (cf. Deutsche UNESCO-Kommission e. V., 2013). This convention needs to be briefly examined with regard to the FCP's guidelines for the realisation of international cooperation in the arts.

The CDCE anchors the human right to cultural self-determination in international law (Article 6 of 7 the UNESCO Agreement, cf. also Schwencke *et al.*, 2009: 87 f.). It serves as a basic international frame of reference for cultural-political action. Every state has the right to formulate and implement its own cultural policy, and to adopt regulatory and financial measures and to shape frameworks in order to protect and encourage the diversity of cultural forms of expression (cf. Schneider, 2011d: 21 f.). Art and culture – not only as goods, but also as carriers of identities, values, and meaning (Article 1 of the UNESCO Agreement) – should above all be protected from a worldwide homogenization and standardisation (cf. Schwencke *et al.*, 2009: 87 f., Unmüßig, 2008: n.p.). The agreement was ratified in 2005 by 154 states (Mattelart, 2006: 141), and entered into force in Germany in 2007.

The 2005 Convention (Article 12) expands on the central goal of UNESCO – the promotion of cooperation between nations in education, science, and culture (Article 1.1 of the constitution cf. Schwencke *et al.*, 2009: 156 f.), since the strengthening and promotion of cultural diversity can only take place on the foundation of international dialogue and exchange. International cooperations in the arts are therefore a condition for and guarantee of the implementation of the agreement. A special importance is placed here on cooperation between countries from the 'Global South' and the 'Global North' (Article 13 to 16 of the UNESCO Convention), as already stressed at the third 'World Conference on Cultural Policies' in 1998. This includes encouragement for the development of independent cultural policies and cultural landscapes in the so-called 'developing countries', as well as stressing the need to protect and promote their forms of cultural expression during the process of international exchange (cf. Schwencke *et al.*, 2009: 160 f., Mataga, 2013: 2). The German UNESCO Commission explains the issues at stake in the 2005 Convention in the following terms:

> The CDCE aims at achieving a fairer balance for the Global South – approximately 150 nations of Africa, Central and Latin America and most of Asia – in the international flow of cultural goods and services as well as in the exchange of artistic expressions. (Merkel, 2013: 13)

The way in which this fair balance for the 'Global South' with regard to the equality of cultural encounters between unequal partners from 'North' and 'South' can be achieved is the subject of this study (cf. Ch. 6.13 and 7). The 'give and take' required by the FCP with regard to exchanges with countries in the 'Global South', which like India often have a history of colonisation, needs to be implemented sensibly.

The CDCE from 2005 draws attention to the connection between artistic creation, cultural training, and processes of social development. This desire to draw cultural and development policy together has been evident in UNESCO world conferences since the 1970s, and remains a point of discussion (cf. Gad, 2012b: 99).[71] Forms of cultural expression and creation are part of the human experience and societal life. UNESCO describes this reciprocal relationship between culture and development in the following terms:

> Culture enables the person to reflect on himself. It is first through culture that we become human, rationally acting, beings with the ability to reach critical judgements and a feeling for moral obligations. It is first through culture that we recognise values and make choices. It is first of all through culture, that the human being expresses himself, becomes aware of himself, recognises his own incompleteness, questions his own achievements, seeks tirelessly after new meaning, and creates works through which he oversteps his own limitations. (UNESCO, 1982: n.p.)

Engagement with culture, which strengthens creativity, and a person's ability to reflect and express themselves, is, accordingly, a development factor (cf. Gad, 2012b: 100, Metzendorf, 2011: 56).[72] Schneider speaks of

---

71 For further detail, see Deutsche UNESCO-Kommission e. V. (1995), Deutsche UNESCO-Kommission e. V. (1998), Deutsche UNESCO-Kommission e. V. (2005), Hamm-Brücher/Auswärtiges Amt (1982).

72 This would be an appropriate point to direct readers to the theoretical concept of the 'Capability Approach', devised by the Indian Nobel laureate Amartya Sen. According to Sen, the person requires capabilities enabling him to develop. These capabilities are multidimensional, and depend on context. Alongside the political, economic,

"cultural help to help oneself" (Schneider, 2008b: 16), which should make individuals and groups available to become the leading actors in their own development.[73] Since culture is, or ideally should be, based on plurality and diversity, it follows that there is no single path to development (cf. Gad, 2012b: 87).

Cooperations are a basic format for the field of culture and development in the FCP (cf. *ibid.*: 85),[74] which should have the functions of qualification, advice, and networking. Cooperation between rich and poor states, or states with varying degrees of cultural political experience, is necessary for the fulfilment of the tasks of foreign cultural policy in the field of culture and development. These include providing support for local cultural infrastructure, or the cultural and creative economy; or through supporting the establishment of robust and independent cultural support networks, and capacity building[75] (cf. Millan, 2012: 94). This once again raises the question of precisely how these partnerships are organised in practice.

Chapter 2.2 has clearly shown that the cultural policy discourse has concerned itself for almost fifty years with the realisation of dialogue, partnership, and equality in the FCP (ambition). However, how this might be practically implemented in line with the needs of the partner countries has not been defined (reality). The exact meaning of the key terms of the FCP remain undefined in the political discourse (cf. Schreiner, 2008: 12, IFAB, 2001: 19). "Stakeholders such as governments, civil society or cultural practitioners are challenged by the task of translating these

---

and environmental dimensions, Sen also uses a sociocultural dimension to describe these capabilities (for more see Volkert, 2005, Leßmann, 2011: 54 ff., Sedmak *et al.*, 2011b: 7, Graf, 2011: 11 ff., 26, Sedmak, 2011: 31 ff.).

73 According to Gad, there are two "directions of impact": "The programs devised and implemented by the donor countries together with the partners, which also means giving over control over the project direction and management to the target group, [and] setting up the donor country's programs to broaden the options to participate for people in the partner countries in the long term, and so to allow the target group a deeper involvement in the direction of the development process." (Gad, 2012b: 58)

74 For more detail on the field of culture and development, see Gad (2012b: 1-127, 273-306), Schneider/Gad (2011), Wilhelm (2010) as well as the websites of the UNESCO Chair in Cultural Policy for the Arts in Development / Department of Cultural Policy at the University of Hildesheim at www.kulturundentwicklung.de and http://tinyurl.com/l7db5bg (Accessed: 02.01.2014).

75 Capacity building can be understood as the strengthening of persons and institutions to enable them to sustainably reach their development goals through the effective use of resources and structures, as well as the growing involvement of civil society. Capacity building should strengthen the problem-solving ability of individuals, organisations, or societies in developing and transformation countries (cf. Schönhuth's definition at http://tinyurl.com/qaecb7k, Accessed: 28.10.2013).

broad political ideas into ground realities." (Steinkamp, 2013: 2) The identification of best practice examples of international cooperation – for example, the "Kaleidoscope on Diversity of Cultural Expressions"[76] or white papers from civil society groups such as "Creating Cultural Diversity. Action Points from Civil Society for the Implementation on the UNESCO Convention on the Diversity of Cultural Forms of Expression (2005) in and by Germany"[77] (cf. Deutsche UNESCO-Kommission e. V., 2009) are intended to reduce the gap between the ideal and the reality. However, these political goals require a gradual implementation; including the time and space to experiment and to fail (cf. Ch. 5.5.4 and 6.10). Chapter 5 of this study will illustrate the state of this implementation with regard to German-Indian partnerships in the arts at the beginning of the 21st Century. The succeeding Chapters 6 and 7 will show how this implementation could take the form of a partnership of equals.

2.2.1 The Goethe-Institut: Key Actor in German-Indian Cultural Relations

The Foreign Office has the leading role in the external realisation of cultural policy. It provides financial resources and creates secure legal frameworks such as international treaties (cf. Maaß, 2009c: 276, Schreiner, 2011: 121). The implementation of the German FCP takes place by intermediary organisations (cf. Kathe, 2005: 18 f.) engaged by the Foreign Office, who are "broadly independent" to "realise and implement" the Foreign Office's political goals (German Bundestag, 1975: 43).[78]

---

76 See http://tinyurl.com/oen79jk (Accessed: 13.01.2014).

77 German: *Kulturelle Vielfalt gestalten. Handlungsempfehlungen aus der Zivilgesellschaft zur Umsetzung des UNESCO-Übereinkommens zur Vielfalt kultureller Ausdrucksformen (2005) in und durch Deutschland.*

78 A "de-nationalisation" of cultural policy is achieved through the interposition of mediators in the form of organisations under private law (Hamm-Brücher, 1980: 112; see also Kathe, 2005: 19). These mediators include, for example, the Goethe-Institut, the Deutsche Akademische Austauschdienst (German Academic Exchange Service – DAAD), the Alexander-von-Humboldt-Stiftung, the Institut für Auslandsbeziehungen (Institute for Foreign Cultural Relations – ifa), the Zentralstelle für das Auslandsschulwesen (Central Agency for German Schools Abroad), the German UNESCO Commission, and the Deutsche Welle (cf. Schwencke *et al.*, 2009: 37 ff., 137 f., Niklas, 2005: 59 ff.). For a critical perspective on the independence of these cultural mediators, see, for example, Wittek (2006: 12), Bode (2002: 157 f.), Roßkopf (2010: 26), Maaß (2009a: 12, 15, 20 ff.). As the question of the dependence or independence of these cultural mediators does not lie within the scope of this study, an extensive discussion will not be presented at this juncture.

German-Indian cultural relations are largely the responsibility of the Goethe-Institut in India (cf. Spiess, 2009: 22).[79] The empirical results of this study have confirmed this fact. Almost all German-Indian cultural cooperations have some kind of relationship with the institutes in India in order to be able to carry out their work (cf. Ch. 5.3).

The organisational mission of the Goethe-Institut is "promoting knowledge of the German language abroad, maintaining international cultural cooperation" and "presenting a comprehensive image of Germany through information on its cultural, social, and political life".[80] Alongside these pre-existing goals, the Goethe-Institut as cultural representative has also received new tasks and fields of work because of developments in the FCP (cf. Maaß, 2009c: 269-280, Ch. 2.2). In a press release from 6.6.2013, the institute explained:

> In a time of new global challenges, the work of the Goethe-Institut is devoted to a deepened understanding between cultures, and the strengthening of Germany's global reputation.[81]

The institute's worldwide presence is one of its trademarks: "At present, the Goethe-Institut has more than 149 institutes and 10 liaison offices in 93 countries. Thirteen of these are Goethe Institutes in Germany" (Goethe-Institut e. V., 2012c: 4).[82] The past decade has seen the institute concentrate on the expansion of its network in over fifty 'developing countries' and 'emerging economies', particularly in Africa (cf. Lehmann, 2011c: n.p., Spiess, 2009: 19), in order to fill a "cultural vacuum" (Goethe-Institut staff member in India, quoted in: Kämpchen, 2004: 33) and to

---

79 Also Ittstein (2002: 34). The institute has been a registered association (eingetragener Verein) since 1951. Its full name is "*Verein zur Pflege der deutschen Sprache im Ausland und zur Förderung der internationalen kulturellen Zusammenarbeit*" (Association for the maintenance of the German language abroad, and for the promotion of international cultural cooperation) (cf. Michels, 2001: 13). For a comprehensive history of the institute, see, for example, Kathe (2005: 65-368), who gives a history of the institute between 1951 and 1990, and Michels (2001). See also Eisfeld (2004: 21-39) and Roßkopf (2010: 29 ff.) on the history, organisational structure, and objectives of the institute.

80 Quoted from http://www.goethe.de/uun/org/ (Accessed: 19.11.2013). The goals of the organisation are in Paragraph 2.1 of the Statutes in the version from 20.11.2009 (cf. Goethe-Institut e. V., 2009: 1).

81 Quoted from http://tinyurl.com/qyta2gg (Accessed: 27.10.2013). On understanding and communication as the basis for the future work of the institute, see also Goethe-Institut e. V. (1998: 206).

82 Also described by Lehmann (2011a) as "saturated". The Goethe-institut is here said to be the largest of the recognised mediator organisations in the Federal Republic of Germany. Because of its large presence abroad, it is also the best known.

open up "the creative potential in developing and emerging countries" (Lehmann, 2011b: n.p.).

The activities of the institute are divided into the fields of program, linguistic, information, and archival work, as well as networking activity, which is seen to be its overarching task.[83] Since artistic cooperation is anchored in the field of program work, it would be meaningful at this point to present the goals of the institute's program work in general, and in India in particular.

The cultural program activity is orientated towards the practical aspect of the implementation of cultural policy measures. At present, the program work is directed principally towards the support of international cultural exchange. That is, in towards an unfolding of cultural life in the intercultural context, which for the purposes of the Goethe-Institut consists of the conception and organisation of cultural events in the established cultural and aesthetic media such as literature, film, theatre, dance, art, music, archaeology, architecture, design and fashion (cf. Maaß, 2009a: 12, Bauer, 2009a: 128 ff.). In keeping with the declared goals of the FCP in the 21st Century (cf. Ch. 2.2), alongside the 'fine arts', this program work also showcases "the public discourses, economic and technical, as well as socio-political culture of the Federal Republic" (Goethe-Institut e. V., 2011b: 3). Accordingly, this program work makes use of the broader conception of culture characterised by Dahrendorf (cf. Schöfthaler, 2009: 317, and Ch. 2.2).

Alongside the management of events, the institute reports that its work to mediate and network between institutes, professionals, and artists in host countries and in Germany, with the goal of establishing and expanding networks, is central to its program work (cf. Goethe-Institut e. V., 2011c: 6).[84] According to Klaus-Dieter Lehmann, President of the Goethe-Institut since 2008, this encompasses support for direct encounters and active exchanges of equal value for cultural workers from various cultural contexts (cf. Lehmann, 2011b: n.p.).[85]

According to a representative of the Goethe-Institut in New Delhi, all of the organisation's activities are undertaken on the basis of a long-term cooperation through dialogue with partners (cf. I_42: 36).[86] Projects in the cultural program were said to be initiated, conceived, and realised

---

83 On the activities of the institute in all three areas, see the press cuttings from the annual press conferences from previous years (cf. Goethe-Institut e. V., 2011b, *ibid.*, 2012c).

84 Also Gad (2008: 12), Sattler (2007: 257), Knopp (2010b: 20).

85 See also Goethe-Institut e. V. (2011c: 6), Kettner (2009: 240), Lehmann (2011c: n.p.), Ch. 2.2.

86 This information "I_###: ###" refers to transcripts of interviews undertaken with experts in the course of this study. See also Lechner (2004: 239), Hoffmann

together with equal partners on the ground or in the host country. A focus was said to be on a common financial or in-kind engagement towards a participation-orientated cooperation (cf. Goethe-institut e. V., 2012b: 7). In order to meet the needs, interests, and problems of each host country in an appropriate way – that is, to implement "demand-driven" program work (Goethe-Institut e. V., 1999: 219)[87] – the institute claims to enter into a dialogue "which demands the trust and credibility of a relationship, which can only develop through long-term cooperation" (*ibid.*, 2012c: 3).[88] However, Lechner questions whether the current structure of the cultural mediator allows such a dialogue, characterised by a long-term commitment, and an emphasis on processes (cf. Ch. 6.9):

> Funds and personnel are not […] invested […] for the purposes of medium and long-term project work with partners. This means that […] forms of working that continuity, professionalism, and exchange in the longer-term […] become difficult if not impossible. (Lechner, 2004: 262 f.)

Is it at all possible to realise a long-term dialogue in equal partnership with actors from the host country? How can the "presentation of Germany as an innovative, modern cultural nation" (Auswärtiges Amt, 2002: 13) be reconciled with cultural activities, which seek to integrate themselves in the context of local culture and society? This study will concern itself with putting this principle of dialogue and partnership into question when it comes to present its results in Chapter 5.

2.2.2 "Max Mueller Bhavan": The Goethe-Institut in India

There are six Goethe Institutes in India:[89] New Delhi (founded 1957), Kolkata (1957), Chennai (1960), Bangalore (1960), Mumbai (1969), and Poona (1961),[90] which have been represented in the country continuously

---

(1996a: 12), *ibid.* (1999), Goethe-Institut e. V. (1996a: 8), *ibid.* (2012c: 3), Knopp (2010b: 16 f.), Lehmann (2013).

87 See also Lehmann (2011b), Lechner (2004: 247 f.).

88 See also Lechner (2004: 247 f.). For further literature on the activities in the program work of the institute see the institute's magazine *Reportagen Bilder Gespräche* (Reports, Images, Discussions) and the yearbooks at http://www.goethe.de/uun/pub/ (Accessed: 27.10.2013). See also Braun *et al.* (2010), Goethe-Institut Inter Nationes e. V. (2001), Lehmann/Zimmermann (2013), Kathe (2005) and Wittek (2006).

89 Institutes with a program and language department, as well as a library as information centre (cf. Schindler, 1997: 151).

90 See Niklas (2005: 78 f., 84 ff.) for an in-depth description of the individual institutes in India, and their respective websites: Bangalore: http://tinyurl.com/m7jumam, Chennai: http://tinyurl.com/kvufcj5, Kolkata: http://tinyurl.com/n3z6ygy, Mumbai: http://tinyurl.com/k22ftjd, New Delhi: http://tinyurl.com/lykhrb3, Pune: http://

for more than fifty years.[91] These are, according to Heiko Sievers, head of the New Delhi Institute, and delegate for the South Asia region since 2010, "very well connected with the local artistic, educational, and academic scenes."[92] The network of institutes is complemented by four *Goethe* Centres, in Ahmedabad, Coimbatore, Hyderabad[93] and Trivandrum, which work together with local German-Indian cultural organisations.[94] This means that altogether, the Goethe-Institut has its strongest worldwide international presence in India. As an MMB staff member in New Delhi explains, this is demanded by the size and complexity of the country:

> If you are based in Delhi, you can't do anything in Trivandrum. It would be the equivalent of sitting in Oslo, and thinking you would be able to do a program in Rome. This is simply due to the size of the country [...] which then comes together with an extremely high level of variety and diversity. (I_42: 26)

Lechner raises the criticism that the close network, resources,[95] and infrastructure possessed by the Goethe-Institut in the world reminds him of "colonial behaviour patterns" and "Western dominance", when he compares the massive German presence in India with the relatively modest Indian presence in Germany – in the form of a single Indian institute in Berlin – the "*Tagore-Zentrum*" (Lechner, 2004: 289).[96] This "imbalance"

---

tinyurl.com/kes7t6s (All Accessed: 20.07.2013). For a history of the institute in India, see Schmid (1997: 66, 73 f.). Schmid (1997), although an older publication, is an important source for this study, because of the focused presentation of the German-Indian cultural dialogue from an ethnological perspective.

91 On the fiftieth anniversary of the institute in India, see http://tinyurl.com/ovu9cga (Accessed: 27.10.2013).

92 Quoted from http://tinyurl.com/q7abll4 (Accessed: 27.10.2013). The South Asia Region incorporates India, Pakistan, Bangladesh, Nepal, Sri Lanka, Afghanistan, and their respective Goethe Institutes.

93 Former institute, which was closed in 1996/7 on financial grounds (cf. Schmid, 1997: 73 f.). Institutes have been closed, and sometimes re-opened in India in the course of the decades (cf. Schindler, 1997: 152).

94 The fifth centre in Chandigarh seems to be closed. For the current locations of the Goethe Centres and Goethe Institutes in India, see http://tinyurl.com/pmx7m2m (Accessed: 27.10.2013).

95 Material and human resources such as, knowledge, abilities, and funds, as well as infrastructure (cf. Steinkamp, 2013: 7, 9) allow the party designing the project to exercise influence over topics, programs, projects, and goals, or to control access to these resources.

96 Named after Rabindranath Tagore (1861-1941), Bengali poet, composer, education reformer, and Nobel Prize winner. For more on India's foreign cultural policy, see Ch. 3.3.

leads to inequality though a lack of "fairness" and an element of "coercion" between the partners (*ibid.*).[97]

The Goethe-Institut in India goes under the name of the 'Max Mueller Bhavan Indo-German Cultural Centre' – shortened to Max Mueller Bhavan or MMB. The Max Mueller Bhavan – or Max Müller House takes its name from the German religious scholar and co-founder of modern Indian Studies, Max Müller, who is himself said to have never been in India (cf. Rothermund, 1995b: 479),[98] despite fostering great admiration for the country and its people:

> If you were to ask me under which skies the human spirit has developed the wisest, and reached the highest point; where it has submerged itself deepest in the greatest problems, and found their solutions, then I would direct you to India. (Max Müller quoted in: No author, 2013: 40)

The Goethe Institutes in India are the only ones in the world that carry their own name (cf. I_69: 130). As Indologist and Sanskrit scholar, Max Müller[99] was a pioneer amongst European intellectuals, who, in his spiritual, romantic, and philosophical search, followed the common traces of Indo-European civilization back to the ancient Vedic cultures of India. His efforts to display the affinity of the Indo-European family, united by their shared roots, has earned him high estimation in both cultural circles to the present day (cf. Schäffler/Mittelstädt, 2008: 46). The German Indologist with iconic status in India (cf. Lehmann in: Breukelchen, 2010: 51 ff.) is a "free entry ticket" for German partners to enter into dialogue in India (Niklas, 2005: 71).[100]

The tradition of the institute, as well as its independence – in comparison to the short lifespans of other European cultural institutions, which depend on their embassies – are appreciated by Indian cultural actors, and highly prized (cf. I_63: 5).[101] They describe the institute as "unique" or "extraordinary" (I_39: 2),[102] and capable of acting as an

---

97 For more detail see Ch. 5.9.1.

98 Despite the age of the publication, the 'Handbook on India' by Dietmar Otto Ernst Rothermund, Professor Emeritus in South Asian History at Heidelberg University, made a valuable contribution to the orientation of this study. Fore more background information on the naming of the Goethe-Institut in India, see in depth Rau (2001) and Lechner (2004: 299 ff.).

99 For more on the person of Max Friedrich Müller (1823, Dessau – 1900, Oxford), see Wessler (2007b).

100 For more on German Indology, see Rothermund (1995b: 479 f.), Wessler (2007b).

101 See also I_47: 8, 26-27, I_43: 15, I_65: 5, I_59: 6, I_44: 11-13.

102 See also I_54: 70, 87, I_75: 26-30, I_43: 15.

example to other Western institutions (cf. I_65: 3).[103] The Goethe-Institut has built itself a good reputation in India during the last fifty years, as one of its representatives puts it (cf. I_69: 130).

Thanks to the specific conditions and current challenges of the host country, each national *Goethe* structure has its own focus with regard to cultural program activities, which takes the local art scene and its own target groups into account (cf. I_63: 10, I_70: 12).[104] In India, this country-specific planning and implementation of cultural exchange is made more difficult by the size and complexity of the country in question, with its huge size and wide diversity of ethnicities, languages, scripts, religions; as well as regional, social, and economic differences (cf. Schmid, 1997: 79, Ch. 3). The focuses of the program activity of the MMB, as well as the selection and sponsorship of projects on the basis of these focuses, also depends – alongside the local conditions – on the personal interest and initiatives of the staff and management of the institution: "I think that [name of the former manager of the Goethe-Institut in Bangalore – author] was also very keen on dance. This was her 'pet thing', it was dance." (I_49: 71)[105]

For several years, the focus of the Goethe Institute in New Delhi has been in the field of contemporary dance,[106] children's and youth theatre, electronic music, and photography[107] (cf. I_73: 22, I_11: 64-65, I_56: 14). It supports and sponsors numerous, and increasingly multicultural projects in these fields (cf. I_42: 80, I_73: 22, I_13: 26), with the goal of qualifying artists and cultural actors, as well as on the expansion of cultural infrastructure within South Asia. These local focuses are, as a rule, renegotiated and renewed as needed every four years, and shifted onto other fields and sectors as required (cf. I_54: 169).

The focus of the Goethe-Institut in India is on the mediation of contemporary art.[108] Accordingly, the institute provides contemporary artists in particular with non-material and financial support, which they do not receive in their own country (cf. I_50: 62, 148, I_15: 13, Ch. 3).

---

103 For justifications, see Ch. 5.3.

104 See also I_50: 16, 67, 165, Hoffmann (1999: 194).

105 See also I_28: 110, Schäffler/Mittelstädt (2008: 46).

106 The institute's focus on dance in India has a long tradition reaching back to the 1980s. Lechner describes the cooperation between India and Germany in dance during the first East West Encounters of the 1980s, and the 2000-1 *Festspiele* in detail (cf. Lechner, 2004: 224 ff., Ch. 4). On the institute's focus on dance in India, see also http://tinyurl.com/odygdwy (Accessed: 27.10.2013) as well as the expert interview I_45, e.g. at I_45: 18, 445.

107 See also, for example, the PIX filmography magazine at http://www.pixquarterly.in (Accessed: 25.09.2013).

108 Sievers quoted at http://tinyurl.com/q7abll4 (Accessed: 27.10.2013).

The global mutual learning process called for by Lepenies is, according to its manager Heiko Sievers, today a part of the program of the institute in New Delhi (Sievers quoted in: Kusch/Beckmann, 2011: n.p.).[109]

Rather than presenting German culture its mission, according to a representative of the MMB, is to engage with contemporary Indian art and "to see how one can work there together with German colleagues" (I_42: 72). The program activities of the MMB are, in this estimation, and according to the principles set out by headquarters, principally cooperation work:

> [Cooperation work] is now the basic idea when we are talking about the cultural field nowadays. That is, just the cultural field, the foundation of our work. When we give that up, we can go home. We now have things that we call strategic goals, but these in no way prescribe the way in which these can be implemented, and so the implementation needs to be discussed again and again, considered, and discussed with the partners, and so on, in every location, every year, and for every sector. But I think that this is absolutely basic for our work, and for the recognition that we have here. That is to say, we are known as being somebody with whom you can develop projects. (I_42: 50)[110]

The focus on contemporary art rests on the fact that the institute "speaks a common language" with Indian cultural actors in this field (I_42: 14, see also I_63: 18) and can therefore engage with them on an equal footing.

In traditional, or classical art, this common language is not in place, because the many years of rigorous training – for example, in classical Indian dance, or ballet in Germany – which often begins in childhood, and incorporates a comprehensive knowledge of tradition, means that the partners are never able to have an engagement on equal terms (see also Panke, 2006: 32). Indeed, contemporary art includes an invitation to experimentation, which the tradition of the classical arts would not permit (cf. I_33: 15). It remains to be seen whether this equality can be preserved when professional European contemporary art meets the young and developing Indian scene, or whether the European art will tend to instruct the Indian to develop in a European direction, and thereby nip the principle of equality in the bud:

> European contemporary thought [...] or international contemporary practice has had a massive influence [...] in all of the artistic fields that [the Goethe-Institut] deals with. (I_42: 72)

109 See also I_73: 22, I_60: 19-24, Bloch (2010: 16).

110 See also I_42: 14, 36, I_54: 187, 191, I_73: 22.

The focus of the MMB in Bangalore is similar to that of the regional Goethe-Institut for South Asia in New Delhi.[111] The Goethe-Institut in Bangalore is distinguished by its residency program.[112] In the spring of 2013, it initiated a 'Residency Offensive' under the name 'bangaloREsidency' – accepting German artists for between several weeks and several months in cooperation with nine various Indian contemporary cultural institutions in and around Bangalore.[113] Alongside space to live and work, the residencies in Bangalore offer intensive and personal supervision through the residency leader, to ease entry into the new culture, and allow for introductions and networking in the local arts scene. The website of the MMB in Bangalore explains that the residence program:

> [...] [s]hould offer German artists space for creative output, and give them the opportunity to cooperate with Indian artists, and face the challenges offered by a pulsing modern Indian metropolis like Bangalore. The residence was created in order to support mutual exchange so that both the German guests and the local artistic community can profit from new perspectives and widen their horizons.[114]

The headquarters advertises the residency programs as "particularly effective formats" (Goethe-Institut e. V., 2011b: 5 f.), because of their ability to encourage long-lasting and sustainable contacts on the basis of intensive local cooperation.

The residencies in Bangalore follow a clear process. At the beginning of their stay, the German artist presents themselves to the art scene in Bangalore:

> [Y]ou start with something where you just introduce yourself as what you've done before, that's interesting because for the younger artists of the city and all of that they get to see someone from outside who has done a very interesting body of work, who I have clearly liked and I have to bring them here. So that's useful more so for the community than for the artist who is staying here. (I_63: 103)

At the end of their stay, the artist presents the content that they have produced during their residency (cf. I_69: 56).

---

111 For detail on the focus of the MMB in Bangalore, see Niklas (2005: 84 ff.).

112 For more on the worldwide residency program of the Goethe-Institut, see http://tinyurl.com/pohqx7y (Accessed: 27.10.2013) and Goethe-Institut e. V. (2012a). On the residency program in Bangalore, see Goethe-Institut e. V. (2012a: 14 f.).

113 Cf. the website of the MMB Bangalore on the residency program at www.goethe.de/bangalore/residency (Accessed: 18.08.2013).

114 Quoted from the website of the MMB Bangalore: http://tinyurl.com/ohakzpz (Accessed: 27.10.2013).

The residency format is open to criticism.[115] One reason for this is so-called residency hopping (cf. I_70: 91-92, I_69: 40-42), whereby invited artists go from one residency to the other "because international experiences are now also essential in artists' CVs in order to achieve national recognition" (Knüsel, 2011: 72):

> When they hop from one place to another, always grazing, but somehow never deliver anything, then there is somehow an unpleasant feeling that stays behind in Bangalore. Now we have given him everything that we have, we have shown him all the fields, he has grazed everywhere, and now he is gone. And what even was that? What have I got now, why was he even here? (I_69: 44)

As this quotation from a *Goethe* member of staff makes clear, the residency program brings with it the danger of short one-time events without any sustainability. This raises the question – what effect can short term artistic exchange formats like residencies have on the cultural landscape and cultural scene in the host country at all?[116]

Indian cultural actors describe the activities of the MMB in India as contributing to the expansion of cultural infrastructure, and the establishment of specific artistic scenes, like, for example, the fields of contemporary dance, children's and youth theatre, and electronic music: "[T]hey [the MMB] [a]re [...] essential to the building of the scene in India." (I_50: 148)[117] Accordingly, the institute does have an effect on the national cultural and educational development through its work (cf. Bode, 2002: 154). However, when asked, the Goethe-Institut in India definitively does not view itself as a cultural-political actor in India (cf. I_42: 50, I_60: 19-24, I_73: 22). This statement can be seen programmatically. "Political

115 The Department of Cultural Policy at the University of Hildesheim engaged intensively with this form of sponsorship in the summer semester of 2013 through Professor Dr. Wolfgang Schneider's event "Residencies. Cultural-political instrument for the processes of aesthetic practice" (*Residenzen. Kulturpolitisches Instrument für Prozesse ästhetischer Praxis*), see http://tinyurl.com/ongag65. For a critical appraisal of the residency program, see Knüsel (2011: 71) and the India Foundation for the Arts at http://tinyurl.com/qhjz4c4 (Both Accessed: 27.10.2013).

116 See the discussion on this question in Ch. 5.7 and 6.11.

117 Also I_15: 219, I_45: 18, 445, I_75: 26-35, I_49: 8, I_44: 2-3, 6-8, 15-16, I_7: 38, I_54: 66, I_60: 19-24. On the expansion of cultural infrastructure through the Goethe-Institut, see http://tinyurl.com/oejaomj (Accessed: 27.10.2013) and Lehmann (2011a: n.p.). Expansion rather than support – that is the expansion of infrastructure – can be thoroughly criticised, since the change ultimately depends on the people on the ground, whereby a cultural mediator cannot claim to 'expand' cultural infrastructure, but at most to 'support' this expansion. This support would be possible through an "equal cooperation of all the relevant actors from the first needs analysis to the evaluation" (2011: 103). See Ch. 3, 5.1, 6.13.

neutrality", and "non-engagement" or "political correctness" is demanded from the cultural programs of mediator organisations abroad (Lechner, 2004: 262 f.). However the activities of the MMB certainly do have an influence on India's cultural landscape (cf. I_60: 19-24, I_54: 84) meaning that it is, however indirectly, involved in the cultural politics of the country (cf. I_69: 125-129).[118] This role as a shaper of public policy can be seen clearly in that the MMB engages in "ongoing cultural – and this also implies political and societal and social – discussions" and leads cultural-political discourses on, for example, the non-existent cultural spaces in India "in dialogue with prominent artists and multipliers" (I_73: 22). Indeed, these are defined as "central tasks for a European cultural institute in India" by a representative of the MMB (I_73: 22, I_60: 19-24).[119] This type of dialogue is also often welcomed by Indian partners (cf. I_58: 4).

2.3 Cooperation: Theoretical Frame of Reference

To be part of a cooperation – that is to have the opportunity to cooperate, and thereby networks – means to possess and to generate social capital (cf. Putnam/Goss, 2001: 22, Lederer, 2005: 20 f.). The theory of social capital has a range of representatives (cf. Putnam/Goss, 2001: 15 ff.). In order to provide a broader scholarly frame of reference for this study of cooperative work in the arts, it suffices to concentrate at this point on the "primary representative" (Lederer, 2005: 3, 20).[120]

At the end of the 1970s, the French sociologist Pierre Bourdieu defined his Capital Theory of Social Capital as "an aggregate of the actual or potential resources that are connected with the availability of a lasting network of more or less institutionalised relationships based on mutual recognition and acknowledgement" (Bourdieu quoted in: Putnam/Goss, 2001: 18, see also Lederer, 2005: 3 f., Seubert, 2009: 162 ff.).[121] This

118 Also I_61: 31-32, I_54: 78, 84.

119 On the political activity of the Goethe-Institut, see also Wittek (2006: 234) and Lehmann (2013: n.p.), who describe culture as "political power" and not a "playground for artists and intellectuals".

120 On the theory of social capital and the history of the idea of social capital, see Putnam/Goss (2001: 20 ff.). Various models of social capital are concisely summarised in Lederer (2005: 3 ff.). For criticism of the term and the theory, see e.g. Seubert (2009: 12), Betz (2005: 20). Social capital can be divided on the level of individual, group, and whole society (cf. Seubert, 2009: 20, 184, 267). This presentation primarily rests on the first two levels, which are of significance for cooperation work. Quality is usually more important than quantity, in order to generate capital, and thereby social status (cf. *ibid.*: 170, 184).

121 Bourdieu's 1982 work *Distinction: A Social Critique of the Judgement of Taste* forms the basis of the theory of social capital.

capital refers accordingly to relations between persons. These relations are the actual bearers of this form of capital. Alongside social capital, Bourdieu proposed three additional forms of capital: economic capital – describing all forms of material wealth,[122] cultural capital – or level of education in its broadest sense (cf. Throsby, 2001: 45 ff.)[123] and symbolic capital – which bestows prestige, reputation, social recognition, and therefore social power. Symbolic capital is also described as a "collective term" for the availability and combined effect of the three other types of capital (Seubert, 2009: 172).[124] The capital forms exist contemporaneously, and mutually determine one another. They can be invested in one another and thereby transformed (cf. *ibid.*: 175):

> The accrual and maintenance of social capital requires time, energy [and money – author]. When individuals […] feel forced to apply their resources in a different place […], social capital will probably suffer as a result. (Putnam/Goss, 2001: 39, see Ch. 3.2.5, 3.4, 5.2).

Similar principles apply to cultural capital, which requires time and money (cf. Ch. 5.4.2 and 5.4.3). At the same time, social capital can also condition cultural and economic capital (cf. Ch. 5.9.1).

The various forms of capital are therefore use and advantage bringing resources (cf. Deindl, 2005: 1 ff.).[125] The nature of social capital as a resource is made clear by the US sociologist James Coleman, who defines social capital "by its function […]: It enables actors to realise particular goals, which without social capital they would not be able to fulfil or, at least not so effectively." (Seubert, 2009: 20, 84)[126] These resources, and their ability to be transformed, determine individuals' social position (cf. Seubert, 2009: 165 ff., Lederer, 2005: 20 f.).[127]

---

122 For more on economic capital, see Fuchs-Heinritz/König (2005: 161 f.).

123 Bourdieu distinguishes cultural capital as being incorporated (through education, upbringing, and science), objective (e.g. books and paintings), and institutional (e.g. academic titles). For more on cultural capital, see Fuchs-Heinritz/König (2005: 162 ff.). Education is the prerequisite for an experience of culture, and culture offers a milieu in which education can be developed.

124 On symbolic capital, see Fuchs-Heinritz/König (2005: 169 f.).

125 See Ch. 2.2 for a definition of resources.

126 For Coleman's definition of social capital see also Lederer (2005: 4 ff.).

127 This social position in turn determines the habits, and individual patterns of perception, thought, and action (cf. Fuchs-Heinritz/König, 2005: 113 ff., Seubert, 2009: 164). The 'social field' is a further central term in Bourdieu's capital theory, which can be understood as "a social constellation in a constant process of change, which refers to a vaguely defined part of society, and can be understood as the setting of struggles between various forces." (Schreiner, 2011: 287) Art is an example of a social field (see also Fuchs-Heinritz/König, 2005: 176 ff.).

The US sociologist Robert D. Putnam understands social capital as the reserve of social trust, reciprocal norms, and networks, which can accrue to people working in cooperation (cf. Putnam/Goss, 2001: 22, Höfer *et al.*, 2006: 270).[128] He thereby defines the conditions upon which social capital is based and out of which cooperations and networks are able to develop (see also Ch. 5):[129] Freedom, or voluntary choice is understood as "the absence of coercion" (Seubert, 2009: 101 ff., 115).[130] This definition of 'freedom' is open to criticism, since membership in networks is pre-structured by the position of actors in the social space. This means that the social standing of an individual determines their access to certain groups (cf. Seubert, 2009: 268).

Trust reduces social complexity according to Luhmann's model. Social capital is based on trust (cf. Ch. 5.4.2, 6.13).[131] Trust can be created through long-term relations, which first serve their own purposes and not immediately a result-oriented strategic action (cf. Ch. 5.5, 6.3, 6.5, 6.9). Trust can also be achieved through institutional frameworks and common understanding through social norms (cf. Seubert, 2009: 22, 190 ff., 267).[132] However, institutions can close the field and thereby, for example, hinder access to new players (cf. Ch. 5.3).

Reciprocity is related to norms, interests, and exchange (above all of goods and information): norms, which serve as the moral basis of cooperations, are ideally discussed by the participants in a cooperation. The interests of the actors also need to be clarified (cf. Ch. 6.2). With regard to exchange, Seubert explains:

> When some are in possession of the goods upon which others are dependant, exchange is a source of power. One basic question of the sociology of reciprocity

---

128 For more detail on Putnam's conception of social capital, see Lederer (2005: 8 ff.), Seubert (2009: 72 ff.). An additional significant representative of the theory of social capital is Francis Fukuyama, cf. Lederer (2005: 11 ff.). Seubert summarises the definition as "the means to act collectively acquired through social connections" (Seubert, 2009: 90, 190).

129 For the extant to which cooperations are based on pre-existing conditions, see, for example, Ch. 5.4 and 6.8; further criteria for social capital according to Steinkamp (cf. Steinkamp, 2013: 16): "Commitment" (cf. Ch. 5.6), "Personality" (cf. Ch. 5, 6, 7), "Ownership" (cf. Ch. 5.4.3), "Responsibility" (cf. Ch. 5.9.1, 6.2, 6.8), "Identity" (cf. Ch. 5.1, 6.2), "Face-to-face meetings" (cf. Ch. 6.5).

130 "Rather than externally imposed norms, cooperation should allow the creation of autonomously determined norms." (Seubert, 2009: 102) For social capital as a relation with shared norms, value-measurements, and convictions, see also Lederer (2005: 7, 17). On the absence of coercion in cooperations, see also Ch. 6.1, 6.2, 6.6.

131 For more detail on trust as a criteria for social capital, see Lederer (2005: 6, 13, 21) and Seubert (2009: 74, 111 ff.).

132 See also Rautenstrauch *et al.*, 2003: 131 f. and Ch. 6.2, 6.6.

> is therefore the evaluation of performance and consideration in a relationship. This directs us to the problem of legitimacy: When can an exchange [...] be regarded as fair? [...] Does this reciprocity refer to material or incorporeal exchange goods? (Seubert, 2009: 107, see here Ch. 5.9)

Consequently, equality, and the equal treatment of partners in a cooperation are central to the question of reciprocity, as are the ways in which these conditions can be achieved where there is an inequality in the goods and services that partners are able to contribute to a cooperation (cf. Seubert, 2009: 110, Ch. 6.13).[133] This reciprocity leads to the following essential question with regard to the theory of social capital, namely: What is the effect of social capital?

The theories of Bourdieu and Putnam diverge from one another in seeking to answer this question. While Bourdieu defines capital as a means of distinction[134] (cf. Radtke, 2011: 50 ff.), which reproduces social inequalities, Putnam works from the assumption that social capital is a resource for social inclusion (cf. Seubert, 2009: 18 f., 190 f.).

According to Bourdieu, social capital preserves or reproduces power relationships and social inequality. This can be strengthened in connection to the other forms of capital (cf. *ibid.*: 11, 131, Radtke, 2011: 11).[135] Actors have differing levels of access to the resource of social capital. The individuals who find themselves within the structure of networks and cooperations, therefore, receive a benefit in their actions and their ability to reach their goals (i.e. the 'elite' – cf. Ch. 3.2.4). Individuals who are excluded from these structures have very little chance to build up a resource of social capital. Seubert speaks of "underprivileged", whereby "persons are engaged in very few networks" and accordingly, experience social capital as a means for exclusion (Seubert, 2009: 11, 130, see also Deindl, 2005: 4). The unequal distribution of capital leads to an inequality in opportunities to participate (cf. Sedmak *et al.*, 2011b: 8 and Ch. 5.2).

We can see the "two-fold nature of social capital" in Putnam's understanding – in contrast to Bourdieu, of social capital as a resource that encourages inclusion and integration (Seubert, 2009: 81, 190).[136] For him, social capital enables "participation in the economic and cultural

133 On the criteria of reciprocity for social capital, see Seubert (2009: 74, 105 ff.), Lederer (2005: 24).

134 Distinction can be understood as discriminating, emphasising, marking out. For more on the term, see Fuchs-Heinritz/König (2005: 192 ff.).

135 Power is here understood as "every chance within a social relation, of imposing one's own will in spite of opposition" (Weber, 1972: 28 f., see also Lee, 2010: 5). Power has its basis, among other things, in unequal access to limited resources. For more on the term, see http://tinyurl.com/m4vt8uo (Accessed: 04.01.2014).

136 On the positive and negative effects of social capital, see Seubert (2009: 10 f., 78 ff.).

prosperity of the community, it forms the condition for social and political participation" (*ibid.*: 141). According to this model, social capital influences the democratisation of a society (cf. *ibid.*: 18 f.). However, Putnam does take up Bourdieu's sociological theory of distinction – drawing a difference between 'bridging' and 'bonding' networks and cooperations (cf. *ibid.*: 81 ff.):

> 'Bridging' social capital is relevant for social networks that bring together completely different people; 'bonding' social capital brings together people who are similar in some respect (such as ethnicity, age, sex, social class, etc.). This is an important distinction, because networks with bonding social capital (which limit themselves to certain social niches) bring with them a greater risk of negative consequences. (Putnam/Goss, 2001: 28 f., see also Lederer, 2005: 10)

According to both Bourdieu's power critique, and Putnam's integration theory, social capital can broaden or limit an actor's creative freedom and scope for action. Whether social capital brings about integration or exclusion is also dependent on the way and means in which the cooperation is initiated and set out (cf. Ch. 5).

The capital theory presented here is not just limited to the field of cooperation in its application. It can also apply to the arts – field of this present study. Here, the 'two-fold nature' of – in this case cultural – capital also becomes clear. The arts have two social functions – on the one hand integration and inclusion, on the other, demarcation and exclusion. The first of these functions is based on the understanding that culture is a means for democratisation, and that cultural policy has an innate potential for democratisation. Insofar as the 'user group' of culture in practice as well as reception expands, the number of people participating in culture grows. Social, economic, and political participation is promoted through this cultural empowerment and association. This expansion of participation enables a contribution towards shaping society (cf. Fuchs, 2007: 57 ff.).

In the second sense, cultural participation continues to be influenced by the social level of the family, the origins of the person, and their social status, as explained by Bourdieu. Art and culture are thereby "means of distinction" (Knüsel, 2010: 47 ff.). The reception of culture is an important social space in which processes of distinction are realised. This culturally produced differentiation, as well as cultural participation, in turn conditions access to political participation, and thereby the ability to shape society (cf. Gad, 2012b: 97 ff.) – analogously to the understanding of culture as a means for inclusion. According to this understanding, culture is an "instrument of domination" and a means for maintaining the power of an elite (Faschingeder, 2010: 35, see also *ibid.*, 2001: 135 ff.).

Actors in cultural policy and practice have a central role to play in that they are able to continuously re-present or change existing power relationships and marginalizations that are brought into being through the means of art (cf. Gad, 2012b: 98). The arts can only be free, when they can be freely accessed.

India:
a Cultural-Political Orientation

In order to investigate German-Indian partnerships in the arts, the context in which these encounters take place needs to be surveyed (cf. Ch. 6.7). This approach is in accordance with the fourth rule of field research according to the Austrian sociologist and cultural anthropologist Roland Girtler: "You should acquire a solid knowledge of the history and the social structure of the culture with which you are concerned." (Girtler, 2008: n.p.) Contextual dependencies in the form of situational influences and structural frameworks help shape the structure of a cooperation, meaning that the individual perspectives of the actors need to be supplemented with an overview of the whole structure in order for the cooperation to be understood within the concrete spatial, temporal, and socio-cultural context in which it is conceived and constructed. Martin Holzberg, researcher into cooperation in business administration, speaks of a "situative approach", whereby local contextual conditions determine the variables of a cooperative relationship, and thereby influence its success or failure (Holzberg, 2009: 23 f., 79). It is only with the help of this holistic approach, which pays attention to external, as well as internal factors, that alternative ways of structuring cooperations can be discerned. The following pages will therefore present the domestic and foreign cultural policy of India, including their specific characteristics and cultural-political challenges. The consequence of these conditions is the concrete reality of work and life for artists in India, which their German partners are required to share when their work together takes place in the Indian art and cultural scene.

Information on the current state of Indian cultural politics were collected in the course of the field research undertaken for this study. German and Indian cultural actors, some of whom with a record of up to forty years of engagement with the Indian art and culture scene, were questioned. The references and sources presented here are therefore frequently interview statements from these experts. It is not the goal of this study to present a complete and exhaustive record of all Indian cultural actors and their activities at home and abroad from the beginning of German-Indian relations.[1] Rather, the goal here is to highlight what

1 For a detailed description of India's cultural policy, see the website International Database of Cultural Policies at http://www.worldcp.org/india.php (Accessed: 16.03.2014).

needs to be observed in the context of the research question on artistic cooperation between India and Germany in its current form.

The German Federal Agency for Civic Education (*Bundeszentrale für politische Bildung* – bpb) describes India as "the world's largest democracy, emerging economic power, and ambitious actor on the international stage" (*Bundeszentrale für politische Bildung*).[2] Its 1.2 billion inhabitants, with an average age of 25 (cf. Palazhy, 2009: n.p.), make India the second-largest country on earth, comprising around one-sixth of the global population (cf. Auswärtiges Amt, 2002: 3). Between 40 and 65 % of the Indian population is illiterate,[3] including most of those living in the countryside, or in the slums of its megacities. The level of education is strongly dependant on a person's background (cf. Mentschel, 2007b: n.p.).

The economic stagnation of India's rural areas, which are characterised by poverty and undernutrition, with no chance of an education, have led a large number of people to move to the cities, driven by the hope of finding work. They dream of "the urban India, the shining India, which is cosmopolitan, global and affluent" (Sundar, 2006: 97). However, the reality is different. Cities like Delhi, with 24 million inhabitants, or Mumbai with 22 million, are bursting at the seams, leading to the growth of huge slums at their edges, which grow by thousands of new inhabitants every day.[4] As the following quotation highlights, the image of urban India is often characterised by extremes of wealth and poverty (cf. Ihlau, 2008: 5, Imhasly, 2008: n.p.):

> The crazy thing about India is that everything is actually simultaneous […], the ancient culture is massively present, and at the same time, so is the hyper-modern bank and internet culture […]. Just a few meters away from each other there are people living in mud huts and cooking on open fires, while a couple of kilometres further along live the I-don't-know-whats in high-tech apartments, walking around on Manolo shoes. (I_25: 34)[5]

This inequality will lead, according to several prognoses, including *India: Between myth and mouse click* (Indien "zwischen Mythos und Mausklick", Punnamparambil, 2002: 30) to further unrest in the future.

---

2 Quoted from http://tinyurl.com/myzqsx5 (Accessed: 06.06.2013).

3 The figure varies: Wagner (2005: 16) speaks of forty per cent. Hillger (2007: n.p.) gives an illiteracy rate of 65.38 per cent with reference to the Indian census of 2001 – see http://www.censusindia.net/ (Accessed: 10.06.2013).

4 Up to fifty per cent of India's urban population lives in slums.

5 The expectation that poverty would be reduced by the growth of the middle class has not been confirmed (cf. Wieck, 2012: 5). On the contrary, global competition has led to a deepening of the gulf between rich and poor (cf. Meyns, 2010b: 49).

India's 34 'problem cities' with a population of over one million, however, are still only home to around 31.2 % of the national population.

Following the Second World War, the state was responsible for meeting the needs of its citizens in all areas of life. From Delhi at the centre, distribution of limited resources was undertaken "from top to bottom and right to left" (I_71: 103). With the end of the Cold War and the economic reforms of 1991, the Indian economy became open to investment from overseas (cf. Auswärtiges Amt, 2002: 3, Müller/Rauch, 2008: 9 ff.). An export-driven policy of integration with the world market led to substantial growth in the previously isolated Indian economy. However, the structures of a market economy developed unevenly from sector to sector. The relationship between state and market, and the respective tasks, instruments, rights, criteria, and institutions of the same remain unclear up to the present, as was made clear in the discussion on direct overseas investment in 2012.[6] India now faces the challenge of survival in a liberalized market accompanied by the simultaneous withdrawal of the state (cf. Singh, 2009: 65).

The booming economy[7] caused by a liberalization that Spiess describes as "an opening to the world" (Spiess, 2009: 12), has catapulted the Indian metropolises in particular into the maelstrom of globalisation. The German Foreign Office has stated with regard to economic volume and growth that India does not need "to be shy of comparing itself with industrialised societies" (Auswärtiges Amt, 2002: 15, see also Arickal, 2012: 11). This has led to the belief that India – described as a "threshold country" in common with the other 'BRICS' states – had "already crossed [...] the threshold" (Garcia dos Santos, 2011: 55) to be an "ambitious force helping to shape geopolitics" (Messner, 2009: 109). Against this stands the fact that this economic growth has been stagnant for a number of years and almost half of the Indian population continue to live below the poverty line, with more than thirty per cent in extreme poverty (cf. Meyns, 2010a: 49).[8] Klaus-Dieter Lehmann sees the reason for this as being that although the developing countries have "taken over the entrepreneurial spirit and the scientific-technical methods [of the West – author]", they have "not, or have only hesitantly, [...] implemented the necessary processes of social change, which are made necessary by economic reform" (Lehmann, 2010: n.p.).

India has been a "focus country" in Germany's international development work since the 1950s (Auswärtiges Amt, 2002: 12, see also Wagner, 2011: 10 f.). In spite of the new light shed by India's economic

6 See http://fdiindia.in/ (Accessed: 10.06.2013).

7 Particularly in the fields of information and software development and biotechnology.

8 Poverty is a violation of human rights.

grown, which began with the market reforms of the 1990s and continues to the present day, as well as the country's efforts to remove itself from the role of a recipient of development aid (cf. Wagner, 2005: 9),[9] it is still not inappropriate to speak of a region in need of further development.

Despite the problems of poverty, migration, and the population explosion, India is often spoken of as the "world's largest democracy".[10] It has an important role to play as a political "anchor of stability" in South Asia (Wagner, 2011: 15, Auswärtiges Amt, 2002: 15) and as a "regional power" (Mentschel, 2007a: n.p.).[11] Compared to other countries in this region, India is a highly modernized society. The nuclear and satellite program which India possesses, in combination with the world's second-largest military, is intended to strengthen this image (cf. Lee, 2010: 3). Around sixty per cent of the state budget is devoted to the military, with the remainder going to the social needs of the population, including cultural-political activities (cf. I_56: 9).

Alongside extreme social differences, India is also characterised by a broad ethnic, linguistic, and religious diversity (cf. Auswärtiges Amt, 2002: 3), which makes itself felt on all levels of life and society (cf. Varma, 2007: 1139, Wessler, 2007a: n.p.). Despite this cultural diversity, India is also supposed to be a united nation, as one Indian cultural worker explains:

> Another big cultural struggle is that India is not a homogenous country, [...] in India every state has a different language, we have different music, different food, different habits, different everything and yet as a whole it's a united nation. (I_26: 9)

India has 28 federal states, which are small nations of their own thanks to their cultural characteristics (cf. Varma, 2007: 1140). The Indian Constitution acknowledges 22 languages officially (cf. Lisbonne-de Vergeron, 2006: 36), which in turn have thousands of various dialects. Hindi and English – as the 'dowry' of the British Empire's colonial power – are the official languages. However only around ten per cent of the population are able to speak English (cf. Punnamparambil, 1999: 30). These are amongst the Indian upper and middle classes (cf. Wieck, 2006a: 2). Chetan Bhagat, a popular Indian writer,[12] illustrates:

---

9 Wagner (2005: 9) refers to the "symbolic independence of external influences" taken up by Indian foreign policy.

10 See, for example, http://tinyurl.com/qb36xca (Accessed: 24.11.2013).

11 It could be asked whether regional power or 'hegemonial power' in South Asia is the case, cf. Wieck on this critical discussion (2012: n.p.).

12 See his website: http://www.chetanbhagat.com/ (Accessed: 28.10.2013).

> Elitism and English are linked and people who speak good English look down on people who don't. (Bhagat, 2012: 117)[13]

Those who speak India's local languages also seek to speak English, even though their ability may be limited, and they may be much better able to express themselves in their local tongue. English is therefore seen as a danger for the local languages, which are viewed as of being less value than English. On top of these considerations comes the fact that the spread of the English language in India is seen as an advantage in competitiveness – for example, against Europe – and needs to be promoted accordingly (cf. Bhagat, 2012: 118).

Alongside this linguistic diversity comes India's religious diversity, with between four and six main religions (cf. Singh, 2009: 76, Sen, 2007: 176 ff.): Hinduism, Islam, Christianity, Sikhism, as well as Buddhism und Jainism. India is a Hindu-majority country with, at the same time, the world's second largest Muslim population. The richness of this cultural diversity is able to live because "Indians […] live a life of convergence and divergence, which orchestrates beautifully." (Varma, 2007: 1140) However these cultural riches are at the same time a curse – preventing a national feeling from arising, even in the presence of strong government support for a national culture (cf. Sengupta *et al.*, s.a.: 3). On the contrary, this diversity is even a source of conflict between ethnicities, religions, castes, and tribes (cf. Sundar, 2006: 97). These tensions are augmented by the Partition of 1947, which continues to leave an impression on India to this day – for example, in the form of the conflict with Pakistan over Kashmir (cf. Wieck, 2012: 11).[14] The Caste System, with its four principal castes and thousands of subcategories,[15] as well as gender-based problems – in particular the low status of women which, for example, received dramatic public attention following the public mass rape in New Delhi at the turn of 2012-13 (cf. Stiebitz, 2013: n.p.) – further intensify regional conflicts (cf. Lisbonne-de Vergeron, 2006: 39). These social problems limit India's democratic structures (cf. Wieck, 2012: 13, Auswärtiges Amt, 2002: 6). According to Amartya Sen, the Indian Nobel Prize winner in economics, India has to find its own way to democracy, whose sources are many and "not a European monopoly" (Lepenies, 2012b: n.p.). The country's

13 For elitism in the spoken languages of India, see Lee (2010: 7).

14 The Partition of the region dates back to 1947. The independent states of India and Pakistan each occupied a portion of Kashmir. Both continue to claim the whole region, the international status of which is unclear. Combined with the regional population's push for autonomy, Kashmir is one of India's largest flashpoints.

15 The Indian Constitution of 1950 formally forbids social hierarchisation on the basis of caste membership. However, the caste system continues to influence daily life in India to this day. For a detail description of the caste system in India, see Skoda (2007).

success does not lie in the imitation of Western 'examples' but in a local chain of cause and effect. Wolf Lepenies, the German sociologist and economist, speaks of the concept "Multiple Modernities", saying:

> Around the world, societies with entirely different historical and cultural starting points have found their way to democracy, the market economy, and the rule of law. (*ibid.*, 2012a: n.p.)[16]

Until India achieves the completion of its democracy and market economy under the rule of law, Public Diplomacy works to give 'polish' to the country on a national and international level in the form of a positive public image (cf. Ch. 4), in particular on the basis of its future role as an increasingly important actor on the stage of global politics.

Jawaharlal Nehru, first Prime Minister of India from 1947-64,[17] whose government stood in the socialist tradition said: "I have tried to understand India. Unfortunately, I have to admit that I have never succeeded."[18] Amartya Sen's *The Argumentative Indian* can be recommended as a good starting point to understand the history, politics, culture, and identity of present day India (cf. Sen, 2005).

3.1 India's Central Government: the "Patroness" of Culture?[19]

In the first five year plans[20] following independence, culture was defined under Indian constitutional law as religion[21] and language: "[Y]ou had a legal definition which is what the constitution says; language and

---

16 See also Meyns (2010a: 46 ff.): Cultural specificities condition the improvement in human living conditions.

17 Jawaharlal Nehru (14th November 1889, Allahabad – 27th May 1964, New Delhi) was an Indian politician and independence activist.

18 Quoted from http://tinyurl.com/mqzhndt (Accessed: 25.11.2013).

19 At this point it is not possible to take into account the structures in the states. The reality is that these regional structures are even more deficient than those at the national level, since artistic sponsorship is focused on the capital and central government.

20 The government developed a five-year plan following its election, which it tried to implement during its term of office. After five years, new elections took place, and the elected government developed a new five-year plan. The current government (from 2012-17) is implementing the twelfth plan. This plan is divided into three areas: growth, economy, social, and can be read at http://tinyurl.com/m3r9tzo. The role of art and culture in the plans has changed from government to government. Specific passages on art and culture were included from the ninth plan onwards. All plans are available at http://tinyurl.com/6vsuset (Both accessed: 04.04.2013).

21 In India, religion is grouped together with philosophy and mythology. The three branches – philosophy, mythology, and religion were also described as the foundation of Indian culture.

religion." (I_71: 5, cf. Singh, 2009: 8-21)[22] The cultural discourse was, accordingly – because of the huge pre-existing diversity of languages and religions in India – already exhausted. The definition of culture did not incorporate other fields or areas of life. Even today, the dominance of language and culture remains visible. For example, the cultural ministry of the state of Karnataka bears the name 'Department of Kannada and Culture'. Kannada is the state's regional language.

At present, an "extraordinarily diverse set" of ministries and government departments are concerned with Indian culture, according to a representative of the Centre for the Study of Culture and Society (CSCS) in Bangalore (I_71: 6, see also I_73: 16). According to the centre, these authorities' understanding of culture can be divided into the following four sectors: archaeology and anthropology; handicrafts; communications and technology; and science and education (cf. I_71: 14, CSCS, 2012: 2, answer to Question 2). These sectors are the responsibility of their own ministries, each with their own cultural policies (cf. I_71: 7, I_73: 16), none of which are, however, official or written down (cf. I_51: 76). Culture is not recognised as a cross-cutting issue for all sectors and ministries.

Following Indian independence and economic liberalisation, old institutional forms of cultural and artistic activities such as temples, churches, and monasteries fell away (cf. Singh, 2009: 52). At the same time, the Indian market was under- and undeveloped, and remains so to this day (cf. Ch. 3.2.4). Accordingly, the state took over responsibility for the cultural needs of its citizens (cf. I_71: 2), and large cultural institutions were established under Nehru in the first two five-year plans, which are still the full responsibility of the Indian government (cf. Klaic, 2009: n.p.). These are above all obliged to the traditional arts.

Two parallel artistic universes have established themselves in India – that of the classical and the contemporary. They draw a self-conscious distinction between themselves, and vie for the same limited financial resources. The government and its sponsorship system strengthen this competition, and tend to favour the traditional arts (cf. I_73: 12).

Similarly, national cultural sponsorship is primarily concerned with the protection of the national cultural heritage (cf. Singh, 2009: 52, Ministry of Culture/Government of India, 2012-2013: 2).[23] According to a young Indian scientist concerned with the possibilities of Indian cultural policy, this has had the advantage of bringing cultural heritage back to the

---

22 For a different treatment of the Indian definition of culture, see Surana (2009: 52 ff.). Religion is also central here.

23 For a justification of the focus on the cultural budget in the policies of countries in the "Global South" with reference to Maslow's pyramid of needs, see Dhanwani (2012: 5 f.) and http://tinyurl.com/btqynnx (Accessed: 29.09.2013).

attention of civil society, and the understanding of culture as a factor in development (cf. I_11 und I_35).[24] On the other hand, a large portion of the limited state arts budget is devoted to cultural maintenance, although the state only maintains a small percentage of the cultural heritage – namely 5000 monuments, of which sixteen are World Heritage Sites.[25]

Today, the state understands its role as being "[...] to guide culture but only to provide an environment which would facilitate dialogue among creative persons and encourage freedom of their expression" (Singh, 2009: xv). According to this model, the political tendency of the state is to withdraw more and more from the social-cultural fields (cf. Arickal, 2012: 11, I_67: 60-67, I_71: 122-126), even though state-managed cultural institutes continue to be in place for the moment. The Indian neoliberal globalisation policy has led to the prevalence of the opinion that culture can be left to the market. An often-cited example for the success of this approach is Bollywood[26] and its worldwide marketing. With this change, the government has completely abandoned the conception of sole state responsibility.

At present – in 2013/14, however, the central instance for cultural sponsorship in India continues to be the state – principally meaning the Ministry of Culture based in New Delhi.[27] Chandresh Kumari Katoch has been Culture Minister since October 2012. The Ministry's vision in 2013 was:

> To protect, conserve and propagate the tangible and intangible cultural heritage of India by supporting and sustaining cultural creativity and expressions, as a unifying factor within our rich diversity. (Indian Ministry of Culture)[28]

---

24 Two interviews were undertaken with the scientist.

25 The example of the maintenance of cultural heritage shows the financial dilemma of the state clearly: Only a few thousand monuments belong to the state, which is a minimum of those that actually exist. The others are supported by religious groups, institutions, or civil society; or they crumble. It is often noted that these facilities are often in better condition when they are left to their traditional function, than when they are taken over by the state (cf. I_71: 128).

26 Bollywood is the popular film industry based in Mumbai. The films produced in Bollywood are characterised by their particular music and style. For more detail, see Spiess (2009: 48 ff.). More than 160 Hindi films are produced in Mumbai alone per year (cf. Stepf, 2009: 24).

27 The Department of Culture was established in the 1970s (I_71: 7). This was assigned to various ministries according to the preference of the government of the day – for example, the Ministries of Education, Human Resource and Development, Textiles, etc. (cf. Singh, 2009: 54, I_71: 14). In 2001, the Department of Culture first became an independent ministry, was briefly a department again, and has been an independent ministry from 2006 to the present. For more on the history of these institutions, see http://tinyurl.com/k4y5eyv and http://tinyurl.com/o2yrsxz (Both accessed: 27.10.2013).

28 Quoted from http://tinyurl.com/owa3x6p, see also http://tinyurl.com/qd46sg7 (Both accessed: 15.04.2013). The mission of the ministry is comprehensively described here.

At present, the Ministry's vision is "an India where cultural diversity and heritage are important pillars of inclusive national development." (Ministry of Culture/Government of India, 2012-2013: 2) The goals and functions for reaching this vision are obliged to cultural heritage, in keeping with the state's understanding that cultural maintenance is its primary task (cf. Ministry of Culture/Government of India, 2013-2014: 142). Alongside this, the traditional arts are the primary source of sponsorship, as the Ministry itself emphasises (cf. I_51: 54),[29] since no funds remain available from the limited state arts budget for the contemporary arts. These are, therefore, broadly excluded from the government's system of financing.

The Ministry works over two channels: its autonomous institutions, as well as its sponsorship schemes:

> Apart from the activities carried out through its Attached/Subordinate Offices and Autonomous Institutions, there are 26 grant-in-aid schemes being implemented directly by the Ministry. (Ministry of Culture/Government of India, 2013-2014: 11)

The sponsorship schemes award stipends to cultural actors and cultural institutions for a variety of artistic and cultural activities: "The grant-in-aid is given to voluntary cultural organisations/individuals in the form of financial assistance who are engaged in the area of promotion of art and culture." (Ministry of Culture/Government of India, 2013-2014: 11) The government redefines the scope and focus of its sponsorship schemes each year. In the budget year 2013-14, 26 schemes[30] were divided into the following six sectors: "Performing Art Sector", "Buddhist & Tibetan Institutions Sector", "Museums Sector", "Public Library Sector", "Memorials Centenaries and Others", and "International Cultural Relations". Together, these constitute India's unofficial cultural policy, whereby the Ministry awards funds to cultural institutions and artists for the establishment of cultural infrastructure (cf. I_51: 47, 76). This model of sponsorship, and network of autonomous cultural institutions, is in keeping with the Ministry's "arm's length" approach (I_71: 16, 63).

In order to fulfil the responsibility as patron of culture that it took over following independence and the collapse of old forms of support for

29 See also I_73: 12, I_45: 201, I_80: 13.

30 As a comparison, in the budget year 2012/13 there were 16 sponsorship programs. For more on these schemes, see http://tinyurl.com/qbaokre (Accessed: 27.10.2013). For more on the ongoing sponsorship programs, see Ministry of Culture/Government of India (2013-2014).

cultural activity, the state founded autonomous institutions in the 1950s that should take over the sponsorship and maintenance of culture on its behalf. The first of these were three academies. In 1953, the *Sangeet Natak Akademi* was opened, with responsibility for supporting the performing arts:

> The *Akademi* acts at the national level for the promotion and growth of Indian music, dance and drama; for the maintenance of standards of training in the performing arts and other related areas. (Ministry of Culture/Government of India, 2013-2014: 436, see also Sengupta *et al.*, s.a.: 12)

In 1954 followed the *Lalit Kala Akademi* and the *Sahitya Akademi*. The *Lalit Kala Akademi* is the National Academy of Fine Art, for the support of the visual arts in India (cf. Ministry of Culture/Government of India, 2013-2014: 438). The *Sahitya Akademi* has the task of supporting Indian literature:

> [...] to work actively for the development of Indian Letters and to set high literary standards, to foster and coordinate literary activities in all Indian languages and to promote through them the cultural unity of the country. (*ibid.*: 437)

In 1959, the National School of Drama (NSD) followed, which "was established by the Government to promote theatre activities in the country, by imparting training in the field of dramatics." (*ibid.*: 436) The NSD has a unique reputation in India, being described as "one of the most prestigious institutions in the country" and "one of the foremost theatre training institutions in the world" (*ibid.*, see also Kumar, 2001, I_42: 64).[31] The advantage of the Academies, including the NSD is the presentation up to the present day, according to an Indian expert on cultural policy, the ability to present a uniform Indian culture (cf. I_61: 3). The art presented are characterised by traditionalism, even though the government presents the program of the Academies as representing "contemporary creativity" (Ministry of Culture/Government of India, 2013-2014: 142). The other thirty of the 34 autonomous institutions founded and still financed by the state consist of archives, libraries, and museums, as well as a few foundations and scientific establishments (cf. *ibid.*: 2-3, 434).

---

31 The detailed history of the three Academies and the NSD can be read in the Outcome Budget 2013-14 report by the Ministry of Culture. This also gives a historical overview of all of the government's autonomous bodies, including a description of their function.

Complementing these institutions are seven Zone Cultural Centres (ZCC), which have been established in various regions of the country. The work of these centres is to maintain the arts from the past in the present on a regional basis, and to support their development (cf. Singh, 2009: 56):

> The essential thrust of Zone Cultural Centres has been to create cultural awareness among the people and to identify, nurture and promote the vanishing art forms/traditions in the rural and semi-urban areas of various states. (Ministry of Culture/Government of India, 2013-2014: 434 f.)

Although the government describes the work of the ZCC as "quite impressive" (*ibid.*: 434), Indian cultural workers describe the concept as a failure:[32] the ZCC are unable to create the urgently needed internal dialogue (cf. Singh, 2009: 56 f.). Art and cultural scenes do establish themselves in India's large cities, however rural regions are neglected by the government. Only two Attached Offices[33] and six Subordinate Offices[34] work under the 34 autonomous government cultural institutions. All of these institutions are one hundred per cent financed by the government which act at arm's length for the Ministry of Culture.

The number of institutions supported by the government changes year on year. In 2012, 48 or 49 institutions were named by experts. In 2013-14, this was just 42. The reduction of the number of state supported institutions has the advantage of slightly reducing the complexity of the "bureaucratic machinery" with which the Ministry of Culture is surrounded (Sengupta *et al.*, s.a.: 12), however it is also a further indication of the withdrawal of the state from the country's cultural-political activity.

In the future, according to the prognosis of a cultural scientist from the CSCS in Bangalore, the state will ask the autonomous institutions to supply between ten and twenty per cent of their funding costs themselves in a form of matching funds, or to supply fifty per cent themselves as co-financing (cf. I_71: 125). In the case of financial crises or bottlenecks, profit-maximization methods such as increases in student fees, entrance fees, or the leasing of facilities are implemented, in order to avoid putting a further burden on the state Cultural Council, which might otherwise prove overwhelming (cf. Singh, 2009: 70). These measures first of all

32 See, for example, in depth the interviews I_11 and I_35.

33 The Archaeological Survey of India (see http://asi.nic.in/) and the National Archives of India (see http://nationalarchives.nic.in/, both accessed: 10.04.2013).

34 Anthropological Survey of India (http://www.ansi.gov.in/), National Museum (http://nationalmuseumindia.gov.in/), National Gallery of Modern Art (http://ngmaindia.gov.in/), National Library (http://www.nationallibrary.gov.in/), Central Reference Library (http://crlindia.gov.in/), National Research Laboratory for Conservation of Cultural Property (http://www.nrlc.gov.in, All accessed: 10.04.2013).

need to be established in Indian society. This requires a large expertise in cultural management that is barely developed (cf. Ch. 3.2.2).[35]

The arm's length model can be viewed critically. State control over the institutions is supposed to be minimal, however because they are fully state financed it is questionable whether they are as autonomous as the state makes out: "[T]hese agencies have absolutely no funding except what the government gives them, the government dominance remains [...]." (I_71: 68) For proponents of the system, the autonomy consists of the fact that the Ministry allows the institutions the freedom to set their own budget and content (cf. I_71: 63).

It is publically known that these institutions and their committees, which make decisions on programs and sponsorships, have members who belong, or who belonged in the past to the Ministry of Culture (cf. I_71: 70, 76, Singh, 2009: 115). These government representatives are able to undertake lobby work in the interest of the Ministry, while they are accorded veto powers in committee. The possibility of censorship is in existence, and places the autonomy of the institution in danger. The following quotation from a Goethe-Institut staff member in India makes these problematic internal structures, which primarily serve to secure the power and privileges of a functional government elite, clear:

> When we work with the National Gallery of Modern Art then we dealing with the Ministry straight away, because the National Gallery as a huge great museum is not independent. Every step has to be approved by the State Secretary, Minister, or whoever. (I_42: 62)

An Indian theatre scientist and director at an institution near to the government, also reports of work being commissioned in the light of upcoming elections (cf. I_37: 70). The explanation of an expert from the CSCS draws a conclusive distinction between "legal autonomy" and "functional autonomy" (I_71: 66). Further, the autonomous status of every cultural institution near to the government requires precise observation, since "where it is there, there is growth, and where it is not there, there is also a lot of stagnation." (I_42: 68)

The Ministry of Culture works through its cultural institutions. The unofficial cultural policy "is actually a result of the sum of these [...] national cultural establishments", according to a Goethe-Institut staff member in India, quoting the description of a representative of the Ministry of Culture. He commented on the Ministry's description in the following way:

---

35 Cultural management can be understood as "the leadership and management of institutions and business sharing responsibility for cultural services" (Schwencke *et al.*, 2009: 107 f.).

> This is of course an extremely defensive answer, however it is extremely telling, because the majority of these establishments are in a very regrettable state. This is perhaps clearest in light of a few criteria. For example, the standard of archivization, which is I believe lamentable in all of the institutions. And these are, by definition, the national institutions in some fields – for example, the Lalit Kala Akademi, which is the national art or fine arts academy, or the Sangeet Natak Akademi for music and dance. This is something that one expects of a national institution – namely to manage and archive cultural heritage on the one hand, and to keep it alive, and provide new impulses. This is something that perhaps two or three of these 48 institutions manage to live up to. And when that is, so to speak, the cultural policy then it has failed […]. (I_73: 12)

The "very regrettable state" of state cultural organisations quoted here was confirmed as long ago as July 1990 by the 'High-powered Committee' that compiled the 'Haskar Report'.[36] The committee evaluated the work of the three largest of the government institutions – the three Academies and the NDS, and determined that these institutions have no identifiable influence on Indian culture, because they do not cooperate with each other or other organisations (cf. Singh, 2009: 54). As a consequence of their intransparent and difficult to assess nature of their dependency on the state, the professionalism, as well as the effectiveness, of these organisations was thrown into doubt (cf. I_76: 11).

The goal of the Academies was to develop civil society as an agent and supporter of culture and creativity. Balmiki Prasad Singh, fourteenth President of the Indian state of Sikkim, as well as scientist and publicist, claims that the facts show these goals have been a success "India today is one of the few countries in the world which can claim it has more than a hundred creative persons who are the world's best in their representative fields." (Singh, 2009: 54) Whether this judgement will suffice to justify the continued existence of the institutions is questionable.

Dragan Klaic, the late Dutch cultural policy adviser, describes the cultural institutes close to the government of India as "public institutions in an advanced state of decay", which have become passive and dysfunctional, "with little output and no policy" (Klaic, 2009: n.p.). India's second-largest English language daily, The Hindu, drew attention to the institutions' lack of autonomy, and the influence of the state in cultural activity in an article on 30th May 2012 entitled "State of Culture": "Since the state remains the biggest patron and taxpayers' money is involved, the government justifies

[36] The Haksar Report is the short title of the "Report of the High-powered Committee Appoint to Review the Performance of the National Akademis and the National School of Drama", cf. Department of Culture/Ministry of Human Resource Development/ Government of India (1990).

its intervention." (No Author, 2012h: n.p.) Indian cultural actors are unanimous that it is only a "de-politicisation of culture" – where the state ends or limits its interventions to an absolute minimal, while at the same time financing more – that will be able to save cultural practice and production in India (CSCS, 2012: 6, Answer to Question 4, see also I_45: 441).

A number of free institutions exist alongside the government sponsored cultural bodies, which finance themselves through private donations from their immediate neighbourhood that have been built up and supported by foreign cultural institutes (cf. I_42: 8, I_13: 17).[37] However these independent cultural institutions[38] are barely quantifiable, and unable to support themselves, despite the wishes of their management (cf. I_54: 157). Administrative work in these bodies is often undertaken by volunteers (cf. I_70: 28). On top of this comes the fact that cultural institutions in India are highly dependent on personality. Bharat Sharma, the Indian artist, speaks of "personality cults" (Sharma, 2000: 16). When this person dies or leaves, the institute is often closed (cf. I_44: 37-38).[39] Indian cultural actors are aware of the need to establish private alternatives to the government sponsored cultural institutions (cf. I_44: 40-43), in order to secure spaces and opportunities for training, two of the scarcest resources in India (cf. I_54: 161 and Ch. 3.2). Ideally, a network of institutions needs to be constructed, in order to strengthen the professionalism and estimation of the arts in India (cf. I_45: 26, 239, 424-430, I_49: 61). However the question of where the funding for such an endeavour might come remains open (cf. Ch. 3.2.3 and 3.2.4).

---

37 For example, the Ranga Shankara Theatre in Bangalore, the Prithvi Theater in Mumbai or the Jana Natya Theater in Delhi.

38 Institutes usually have their own technical infrastructure in order to avoid the horrendous rental costs, and avoid doubts as the availability and functionality of the equipment (cf. I_45: 239).

39 Faced with this problem, the founder and former director of the India Foundation for the Arts, Anmol Vellani, advocated for the establishment of 'polyphonic' institutions: "What you find generally [...] in institutions is that one voice speaks and the others listen and respond. So what you need is to build institutions with a culture where there are multiple voices speaking. It is very common abroad for any cultural institution to have more than one artistic director. It's so uncommon in this country. We seem to be un-able to tolerate multiple sources of authority with institutions. Multiple voices within an institution can make a difference at the policy level, can effect change at the highest level in the institution. When you do that, then when the person who leads goes, then there are other people who have taken ownership of the institution and there is no reason to believe that it will collapse. So an institution must become fearlessly and reflexively dialogic within, in order to survive." (Vellani, 2009c: 195)

3.2 Current Challenges of the Indian Cultural Landscape

India's cultural landscape is characterised by a range of challenges, which have an influence on the actions and considerations of agents in the cultural scene.

One of the central challenges is the national cultural policy itself. Culture is interwoven with daily life in India in a variety of ways (cf. I_25: 32). At present, the military, and economic market are the driving forces. Most state expenditure continues to go towards the military, while the Indian market continues to be characterised by the legacy of communism. The role of culture in this mix is developing: "[C]ulture is emerging as a third factor." (Singh, 2009: xlv) Spiess predicts that India's focus will shift in the future from 'hard' power – military and economic – to 'soft' power in the forms of diplomacy and culture.[40] This will require a restructuring of policy fields – in particular that of cultural policy (cf. I_21: 9). However, at present the discourse on culture, its quality, and politics, remains outstanding:

> There is no really broadly open discussion about culture, or about quality, which is also a question. Any real discussion about these things is almost invisible. (I_73: 18)

Only very few Indian cultural actors engage with the concept of a possible national cultural policy.[41] Which is, in India as in many other 'developing' or 'emerging' countries, inexistent:

> Cultural policy makes itself best known by its absence. Because cultural policy implies an agenda, goals, and measures, as well as financial, structural, and human resources. (I_73: 8, see also I_61: 5-9, I_49, 31, 33, I_51: 76, Kapoor, 2009: 186)

---

[40] See Spiess (2009: 18). The term 'Soft Power', which is now established in the political sciences, was coined by Nye. Soft power rests on the ability to appeal and convince through image campaigns and the maintenance of international relations in the form of cultural exchange and dialogue on values (cf. Nye, 2004: n.p.).

[41] Singh (2009) – not to be confused with the Indian Prime Minister – as well as Sengupta *et al.* (s.a.: 20 f.) are two of the few authors or editorial teams, who try to reflect on and discuss the history and present state of Indian culture. Knopp (2013) makes the point that English language information on India is primarily the product of US and European authors. The Secretary General of the International Federation of Coalitions for Cultural Diversity in Canada also points out that India and the EU call for dialogue on cultural policy in the framework of the mutually-ratified UNESCO Convention of 2005 (cf. Ch. 2.2). A Joint Declaration was signed to this effect at Brussels in December 2010 (cf. Singh [Prime Minister of India], 2010).

Three reasons are given for the non-existence of a written or stated policy:[42]

First of all, India's five thousand year old culture has survived for this long without a policy, proving that none is required:

> Personally I feel the greatest burden we carry is our 5,000-year old culture. Today we believe that since it has survived so long with no policy, it can continue to survive without any in the future as well! (Kapoor, 2009: 190)

Second is the difficulty of developing a cultural policy that includes and pays attention to each of the ethnicities, religions, and linguistic communities that make up India's highly diverse and pluralistic cultural landscape (cf. I_67: 60-67). There is a high level of anxiety that minorities such as the Dalits or Adivasis will suffer from marginalization (cf. I_76: 2-5, 13-14).[43] This cultural diversity makes the definition of a policy difficult (cf. I_11: 62-64).

Third, according to a Joint Secretary of the Ministry of Culture in Delhi, no Indian government has the desire to open the debate about cultural policy (cf. I_51: 74). An Indian artist comments: "[T]oo many bureaucracies, too much ministry, the entire sort of messy situation in a place like India in defining what is culture itself." (I_71: 52)

These justifications seem advantageous for the Indian government in that the state cannot thereby continue to be obliged to strengthen art and culture, which can then be left to the free market. These justifications also apply to the creation of "a broad set of guidelines on what [the Indian government] would consider the essential aspects of culture in relation to human dignity" (I_71: 16, see also I_71: 49). The fact that the precise content of these guidelines remains unclear (cf. I_76: 2-5) means that the Indian state cannot be held responsible.

The maintenance of cultural heritage, where the state is required to fulfil certain legal obligations, is exempt from this schema (cf. I_76: 2-5). A policy for the financing and institutionalisation of cultural heritage, as well as legislation on this topic is currently being developed in the Punjab,[44]

42 'Policy' can here be understood as political concept with strategies and goals.

43 Dalit is the term chosen by the descendants of the aboriginal inhabitants of Indian subcontinent who were classified as 'untouchables' in the Hindu caste system of the Indo-Aryan migrants or invaders to describe themselves. They continue to be the subject of social discrimination in Indian society of the present day. Around 160 million Dalits live in India, and make up around sixteen per cent of the total population. Adivasi is the term chosen by the indigenous population of the present territory of India to describe themselves.

44 Punjab was the name of a former province of British India from 1849 to 1947, which was divided between the Dominions of India and Pakistan as the state and province

on the basis of an intensive regional analysis. This project seeks decisively to pay attention to all of the region's ethnic groups and history in order to incorporate a representative diversity in the policy. This will not be able to serve as a model for other regions or branches, say those responsible, because it is "too specific" in its area and subject matter (I_76: 10).

The development of a cultural policy in the face of the social problems like poverty, malnutrition and illiteracy which deeply characterise the financial and substantive makeup of the country is frequently deferred – even from the directly affected stakeholders, such as the culturally-active elements in the country (cf. I_50: 114, I_11: 67). However, this shows a recognition in India that development cannot simply be measured according to political and economic factors, but that cultural and social dynamics play an important role in the realisation of development: "[C]ulture indeed constitutes a crucial input to the overall process of development." (Singh, 2009: 72) However, against this comes the question: "Is it not permissible to pursue culture in a city where so many people live in misery?" (Kämpchen, 2004: n.p., see also Hardie, 2011: 22 ff.)

Kämpchen answers his own question by pointing to the contribution that culture can make to self-discovery and strengthening identity, through which a situation of poverty can be overcome. He folds social and cultural poverty into material poverty, which can therefore be overcome through cultural formation. The Indian scientist Chaitanya agrees with him: "Somehow we have to manage to spare some of our energy for art even while we are struggling for bread." (Chaitanya quoted in: Singh, 2009: 58) He justifies his position by saying:

> Poverty has been there since the beginning of history. Should art and creativity be totally suspended till a better social order is created? If we decide it that way, life will be infinitely impoverished. (*ibid.*)

The central question, therefore, is not whether the country is in need of a cultural policy, but which cultural policy, according to which theoretical framework, can and must be implemented practically, especially in light of the challenges facing the country in the form of an explosive population increase, environmental destruction, and violence – particularly against women and children. This would have the vital role of developing criteria and institutions that work transparently (cf. I_21: 2), so that actors in the cultural scene, who are not lacking in creativity, no longer have to work in a "vacuum", as one Indian cultural worker described the situation in winter

---

of Punjab respectively upon independence and partition. More on this project can be found at http://tinyurl.com/psd36ru (Accessed: 13.06.2013).

2012: "[Y]ou are not working towards anything. You are just responding or reacting." (I_45: 323, see also I_54: 74)

Even though there may be no official written cultural policy,[45] there is an "unstated policy" (I_57: 3), which provides a basis for the actions of the government. The Ministry of Culture and the Indian Council for Cultural Relations (ICCR)[46] have both developed selection criteria for the sponsorship of artists, institutions, and projects which are recognised as an indirect cultural policy.

Cultural workers criticise the fact that this 'unwritten' cultural policy is dominated by the government – who formulated it without consultation in an intransparent, and financially limited exercise of 'top-down' bureaucratic power, which has the potential to interfere with the national culture (cf. I_57: 3, I_58: 5, I_35: 12). According to a representative of the India Foundation for the Arts in Bangalore (IFAB), government cultural sponsorship is unrealistic and inefficient, because it is not engaged with local realities[47] (cf. Sengupta *et al.*, s.a.: 12). At the same time, the state remains the "primary supporter" of culture because of the lack of alternative sources of finance (Vellani, 2006: n.p., cf. Ch. 3.2.4). There are only few local cultural institutions which act indirectly – for example, by enabling frameworks for culture (cf. I_61: 1-2, I_44: 4, Sengupta *et al.*, s.a.: 12). While civil society initiatives are also lacking.[48]

The majority of those questioned were unanimous that democratic forae are required where civil society actors including scholars, managers and artists are able to organise themselves in order to encourage the development of a cultural policy. Content, instruments, and resources need to be discussed and negotiated, and carried into the political instance in order to allow an "official system of governance" to arise (I_59: 18-19).[49] These forae should strictly speaking be financed by the government-sponsored cultural institutions that have done so little for the Indian cultural landscape "in order to facilitate a dialogue among persons

45 The attempt to establish a government-level cultural policy in 1992 failed (cf. I_57: 1-3). It was based on the *Approach Paper On The National Policy On Culture & Observation, Comments, Recommendations Thereon* from the National Colloquium on Culture Policy. A copy of the document is held by the author. For a history of Indian cultural policy, see also Malik Vatsyayan (1972). The CSCS drafted a report on the activities, institutions, and goals of the current and former Indian cultural policies in December 2012 (cf. CSCS, 2012).

46 See the ICCR website at http://www.iccrindia.net/index.html (Accessed: 13.05.2013) as well as Ch. 3.3.

47 The IFAB is a unique philanthropic cultural foundation in India in Bangalore (see Ch. 3.2.4 as well as http://www.indiaifa.org/, Accessed: 19.07.2013).

48 For more on the role of civil society in India, see Kuhn (2006).

49 Also I_44 3-4, I_58: 5, I_21: 13-18, Singh (2009: xvi).

engaged in creative activity, and for the publication and display of their work" (Singh, 2009: 53).

The participation of civil society actors in devising and implementing natural cultural policies to support cultural creation is a core element of the 2005 UNESCO Convention. India ratified this convention in 2006,[50] but the relevant governmental actors have nevertheless been unable to submit a report on the national implementation of the convention up to the present.[51] Here too, the same arguments are used as are voiced against the establishment of a national cultural policy: India is too large and diverse to make a report possible. It therefore remains questionable whether the convention will have any effect on the unsatisfactory cultural-political situation in India.

According to a cultural worker from Delhi, the lack of state action and activity in the sphere of cultural policy gives the impression of a government without a plan; while regular changes of government every five years prevent the establishment of continuity in the cultural policy discourse. This has led to series of informal cultural-political initiatives within existing artistic networks to promote a national cultural policy (cf. I_49: 59). These advocates and lobby groups for a national cultural policy, such as the Gati Dance Forum in New Delhi in the sphere of contemporary dance,[52] and the India Theatre Forum in Delhi[53] are working for the implementation of the necessary cultural policy structural frameworks.

The Gati Dance Forum was established by the Gati Dance artists collective, which is dedicated to the establishment of networks in the Delhi contemporary dance scene, including to disseminate knowledge of the theory and practice of dance (cf. Spiess, 2009: 64). In cooperation with the MMB in New Delhi, it runs its own research program entitled

---

50 See the UNESCO website at http://www.unesco.de/864.html (Accessed: 13.06.2013).

51 The report on the status of the implementation of the convention is, as a rule, to be submitted every four years (cf. Fuchs, 2007: 83).

52 See http://www.gatidance.com/wrap.html (Accessed: 13.06.2013). "The Gati Dance Forum is an autonomous arts initiative based in New Delhi, working in the field of contemporary dance. Founded in 2007, in response to the glaring absence of opportunities and infrastructure for independent dance in India, the organisation has consistently searched for avenues to create a supportive environment for the development of contemporary dance practice in the country."

53 See http://www.theatreforum.in/ (Accessed: 13.06.2013). The India Theatre Forum was developed from the Prithvi Theatre. Its goal is: "[...] to reflect and deliberate on various issues in their chosen field of work. An important focus of the Forum is to discuss and document the various conditions under which theatre survives in India and explore different models of economic sustainability for theatre institutions." (Sengupta *et al.*, s.a.: 17 f.) In 2009, the Forum published a documentary on India's theatre landscape on the basis of one of its seminars, see Deshpande *et al.* (2009).

'W.R.A.P.',[54] whose role in the first instance is the identification of the needs of the dancers and their target groups: "What needs to be completely revamped or redesigned so that it caters to our generation of artists?" (I_49: 33, see also I_49: 29, I_54: 85) The identification of common needs leads to an identification with one another, and the welding together of an interest group from a collection of individual members: "You all have the same needs. Then you start seeing yourselves as a team. When you're divided, nobody listens to you. When you are united, people will listen." (I_54: 85) The purpose of W.R.A.P. is to assess the lack of cultural infrastructure in line with the Forum's desire to initiate cultural projects which encourage the growth of local cultural infrastructure (cf. I_49: 33, I_13: 12). Their intent is to then use these best practice examples to show the importance of culture to national development, so that the government has to discuss cultural policy measures and content with cultural agents (cf. I_54: 85, I_47: 24). However, these cultural workers recognise that responsibility ultimately lies with them, and that they are therefore not dependent on the state:

> Of course the other thing is that we realised by creating this, you don't need the government at all. That, you know, you can actually create what you need as a community. The infrastructure you need, [...] the resources you need, the kind of education you need. Everything can be created by us as a community. (I_49: 61)

Amongst the weaknesses of the groups lobbying for an Indian cultural policy are their regionally limited focus on the capital, in comparison to the size of the country, the small size of the little groups of cultural actors in comparison to the huge national population, and their branch-orientated thinking (cf. I_55: 5).[55] Although taking the various branches of culture one at a time (cf. I_76: 13-14) and first, for example, developing a policy for the theatre, before considering general concept, may appear to be a sensible approach, many needs are the same across all fields of culture. These include, for example, development opportunities, and spaces for rehearsal and performance. In this sense, such a sectional approach undermines the credibility of the intention behind the creation of a cultural policy – giving rise to the impression that the various branches are in competition, and acting out of concern for their own resources (cf. I_57: 4-5, I_61: 5-9).

The number of cultural actors in these few lobby groups is minimal due to the generally poor level of development in India's cultural scenes.

---

54 Abbreviation for: Work in Research and Policy. For more detail on the research program, see http://www.gatidance.com/wrap.html (Accessed: 17.06.2013).

55 This also refers to the division of the arts into the traditional and contemporary.

On top of this comes their limited reach due to the size of the country and their regionally-based approach; their limited financial resources (cf. Sengupta *et al.*, s.a.: 21), which force actors to undertake lobby work on a voluntary basis alongside their professional work; as well as personal antipathies amongst the artists (cf. I_56: 19),[56] which hinder the likelihood of cooperation. The consequence is that the cultural stakeholders are required to fight for the recognition and appreciation of art and culture in their own country.

3.2.1 Cultural Spaces: No Room in a Huge Country

> Cultural spaces are an important point. This also used to be a focus of [the Goethe-Institut] a couple of years ago: Cultural spaces with the study, or shall we say, investigation of existing spaces, and the search for new ones. (I_73: 18, see also I_49: 33, I_42: 74)

Existing spaces are almost exclusively in the possession of the government – such as, for example, the 49 cultural institutions sponsored by the government, which have their own stages and auditoria, which are difficult for most of the artist and cultural actors in India – even the Goethe-Institut – to rent for a range of reasons. Firstly, they are very costly, secondly, a lot of notice is required, thirdly, the government is unpredictable – meaning that long planned events can be cancelled at short notice when the government needs the spaces itself (cf. Sengupta *et al.*, s.a.: 4, 9 f.). In this context, a member of staff at the Goethe-Institut reports on the following case:

> There was a space there that we wanted to have. So because we wanted to have a public space, I got together with the policy side. We had everything ready, and then there was a political decision that they urgently wanted to do their own event, which since then has been postponed or whatever, I'm not so sure. In any case, from one day to the next, we were out. The decision just came down from on high, and it seems like that's how things work here. I have to pay a little more attention, and see how you can get yourself hooked in. (I_69: 140)

There are a huge number of public spaces, or simple empty buildings, which can be used as rehearsal and performance spaces in India's cities (cf. I_54: 85). However the government has the opportunity to prevent the use of these spaces and places. It can forbid cultural events because of

---

56 On the basis of differing ideologies, languages, classes, and castes, cf. Sengupta *et al.* (s.a.: 21).

their content, or refuse to issue permission for artistic productions and receptions:[57]

> Like there are hundreds of houses within the city which are dilapidated and just lying there. And if for one night we have a gig there, why not? But the whole licensing and permission regime is so strong in India, that they will not let the musicians or the arts to take over these spaces. (I_54: 66)

The permission of the government is required for every cultural event. Ensuring that this is in place takes up a large amount of the working time of cultural actors. These restrictive administrative practices in effect cut off cultural freedom (cf. I_73: 18-20, see also I_63: 115), as a representative of the MMB explains:

> There are a large number of limitations with an indefinite background. Permissions are required for a lot of things – whether for locations, or certain content, and there is a lot of very nervous bureaucracy. This all means that artistic freedom is often challenged by administration, which is also […] a limitation for the presentation and discussion of culture. (I_73: 18-20)

The result of this is that cultural workers and artists often work illegally, without permission. It follows that the development of artistic production – and the presentation of these products – will require a professional infrastructure in the future (cf. I_73: 18).

The technical suitability of a space – including electrical supply – cannot be taken for granted. Renting the required technical equipment therefore poses an additional challenge: "[T]o get the technical things, it [is] […] so difficult for us to do […]." (I_45: 325) Because of the lack of spaces, available rooms are often so tightly-booked that dance and theatre choreographers and directors report that they are often forced to take them over with their actors and dancers the night before their performance, make their preparations and set up their equipment, and then remove everything again immediately afterwards (cf. I_45: 327, 333, I_44: 21): "This is […] how we organise things in a short time, put up a show." (I_44: 39, see also Sengupta *et al.*, s.a.: 4, 9 f.) On top of the requirement to rent spaces and apply for government permission come the required costs for security personnel and 'waste managers'.[58]

---

[57] For example, the Performance Licence from the Licensing Unit of the Delhi Police and No Objection Certificates from agencies like the Entertainment Tax Department.

[58] See, for example, the content of the contract between the MMB in New Delhi and The Just Environment Charitable Trust for the Yamuna.Elbe project (cf. Goethe-Institut e. V. New Delhi, 2011).

Interviewed musicians reported that in order to be able to present their work, they were required to resort to "star hotels" or "nightclubs" (I_28: 56), where music is nothing more than "a supplementary program to dinner" (I_50: 17) or the consumption of alcohol, where the public is limited to an elite circle of listeners from the Indian upper-middle class because of the high entry prices (cf. I_50: 97, I_28: 24).

Since the turn of the century, a change has been observable in the space situation in India, according to a member of staff at the MMB in New Delhi:

> In the meantime, there are an increasing number of rich, private cultural actors – collectors, who build their own museums, who we work with, because they suddenly offer their rooms for international exhibitions. Or there are private theatre producers, who put up their own theatre. They have bought land, and will build their own theatre sometime in the next few years. These private structures which are coming about, which have come about, these are the type of things that people want to work with. (I_42: 74, 78, see also I_59: 15-17)[59]

Alongside the establishment of these private houses, state structures need to professionalise. In its report on the planned activities 2013-14 entitled 'Outcome Budget 2013-14', the Ministry of Culture lists professionalization as one of its targets (cf. Ministry of Culture/Government of India, 2013-2014: 142 f.), however this is entirely limited to its role in cultural heritage. On top of this comes the fact that professionalization through the establishment of cultural facilities is not sufficient. Qualified personnel are required who are able to manage these cultural institutes, use their technology, and organise their programs, in order to attract a public willing to pay to visit cultural events (see Ch. 3.2.2 and 3.2.4).

3.2.2 Professionalism through Passion: Limited Chances for Training

> You are expecting people to create work and be artist, but without actually supporting a training and dance-making. (I_49: 57)

The term 'training' can be distinguished between training in cultural practice, as described in the quotation above, and training to organise,

59 Private cultural actors include, for example, the Devi Art Foundation, which in 2008 opened a museum in Gurgaon – the new satellite town south of Delhi. The Foundation's museum presents a collection of Indian contemporary art, and is thereby India's first modern art museum (cf. Ulmer, 2008: n.p.). The collection is that of the Hotellier and Industrialist Anupam Poddar and his mother Lekha.

manage, or mediate culture (cf. I_70: 3). What both have in common is that there are very few or no opportunities for such training to take place on a formal base in India, although there is by no means a lack of creative talent with the desire and ability to work towards a career in culture.

Training in cultural practice can be further divided between training in the traditional and the contemporary arts. Artists in the traditional branches of culture have the opportunity to train at one of the autonomous government sponsored cultural institutions such as the Centre for Cultural Resources and Training in New Delhi,[60] or to complete the many years of training often required by a Guru.[61] While certain avenues are accordingly open for training in the traditional arts (cf. I_11: 4, Velayanikal, 2011: n.p.), opportunities for practitioners of the contemporary arts are much more limited (cf. I_49: 13).[62]

A further gap in the lack of training opportunities means that the abilities which make artistic practice complete, and encourage independent participation in an art form are not encouraged or developed:

> By the end of the day when you stop dance you cease, there are no other skills you know. […] In terms of capacity building, skill development, education, those things are not being developed […]. (I_11: 66, 60)

Among these skills, for example, is training in the abilities such as "the writing and choreography" of theatre and dance pieces (I_49: 57), in order to escape Western adaptations and be able to produce independent works of art.[63] Technical abilities, like working with light and tone, or making use of space, or public architecture – for example, in stage design, also come under this heading (cf. I_11: 6-8, Sengupta *et al.*, s.a.: 20). These abilities would also have the important effect of helping artists to continue to earn a living after or alongside their careers as dancers or actors.

The Gati Dance cultural institution has decided to take on the challenge of the lack of professional training for cultural actors in India. An

---

60 See http://ccrtindia.gov.in/ (Accessed: 13.06.2013). The number of training opportunities is however minimal when compared to the number of applicants, even though training in the classical arts is generously supported by government grants (cf. I_49: 51).

61 Alongside those providing purely spiritual leadership, the term 'Guru' applies to all those who teach arts such as singing, music, etc. since these continue to have a strongly religious aspect.

62 Since this study is focused on the contemporary arts, training opportunities in the classical branches will not be dealt with in detail.

63 Bertolt Brecht and GRIPS are, for example, often copied in Indian theatre (cf. Lechner, 2004: 51, Spiess, 2009: 60). An Indian theatre producer estimates that 75 per cent of the training is based on Western theories, which makes it difficult for the students to develop originally (cf. I_72). See also Ch. 5.5.3.

employee of the organisation describes the activities that the organisation has taken on for the professionalization of dance in the following terms:

> We had the skill-building workshops where we have a workshop each month and it could be to do with choreography, it could be to do with anything associated with dance, like lighting or dance-writing or scenography, music. (I_49: 13)

These efforts show the first signs of change. But this opportunity for professional training remains one of the very few open to the huge number of Indian cultural actors who wish to enter this field.

Even training at a government-sponsored cultural institute is still no guarantee, that the professionally trained artist will make a contribution to the establishment and development of a cultural landscape that is not dependent on the market, but which remains dependent on the state or foreign cultural institutes. Although an artist is admitted to one of the sought-after training courses – for example, like the twenty to thirty per year who are accepted into the NSD (cf. Bandyopadhyay, 2009: 198),[64] the reality is that at the end of their training, these students leave the theatre and look for jobs in television or Bollywood. It is only there – in market-driven art – where it is possible to earn enough money with a full time artistic career to allow "a good standard of living" (*ibid.*: 197, see also Sengupta *et al.*, s.a.: 15). A young actor confirms: "Theatre is not getting much out of it [i.e. the training offered at institutions like the NSD in New Delhi – author]." (I_80: 12, see also I_80: 2, I_62: 36) Samik Bandyopadhyay, a theatre and film scholar from Kolkata, comments: "Somehow this has become the definition of professionalism. Usable tools are being produced by the National Drama Factory and being offered to the entertainment industry." (Bandyopadhyay, 2009: 198)

Although art is organised, managed and mediated every day in the country's cultural institutions and their programs, "art management as a profession is not yet recognized in India" (Singh, 2009: 63, see also I_11: 10). Those working as arts managers are usually either artists without management training, or managers with no training in the arts. The manager of an artists' platform in Bangalore – himself one of the former, explains:

> And I'm not equipped, I'm not a business person, I have an arts background. I studied art, history and painting and animations so I have no business acumen or legal expertise or organisational and management expertise. (I_63: 27)

---

[64] Two of these places are reserved for non-Indians. These are seldom occupied.

On the other hand, a theatre administrator working in Bangalore states: "I haven't studied arts. I don't come with a creative background." (I_7: 16-18)

Support for the skills in cultural management, cultural education, and cultural mediation is urgently needed, according to the majority of the Indian cultural actors who were interviewed (cf. e.g. I_59: 16-17, 24-25), however this type of training is non-existent in India: "[W]e don't have any courses in Arts Management in India […], it would be difficult […] to find someone who's trained to do that […] in India." (I_7: 24, 180)

Faced with this situation, the Goethe-Institut has created a program for cultural managers in the context of its *Kultur und Entwicklung* (Culture and Development) initiative (cf. I_39: 9).[65] In India, this training program is entitled 'ARThinkSouthAsia (ATSA)'.[66] The cultural institute formulates the goal of this program as follows:

> To support potential leaders in the South Asian cultural sector in broadening their knowledge, international networks and experiences. In the long term it should help to establish a pool of professional trainers able to function as multipliers, who will be able to conceive and implement cultural management programs in South Asia independently. (Goethe-Institut e. V.)[67]

This course provides two weeks of training in competences including "strategic planning, policy processes, financial planning and fundraising, marketing, communication, and internet technologies" (Goethe-Institut e. V. New Delhi, 2012b: n.p.), while the participants from South Asia work to develop a project, which following a year-long trial period can be brought to their own cultural institutions or tested independently. The program is rounded off with a four-week placement at a cultural institute in Germany – from 2013-14 also in the UK, since the program is a partnership between the MMB in New Delhi as well as the British

65 This initiative was started by the institute at the end of 2008. It is focused on four areas of activity in developing countries, namely: vocational qualification, educational advice and cooperation, the creation of cultural spaces, and cooperation with civil society. See http://tinyurl.com/oejaomj (Accessed: 27.10.2013), Goethe-Institut e. V. (2011c: 6), Eisfeld (2004: 88 ff.). Projects in this field are developed with the need for long-term and sustainable engagement in mind, and developed in cooperation with partners on the ground with regard to their needs (cf. Ch. 2.2, 2.2.1, 2.2.2).

66 See the program website http://www.arthinksouthasia.org/ (Accessed: 13.06.2013).

67 Quoted from http://tinyurl.com/l2v9x8t (Accessed: 28.10.2013). It should be noted here that the participants value the national network being developed through the training program, since actors in the various branches and scenes are rarely connected, even in the same city.

Council.[68] For its participants, this program is one of the few opportunities to take part in training in the field of cultural management and mediation in their own country: "This [ARThinkSouthAsia – author] is, probably, the first course of its kind in India." (I_7: 170)

Because of the lack of cultural managers in India who are able to tech, teachers from abroad are invited to allow the program to take place in India (cf. I_11: 8). However, their working practices and contexts are not comparable with those in India. Following the conclusion of the training, Indian cultural practitioners are therefore also invited, in order to ensure that the knowledge can be transferred into the local context:

> So we have practitioners who could bring their experience, […] which is what we've been doing in the evening lectures. […] [I]t was great that [name of an Indian cultural actor – author] was there to keep […] bringing us back to our context. (I_7: 172, 178, 182)

It remains questionable whether European cultural management – despite the efforts at 'translation' – can function with the flawless success that one might hope (cf. Ch. 5.5.3).[69] According to a member of staff at the MMB, there is a growing need for professional cultural actors in India who are able to teach comprehensive context-specific cultural management (I_73: 62).

Until this vision is realised, the lack of trained staff in cultural management and education will continue to be a problem. The reality is that India's well known cultural institutions – for example, like the National Museum, which was founded in New Delhi as an autonomous cultural institution by the government in 1954, and which forms one of the government's Subordinate Offices (cf. Ch. 3.1) – has been working understaffed and "without leadership" for years (I_61: 17). The permanent staff of the National Gallery of Modern Art in New Delhi, for example, consists entirely of one manager and one conservator (cf. I_42: 62-64). This state of affairs means that the opportunities for moderation "between artistic production and reception, as well as between the art sector and other social branches remains […] underutilized" (Gad, 2012b: 293).

---

68 The British Council is a non-profit establishment for the fostering of international relations. Its goal is the expansion of mutual relations between the people of the UK and other countries (cf. Chakraborty, 2013: 20). See http://www.britishcouncil.org/ (Accessed: 29.09.2013).

69 For a comprehensive evaluation of the Goethe Institute's program for cultural managers, see the *Diplom* dissertations of Jennifer Emmrich and Marianne Kreuzig at the Department of Cultural Policy at the University of Hildesheim at http://tinyurl.com/o579h6x (Accessed: 27.10.2013).

Even the artists who are privileged with the chance to study abroad (cf. I_45: 453) are unable to balance out this lack of "good culture managers in the country" (Singh, 2009: 79). Until recently, these artists often did not even return to India, but remained abroad in environments where they were able to make a living with their art. However, Indian artists are increasingly making the conscious choice to live and work in India, according to the observations of many of those interviewed.

At the same time, many of the artists and artistic mediators who have not had the chance to study abroad work to achieve a certain level of self-taught professionalism as passionate practitioners of their art form (cf. Sengupta *et al.*, s.a.: 1, 4 ff., 10, Roy, 2011: n.p.). This type of training is entirely different from that of Western artists, which can often lead to differences and hierarchies in cooperations with them (cf. 6.6 and 6.9.1).

3.2.3 State Financing of Culture: Complex and Corrupt

State activity as a financial sponsor of art and culture is almost not worth mentioning. Only 0.16 per cent of the state budget is assigned to cultural activities, and this proportion is falling (cf. Singh, 2009: 70). The government is thoroughly aware of the small size of the cultural budget (cf. Ministry of Culture/Government of India, 2013-2014: 143). However, even this tiny proportion is not being used completely. Only seventy per cent of the state funds assigned to culture are actually expended (cf. Ghosh, 2013: n.p.), according to an internal government audit:

> While reviewing the Ministry's demand for grants (2012-13), the committee found that year after year, even the meagre funds allotted remain underutilized. Of the Rs. 805 crore sanctioned last year, only about Rs. 570 crore was used. This has seriously undermined the demand for more government spending on cultural activities, which is as low as 0.16 per cent of the total Eleventh Plan allocation. (No Author, 2012h: n.p.)[70]

According to Arundhati Ghosh, Director of the India Foundation for the Arts (IFAB)[71] since June 2013, the reason for underuse of the cultural budget is the consequence of a state that refuses "to change its programming and modes of operation in keeping with the changing needs and aspirations of the arts world." (cf. Ghosh, 2013: n.p.)

---

70 "Rs." is the abbreviation for Indian rupees. 805 crore is 8,050,000,000 Indian Rupees, or around 100 million euros. Only around 74 of these 100 millions was expended on art and culture. "Eleventh Plan" refers to the eleventh Five-Year Plan (cf. Ch. 3.1).

71 Unique philanthropic Indian cultural foundation based in Bangalore. For a description, see Ch. 3.2.4 and the institution's own website http://www.indiaifa.org/ (Accessed: 19.07.2013).

Indian cultural actors confirm the loss of potential funding because of the "complex" and "dysfunctional" government sponsorship system, which lacks a systematic plan, and does not fund art in a needs-orientated way (I_49: 53-55, see also I_11: 62-64).

This lack of government funding stands in stark contrast to the Ministry of Culture's current reports, which describe culture as an agent of national integration and social development (cf. Ministry of Culture/Government of India, 2013-2014: 142). According to the comments of a Goethe-Institut employee in India, one would be justified in the opinion that the government needs to be reminded of the importance of culture.[72]

The Ministry has introduced committees of experts for every branch of culture, to decide on the artistic quality of program applicants, and to decide whether or not to agree to a request for sponsorship (cf. I_51: 35). For artists and cultural workers, applying for state support requires much more effort than applying at a foreign cultural institute (cf. Ch. 3.2.4). The tough and complex bureaucracy of the Ministry prevents many cultural actors from applying for support at all – putting them directly on the search for other funding opportunities (cf. I_11: 13, I_66: 120-121).[73]

On top of this comes the criticism that the award of grants by the Ministry of Culture is neither serious nor transparent. The members invited to join the committees of experts promote artists known to them on a personal or professional level: "You know a lot of the things are going through connections that I know this person or this person." (I_45: 315, see also I_63: 116)[74] Artistic quality, according to an Indian cultural worker, plays no role whatsoever in the selection process: "[T]here's no follow-up on whether the work gets done, there's no follow-up of the quality of the work that gets done [...], it doesn't actually positively impact the field [...]" (I_49: 57, see also I_55: 2-4). There are no transparent public principles that define eligibility for funding, or support applicants (cf. I_73: 18, I_45: 538).

One of these criteria seems, however, to be that the government supports projects and events, which have already received financial support from other overseas cultural institutions and embassies, since their support provides proof of high-quality work:

72 This statement was made in the course of an informal discussion between the author and the employee.

73 See also I_50: 110, I_72: 41, I_63: 110.

74 See also Sengupta *et al.* (s.a.: 12): "And it is common knowledge that political influence and bureaucratic caprice play a key role in determining who gets awards and fellowships from the government."

> One of our last residencies finally got supported from the Ministry of Culture [...]. That was quite novel. They see Goethe-Institut, they see Norwegian Embassy supporting the missions and that [...] innovate the credibility of the project itself. It is a law being. If these organisations are supporting them, they must be doing some kind of good work. [...] No matter, how much we try to deny it, it is always that some sort of international endorsement and some sort of international support always helps you leverage your voice in the community and governmental circles [...], so it definitely has an impact. (I_11: 14, 26)

The Ministry responds to this criticism with the attitude that since it publishes all of its expenditure, a transparent distribution of the funds is ensured. However the seriousness of the government seems doubtful. Even when funding is approved, it is not certain that this sum will be received in full and on time by the sponsored project. For example, Gati Dance received a state grant for the IGNITE! dance festival in autumn 2012, but did not receive any funds until the end of November – forcing institution staff to invest private funds, and ask for financial support from the Goethe-Institut (cf. I_35: 9, I_11: 71). One self-employed cultural worker from the Indian children's and youth theatre confirms these statements, and lays out his approach following the award of government funds:

> If I receive a grant of 300,000 Rupees, and give assurances that thirty per cent will go back to the Ministry, if I am lucky, I will get the promised funds at the end of the project, otherwise one or two years after the end of the project if at all. (I_56: 18)[75]

This is one of many examples of the corruption that exists in India (cf. Auswärtiges Amt, 2002: 1 f., Bhagat, 2012: 141), which cultural workers in the country are forced to deal with, and which they are powerless against.

Further government restrictions severely limit the number of actors who are eligible for state support in the first place, particularly in the contemporary arts (cf. I_63: 18, I_51: 54-58, I_49: 51). These include laws stating that cultural institutions are only allowed to apply for state support after three years of existence (cf. I_49: 39-41, I_11: 72-74, I_39: 29), or the ministry's stated goal of supporting the traditional arts and maintaining cultural heritage.

[75] Accordingly, 1,200 euros of the 3,900 sponsorship awarded by the government would need to be paid back.

3.2.4 Alternative Sources of Funding: Their Limits and Potential

Patronage for the arts is very low in India. (I_13: 30)

Few alternative sources of funding are available, particularly for the contemporary arts. Businesses and private individuals, foundations, and the market all present opportunities, and their current development as alternative sources of funding for cultural activities in India will be analysed in the following pages.

The Indian government has been living through a period of change for some years. Since the economic liberalisation in 1991, the government has been gradually withdrawing from sectors such as art and education, with the intention that these 'soft' sectors can and should be taken over by the country's new economic powerhouses – such as wealthy firms (cf. I_67: 70-71).

The support of culture by businesses under the principle of Corporate Social Responsibility (CSR) is not popular in India, and almost inexistent (cf. I_44: 19-20, 23).[76] Companies that give a portion of their profits to social causes tend to favour the education sector – specifically universities – seemingly in the interest of the development of their own human resources. Art and culture receive support only seldom (cf. I_45: 171). When they do fund culture, their focus is usually on India's cultural heritage – for example, in the maintenance of temples and so on (cf. I_71: 91).

This tendency confirms the government's work to free itself of the financial burden posed by culture through the model of Public-Private Sponsorship (PPP).[77] The Ministry of Culture's budget report from 2013/14 presents 28 projects supported by them in a PPP framework as evidence of the success of this model. It is obvious, however, that the named partner companies have overwhelmingly supported projects that serve the protection and maintenance of cultural heritage (cf. Ministry of Culture/Government of India, 2013-2014: 144 f.). Sponsorship from well-known Indian companies such as TATA[78] represents a large amount

---

76 "[CSR is a] form of corporate self-regulation aimed at managing the impact that business activities have on different stakeholders, in order to produce an overall positive impact on society." (Chakraborty, 2013: 27) See also Sengupta *et al.* (s.a.: 11 f.), who provide a detailed description of when and why businesses sponsor Indian culture.

77 The intention behind PPP is to allow exclusively state-supported structures, such as cultural institutes and schools, to be added to and expanded by forms of organisation incorporating the trusteeship of local, private, and public partners. For a precise definition of PPP, see Ittstein (2002: XXXII) and Schwencke *et al.* (2009: 141 ff.).

78 TATA is India's largest industrial conglomerate, with more than 90 firms in fields such as metallurgy, car manufacture, IT and communications. Its head office is in Mumbai.

of bureaucratic effort, which leaves cultural sponsorship from overseas institutions looking more attractive than ever (cf. I_65: 7).

Why is CSR not an alternative sponsorship model in India? "The tax environment, however, does not encourage corporations to support the arts unless they can find a strong business reason for doing so." (IFAB, 2001: 8)[79] Tax breaks for cultural sponsorship, which are common in the USA or Germany, do not exist in India (cf. I_71: 91), meaning that cultural sponsorship can only be justified by a good deal – such as, for example, the use of art as entertainment in brand profiling (cf. Ghosh, 2013: n.p.). Businesses promote "finished art" (I_45: 475), if it can help them to promote their brand. Art is thereby used as an important medium for communication and advertising for increased sales. Popular music and Bollywood profit from this form of sponsorship in particular: audiences of thousands at pop concerts are subject to advertisements from soft drink brands, while well-known car manufacturers place their products in Bollywood films (cf. I_15: 13-17, I_80: 14). For these cultural branches, businesses are "major patrons of the arts with varying interests and goals" (Singh, 2009: 61).[80] However, to view Bollywood's success as evidence of the success of art and culture in the commercial market would be too shallow a judgement.[81] For other art forms – in particular modern ones – this market simply does not exist:

> [A]rt processes, art collaborations, performance art, design interfaces, all the kinds of experimental stuff you're talking about, there's no market for. So you need a very, very different idea of an art market then the state of art objects and I'm not sure right now that the art market in India has extended to accommodate all these definitions. (I_71: 106)

The often-cited 'cash value' success of Indian visual art needs to be approached differently. Although the past decade has seen a "gallery boom" in the Indian visual art market (Ulmer, 2008: n.p.), a lack of institutions in the art market means that opportunities and room for manoeuvre are limited in this sector (cf. Spiess, 2009: 9). The result of this is that although a market does exist for Indian visual art, it is not in

---

79 Excepted are the National Cultural Funds, founded by the state, which have begun to give businesses a 100 per cent tax break. These funds are primarily used to finance the maintainance of cultural heritage (cf. I_67: 69).

80 Also Kapoor (2009: 190), however even here, foreign companies familiar with sponsoring are often contacted, rather than Indian ones, who continue to be mistrustful of the success of sponsorship in cultural events (cf. I_15: 9-11).

81 Bollywood is the world's largest film industry, which owes a large degree of its success to the two million strong Indian diaspora, a large part of which lives in the USA (cf. Frieling, 2000: 34 f.). The Indian diaspora in Germany consists of around half a million people (cf. Rana, 2002: 23).

India, but overwhelmingly in the 'Global North' (cf. Ulmer, 2008: n.p.).[82] The gallery boom has, furthermore, led to mass production, which has had a negative effect on the quality and reputation of Indian visual art (cf. Singh, 2009: 64). Leading Indian cultural actors to fear a 'selling out of culture' on the market.

The non-existence of an Indian art and culture market is partly due to the impossibility of levying entrance fees. Eighty per cent of all cultural events are free to enter, according to the estimation of an established theatre producer in Delhi (cf. I_59: 27-28, I_45: 171). Raising entrance fees is not possible because "ticketed programmes are still regarded as less prestigious then invitational programmes" (Singh, 2009: 63). Invitations as well as entrance fees are a both a means of exclusion, because there are many Indians who would be unable to afford even a cheap ticket for a cultural event:[83] "Any price of course has the effect of excluding some people." (I_73: 16) In a country where art belongs to the elite (cf. I_49: 17, I_35: 24-25, I_61: 9), any type of exclusion in the arts is a sensitive topic (cf. Ch. 2.3).

There is a growing awareness amongst Indian cultural actors that art and culture can and have to cost something so that they can support themselves, and not depend completely on the support of the state or foreign institutions. The tradition of having to buy a ticket for a cultural event is a relatively new one, adapted from the West like many other conventions around the presentation of art (cf. I_72: 43): "Needless to say, all forms of contemporary performance rely on conventions of staging that India inherited through its contact with the West." (Sengupta *et al.*, s.a.: 3)[84] The West has transmitted an understanding that an audience needs to pay for culture, and that producers are able to draw profit from culture. However, in order to be able to demand an entry fee, as the theatre producer from Delhi points out, the work that is shown needs to have a certain level of quality, which is questionable in the case of many events (cf. I_59: 28).[85]

US-style private philanthropy in the arts is rare in India:

---

82 Also I_42: 72, I_61: 10-14. The international recognition achieved by Indian visual art, meaning that Indian artists are able to work on an equal footing with their US and European counterparts, was in evidence, for example, in the Indian participation at the Documenta, or at the Indian Biennale in Kochi, which took place for the first time in 2012. On the boom in Indian visual art, see Spiess (2009: 27 ff.) and Sonna (2009).

83 The price of entry is also subject to tax (cf. I_29: 17).

84 Also I_45: 171. Meant here are also stylistic conventions such as a frontal stage, a curtain, and low lighting (cf. Palazhy, 2009: n.p.).

85 Also I_47: 17, Kapoor (2009: 185). See also Vellani (2006) on the relationship between art and culture in India.

> Out of a total of 104 Indian donors surveyed in terms of their areas of philanthropic interest, a recent compilation [...] lists 13 institutions interested in supporting 'Arts and Humanities'. (CSCS, 2012: 1, Answer to Question 6)[86]

One reason for the lack of philanthropy in India could be that the concept of giving to those in need does not form a part of the Hindu worldview (cf. I_71: 85). One exception is the philanthropic India Foundation for the Arts Bangalore (IFAB) founded in 1993, which remains unique to this day. IFAB describes itself in the following terms:

> India Foundation for the Arts [...] is an independent, professionally managed grant-making agency with the goal to enrich the practice, knowledge, public access to, and experience of the arts in India.[87]

One letter written to IFAB by an Indian artist makes the need for an institution of its kind clear: "There are few institutions in India offering much-needed support in the field of art and culture, as you are doing." (IFAB, 1999: 5) Despite the passage of fifteen years, private-law institutions for cultural sponsorship continue to be virtually non-existent. IFAB accordingly defines its principal task as:

> Mobilising funds for the arts is a daunting challenge in a country where charitable assistance has traditionally focused on building health, educational and religious infrastructure, or providing relief from various forms of adversity and suffering. (IFAB, 2001: 8)

In order to strengthen the engagement of Indian firms, organisations, and individuals in cultural sponsorship, IFAB has tried to introduce the "draw-down funds" model of sponsorship, whereby funds are awarded when the sponsored body is able to contribute the same amount of resources (IFAB, 2001: 8), with a very limited degree of success.

Private persons in India have no advantage from leaving a legacy to a cultural establishment rather than their descendants, since gift and inheritance takes similar to those in Germany or the UK do not exist (cf. I_71: 86-89). In the absence of favourable tax conditions for private persons and organisations, the government itself is responsible for conditions that hinder the development of cultural infrastructure.

---

86 On this exhibition, cf. Indian Centre for Philanthropy (1999).

87 Quoted from http://tinyurl.com/o998xf3. See also http://www.indiaifa.org/ and Ghosh (2013: n.p.). IFAB's projects and programs, as well as the size of their various grants are listed in the 'Annual Reports' of the public foundation under http://tinyurl.com/pnexr4f (All accessed: 15.07.2013).

Arundhati Ghosh, the director of IFAB since 2013, illustrates the potential role of private donors as a future source of funding for art and culture:

> [T]he individual donor is emerging as a key supporter and partner of the not-for-profit sector, including the arts. [...] This is true not only of high net-worth individuals capable of giving large sums but also of people from the middle and upper-middleclass who have started donating smaller amounts. I believe this is where the future of resource mobilization lies in India for the arts and culture sector. (Ghosh, 2013: n.p.)

Alongside cultural sponsorship from abroad, philanthropy and the art market are additional alternative sources of finance for Indian cultural actors.

> I actually honestly don't think [name of an Indian cultural institution – author] could survive without *Goethe*. (I_63: 25)

This quotation makes clear how (existentially) important the support of foreign cultural institutes – especially those from Europe – are for India's cultural actors (see also I_50: 148). In particular, the innovative and contemporary art and cultural scenes require this assistance as an alternative to the lack of local support (cf. I_65: 2).[88] Shuddhabrata Sengupta, member of the artists' and media group, the RAQS Media Collective (RAQS),[89] explains: "[W]hat is really starved of support is any practice that foregrounds contemporary art." (Sengupta, 2002: 1) On top of this comes the fact that financial support from Western institutions is less bureaucratic to manage and obtain than that from the Indian government and commercial entities (cf. I_65: 7).

Foreign cultural institutions and the cultural departments of foreign embassies are therefore responsible for supporting a large part of India's contemporary cultural landscape.[90] Rather than just providing the publicised start up financing to complement the efforts of the beneficiaries themselves (cf. I_70: 68), they are increasingly providing core funding

---

88 See also I_56: 12, I_47: 1, I_42: 28, Varghese Mathews (2000: 9).

89 RAQS Media Collective is a group of three media artists (Jeebesh Bagchi, Monica Narula and Shuddhabrata Sengupta), located in New Delhi. The Collective is known internationally for its work in the contemporary visual arts, having taken part, for example, in the *Documenta* and the Venice Biennale. For details, see http://www.raqsmediacollective.net/ (Accessed: 19.06.2013).

90 In contrast to the widespread perception amongst those interviewed that European cultural institutes have a significant supportive effect on the cultural landscape, Arundhati Ghosh comments: "[B]ilateral agencies, embassies, consulates, and cultural arms of countries that have diplomatic relations with India still form a very small percentage of the supporters for the arts." (Ghosh, 2013: n.p.)

to the Indian cultural landscape. Indian cultural workers and their institutions are often already the recipients of several years of financing from a range of foreign cultural institutes and embassies, as the foreign funding history of one Indian cultural actor illustrates:

> And then we've worked with the British Council and we've worked with Pro Helvetia which is the Swiss Arts Council. We worked once with the Austrian Culture Forum, and […] we've worked with […] the Dutch […] Design Fashion Architecture. We've worked with them. There was a lot of collaboration and participation from the international community. (I_15: 5)

An additional example for the influence exercised by foreign donors on the Indian cultural scene is the work of KHOJ.[91] The international artists' platform in New Delhi received financial sponsorship from the Dutch development organisation HIVOS[92] for ten years before receiving a three-year sponsorship from the Norwegian Embassy in 2012 (cf. I_13: 13-14). SPIC MACAY[93], an Indian society for the support and maintenance of Indian classical music and culture amongst young people is only able to act thanks to the support of the Norwegian Embassy, although it supports the classical arts and would be able to ask for support from the Indian state (cf. I_48: 5-7, 21-22).

However support from abroad is a two-edged sword. It creates dependencies on funds from richer countries, which purchase the creative potential of poorer countries (cf. I_44: 33, I_59: 21). This has been described by some Indian cultural actors as a 'second' or 'new' colonisation (cf. e.g. I_45: 504).[94] These renewed dependencies are strengthened when

---

91 With the full name "KHOJ International Artists' Association". For details, see http://khojworkshop.org/ and CSCS (2012: 16, Answer to Question 3) as well as information at http://tinyurl.com/c833ap6 (Both accessed: 14.04.2013).

92 HIVOS stands for "*Humanistisch Instituut voor Ontwikkelingssamenwerking*", see http://www.hivos.org/ (Accessed: 15.05.2013).

93 Short for: "Society for the Promotion of Indian Classical Music And Culture Amongst Youth", see http://spicmacay.com/ (Accessed: 13.06.2013) and Ittstein (2009: 98 f., 126 f.). For a comprehensive description of the cooperation between SPIC MACAY and their Norwegian supporters, see I_42: 38-40. The Norwegian Embassy has been a strong and generous supporter of Indian culture in recent years – above all of cultural institutions. It supports projects on an institutional basis, most often over a period of three years.

94 It would not be possible to thoroughly document the colonial history of India at this point. However its effects can still be felt today (cf. Sen, 2007: 100 ff.), and this history still plays a role in conditioning India's present. For the current scholarly debates on colonialism, see Postcolonial Studies. An overview of this discipline can be found at http://tinyurl.com/ox4rvmx (Accessed: 18.01.2014). Leela Gandhi provides an insight specifically into Indian-British colonial relations in her foundational work on postcolonialism (Gandhi, 1998).

the support is conditional on a personal relation to a leading foreign institute staff member, or is only available for a specific branch, which is the subject of an institute's long-term focus (cf. Ch. 2.2.2).

Some artists feel themselves to be in the role of supplicant (cf. I_59: 21), when they apply for financing from foreign cultural institutions. Even though there may be no other opportunity to finance their projects – above all in the contemporary arts – in their own country. According to an Indian theatre director, this lack of an alternative is no protection from the loss of prestige that support from abroad can imply: When a project receives overseas support, it is unable to support itself, and is therefore not worthy of assistance. The artist embarking on such a project loses his reputation amongst his peers (cf. I_15: 219, I_32: 11, 29-31, Klaic, 2009: n.p.). As a consequence, artists often hide the fact that they are supported by Western cultural institutions. Pride too, and the desire to finance a project from one's own resources, also has a role to play here (cf. I_32: 31). Meanwhile, this subsidization of art through foreign funding because of a lack of access to other sources serves to strengthen the position of the existing local cultural elite (cf. Knüsel, 2011: 72).

The feeling of dependence and the role of supplicant are made stronger by the behaviour of some institutes, which is reminiscent of '21st Century colonial masters' (cf. I_61: 26, I_47: 16-17).

At the same time, there are institutions, like the MMB, whose international activities are engaged with the severe challenges and deficits of India – for example, through the training and education of artists and artistic actors (cf. I_44: 27-29), and the mediation of access to art and culture without regard to the elite (cf. I_73: 16). This is in keeping with the approach already adopted in the Mexico City Declaration on Cultural Policies in 1982 (cf. UNESCO, 1982: n.p. and Ch. 2.2). At the same time, Indian cultural actors are aware of the institutes' limited cultural budgets (cf. I_61: 29-30, I_56: 14), which are unable to provide long-term support, and do not view them as being under the obligation to provide further funding: "[I]t's probably unrealistic to expect […] from Goethe-Institut and the German government when the Indian government should do that job." (I_45: 253) Foreign cultural institutions give a sufficient amount of conceptual and financial support (see e.g. I_44: 11-13), and thereby show Indian artists and cultural workers more recognition and estimation than their own country (cf. I_43: 20-21, I_49: 79). The institutes strengthen the self-confidence of cultural actors, and encourage them to believe in themselves and their art (cf. I_15: 93), giving them the feeling of belonging to Indian society, and the opportunity to show themselves and their work in public.

In summary, with regard to the financial structures that underpin art and culture in India: Government sponsorship is almost non-existent.

The government does not see itself as being under an obligation (cf. I_37: 32-46, I_43: 20-21, I_49: 79), because it does not seem to recognise the socio-political value of cultural sponsorship (cf. Gad, 2012b: 281 f.). Accordingly, instruments for the support of culture have a largely marginal and undifferentiated existence.[95]

There are very few local alternatives to state support, such as civil-society initiatives. Because of the lack of appropriate public and private financial support, the only alternative is for the contemporary art and culture scene to seek funding from overseas. However funds from abroad are limited and "can only ever be limited with regard to the partner's responsibility for themselves" (*ibid.*: 306).

This lack of support, and the absence of any prospect of long-term financing that would allow a certain degree of security and stability for artists in their private and professional lives, has the effect of limiting artistic freedom, and preventing artists and cultural workers from putting their creativity to use in artistic processes: "[C]onstantly begging for money. Constantly fundraising takes away from the work itself. You are tensed to compromise on the quality of work." (I_11: 30)[96] The development of strategies for stable and long-term local financing for culture in accordance with the needs of the cultural landscape on the ground is therefore of the greatest importance: "The time has come to make appropriate adjustments and innovations in the pattern of cultural funding in India." (Singh, 2009: 71, see here Ch. 6.13)[97]

3.2.5 The Indian Cultural Worker as Master in the Art of Living: The Consequences

> We made it work with what we had. And this is the single most important concept we learned during our time in India: jugaad. Making do. [...] Improvising a solution. Creating options where there is none. [...] Artist Sanjeev Shankar describes it as 'attaining any objective with the available resources at hand'. (Prager, 2011: 258)[98]

The lack of infrastructure and resources force Indian artists to implement their artistic ideas in a creative manner, according to the concept of "jugaad" described in the quotation (cf. I_50: 30, I_45: 149).

---

95 See also here Narayan (2013), who reports on the value of the arts in India in the article "Why we don't value our arts enough".

96 See also I_49: 143 as well as Ch. 3.2.5 and 5.4.3.

97 For more on cultural financing in India, see Ghosh (2013: n.p.) and Sengupta *et al.* (s.a.: 11).

98 See also www.sanjeevshankar.com/jugaad.html (Accessed: 02.05.2013).

They are required to fulfil the conditions for artistic activity by themselves, since they only belong to institutions or organisations in the rarest of cases. This includes challenges such as finding real estate; rehearsal, and display spaces; applying for official permits, managing and securing financing opportunities, as well as promoting their projects and themselves. This range of tasks has the consequence that only a limited amount of time then remains left over for their cultural activities and the professionalization of their work. According to the estimation of one staff member at the Goethe-Institut,[99] eighty per cent of an Indian cultural worker's time is occupied with administrative tasks like those named above; while at most twenty per cent of their time remains available for creativity and engagement with artistic projects and processes. This is confirmed by an Indian dancer (cf. I_49: 39). In particular, finding sources of funding in India is described as "the hardest of work", because they simply do not exist (I_46: 4), meaning that the creative ideas of many Indian cultural actors are primarily concerned with the question of financing (cf. Ch. 3.2.3 and 3.2.4).

Teaching one's own cultural practice is an alternative way of earning a living, independent of institutional grants (cf. I_45: 149-152, 245, 385-387, see also Velayanikal, 2011: n.p.). In the traditional arts, the model of the student-teacher relationship continues to be practiced.

However the ability to teach requires professionalism in one's own field, based on training, which – because of the lack of infrastructure – is practically impossible to receive in India:

> I always tell my dancers to have other skills like [...] teaching, choreographing, management or project management [...], even personal training or therapy; having said that we don't have enough infrastructure to effect that. (I_45: 281)

This produces a vicious circle – because of the lack of infrastructure in the form of funding sources, artists want to teach in order to finance their art. But because of a lack on infrastructure in the form of training opportunities he is unable to do so, because it is impossible to acquire the professionalism required in his own country.

Furthermore, the teaching concept cannot apply to young artists at the beginning of their careers, because professionalism in their art form arises first of all from experiences of working nationally and internationally. It is only by performing dance, theatre, or music, or undertaking art exhibitions that these experiences can be gained. These also require an infrastructure of spaces and locations that is hardly

---

99 This information comes from an informal conversation between the staff member and the author.

present in India (cf. I_11: 17, Ch. 3.2.1), as well as the ability to be mobile – which is only possessed by privileged artists (cf. I_50: 101, Ch. 5.2). Daniel Gad summarises the reasons for this lack of mobility: "The mobility of artists is limited by small budgets, as well as poor transport infrastructure in many places, and partly by restrictive visa policies." (Gad, 2012b: 185 f.)

When artists are able to teach, their teaching function – particularly in state-sponsored cultural institutions – often takes so much of their time and energy that there is little left for their own creative processes, according to a German artist's estimation of his Indian partner who teaches as a scholar at the NSD (cf. I_32: 85).[100] This double burden also has a negative effect on German-Indian partnerships. Backed up by good funding,[101] the German partners are able to give the cooperative project their full attention, while the Indian partner needs to balance this with the other obligations of their personal and professional lives. This creates a gap, because the German partner is able to invest more time into the cooperation than the Indian one. This means that the German partner can often feel misunderstood: He has come the long way to India for the privilege of working on a combined project to which the Indian partner gives only half of their energy: "He was not really available. If only he had just worked for this performance." (I_32: 95) German partners often summarise their Indian partners with a lack of engagement or application. However the Indian partner can in turn thereby feel misunderstood in his situation (cf. Ch. 5.4.2). This gap is also problematic for relationships between Indian artists and German supporters, which extract Indian artists from their daily life completely for the purposes of cooperation. For Indian artists, this kind of sponsorship is almost impossible to accept, because of the need for them to continue to work their income sources outside of their artistic activity, which they will continue to rely on following the conclusion of the cooperation.

Furthermore, it is doubtful whether there exists a (large enough) market for costly artistic training in India to make work as a teacher viable. The vast majority are not in possession of significant privilege, and do not need or wish to make a living through art and culture.

The members of certain social groups, in possession of the necessary resources in terms of time and money, are able to practice and concern themselves with the arts. In these cases, the family is often responsible for

100 Cf. the statements from the Indian side, which confirm this impression: I_37: 13.

101 E.g. through the 'Federal Cultural Foundation' (Kulturstiftung des Bundes), Goethe-Institut, or the various cultural foundations of the federal states (cf. Schwencke *et al.*, 2009: 125 f.).

providing the necessary resources, under the condition that the art of their son or daughter is acceptable. This is the case where a family is privileged and either an artistic dynasty, which values art for its own sake,[102] or merely wealthy and able to afford it (cf. I_35: 35, CSCS, 2012: 4 f., Answer to Question 4). The latter are often those with connections to 'the right kind' of important and influential people, who are able to make some of the limited resources in terms of space and funding available for their work, regardless of whether or not the artist is talented or not (cf. I_35: 30, Ch. 3.2.3). The types of capital here condition one another simultaneously. For artists from poorer background, an artistic career is something like a lived art of survival: "People are surviving in whatever way they can survive." (I_71: 112)

The limited nature of financing opportunities in the cultural field means that many artists are forced to earn a regular income from other sources – co-financing and subsidizing their art with money from other branches:

> [W]e have to do other professional, we do a lot of other work to earn money. That I can sustain, by recovering the cost from other sides. (I_59: 22)

As a consequence, their professional artistic practice is first of all limited to taking place on a voluntary basis in the evening, and at weekends, on a voluntary or amateur basis.[103] The founder of one platform intended to serve artists and the technology community in Bangalore financed their project from income saved from their previous employment in a multinational IT company, income from work as a consultant to the state government in cultural and environmental issues, and from the income of their life partner (cf. I_63: 121-131). But even when these artists are successful with their work, they are unable to profit from it: "[I]f you're good and careful and solid you don't lose money but you don't make money." (I_63: 121)[104] One Indian actor reported that he paid 95 per cent of the costs of a community production "from his own pocket", and that ticket sales covered a mere five per cent (I_80: 7).[105] Putting the situation positively, an actor from the Indian children's and youth theatre in Delhi

---

[102] E.g. the prominent Kapoor family with a long Bollywood history. Many family members were and are successful actors, directors, and producers. See, for example, http://tinyurl.com/yd5ze58 (Accessed: 27.10.2013).

[103] The term "amateur" is not intended to degrade the work of Indian cultural actors. On the contrary, these artists are often characterised by a great devotion to their work. Furthermore, many achieve a high level of professionalism through independent learning (cf. Ch. 3.2.2).

[104] Also I_63: 131, I_35: 34-35, I_21: 4.

[105] On the use of private means for cultural practice, see also I_37: 54.

said: "Nothing is lost through art, but there is no profit either." (I_44: 26-27, see also I_37: 54-59, I_59: 22)

Since an artistic career is not seen as a full-time occupation, immediate financial insecurity is joined by a complete lack of social security (cf. I_21: 4). The India Theatre Forum – the independent network of those associated with the theatre – presented a petition to the Ministry of Culture entitled "Kala Kalyana: A Social Security/Welfare Scheme for Artists", in order to advocate for the social role and rights of artists. It states, in part:

> However, artists are typically under-resourced despite the work and services they provide, and they are often undervalued and under-recognized for the roles that they play in society. [...] Presently, there are systems of support for artists like awards, fellowships, pensions (administered by the state and central governments), aid to individuals and organizations but none of the above systems offer a comprehensive social security module in which artists are not just beneficiaries, but active premium-holders. (India Theatre Forum)[106]

According to a theatre producer from Bangalore, the establishment of the idea that art can be a vocation is a relatively new phenomenon in India (I_72: 39-41). Being able to practice art as a full-time occupation with a regular income, as is the case in the West, is not yet realistic or practicable, since the conditions required for this model of living and working do not yet exist in India (cf. I_44: 25-26, I_20: 19). The constant struggle for survival limits the freedom of artists, who need the ability to concentrate completely on their creative work. This means that for most artists, even those with great talent, learning and practicing art remains a hobby. This reality also conditions German-Indian partnerships in the arts, where professional German artists encounter Indian amateurs. A German *dramaturg* describes the following scenario:

> The *Schnawwl* actors [from Germany] [...] are actually more or less actors the whole day long, and do the job professionally, while the *Ranga Shankara* actors [from India] often had other jobs, or were working on more of an amateur basis. (I_70: 29, cf. Ch. 5.9.1)

Supporting the vocational position of artists and cultural workers – including through the sponsorship and reinforcement of appropriate training formats, as foreseen in the 2005 UNESCO treaty – would have to be a decisive part of a theoretical Indian cultural policy.[107]

---

106 Quoted from the petition at http://tinyurl.com/q4doa7g (Accessed: 11.06.2013).

107 Article 10: Paragraph c and Article 14: Paragraph b, see http://tinyurl.com/nnpc98x (Accessed: 12.09.2013).

3.3 India's Cultural Foreign Relations: Conservative and Invisible

India's foreign cultural policy distorts the perception of the country abroad. First of all, India's foreign cultural policy receives only a small amount of state funding, which are not appropriate to India's large population or strategic importance (cf. Wagner, 2005: 17). The country's few activities in the field of foreign cultural policy are not visible. Amongst other issues, support is exclusively provided to the traditional arts – similar to the situation under the domestic cultural policy – giving a highly conservative appearance to the foreign cultural policy's representations (cf. I_73: 14).[108] One MMB staff member asks provocatively:

> If there is so much cultural richness, which is possibly primarily represented through classical music and dance on an international level, then why not something contemporary? (I_73: 12)

The Ministry of Culture and the Indian Council for Cultural Relations (ICCR) are the two organs that pan and implement India's foreign cultural policy (cf. Spiess, 2009: 19). The following pages will give an analysis of these central institutions and their activities with regard to India's foreign cultural policy.

Amongst the goals and functions of the Ministry of Culture is care for international relations: "Develop and promote international cultural relations" (Ministry of Culture/Government of India, 2012-2013: 2, 5, 12, 20). However, the Ministry's staff have the aim of supporting Indian culture abroad, and not international relations. The Ministry exists, "[b]asically to promote Indian culture abroad" (I_52: 56).[109] Its international relations are based on bilateral agreements: "The Ministry signs a cultural exchange program; it's like a memorandum of understanding with many cultures." (I_51: 40, see also I_52: 1-10) At present, joint declarations for cultural cooperation are in place between India's Ministry of Culture and 121 partner countries.[110] These agreements define the temporal and financial scope of a range of highly specific cultural exchanges. Favoured branches include archaeology and visual art (cf. I_51: 56). India signed its first Memorandum with Germany in 1969 (cf. Ch. 4), and its most recent was renewed in 2003

[108] Also I_61: 2, 14-15, I_50: 114-119, 121-123.

[109] The CSCS concludes regarding the government's activities in international relations: "[T]he Government of India has been aggressively promoting various kinds of both bilateral and multinational strategies for the promotion of Indian culture internationally." (CSCS, 2012: 4, Answer to Question 3)

[110] See the website of the Ministry of Culture at http://tinyurl.com/qdx3u5n (Accessed: 12.06.2013).

for the period 2003-5. The Ministry recognises that these agreements have very little effect on mutual dialogue – even though they provide decisive legal security for cultural-political work on foreign soil (cf. I_52: 80-82). In order to implement these agreements with foreign states, the Ministry commissions its independent institutions like the Academies and the NSD (cf. I_52: 14). These institutions do not receive any additional financial support from the Ministry for their work in support of the national foreign cultural policy. According to their understanding, these commissions to engage in exchange require nothing more than travel costs (cf. I_52: 46-51), since they are solely intended to deliver "finished productions" to foreign countries (I_44: 17). The complete financial dependence of the institutions on the Ministry mean that they have no choice but to support the politically planned cultural encounters, although the Ministry stresses that the commissioned institutions are left a free hand as far as the content of these exchanges is concerned (cf. I_52: 41-42, Ch. 3.1). It is doubtful whether the 'exchanges' that take place within the framework of these commissions, which are above all intended to promote India and Indian culture, do indeed encourage dialogue and thereby relations – especially since the Indian government and its foreign cultural policy engages exclusively with partner governments and their embassies (cf. I_52: 105, Ministry of Culture/Government of India, 2013-2014: 13).

The ICCR is the second central instrument of Indian foreign cultural policy (cf. Spiess, 2009: 25, Ittstein, 2009: 103). It serves as an 'executive organ' and 'event manager' for the Ministry:

> So we [the Ministry of Culture – author] work very closely together, our organisations help the ICCR by providing resources like artists and they arrange the program, the event, so the event management is what ICCR is good at. (I_51: 68)[111]

The ICCR was founded in 1950 by Maulana Abul Kalam Azad, the first Minister for Education in independent India, and is subject to the Ministry of External Affairs.[112] This means that foreign cultural policy is "formally foreign policy, and not cultural policy", according to a Goethe-Institut staff member in India (I_73: 12). This structure means that there

111 Cf. also I_52: 58. On the relation between the Ministry of Culture and the ICCR, see Ittstein (2009: 103 f.), Spiess (2009: 18).

112 See http://www.iccrindia.net/index.html (Accessed: 13.05.2013). The ICCR was originally under the control of the Ministry of Culture, but was then assigned to the Foreign Minister (cf. I_51: 68). For detailed information, see http://meaindia.nic.in/ (Accessed: 14.04.2013). A comprehensive description of the ICCR including its locations and activities, is provided by Ittstein (2009: 103 ff.). For the history of the ICCR see http://www.iccrindia.net/founder.html (Accessed: 12.05.2013).

is no unified cultural policy across the foreign and domestic spheres, even though the Ministry of Culture stresses that it works in close cooperation with the ICCR, as the quotation above makes clear.

The purpose of the ICCR is to encourage encounters with other countries and people. The institution's website states: "The ICCR is about a communion of cultures, a creative dialogue with other nations."[113] However this creative dialogue is questionable. Every year, the ICCR receives an action plan drafted on the basis of reports from Indian embassies abroad, which it is required to implement using the limited financial resources at its disposal.[114]

The ICCR has a committee of experts, whose role is to "[...] decide on the groups' status and standard or level of performance. That level has to be reached by any artist to represent India abroad, in each dance form, or each music genre. So they have to reach that level before they perform abroad." (I_53: 27)[115] The ICCR exclusively selects artists with a classical tendency to represent Indian culture abroad (cf. Spiess, 2009: 62).[116] The involvement of an expert committee in the selection process is no guarantee of a fair chance of securing a commission overseas. Relationships play a decisive role: "[Y]ou are sending people who you favour." (I_61: 19)[117] Chetan Bhagat makes the following comment on this state of affairs: "[India is] a society where connected people do better than people with ability. It leads to a lot of talent being unused, a tremendous waste of national resource." (Bhagat, 2012: 142)

The concept of exchange favoured by the Ministry of Culture, and therefore also by the ICCR, is based around sending selected artists to present India's classical and traditional art at large events such as festivals and concert tours (cf. Ministry of Culture/Government of India, 2012-2013: 8). The available funds are largely expended on flight tickets (cf. I_48: 26-27, I_55: 15). The development of long-term supporting structures such as policies and programs is not part of this understanding of exchange (cf. I_44: 9, 17-18, 27-30), even though this concept may be the official line of the ICCR: "[...] to participate in the formulation and implementation of policies and programs relating to India's external cultural relations."[118]

113 Quoted from http://www.iccrindia.net/index.html (Accessed: 13.05.2013).

114 The ICCR annual budget for 2010-11 was, for example, 175 million euros (cf. CSCS, 2012: 29, Answer to Question 4).

115 On the selection of artists by the ICCR, see also Ittstein (2009: 110).

116 Traditional arts are supported, but contemporary ones barely so, even when they are placed in a prominent position alongside India's cultural heritage on the ICCR website.

117 See also statements in the interviews I_29 and I_55 and Ch. 3.2.3.

118 Quoted in: http://www.iccrindia.net/constitution.html (Accessed: 15.06.2013).

Alongside the sponsorship of individual artists or groups of artists, the ICCR supports twenty domestic offices which are supposed to cover the various regions of India, and thirty overseas offices around the world.[119] The mission is: "[…] [to] organize outreach programmes including panel discussions, lectures, exhibitions, essay competitions, performances, screenings, and language learning courses."[120] The Tagore Centre in Berlin, opened at the beginning of the 1990s, is the institute's office in Germany. The centre formally belongs to the German Embassy, and is run by the ICCR (cf. Rothermund, 1995b: 480). Hans-Georg Wieck, former German ambassador in India, and former president of the German-Indian Society ("*Deutsch-Indische Gesellschaft*") praised the opening of the centre in 1996, describing it as an institution "that promotes dialogue in a form where content is relevant, and not steamrollered by the zeitgeist of 'show-business'." (Wieck, 1996: 80) What Wieck calls the "long-term effects" of this "investment" remain to be seen. The fact is, that the centre has received very little financial support or personnel since its opening, meaning that it now serves as little more than a point of contact for Indian cultural actors in Germany (cf. *ibid.*, 2010: 31).

Alongside these domestic and overseas cultural institutions, the ICCR supports 93 academic chairs for modern Indology – Chairs of Indian Studies – at foreign universities. The task of these is to offer lectures on Indian politics, economics, and culture.[121] Although the ICCR makes use of this overseas infrastructure in the implementation of its policies, it cannot distract from the fact that it has very little infrastructural clout overseas. The richness of Indian culture – the "Cultural Superpower" – stands in stark contrast to the condition of Indian cultural institutions abroad (Varma, 2007: 1137, see also Spiess, 2009: 18).

The current challenges of the Indian foreign cultural policy are conditioned by three discussions. The so-called cultural dialogue promoted by the Ministry and the ICCR is limited to the presentation of Indian culture abroad (cf. Wieck, 2006b: 1079). It is legitimate to ask whether the reason for this presentation of traditional art overseas is not – alongside the Indian understanding of foreign cultural policy, and the wish to attract

[119] Cf. the list of regional institutes at http://www.iccrindia.net/regionalofficeslist.html. The tasks of the various institutes are also described here. The list of the thirty overseas institutes is available at http://tinyurl.com/ppgqbfe. This was only 24 cultural centres in 2010 (cf. Lee, 2010: 14). The objectives of the Indian cultural institutes are comprehensively described at http://www.iccrindia.net/culturalcentres.html (All accessed: 20.06.2013).

[120] Quoted from http://www.iccrindia.net/regionaloffices.html (Accessed: 20.06.2013).

[121] See also http://www.iccrindia.net/chairs.html and http://www.iccrindia.net/chairslist.html (Both accessed: 21.06.2013). The ICCR also provides grants to Indian scientists and students overseas (cf. Wieck, 2006a: 2).

foreign tourists to 'exotic' India (cf. Sengupta *et al.*, s.a.: 16) – does not owe something to the fact that foreign audiences are expecting to see the well-known cliché laden image of India. That is, the exoticism of Indian classical music and dance – two art forms, which have also helped to make Bollywood so successful (cf. Kämpchen, 2012: 14, Spiess, 2009: 58, 67 f., 128).[122] However, in order to project a 'real' image of India into the world, contemporary art must be able to maintain its place alongside the classical.

India's cultural foreign relations are characterised by the principle of reciprocity, as a representative of the ICCR makes clear:

> [I]f we've worked with the German group [...] brought by Max Mueller Bhavan in India, and they work with ICCR, [...] and you want us to host them, so we would like Max Mueller Bhavan to also look for a partner in Germany to host our own groups. It's on a reciprocal basis. (I_53: 116)[123]

When the reciprocity called for by the Indian government cannot be fulfilled by the partner country, the Ministry of Culture is not prepared to undertake an exchange, as one staff member makes clear:

> [B]ecause of this recession, [...] the exchanges on cultural level bilaterally [...] was pretty bad with Europe, I mean we did not have much exchanges, for the simple reason because reciprocity was not possible. (I_52: 88)

In the last ten years, this policy has led to a multiplication of reciprocal bilateral cultural relations with 'developing' or 'emerging' countries, and a continued reduction of those with the countries of the 'Global North'. On top of this comes the fact that the "parallel structures" required by the Indian approach often do not exist – "because in Germany these centralized structures do not exist; there is no ICCR, there is no central federal agency for cultural exchange", says a Goethe-Institut staff member in India (I_73: 12).

This means that the need for reciprocity, based on an equality of structures and financial resources puts limitations on India's ongoing

---

122 See also I_75: 24, I_15: 33-35, 230, I_38: 7.

123 See also I_52: 43, I_51: 45, I_53: 3-5. The meaning of reciprocity was, for example, clearly highlighted in the minutes of the 11th meeting of the Standing Committee for Cultural Cooperation between the Federal Republic of Germany and the Republic of India ("*Ständiger Ausschuss für Kulturelle Zusammenarbeit zwischen der Bundesrepublik Deutschland und der Republik Indien*") from 16th-17th June 2003 (Paragraph 5.1). Paragraph 9, with the heading "Financial Provisions", lays down the financial rules for the visits of individual persons, which continue to be accepted by ICCR and the Indian Ministry of Culture. According to these, the 'dispatching' partner is responsible for the costs of return travel, while the 'receiving' side takes over the costs arising in the host country, including domestic travel.

cultural exchange with other countries from the start (cf. I_51: 37, Spiess, 2009: 18 f.). Instead of a free space for dialogue between nations, cultural agreements are negotiated by civil servants purely out of an obligation to provide a framework for a 'dead' exchange.

The importance of South Asian partnerships alongside international cooperation is currently being discussed and advanced more strongly (cf. I_69: 106, I_54: 58). Such regional networks bring a range of advantages based on closeness. Similar contexts and structures, as well as a shared colonial history mean that artists and cultural mediators often face the same kind of challenges (f. I_56: 16),[124] meaning that regionally networked cultural activity can "bring local actors to a point [...] where they are able to become active themselves" and form "a source of cultural policy frameworks that are sustainable in the long term" (Gad, 2012b: 298 f.). However these so-called "South-South" cooperations at present barely exist in India, according to the experts consulted, even though they offer a cheaper alternative to "North-South" cooperations, and being promoted by cultural mediators from the 'Global North', as the following job description for such a cultural mediator makes clear:

> [...] contribute to the program through the establishment of networks that enable exchange and cooperation between cultural actors from neighbouring countries and regions.[125]

South Asia's ongoing conflicts – for example, in Kashmir (cf. Auswärtiges Amt, 2002: 2 ff.) – and the variations between the subcontinent's national economies, political systems, and cultures make the creation of this network more difficult. However, these local cooperations remain meaningful for Indian cultural actors in order to help promote the diversity of India and the South Asia region.

3.4 India's Cultural Metropolises

As in many countries, India's capital cities are home to many of the most important artistic centres. In India, these are to be found in the cities of Chennai and Kolkata, alongside the 'golden triangle' of the Indian cultural landscape – Delhi, Mumbai, and Bangalore.[126] Many artists have

---

124 Also I_44: 32, I_13: 3, I_58: 9. Regional trade policy initiatives like the South Asian Association for Regional Cooperation are good examples here.

125 Quoted from http://tinyurl.com/qadnpsn (Accessed: 13.01.2014).

126 This study is limited to Delhi, Mumbai, and Bangalore in its scope, and will not go into detail on Kalkutta – India's 'intellectual centre', or Chennai – India's 'city of culture'.

to have a foot in two of these cities in order to ensure their survival. This means that the artistic scenes focus on a few large cities (cf. Spiess, 2009: 128). Because as a rule, state, private, and foreign sponsors are also located in these centres, and prefer to give their support to artists in the city where they are located (cf. I_55: 22-23), many artists feel forced to move to the metropolises (cf. I_58: 7). These large cities are the primary seats of economic, cultural, and social capital. This means that these resources are only available to an exclusive circle of actors (cf. Seubert, 2009: 139, Ch. 5.2 and 2.3).

The cultural scenes in India's major cities are very small in comparison to that of European ones (cf. I_7: 348, 352). A representative of the Goethe-Institut makes the following comment:

> Essentially, one can say that for such an enormous city like Delhi, there is relatively speaking very, very little culture taking place. If you were to compare it with Paris, New York, London, or Berlin, and then take the comparative size of the population into account, it is extremely thin [...]. There is no film library, [...] no theatre, [...] no stages, [...] no literature house, etc. But like I said, this is all from the point of view of a European, who can only somehow see what would be lacking in a Western cultural landscape, [...] theatres are rare, and there is no opera in the whole of India. (I_42: 2, 8)

The various branches of culture in the individual cities are barely connected (cf. I_28: 8, I_11: 16-17, I_57: 11). This can be traced back to, amongst other things, the artists' poor financial situation, which prevents them from travelling here and there, because it is too expensive – even within their own country, unless they take a two or three day train journey. Even connections within the major cities are difficult because of their large size (cf. I_28: 26), especially when there are no platforms or dialogue or exchanges between artists (cf. I_63: 11-13, Ch. 5.8 and 6.12).

The various cultural scenes are very different, depending on the city and its specific context and local characteristics – such as the level of infrastructure on the ground, the actors that live there and engage in the cultural scene, the local audience, and regional culture (cf. I_50: 105). Local political cultures are also highly variable, from liberal to conservative, and each Indian state has its own regional government. All cultural institutions on the national and international level are based in Delhi, India's capital and government city since 1947 (cf. I_58: 2), giving it a certain degree of power and esteem. Cultural events draw a relatively large crowd above all made up of the expatriates sent to live and work in

Delhi by foreign governments and firms.[127] According to the impressions of a Goethe-Institut staff member in New Delhi, music and classical dance "[…] are alongside exhibitions of visual art the main ingredients of the city's cultural life" (I_42: 8).[128]

The city of Mumbai is known for its visual art scene and its Bollywood film industry – which also incorporates elements of dance and music. Mumbai, formerly Bombay, is on an equal footing with Delhi when it comes to the size and importance of its cultural sector. "Bombay is media hub of the country; […] like the New York of America […]. So it has its own amount of wealth and kind of infrastructure for the arts and buying power." (I_63: 135) Strict regulations from the city government like early closing times, or limits on assembly, however, make it difficult to offer any kind of cultural events, which discourages artists wishing to establish themselves in the scene (cf. I_54: 66, I_28: 26, 86).

Bangalore – the 'garden city', known in the regional language Kannada as Bengaluru – is India's third-largest city after Delhi and Mumbai.[129] In order to maintain its dominance in the IT sector – which has India's best paid, best educated, well situated and intellectual workforce – the city is required to play location politics with an attractive contemporary cultural program. This is mostly realised by foreign cultural institutions with their modern programs (cf. I_69: 130).

The development of Bangalore's contemporary art scene began around fifteen years ago, and is not yet concluded, as one local cultural actor points out:

> [A]rt and technology and that kind of thing, contemporary art, especially avant-garde art in some sense, it's still got a youth factor to it that's interesting which maybe Delhi or Bombay don't have […], it's not a very formalized sector yet. (I_63: 135, see also I_28: 44)

Bangalore's cultural landscape is "experimental", "alternative", and "interdisciplinary", according to one Indian cultural worker (I_63: 135-140). It is characterised by young, technologically astute artists,

---

127 Expatriates are people "who live in a foreign country or culture without becoming citizens. The length of the stay is not decisive. Expatriates are often employees who have peen posted abroad. In contrast to immigrants, they do not wish to settle into a new culture, but maintain their own, since they can expect to return home in a relative short time." (Quoted from http://tinyurl.com/mypqtef, Accessed: 20.06.2013)

128 The annual India Art Fair is located in Delhi. However, in 2012-13, the Art Fair received its first competition in the form of India's first ever Biennale in Kochi. See the Biennale website at: http://kochimuzirisbiennale.org/ (Accessed: 13.05.2013).

129 For a detailed description of contemporary Bangalore, see Groll (2011). A large number of gardens is one of the city's characteristics.

who work in fields such as video and graffiti art. Contemporary dance in particular belongs to Bangalore (cf. I_69: 122), which is home to the only dance training centre in the whole of South Asia – the Attakkalari Centre for Movement Arts (Attakkalari), which has been called "the hub of contemporary dance in the South Asia region" (I_45: 438). Also located in Bangalore is the Centre for the Study of Culture and Society (CSCS) – a scholarly institute, unique in India, for the social and cultural sciences.[130] Because of the almost 2,000 kilometre distance between Bangalore and the central sponsoring institutions in Delhi, and with virtually no sense of responsibility for art and culture among local businesses, cultural agents in Bangalore support one another – for example, through the foundation of artistic collectives – in order to be able to exist (cf. I_63: 140).

3.5 The Cultural-Political Orientation: A Conclusion

> India is [...] rich enough to support its own artists [...] but it is not a question of richness, it's a question [of] attitude. (I_45: 45)

The challenges in the Indian cultural landscape are numerous and complex. There is a lack of cultural infrastructure in the form of potential sources of finance, training, and professional development opportunities for artists and cultural actors. This even extends to a lack of spaces for rehearsals and exhibitions, and of long-term established institutions that are not dependent on a specific personality for their continued existence. These challenges limit the presentation, spread, and professionalization of cultural activities in the regional and international spheres (cf. Sengupta *et al.*, s.a.: 9). The non-existence of a cultural political discourse in India, which marginalizes art, makes the lack of institutions and professionalism in the art and cultural sectors worse (cf. Spiess, 2009: 131).

India's pride in its cultural riches stands in stark contrast to the government's censorship and disregard of cultural practice,[131] as well as the indifference of large businesses to the sponsorship of art and culture. The role of cultural and social dynamics as "game changers" in society (I_45: 173)[132] stand in contrast to the government's national ideology of presenting traditional art at home and abroad. Anmol Vellani highlights

---

130 See http://cscs.res.in/ (Accessed: 13.05.2013).

131 The government also makes use of censorship when it forbids artists to appear at festivals like the Jaipur Literature Festival 2013, or when it imprisons individuals – like Deepak Dengle and Sidharth Bhosale from the Kabir Kala Manch, for example. On the topic of censorship in India, see also Kusch/Beckmann (2011: n.p.).

132 Game changers or 'change agents' are people "who are capable of initiating transformations" (cf. Sedmak, 2011: 44).

this difference using the example of work contracted from theatre directors close to the government, and the artistic understanding of contemporary artists:

> Celebrating 'Indian-ness' rather than engaging critically with India's present-day realities, this theatre projected India as folksy and exotic, instead of as a society confronting the contradictions and strains of being tribal, feudal, modern and post-modern all at once. (Vellani, 2006: n.p.)

According to the experts consulted, instead of continuing to promote broad cultural export, the state should help create working long-term structures for an accented regional and international Indian cultural program (cf. I_11: 38-39, I_39: 58).[133]

At present, the approach of bringing artistic discipline into the state school curriculum is being followed. This should allow the appreciation of art and culture in the country to increase. The instruction of teachers in art education and creative methods and techniques should allow them to act as multipliers and advocates for comprehensive development, of which artistic education forms an important part.[134] How an if teachers in reality are able to serve as multipliers for cultural and artistic content in their daily teaching routine remains questionable, since the newness of this approach means that a study has not yet been possible (cf. I_47: 14-15, I_55: 12).[135]

In order to encourage the Indian cultural landscape to unfold, and give the chance of realisation to the available forms of cultural expression, it is necessary to create the cultural policy frameworks that are required for the free performance of cultural activities (cf. Lehmann, 2011b: n.p.). Concrete cultural policy advice from overseas partners could contribute to the establishment of these conditions, as the agreement on the Protection and Promotion of the Diversity of Cultural Expressions from 2005 envisages (cf. Deutsche UNESCO-Kommission e. V., 2005, Article 14 to 18).

Gandhi describes the vision of a possible Indian cultural policy in the following terms (cf. Singh, 2009: 66):

> I do not want to wall up my house on every side, and I do not want to block up my windows. I want the culture of every country to be able to come

[133] Infrastructure, as well as opportunities for training and research should be supported instead of festivals.

[134] Cultural education as an obligatory part of the school curriculum continues to be the government's intent from 2012-17 (cf. Government of India/Planning Commission, 2013: 64).

[135] Also I_45: 168-169, I_62: 35, Schäffler/Mittelstädt (2008: 45).

into my house without any kind of hindrance. But I will not let any culture influence me so strongly that I forget my own. (Mahatma Gandhi)[136]

"Various cultures living together in a melting pot, and the irreducible diversity that results therefrom, that runs out into all areas of society", makes the creation of an Indian cultural policy a complex and many-layered challenge (Ittstein, 2002: 137). The ideal is difficult to define, however, the Indian cultural workers that were interviewed all have a clear vision of their country's future cultural policy. It is their aspiration to create an infrastructure, which is evidently still lacking (cf. I_28: 20, 26, I_42: 2). This should involve the sustainable development of India's artistic scenes (cf. I_11: 20-21), so that they are able to finance and unfold themselves, independent of the Indian government and foreign cultural sponsors (cf. I_59: 23). Instead of project sponsorship for traditional artistic practice, it would be desirable to establish networks. Over and above this, according to an Indian dancer, young artists should be given the opportunity to test their creative talent in society or on the market (cf. I_35: 18, Sengupta *et al.*, s.a.: 20).

This change in Indian cultural sponsorship was already called for in the 1990s by the Haksar Report (cf. Department of Culture/Ministry of Human Resource Development/Government of India, 1990: 149 f.), which investigated the activities of the Indian Ministry of Culture and its associated cultural institutions. According to the report, state support should be invested in "[...] creating and maintaining a useful infrastructure for cultural activities [...] rather than in organizing cultural events" (Singh, 2009: 57). This significant report was apparently unable to convey the importance of cultural infrastructure to the Ministry, since a government representative explained: "[T]he Ministry by itself is not interested in building infrastructure." (I_51: 50) The sponsorship program for the budget year 2013-14 contains only isolated points concerning infrastructural expansion – for example, through the building of cultural institutions, in order to take some action against the lack of cultural spaces. The expansion of training opportunities is not mentioned (cf. Ministry of Culture/Government of India, 2013-2014: 11 ff.). The lack of a defined state cultural policy for the foreign and domestic spheres remains unchanged.

India's attempts to establish a cultural policy may be successful; however integrating the various cultural orientations of its population into a national identity is a more difficult and complex process. With regard to the development of such a cultural policy, one Goethe-Institut staff member had the following idea:

136 Gandhi quoted from http://tinyurl.com/oohp2bt (Accessed: 27.10.2013).

> Perhaps it would be possible to take the Constitution as a basis. The Indian Constitution is widely praised as a constitutional ideal that could not be better. I think there is a lot that speaks for that. The Constitution carries all of these diversities that there are in India. The calculation is ideal. It is just the way it is put into practice, the famous implementation, that is the difficulty [...]. (I_73: 16)

A cultural policy for all – and perhaps from all – would be a great achievement, and "[one] answer to the question: What can India teach us?" (Lotz, 2001: 137, see also Jain, 2007: 38 ff.) Indeed, the German cultural landscape is also struggling with some of the same questions and challenges – including the diversity of cultures created by immigration, the artist's struggle to survive, the elitist European conception of art that continues to dominate cultural sponsorship in many cases, and the role of the arts in the school curriculum.

German-Indian Cultural Encounters

Cultural relations between India and Germany have a long tradition. They are stable and institutionalised (cf. Spiess, 2009: 16, Wagner, 2005: 17).[1] The 19th Century German tradition of Indology, has been the most significant influence on this close connection (cf. Niklas, 2005: 73 and Ch. 2.2.2).

The basis of German-Indian cultural exchange is the bilateral cultural agreement between Germany and India, which has been in force since September 1969, and on the basis of which the activities of German cultural institutions and brokers in India take place (cf. Wieck, 2006a: 2 f., Niklas, 2005: 41). This agreement envisages a regularly-occurring German-Indian cultural consultation, whose commission should audit activities under the remit of the cultural agreement, and recommend the pursuit of projects and exchange mechanisms in the fields of art and education. The most recent cultural consultation took place in October 2005, and the cultural agreement has not been renewed since that year (see here Ch. 3.1 and 3.3).

Alongside cultural mediators and institutions, civil society initiatives have a significant role in determining cultural relations between India and Germany.[2] These are able to contribute to the revision of the traditional image of the Indian subcontinent by offering insights into modern India and its rapid development (cf. Wieck, 2006a: 2). The *Deutsch-Indische Gesellschaft* (German-Indian Society – DIG) with its more than thirty branches in Germany is worthy of mention.[3] The DIG was founded in Stuttgart in 1953, where it maintains its headquarters to this day (cf. *ibid.*, 2010: 32). The mission of the organisation is the "maintenance of relations between India

[1] On the history of German-Indian institutional cultural relations, see Wieck (2006a: 1 f.), Gupta (2012: 17 ff.), *Indien-Institut* (Munich) (2004: 12 ff.). For further reading on German-Indian partnerships in the arts, see Spiess (2009), Kämpchen (2013b: 46 ff.) and Subramaniam (2001: 125 ff.).

[2] Rothermund (1995b: 479 ff.) gives an overview of the most important actors and activities in the field of cultural relations between India and Germany. Wieck (2006b: 1071 ff.) provides an overview of the most significant civil society actors in German-Indian partnership. On the twin city agreements between Bremen and Pune, Stuttgart and Mumbai as well as Berlin and New Delhi, see Niklas (2005: 77) and Wagner (2011: 9).

[3] See www.dig-ev.de (Accessed: 16.06.2013), for a history of the DIG, see Deutsch-Indische Gesellschaft e. V. (2003), for an extensive description of its activities see Ittstein (2009: 120 f.) and Wieck (2006b: 1071, 1075).

and the Federal Republic of Germany"[4]. The DIG is distinguished by "an active program of engagement with the Indian cultures" (*ibid.*, 2006a: 32), which has contributed to German-Indian dialogue throughout the decades (cf. Spiess, 2009: 11). The activities of the organisation are financed through donations from businesses and private persons (cf. Wieck, 2006a: 1). The DIG works in a close and continuous manner with the ICCR, and presents "programs in the field of Indian dance and classical music [...] in fifteen to twenty German cities" (*ibid.*: 3).

The "East West Encounters" from 1983 to 1986 in Mumbai were the beginning of the intercultural encounters between India and Germany, and the "attempt to take seriously [...] the calls for an intercultural dialogue", according to Georg Lechner, who initiated the series of events (Lechner, 2004: 91). The encounters consisted of six international encounters between 1983 and 1986, each lasting one week. The declared goal of the encounters was, according to their founder:

> [A] series of East-West dialogues, involving authors, composers, musicians, theatre experts, choreographers, dancers, painters, sculptors, philosophers and scientists, who are invited to participate in an enquiry into the possibilities of creative work and thought today, drawing from Indian and Western sources. (*ibid.*: 92)

Contemporary dance in particular was able to establish itself through the framework of German-Indian partnership offered by the Encounters (cf. Spiess, 2009: 57, Palazhy, 2009: n.p.). The Encounters had an invigorating effect on cultural relations between India and Germany at the time, however, as a representative of the MMB explains, this form of event would no longer be appropriate:

> I do not see this polarization [between East and West – author] any more. We do not have East and West any more, we have, of course, very, very different traditions but these are so connected and blurred together in so many ways that it would be senseless to come out with such a term these days. (I_42: 14)

The German-Indian partnership is characterised by a mutual fascination, and uncritical admiration. This mutual admiration has been strengthened by the marketing campaigns "Incredible India" launched by the Indian government in 2002 to encourage worldwide tourism (cf. Oranskaia, 2006: 1093 ff.), and its German equivalent – "*Deutschland – Land der Ideen*" (Germany – Land of Ideas).[5] Depending on the point of view

---

4 Quoted from http://tinyurl.com/ozcs59k (Accessed: 01.12.2013).

5 See http://www.incredibleindia.org/ and http://www.land-der-ideen.de (Both accessed: 01.09.2013).

of the observer, the relationship is characterised by negative or idealised perceptions on both sides[6] (cf. Wieck, 2010: 41, Schäffler/Mittelstädt, 2008: 46). Both the German and Indian points of view are littered with pre-judgements, misunderstanding, and misconceptions regarding the partner country. These are not completely wrong, but they are one-sided, and not balanced out by a broader perspective – meaning that they cannot bear the weight of a 'real' cultural exchange (cf. Kämpchen, 2013a: 65).

Kämpchen explains the respective perceptions of the partner countries in the following way (cf. *ibid.*: 65 ff.): For Germany, because of its over five thousand year old culture, India has been the 'cradle of humanity' since the German Romantic movement of the 19th Century. In reaction to its until recently pre-industrial culture, it was often held up as an ideal alternative model in contrast to European civilization (cf. Kämpchen, 2012: 13). For many, not just Germans, India is 'exotic' (cf. Arzoglou, 2006: 981).[7] However, the media and digital revolutions in the West helped to present an alternative image – showing India's poverty and structures of injustice in a clear light, and helping to collapse this image (cf. Punnamparambil, 2012: 3).

For Indians, Germany's high level of civilizational and technical development, and above all ideals of virtue including punctuality, reliability, and enthusiasm for work, which are not characteristically valued in India, are the subject of admiration. Germany's Nazi past is either ignored or played down. Nevertheless, a significant element of anti-Western feeling – above all in some Hindu circles, which contrast India's 'spirituality' with Western 'materialism' – provides a counterweight.

As a rule, Indians are more knowledgeable about Germany than Germans are about India. Even young schoolchildren in India receive lessons in European history and culture – a legacy of colonialism. Indian history, on the other hand, is barely covered in German schools (cf. Ch. 5.5.1).

Both countries seek to present an image that reinforces the existing positive stereotypes of their partners, and counteract the negative. India presents itself as a future technology-driven industrial power, with a valuable ethnic and cultural diversity. Indian society's problems are simply not admitted. This latter strategy is increasingly problematic in the face of an increased media awareness – as shown by the Delhi gang rapes in winter 2012. Meanwhile, the presentation and discussion of public problems

6 Stereotypes can be understood as a significantly simplified image of a nation, positive or negative (cf. Maletzke, 1996: 109).

7 Exotic is meant here in a positive sense: "Exoticism describes a predilection of individual elements […] of a new culture, but not necessarily for the whole culture or lifestyle of the people." (Roßkopf, 2010: 67)

such as migration and unemployment, or its poor record on ecology and climate change are not unforced matters for Germany (cf. Kämpchen, 2012: 14).

According to Kämpchen, both countries have an identity problem, which also has an effect on cultural relations. At the same time, handed-down stereotypes of one another continue to dominate (cf. *ibid.*, 2013a: 65 f.). This situation underlines the necessity for both countries to show a realistic, current, and differentiated image of themselves in the future. Meanwhile, according to Kämpchen, cultural relations offer an ideal opportunity to undertake a free discourse on these cliché-laden and one-sided identities (cf. *ibid.*: 66 f.).

Georg Lechner, an India expert, and former head of the Goethe Institutes in Kolkata, New Delhi, and Bombay[8] outlines a few basic parameters that "form the institutional background for German-Indian cultural relations in the last few decades, and gave them firmness and support." (Lechner, 2012: 4 f.) These facts are taken from a period of only one generation, according to Lechner, but the "necessary cultural relationship remains the work of a century" (*ibid.*: 8). For its purposes, this study will set out the most important milestones of the cultural relations between India and Germany, specifically with regard to cultural exchange from the German as well as the Indian side from the last forty to fifty years in the following pages:[9]

> At the beginning of the 1980s, faced with a negative, lacking, or indifferent media opinion about the Indian subcontinent, particularly in the West, India developed a cultural policy based on the instrument of the 'Festivals of India' intended to counter this image in the most important partner countries. (Lechner, 2004: 165 f.)

Germany had the pleasure of this Indian cultural-political charm offensive at the beginning of the 1990s. From 1991 to 1992, the festival was exported to more than fifty German cities. Around 600 artists representing India's "folk traditions and arts" (Singh, 2009: 55 f.), took part. There were almost 1000 cultural events – in particular music and dance displays – as well as 500 film screenings (cf. No Author, 1998: 154). In retrospect, the festival was described as an eight-month "mammoth program" under pressure for time and funding, which was intended "to promote an increased understanding of this great nation, and to work

8 Lechner had leadership positions in all of these institutions between 1966 and 1995, cf. Indien-Institut (München) (2004: 38).

9 These include the opening of the *Tagore-Zentrum* in Berlin, as well as the Year of India in Germany in 2006 (cf. Cg. 3.3 and Spiess, 2009: 13).

against cliché ridden prejudices" (Schödel, 1997: 176 f.). This festival had the goal of revising stereotypes about India in the public imagination, and broadening knowledge about the country (cf. Singh, 2009: 55 f.). On the Indian side, the Ministry of Culture and the ICCR exercised a significant influence on the running of the festival (cf. Ch. 3.3), and the House of the World's Cultures ("*Haus der Kulturen der Welt*" – HKW) in Berlin – described by Lepenies with regard to the import-focused cultural policy as the "most important Goethe-Institut" – on the German[10] (Lepenies, 1996c: 204). With around 350,000 visitors, this was "the largest cultural presentation realised by any single country in Germany" (Ittstein, 2002: 37). The requirement of reciprocity required that the Indian Festival in Germany should be followed by a German Festival in India:[11]

> Between September 2000 and March 2001, a range of events from the fields of dance, theatre, music, art, film, and entertainment were offered in a total of 28 Indian cities, accompanied by side events and newly prepared publications. Around a dozen German credit institutes and large firms served as sponsors. (Niklas, 2005: 82 f.)

This festival was the largest bilateral German exchange project to date, and is described as a high point of German-Indian relations in scholarly literature. It was "very useful" in the process of intensifying the German-Indian connection to the envisaged strategic partnership. "This festival was worth 2.7 million euros from the Foreign Office's cultural budget", pronounced Daniel Niklas following the sixth Federal Government report in 2001 (Niklas, 2005: 83). Leadership of this project was in the hands of ICCR and the Goethe-Institut. Martin Kämpchen speaks of an "in general [...] highly diverse and balanced program, based on reflection and its long term effects, and not sensationalism." (Kämpchen quoted in: Diözesan-Caritasverband für das Erzbistum Köln e. V., 2000b: 8) Critics of the festival have described the program "which [should] reflect [...] a broad and representative spectrum of the German cultural scene" as "colourfully thrown together" (Lechner, 2004: 170).[12]

Pupual Jayakar, President of the Festival Committee in the 1980s, compared intercultural exchange in the festival format with oil lamps:

---

10 "The HKW primarily presents the culture of [so-called – author] developing countries through exhibitions, theatre, and musical guest events, as well as literary and other programs. Its mission is to deepen and promote understanding of these cultures." (Ittstein, 2002: 37) See http://www.hkw.de (Accessed: 26.12.2013).

11 On reciprocity, see Ch. 3.3.

12 For a comprehensive description and critical evaluation of the German *Festspiele* in India from 2000-1, see, for example, Ittstein (2009: 68 ff.) and Lechner (2004: 165-201).

> To organize a festival is to float oil lamps in tiny boats on a river; for an instant to illumine the ripples on the water and the rapt faces for those that participate in the launching; to set before the mirror of attention, times past and times presents; and when the festival ends, to disappear, like the boats, into the night. (Jayakar quoted in: Singh, 2009: 56, see also I_45: 269-275)[13]

A brief review of the most recent highlight of the German-Indian partnership – the Year of Germany in India – should help to determine whether the boats with lamps remain one-time events without effect, which now belong exclusively to the past.

4.1 "(In-)Finite Opportunities":[14] The Year of Germany in India from 2011 to 2012

The Year of Germany in India, opened in May 2011 and lasting until early 2013, was a further important milestone in German-Indian relations. The interdisciplinary event series brought together thousands of projects from the fields of politics, industry, education, research, science, and culture.

Every Year of Germany has a motto and a primary topic, which provide a frame for the program. The Year of Germany in India was entitled "Germany and India 2011-2012: Infinite Opportunities" ("*Deutschland und Indien 2011-2012 – Unbegrenzte Möglichkeiten*"), and focused on the theme "StadtRäume – CitySpaces".[15] The fifteen month[16] program focused on events and German-Indian projects in various facets of urban development, such as mobility, social structures, architecture, migration, energy planning, and cultural infrastructure. Public spaces played an important role. Their significance in urban life was made visible through a number of projects, which were intended to allow the development of new city spaces and target audiences at the same time.[17]

---

13 For more on the development of the festival format in India, and a critical appraisal of the same, see Sengupta *et al.* (s.a.: n.p.) and Vellani (s.a.).

14 "Infinite Opportunities" is the motto of the Year of Germany in India (Quoted from www.germany-and-india.com, Accessed: 28.09.2013). It is questionable whether German-Indian partnerships are in reality so infinite (cf. Ch. 4).

15 For detailed information on the Year of Germany, see www.germany-and-india.com (Accessed: 07.07.2013). For a comprehensive description of this event from the point of view of the Goethe-Institut, see Goethe-Institut e. V. (2011b: 10).

16 The official program of the Year of Germany was for fifteen months from May 2011 to November 2012. However the program in fact ran until early 2013, and ran for a total of eighteen months (cf. I_74: 6, No Author, 2013: 40).

17 See http://tinyurl.com/lk2qdku (Accessed: 07.07.2013).

The heart, crowd-puller, and "programmatic flagship" (Auswärtiges Amt)[18] of the Year of Germany in India was the "Indo-German Urban Mela" (often simply 'Urban Mela' or 'Mela'), a mobile program with around fifteen 'moving pavilions', which made a tour of five Indian cities.[19] A range of events took place in these pavilions, including symposia, speeches, conferences, expert panels, workshops, and concerts, across the fields of politics, industry, economy, culture, education, and research. These tents gave German actors a stage to present themselves as "innovative", and "creative" partners of India in the frame of the "StadtRäume – CitySpaces" theme.[20]

The business partners and project promoters of the Year of Germany – including well-known businesses like BASF – had the opportunity to buy a place in a pavilion (cf. I_74: 25) and become a part of the Urban Mela.[21] The cultural program was presented by the Goethe-Institut in a cultural festival pavilion, and at two Urban Mela open-air stages.[22] These cultural events were primarily there in order to attract visitors (cf. I_69: 22-26, Tan, 2011: 71).

The goal of the Urban Mela was to make the Year of Germany accessible to a large audience (cf. I_69: 18-20).[23] For this reason, entrance to the Urban Mela was free. The concept was successful, and "visitor records" were set (I_43: 8): "[T]he Indo-German Urban Mela Delhi saw more than 1,400,000 visitors over the nine days [...]. The Urban Mela in Delhi captured the hearts."[24] However, the well-known German firms and educational institutions that bought pavilions had the goal of attracting "quality visitors" with their presence (I_74: 21, see also I_42: 54): the educated, English speaking young members of the upper and

18 Quoted from http://tinyurl.com/p5bzdsx (Accessed: 01.07.2013). See also Sievers in: Vaid (2011: n.p.).

19 Delhi, Mumbai, Chennai, Pune and Bangalore. The city tour began on 13.4.2012 in Mumbai, and ended in January 2013 in Pune. See Nandi (2012: 8), Punj (2012: 3), Chaterjee (2012: n.p.) and the websites http://tinyurl.com/lo82anc and http://tinyurl.com/ly4tod8 (Both accessed: 05.09.2013) for detail.

20 Quoted from http://tinyurl.com/jwojvsb and http://tinyurl.com/p5bzdsx (Both accessed: 01.07.2013).

21 The price for one pavilion was around 700,000 euros, rising for larger tents. A further 700,000 euros were required for equipment, staffing, security, and furnishing of each tent. This meant businesses faced a total cost of around 1.4 million euros for each pavilion (cf. I_74: 25).

22 On the role and program of the Goethe Institutes during the Urban Mela see Sunavala (2012: 62).

23 See here the statements of Heiko Sievers at http://tinyurl.com/q7abll4 (Accessed: 18.05.2013).

24 Quoted from http://tinyurl.com/m2vxjn3 (Accessed: 01.06.2013). For more on the Urban Mela in Delhi see, for example, Sunavala/Arasu (2012: 69).

middle classes – in order to encourage their interest in potential career opportunities in Germany, and to raise the attention of these future decision makers in business and politics, with a key role to play in future Indian-German partnerships (cf. Sievers in: Vaid, 2011: n.p., I_42: 57).

The Urban Mela was explicitly praised by both the German and Indian governments in their joint declaration on the further development of their global strategic partnership on 11.04.2013:

> Both sides take the opportunity of the high interest in the mobile exhibition "Urban Mela" with the theme "StadtRäume – CitySpaces", which became the key event of the Year of Germany in India, in order to found a German-Indian forum on urbanization. This should have a range of working groups for the discussion of themes such as urban planning, architecture, mobility, transport, goods, and infrastructure. (Auswärtiges Amt, 2013: 4)

In light of this positive assessment by the German Foreign Office, it is remarkable that the Urban Mela remains a unique feature of the Year of Germany in India, and that the concept was not used for further Years of Germany (cf. I_74: 15).

Parallel to the Year of Germany in India was the 'Days of India' event in Germany. This opened as part of the Hamburg Port Anniversary Celebrations on 11th May 2012, under the motto "Connecting Cultures". Events took place in numerous German cities up until March 2013 in order to, in the words of Manmohan Singh, Indian Prime Minister at the time, "support, explain, and educate" (Singh quoted in: No Author, 2013: 41). The Indian cultural actors that took part in the cultural program of the Year of Germany in India were not aware of the existence of the Year of India in Germany (cf. e.g. I_54, I_59). The ICCR, which programs the Days of India, neglected to involve Indian contemporary artists in the programming: missing the chance, according to the cultural authorities in Hamburg, which cooperated with the ICCR in the planning and implementation of a variety of events during the Year of India – including the opening, to present themselves in Germany in a differentiated way, and to make themselves visible to the German population.

4.2 German-Indian Partnerships in the Arts: A Conclusion

Relations between Indian and Germany, founded on a handful of bilateral agreements and large events such as the festivals discussed above, are generally good. However they continue to perform "markedly beneath their potential" (Wagner, 2011: 5). Amongst the reasons for this are the "minimal budget", which is made available for cultural exchange, and the lack of long-term supporting structures for cultural dialogue:

> Experience shows that it is only a strengthened exchange [with India – author] that is able of establishing long-term connections [...]. The enormous significance of cultural exchange, however, stands in contrast to the small amount of funding for foreign cultural policy, which does not even begin to approach India's huge population and strategic significance. (*ibid.*: 17)

This argument does not apply to formats such as the Year of Germany because of their large volume of funding, however, many observers and participants often question the sustainability of such 'spectacles'.

On the other hand – and this seems to be a decisive argument – German-Indian cultural relations continue to reflect "inequality in many respects" (Spiess, 2009: 13). This can be seen in the first place that the partner's mutual perception of one another is characterised by ignorance and second-hand impressions (cf. *ibid.*: 9). The cause of this inequality, however, lies elsewhere: German-Indian relations are described in scholarly literature as "unencumbered cooperation", since Germany, in contrast to the UK, does not have a colonial history in India, meaning that it can enjoy an ostensibly "neutral" position (Wagner, 2005: 17, see also Wieck, 2006a: 3). "These cultural relations are therefore able to unfold themselves in freedom", according to Kämpchen (Kämpchen, 2012: 14). However, the previous rule of European colonial powers in India means that the perspective of the two sides is not equivalent, and the structure of encounter is asymmetrical from the beginning of any exchange (cf. Lechner, 2004: 272).

A large number, if by no means all, of the causes of these conditions of inequality, are rooted in this history. It also bears consideration that relations between the 'Global North' and the 'Global South' are conditioned by an unequal distribution of power. These asymmetries have manifested themselves in the past, and continue to do so, in the form of the unequal development of cultural infrastructure in the donor countries of the 'Global North', and their partners in the 'Global South' (cf. Gad, 2012b: 68 and Ch. 5.9.1).

When this inequality is supplemented by the fact of intercultural differences between both countries, it is apparent why the potential of German-Indian partnerships are limited, and therefore unable to unfold themselves to their full extent when those responsible for managing these partnerships do not take on responsibility for changing the framework in which their relationships take place (cf. Ch. 6).

“Cooperative Partnerships” under the Microscope

An Analysis of the Practice

The previous chapters have made clear that the cultural discourse since the 1970s has called for dialogue, partnership, and an engagement on equal levels in international cultural cooperation. However, the way in which this dialogue, these partnerships, and this equality is to be implemented in practice – or, indeed if these ideals are practically possible – has been left indefinite. Since we have determined the extent of the FCP’s ambitions for cooperative work, Chapter 5 of this study will use practical examples of the cooperative work in India, in order to undertake a qualitative and empirical examination of the implementation of these principles. The conclusions drawn from this examination of the practice will help to determine the actual relation between ambition and reality. This chapter will make a focused presentation of how cooperation between German and Indian cultural actors is in fact implemented on the basis of 81 interviews with the experts involved.

The experience of these interviewed experts have crystallised several moments, phases, and aspects of the planning and realisation of artistic cooperations, which can be seen as centrally important in the cooperation between German and Indian cultural actors. The challenges, problems, and deficits of international partnerships lie within these criteria. The presentation of the results of this study lays out the epistemological conclusions of the investigation in a focused way on the basis of the theoretical frame of reference for the research project set out in Chapter 2.3. These results allow for the extrapolation of a range of cultural policy measures for the future planning and implementation of artistic cooperations under the German FCP which would allow cooperation to move beyond a dependence on the personal motivations and interpretation of individual actors (cf. I_42: 50), to being a concrete practice within the structure of international cultural encounters (cf. Ch. 6).

Why, and with whom do cultural creators cooperate? Where and on which subjects do they cooperate? How much time and funding are at their disposal for their work together? What do the internal processes look like in cooperations as they currently exist? What is the relationship between those cooperating? Which current challenges mark out the borders of international cooperations? What is the role of institutions in cooperation?

Are cooperative relations sustainable? And last but not least – how do cultural actors define cooperation? Is the equality in international cultural cooperations that is called for by sponsors and politicians actually realistic?

These questions on the conditions, processes, and structures of cooperative work in the arts have up until now been hardly touched by research, and are often not even asked by directly involved cultural actors (cf. Ch. 1). In order to understand artistic cooperations, and to frame and shape them through cultural policy in the best way possible in the future, it is necessary to identify and show the current state and condition of cooperative work. The directly involved stakeholders in these cooperations play a central role in this process, because these "artists [...] usually know best themselves which initiatives and projects are forward looking" (Quoted from Claudia Roth [Bündnis 90/Grüne] in: Deutscher Kulturrat e. V., 2012: 20). The interviews with German and Indian cooperation partners do not just provide information on the artistic interest in international cooperation. It also contains concrete cultural political statements, such as ideas for cultural policy frameworks that need to be implemented (cf. Ch. 6).

5.1 The Interests and Goals of German-Indian Cooperation

Cooperative work means realising interests (cf. I_15: 93, I_70: 50, I_43: 25-26).[1] Accordingly, the first step is to find out what the interests of the partners have, and whether any of these are shared. The second step is to consider how the interests of the partners, which can also be thoroughly different, can be dealt with best (cf. Ch. 6.2).

> [W]hy should I collaborate? I can work locally in my country, but the only reason to collaborate is for this, to improve our intellectual pool and to raise the bar for art and therefore to make a better world. (I_26: 38)

The motivation for Indian partners to enter into cooperation with German ones consists above all, in the desire to learn – as the quotation above states. A distinction can be drawn here between Indian cultural actors who wish to learn how to be more professional from their German partners, and Indian artists who represent the opinion that both sides have something to learn from one another, since both have something to offer (cf. I_54: 195). The first point of view, which sees partnerships as a form of student-teacher relationship (cf. Ch. 5.9.1), can be seen clearly in the following description of motivation:

1 Interests can be understood as "the pursuit of independent existence-securing goals" (Niklas, 2005: 26).

> [T]here are two aspects to it. One, of course just to learn from other people and to see what they are doing in other parts of the world. […] [E]specially in what we are doing let's say with electronic music or digital art […] it's a very short history of these things in India. You know, growing up, for example, we didn't really experience these things first-hand […]. So I think especially for Indian artists we always feel like we should collaborate because we feel like we can cover up for some lost time. (I_15: 21, see also I_50: 153)

Here, German partners take over the role of mentors – providing inspiration and motivation for the Indian cultural actor (cf. I_66: 167, I_68: 4)[2] to implement 'innovative' concepts from abroad (cf. I_50: 16, 36)[3] or to make themselves known with a branch or genre that is not (yet) extant in their own country: "I'm extremely happy that I had been able to collaborate with an artist about which, about whom and about whose art work I was not much exposed to." (I_10: 70, see also I_10: 61-68, 75) In particular, interdisciplinary cooperation has a particular meaning for the Indian stakeholders interviewed in this context (cf. I_45: 208-210, 297, I_67: 36). Indian artists often see cooperation as offering them an opportunity to broaden their creativity, and the possibilities for expression in their own cultural practice (cf. IFAB, s.a.: 5).[4]

In contrast to this is the view of the cooperation process as one of learning from one another on equal terms: "Value each other's learnings and best practice! You know we have something to give and you have something to give." (I_13: 31)[5] The experts interviewed see commonalities in the challenging working conditions of the art scenes of both Germany and India: "Being artists with different backgrounds, we are finally all confronted to similar existential questions." (Goethe-Institut e. V. New Delhi)[6] For them, it is important to share strategies for dealing with these challenges (cf. I_11: 18-20, 23-25). Going along with this is also the wish for an exchange of perspective – to review one's position from the point of view of another (cf. I_15: 21, I_39: 59, I_56: 5). From this Indian perspective, the exchange of content offered by an international

2 Also I_11: 36, 40-41, I_10: 72, I_7: 58-62, I_39: 59, I_73: 26, I_49: 89, I_25: 2, 68.

3 See also Ch. 5.5.3 and 6.7.

4 See also IFAB (2002b: n.p.) and http://tinyurl.com/odygdwy (Accessed: 01.07.2013). The IFAB operated a sponsorship program to support cooperation with India between 1997 and 2003, and documented the experiences gained during this process. These experiences have been taken into account in the presentation of these results.

5 Also I_31: 18, I_72: 31, I_11: 35, I_58: 10, I_43: 3. It should be noted that the mutual learning perspective is predominantly represented by the staff and management of Indian cultural institutions, and less so by independent artists (see also Ch. 5.9.1).

6 From the Goethe Institute's unpublished project report on the cooperative project 'An Actor Exits'. A copy of the report is archived by the author.

cooperation is essential, because artists like them are a minority in their own country (cf. I_7: 282).

For Indian partners, an additional important reason for cooperation is the fact that they only have the opportunity to practice their art with support from abroad (cf. I_48: 24, I_25: 24, I_56: 7). One condition of this overseas support is often cooperation with artists from the donor country. The reason for international cooperation is to drive the local scene with foreign funding, and to expand local cultural infrastructure (cf. I_50: 26-28, 84, I_13: 19, I_15: 211, I_49: 87). For Indian partners, cooperation means more than working together. For them, international cooperation is a means of achieving the cultural-political framework for a 'living' cultural landscape in their own country. Cooperative work therefore becomes an instrument of cultural empowerment[7] – exercising a positive influence on the professionalization of artists (cf. I_16: 11) as well as the establishment of special art forms and scenes, which did not really exist before such as, for example, children's and youth theatre, or the electronic music scene (cf. I_50: 45, 62, I_44: 9-13).[8]

International cooperation exposes Indian cultural workers and their work to the esteem of foreign partners on their own soil – in a country where art in general is not accorded a high level of prestige, and only a minimal degree of affirmation (cf. I_31: 34, I_68: 6, I_66: 85). Whether over the internet or, when possible, by taking the cooperation to Germany, Europe, or Western countries such as the USA in person (cf. I_26: 6, I_50: 3, 31), there is the possibility of making a worldwide name for Indian contemporary art (cf. I_75: 25) and establishing an international personal network (cf. I_50: 64, I_11: 24). A distinction can be made here between Indian artists who want to have access to an international network, and those already in possession of one, and who are able to make use of this network in their cooperative projects (cf. I_47: 12, I_48: 26).[9]

Despite strong interest from the Indian side, there are also risks inherent for Indian actors engaging in partnerships with contemporary Western partners. A German artist has observed how his Indian partners ran the risk of losing their 'good reputation' – which in India is usually built up in the practice of classical art – through participation in a partnership project in the contemporary arts:

---

7 "Empowerment describes strategies and measures designed to raise the level of autonomy and self-determination in the lives of people or communities. Empowerment describes the process of self-empowerment, as well as professional support intended to help people to appreciate and make use of their resources and scope for action. In Germany, 'empowerment' is sometimes translated as 'self-competence' ("*Selbstkompetenz*")." (Quoted from http://tinyurl.com/p8znjdq, Accessed: 30.07.2013)

8 See also I_7: 114, I_56: 2-4, I_45: 26, I_54: 66, I_73: 48, Ch. 3.

9 See also I_63: 45, I_50: 22.

> Because he is enormously dependent on such engagements [...] and on a good reputation. Here [in India], I can ruin my reputation with one person or another, because I somehow have to do my projects myself. I am asked very rarely, there are some times, but my entire artistic existence is not based on other people calling me up. I don't sit next to the telephone waiting. But he does. He is a quite well-known actor, he has worked a lot with the current Director of the NSD [National School of Drama]. She engaged him in a lot of pieces, and he was also there [at the presentation of the cooperative project – author] [...] as well as colleagues of his. There were a huge number of people there that were very important to him. And I suspect [...], that he was much more involved in the whole thing in the rehearsals, and held back at the performance, because he was not one hundred per cent sure whether he could show that. (I_32: 57, see also I_9/I_10: 125)

Some of the Indian cultural actors interviewed reported that they wanted to use international cooperation work to help break down stereotypes about India (cf. I_43: 28, I_15: 21, I_75: 9) and to present a true, or at least more realistic, perspective of both countries (cf. I_45: 101).[10] Cooperative work for them is a tool in the fight against the clichés that dominate their own culture.

The Germans interviewed for the most part suspected that their Indian partners were acting on a financial motivation:

> Of course they wanted to do a project with us, because there is money in it. It was clear – they were able to bring Indian artists into the project that they normally wouldn't have been able to afford for a children's theatre project. [...] It is just about the money [...], for them it is a great opportunity, but they are not really interested in us as artists. That's why I was also a bit insulted [...]. (I_25: 82, 24)

A German theatrical choreographer qualifies this: "Even when they are doing it for the money, that doesn't mean that they don't bring enough of their own energy with them." (I_1: 14-16)

Some German cultural actors also see their artistic expertise, which they are able to present in India, as being the decisive factor in the desire to cooperate from the Indian side: The Indian partners were impressed by the artistic quality presented, and wanted to cooperate with the German partners for that reason (cf. I_70: 18, 34, I_25: 2-4, I_32: 81, 93).

The German interest to enter into cooperation with Indian partners lies in the first place in the experience of the unusual as an inspiration

---

10 Geesche Wartemann describes this deconstruction of stereotypes as a "condition of an intercultural dialogue" (Wartemann, 2002: 95 ff.).

(cf. I_20: 63, I_28: 76). On top of this comes personal and professional development through encounters with others, as the following quotation makes clear:

> One wants to engage with the foreign, and this engagement with the foreign, with foreigners, is a gain, and that is enough. […] My horizons have broadened. They can of course get even bigger. I don't want to say that I am sitting here like the "*Ober-Guru*". I am thankful for the little things that I have learned. That is just great. (I_25: 82, 44)[11]

The investigation, or sharpening of one's own identity in the mirror of the foreign, insofar as artists are willing to enter into the work of their partners, however, also means having the ability to put one's own identity and working methods into question, and to deal with this uncertainty (cf. Wartemann, 2002: 98 ff., Maletzke, 1996: 68, Knopp, 2006: 119).

It became evident through the interviews, that interest in cooperation from the German side was highly country-specific. That is to say, that the interest in cooperation was connected to the partner country: "We all really wanted to work in India. That is an exciting country." (I_25: 82) German artists are interested in Indian culture. The tendency towards a foreign culture or other cultural space is conditioned by their individual affinities (cf. I_70: 96-97, I_20: 27). This means that cooperative work is highly dependent on the persons concerned.

These working visits also allow the visitor to engage with India in a different way than in the role of tourist (cf. I_25: 44, I_28: 100)[12]:

> There is a whole other kind of depth in encountering a country in this way, that is, by cooperating with somebody, with whom one has an […] artistic commonality. (I_9: 1)

As for the Indian partners, the motivation of exchanging artistic interest and expertise between the artists plays a meaningful role:

> If you tick in a similar way […] you don't just want to stay within your own four walls. You want to bring that out. You want to look and say 'here, look, there is something in Chile that sounds like that thing from Madras' and that kind of thing. You have to get to know each other. (I_28: 80, see also I_32: 95, I_22: 28)

---

11 See also I_9/I_10: 129, I_19: 17-19, I_31: 42, I_32: 24-28, 93, IFAB (2001: n.p.), *ibid.* (1999: 9 f.).

12 On the other hand, there is a danger that cooperative work can "fall into being a kind of cultural tourism", as a German musician considers (I_19: 34).

Indian experts report that German cultural actors also look at the work of future Indian partners – primarily in India – and that this awakens their interest in cooperation:

> So this piece by him that I saw, that was really somehow totally exactly right [...]. We talked and chatted about our artistic experiences. And about all of these artists who are totally important to us, Pina Bausch and so on. And then we noticed how much we were actually interested in exactly the same things. (I_32: 59, 119)

Last but not least, artistic cooperation on the international stage is "a step towards a new visibility" for German artists (I_19: 25).[13]

Indian cultural actors are often of the opinion that German artists are only interested in cooperating with them because they want to travel to India (cf. I_26: 6) and because they can receive sponsorship for the "exotic" elements of the cooperation that the Indian participation promises (I_56: 8). On top of this, they can earn more money with the exportation of this exotic product than with an exclusively German production (cf. I_37: 30-32). This type of relation is viewed as lacking respect by Indian cultural workers (cf. I_37: 34): "This is like going shopping. The Westerners have the money and go shopping [...]" (I_72: 25-26, cf. Ch. 5.9.1). The variety in the impressions of Indian cultural workers becomes clear when opinions are sought on the motivation of an Indian artist from the youth and children's theatre: The German partner enjoys playing with a variety of cultures like the Indian in his aesthetic practice, and exploring them (cf. I_39: 16).

In summary, the interests upon which cooperation projects are based are varied. The most important and primary common interest is often said to be a shared understanding of art, or the same thematic or aesthetic interests in art (cf. I_9/I_10: 12, I_75: 3).[14] According to one Indian artist, artists who share a vision of artistic or aesthetic process have a tendency to find one another (cf. I_47: 4, 11). For cultural creators, aesthetic practice stands in the foreground. It is on this basis that they know who is working with whom, or who would like to work together. The partners are less interested in one another just because they belong to a certain culture or region (cf. Knopp, 2013: n.p.). On the contrary, in the course of a cooperative project, these various cultures seem to disappear, and the similarities come into the foreground:

> Sometimes we still say that the Indians are coming [...], but actually we look at people [...], that is quite different [...]. This 'Indianness' actually falls into

---

13 On interests from the point of view of German creative, see Roßkopf (2010: 90 f.).

14 Also I_32: 95, I_43: 10-11, I_45: 105.

the background. We meet as people who are interested in one another, and above all, I can see the things that connect us. (I_25: 44)

With this comes the recognition, that the cooperative work is dependent on persons and interests. It cannot be 'produced'. The work of an artist, or the genre in which they work, either interests potential partners and sponsors, or it does not (cf. Ch. 6.1).

Further shared interests include the development of both partners through the exchange, and that the cooperative work allows them to develop their networks and reputation. However in this regard, the Indian actors feel inferior to their German partners, since they feel that it is only they who have to learn from their German colleagues, and that they have to build up networks in international cooperation, because they need to 'catch up'. Without knowing it, this posture fulfils the first step in creating power relations (cf. Ch. 5.9.1).

It is questionable whether the interest in strengthening and expanding the infrastructure in their home country amongst the Indian partners (cf. I_13: 6, I_43: 19-20),[15] is well known on the German side. If there was an awareness of this interest on the part of the German partners, in particular on the part of sponsors, they may cease to regard and carry out cooperative projects as short-term, large-scale spectacles, and start implementing them in a more sustainable manner.

Instead, partners seem to tend to guess at the interests of their collaborators, which can lead us to the conclusion that little or no exchange takes place between them on the subject of these interests, or of the motivations for their entering into cooperation. Potential shared interests are not identified at the beginning of the cooperation. A comparison with others makes clear how many parties engage with their partners in an atmosphere of prejudice and mistrust – for example, on the assumption that the financial aspects of the cooperative project are their partner's primary motivation for participating.

5.2 Partner Selection: Exclusive and One-Sided

According to the performer, director, and scholar Sibylle Peters at the workshop "Examples of Successful Cooperation (1) – Artistic Practice and Improvisation"[16] at the 2012-14 *Ruhrtriennale*, "the choice of whom I choose to cooperate with is already part of the artistic process". Indeed, this choice of partner is almost impossible to alter in the course of the

15 Also I_54: 66, IFAB (s.a.: 5).

16 German: *Beispiele gelingender Kooperation (1) – Künstlerische Praxis und Improvisation.*

cooperation, and therefore represents a "critical point" in every cooperative project (I_58: 12). This means the step of initiating a creative partnership deserves special attention.

Cooperations, as this study shows, are not per se participative. The selection of partners is dominated by Western actors – by cultural institutes like the *Goethe* who finance their work, and by the German artists that bring funding with them. The German partners lead and determine the dialogue through the selection of their Indian partners (cf. I_25: 50, I_49: 129).[17] Jütte examines this process in the following terms:

> The process of filtering potential partners – in the sense of a person who participates or takes part in a project or program – on the part of more powerful cooperative actors is perceived to be unfair. (Jütte, 2006: 215)[18]

Since the cultural institutes are based in the large cities and communicate exclusively in English, the circle of actors that these institutes invite to participate in events and projects, or who are perceived as potential partners for German actors, is limited and highly exclusive as confirmed by many of the interviewed experts.[19] The Indian partners belong to the upper class (cf. I_25: 20, I_61: 20-22).[20] The case of cultural producers is similar to that of cultural consumers, and the MMB fails to reach ninety per cent of potential Indian partners (cf. I_35: 29, I_58: 15).

This situation is exacerbated by the fact that the cultural institutions tend to repeatedly select and sponsor the same artists (cf. I_16: 21-22), whether this is because of their proven reliability or personal connections or inclinations.[21] Goethe-Institut representatives in India stress that such a 'closed circle' no longer exists (cf. I_69: 148-150, I_42: 46, 80). However, in reality the opportunity to engage in international cooperation is a privilege enjoyed exclusively by a limited circle of artists. This elite group is strengthened through the selection of partners by the foreign cultural institutes, as one Indian cultural scholar remarks:

> [...] the same people over and over again, [...] the same people and then [...] their children. [...] In that sense the MMB is functioning like the rest

17 Also I_78: 16, I_50: 17, I_39: 28, I_28: 4, I_55: 16-18, I_69: 4, I_20: 12, Singh (2012: n.p.), Majumdar (2012: n.p.), Schmid (1997: 19).

18 Cf. here the statement of a representative of the Goethe-Institut in India at I_69: 84 and Ch. 5.9.1.

19 Cf. I_69: 36, 84, 142, I_32: 23, I_28: 3, 16, 32, 76, I_43: 6, I_39: 17, I_13: 21, I_49: 87, 125, 129, I_50: 10-12, 16, I_15: 211, I_58: 6, I_9/I_10: 136, I_1: 7.

20 See also I_10: 134-135, I_35: 24-25.

21 Also I_28: 38, I_37: 84-85. See also Ch. 2.2.1.

> of India, it is a certain elite that is constantly being circulated over and over again. (I_61: 20-25)[22]

Since German artists frequently use the Goethe-Institut as a 'door opener' to the local scene, they are necessarily also bound up in this closed circle unless they choose to strike out on their own and expand its boundaries (cf. I_20: 7). However this demands research costing time and money which, because of the limited financial and temporal resources of most cooperative projects, is only seldom undertaken (cf. Ch. 5.4.2, 5.4.3, 6.3).

The exclusive and privileged nature of participation in international cooperative projects is reinforced through the highly personal nature of many contacts. According to many of those interviewed for this study, friendship is a condition for cooperating with one another (cf. I_47: 14-15, I_75: 18, 37).[23] This friendship guarantees understanding, even in challenging periods: "[T]he personal relationships also help because they pull you through a lot of tough times." (I_15: 161, see also Sennett, 2012: 160) Here, cooperation does not arise out of a "systematic process of searching" (Rautenstrauch *et al.*, 2003: 87), but on the basis of existing relationships. That is to say in terms of social capital according to Bourdieu's definition (cf. Ch. 2.3). This raises the question of who is capable of building and maintaining this kind of international connection. Friendships, according to Georg Lechner, are thoroughly subject to the conditions of one's circumstances in life (cf. Lechner, 2004: 324). These circumstances are various, as are, accordingly, the conditions for acquaintanceship. Global friendships and cooperation with artists of an 'international stage' are privileges enjoyed by a very few Indian artists who are able to afford the required mobility (cf. I_45: 24, 70, I_16: 18-20), and for the globally connected Western elite (cf. I_16: 18-20, I_49: 171).[24]

This privileged access also applies to workshops, festivals, and conferences that apply a high selection standard (cf. I_47: 6-7) and which offer their participants the opportunity of meeting potential partners for future cooperation (cf. I_9/I_10: 29, 53-55, I_58: 3),[25] in that they are

---

22 See also I_9/I_10: 139, I_29: 5, I_16: 17-18, I_35: 24-25, I_61: 38.

23 Cf. I_15: 95, I_6: 6, I_54: 195. Friendship is based on trust. Trust is a precondition for cooperation (cf. Ch. 5.4.2). At the same time trust and friendship are also products of working in cooperation (cf. I_72: 8, I_16: 3, Majumdar, 2012: n.p., Holzberg, 2009: 88 f., 140, 181, Rautenstrauch *et al.*, 2003: 85).

24 Also I_69: 142 and I_19: 24. Physical ease – the ability to move freely in a global space and access its economic, legal, and social resources – is one of the main criteria of postmodern power for the Polish-British philosopher Zygmunt Bauman (cf. http://tinyurl.com/pzdgfef, Accessed: 04.01.2014 and Ch. 2.3).

25 Also I_65: 12, I_63: 47, I_31: 4, I_28: 36, I_75: 2.

able to present their art and co-workers, examine the practices of their colleagues, engage in technical exchanges, and potentially discover shared interests (I_25: 2, I_9/I_10: 12, 132).[26] However, these discussions around possible cooperation are only open to those who are able to engage in platforms of this kind. Participation in festivals is often subject to a kind of 'domino effect': Actors engage across these platforms, and thereby become known amongst their peers. International cooperations then increase their level of recognition, and they are invited to other festivals where they are able to further expand their networks (cf. I_45: 79, 103, I_47: 2). Thus arises the already described 'closed circle'. This effect is strengthened by the assurance of international participation in these types of festivals by the bilateral cultural institutes that finance them (cf. Vellani, s.a.: 4, I_47: 18-19, I_54: 135), making the selection of available partners dependent on the institutes as 'enablers' of the cooperation (cf. I_45: 13 and Ch. 5.3).

Artistic residencies are another form of exchange in cultural diplomacy (cf. I_42: 30, I_69: 48, 54, I_13: 18). This "mode" is financed (cf. I_63: 37-41, I_49: 133)[27] and supported by the Goethe-Institut through its residency program (I_69: 40-42, 54).[28] This enables a unilateral residency of primarily German artists in a foreign country, allowing them to work together with local artists for a period of between several weeks and months, and thereby to engage with their context and the local artistic scene (cf. I_44: 6, I_49: 13-15, 89).[29]

Ideally, the delicate process of self-discovery in a residency of this kind should be supported "without having any expectations" (I_67: 45-46). However, the requirement of many sponsors that artists present results from this kind of residency stands in stark contrast to this ideal (cf. I_42: 30, I_69: 36, 84, I_28: 10). Residency programs, like other platforms for engagement, embody the contradictory desire to be both process and results oriented at the same time (cf. I_49: 15, I_69: 54, 106).[30]

---

26 Also I_49: 15, 29, 45, 87, 129, I_54: 135, 145-147, I_67: 47, I_19: 3, I_62: 15, I_45: 5, 70, 86, 92, 122, I_39: 48-49, I_56: 6, I_72: 10, I_70: 56-57, 105-106, I_69: 4, I_26: 4.

27 Cf. I_69: 44, 54, 64.

28 The Goethe-Institut has recognised the significance of the residency program by establishing a desk for managing residencies at its headquarters in Munich (cf. I_69: 54). For more on the institute's residency program in India, see Ch. 2.2.2. An insight into the popularity of residencies can be gained on the website 'Res Artis – Worldwide Network of Artist Residencies' at http://www.resartis.org/en/ (Accessed: 11.10.2013).

29 Also I_63: 47, 148-150, I_13: 18.

30 Cf. I_65: 9-10, I_73: 26, Ch. 5.5.2.

5.3 Cultural Institutes: Organisers and Founders of Cooperative Projects

> The project first became realistic thanks to the support of the Goethe Institute's Max Mueller Bhavan in Delhi. The Goethe-Institut enabled intercontinental cooperation between the choreographers by providing financial support, access to infrastructure in India, connection to the "Germany and India 2011/12: Infinite Opportunities" project, as well as help in planning additional guest performances in India: Indeed, the institute laid the tracks for a long-term, intensive cultural exchange in the future. (Ben J. Riepe Kompanie e. V., 2012: 4)

Cultural institutes like the *Goethe* initiate, finance, organise, and moderate international artistic cooperation, as the quotation from a German partner above illustrates. In this way, the institutes fulfil a number of roles in the cooperation process. The questions of which roles the institutes perform, and how these effect the work of cooperation, are central to this chapter.

For both the Indian and German artists engaging in cooperation, the MMB is viewed first of all as the financier of their artistic practice and cooperation (cf. I_54: 135, 145, I_49: 19, 73).[31] This is accompanied by the role of the institute as a 'travel agent' for flights and accommodation for Germans travelling to India and for Indians travelling to Germany (cf. I_15: 13, I_50: 157).[32] Not only does the institute secure access to the partner country, its intercultural expertise and local network provide an entry point to the host culture and the local cultural scene in Germany as well as in India. In this way, the Goethe-Institut can serve as a 'door opener' (cf. I_28: 100, I_20: 6, 10).[33] The question remains, which doors are opened, and which ones remain closed – although potential partners are also certainly to be found behind these closed doors (cf. I_58: 13, Ch. 5.2).

Indian cultural actors value the MMB as "mentor" (I_66: 29-32, 167, cf. Ch. 5.3) and as advisor and contact point in the development of ideas and projects (cf. I_15: 13, 211, I_47: 10):[34] "[O]ften we have gone back to Max Mueller Bhavan, and I think a lot of the time we were really lost, because this is a large project and we didn't know how to make things specific in it." (I_49: 33) An MMB staff member describes this

---

31 Also I_66: 65, 81, I_11: 3-4, I_28: 128, I_42: 41-44.

32 Because of the high costs for Indians to travel to Germany, the institute often offers the only opportunity to do so (cf. I_44: 14-15, I_66: 88, I_45: 26).

33 Also I_22: 13, I_47: 20-22.

34 Also I_49: 19, 35, 71, I_63: 89-94, I_54: 149, I_11: 3-4, I_39: 2, I_9/I_10: 118-119.

dialogue with Indian artists: "[T]hey come and discuss ideas with us and we're involved in developing the ideas as much as they are [...]. So we actually, in certain ways, are attached to the ideas [...]." (I_54: 149) Many German artists, however, have a critical view of this part of the MMB's role – raising the concern that cultural institutes like the *Goethe* may not have the necessary artistic experience to participate in the development of artistic projects (cf. I_29: 3).

A further part of the role of the MMB is to provide a much-needed space for rehearsals, performances, concerts, and exhibitions – particularly for the contemporary or experimental art forms that do not enjoy widespread acceptance and appreciation in India, as well as for critical art liable to be censored (cf. I_42: 40, I_73: 22):[35]

> They [the MMB – author] also give their space for, many, many artists have gone and perform there, where they would never have performed anywhere else. That's a safe space where you know that you can go and really express yourself. You can really go and do whatever it is no matter how controversial it is. (I_49: 87)

This has led to a situation whereby an exhibition of visual art at the MMB can damage the reputation of an artist rather than form a stepping stone to success: "This is one function that the Goethe-Institut have lost completely. Whoever still wants to exhibit here is actually admitting that he won't make it." (I_42: 72)[36]

Alongside offering its own facilities for use, the institute organises other provide or public spaces for the presentation of the results of artistic collaboration (cf. I_28: 72). A renowned institution like the MMB is able to gain access to prestigious cultural spaces where access is otherwise often hindered by the government (cf. Ch. 3.2.1). The reason for this is the aura of political power lent to the institute by its status as an institution of the German government. This has a similar effect on the visa application process: "If somebody has been invited by the *Goethe* it is much more difficult for the authorities to refuse them a visa." (Kusch/Beckmann, 2011: n.p.) In this sense, cultural institutes can be helpful in overcoming bureaucratic hurdles, and thereby contribute to simplifying the process of practicing art both at home and abroad (cf. I_28: 20, I_1: 9-10, I_43: 14).

A cultural institute like the *Goethe* is the primary organiser of a wide range of cooperative projects (cf. I_54: 135, I_43: 9-10). According to one

---

35 See also I_49: 71, I_54: 135, I_31: 15, 22-23, I_16: 16-17, I_39: 3, Roßkopf (2010: 78), Balla (2008: 147).

36 In contrast to other branches of contemporary art, contemporary Indian visual art enjoys international recognition and therefore needs to be addressed separately since it functions according to different mechanics than the performing arts (see Ch. 3.2.4).

Indian artist that has lived in Germany for decades, this has the advantage that "one is insured": Everything is "organised" when the artists arrive in their host country (I_29: 12-14). However, this means that the MMB is required to take on a decision making function in its role as cultural event manager – for example, on issues such as the location and timing for the presentation of cooperative works (cf. I_9/I_10: 118-119, 137, I_32: 19, 24-27). The selection of the venue and the institute's publicity for the event speak to a limited target audience favoured by the institute. This state of affairs tallies with the criticism that cultural organisations dominate cooperative projects, thanks to their role in providing finance, by selecting partners for projects instead of allowing the actors themselves to decide with whom and on what topic they want to cooperate (cf. I_9/I_10: 141-142, I_43: 5-6 and Ch. 6.1).

5.4 Time, Money, Space: The Parameters of every Cooperation

Alongside their finances, location and timeframe are the key parameters of most partnerships. These three forms of influence on German-Indian partnerships will be analysed in the following section.

5.4.1 The Location: India

From the first encounter of the partners through the project development to the presentation of its results, current German-indian cooperative projects overwhelmingly take place in India. As a rule, it is the German partners that come to India (cf. I_48: 6, I_69: 84, I_5: 10). One Indian artist describes the advantages of working in India in the following terms:

> [W]e begun rehearsal in India, so that really loosened things up. I think if we had done it the other way round it may not have been so easy because the format was left loose and it was not so absolute, this would have been tougher to do in Germany; the format would have been quite rigid. But because we started it there [in India] and anything can go wrong, the current electricity can go, maybe the food is too hot, maybe a dog runs through your rehearsal space, so there are infinite possibilities. So it gave the group a sense of fun: 'Oh okay, so there's no electricity, what do we do? We bring a lamp.' Or: 'A dog is here, now what do we do?' It made us more […] loose. (I_26: 12)

In addition, India offers cheaper production conditions as a rehearsal location because of the reduced cost of accommodation, food, and travel (cf. I_72: 38-39). Despite these advantages, it is important for the Indian artists to develop part of the cooperative project in Germany, in order to be able to experience the reality of life and work for their partners (cf. I_58: 11, I_45: 111).[37] However this exchange only takes place in the rarest of cases, for example, in the case of one German-Indian cooperative dance production, which divided the two months available equally into six weeks in India and six in Germany (cf. I_75: 7).[38] Cooperation, in other words takes place overwhelmingly in a single direction – from West to East. The reason for this one-sidedness is that the Western partners are able to afford mobility, and the Eastern are not. Their financial opportunities make the German artists mobile (cf. Kämpchen, 2013a: 66). They have the freedom to be able to travel to India (cf. I_75: 4, I_45: 94). Indian artists on the other hand are as a rule not able to afford the mobility required for an exchange (cf. I_28: 36, 77-80, I_44: 16-17).[39] Mobility is limited to a small number of successful and economically well-placed artists (cf. I_28: 44, Vellani quoted in: *ifa*, 2013: 15). Meanwhile, the difficulties of international exchange are made worse by complicated visa application processes (cf. Jain, 2007: 38).[40] These conditions of limited mobility and freedom to travel stand in stark contrast to the vision of a world connected by culture, as, for example, formulated by UNESCO. On the other hand, Kämpchen sees limits even to the apparently unlimited mobility of the Germans, which leads them to neglect preparation for the cultural encounters, and to visit one location for only a short time without engaging with their host country:

> Spontaneous travel for short periods leads to the case that the experience of India remains accordingly superficial and ill-defined. There is a tendency to believe that one has understood 'everything' at once, producing immediate opinions and judgements and leading to a lack of reflection on one's own weakness – for example, in specialist knowledge and language skills. One

---

37 Cf. Ch. 6.3 and 6.5.

38 Also Ben J. Riepe Kompanie e. V. (2012: 4), I_50: 137.

39 Also I_20: 48, I_11: 56-57.

40 See also Auswärtiges Amt (2002: 15). On the challenges to international mobility in the form of borders as barriers see Burke (2005: 172 ff.). On visa restrictions in the context of global artistic cooperation, see Mataga (2013: 15). For more on the theme and challenges of the international mobility of artists, see the information portal 'Touring Artists' at http://www.touring-artists.info/home.html and the websites of 'On the Move' at http://tinyurl.com/p6luuvl and http://tinyurl.com/oelpdfk (All accessed: 11.10.2013). There are additional organisations concerned with the mobility of artists (cf. Mataga, 2013: 14 ff.). Alongside visa regulations, copyright is a significant topic in international cooperative work. See Mitra (1998a: 1) and the India Theatre Forum (2010: n.p.). The debate on copyright is not within the scope of this study and will therefore not be followed.

> overlooks the fact that understanding of another cannot be based on a simple 'I like it' or 'I don't like it', but needs to rest on a deliberate engagement with the unfamiliar, which requires a certain time to mature. Otherwise, one might return with a hardening of his already held prejudices, since he has 'seen everything' already. (Kämpchen, 2013a: 66)[41]

The location is not only a consideration for the rehearsal phase, but is also significant for the presentation of the results of the cooperative project. As a rule, this presentation takes place in India (cf. I_69: 32, I_70: 87), however reciprocal 'return performances' in Germany, and tours within the German cultural landscape rarely take place (cf. Schäffler/Mittelstädt, 2008: 48). This is despite the fact that with its active infrastructure, this landscape offers an inviting prospect for the domestic presentation of what was created through overseas cooperation. Despite the fact that this loss has been sufficiently marked out (cf. Schneider, 2011a: 6), a change to the situation does not seem in sight, and cultural institutes moderating cooperative projects such as the Goethe have been thoroughly aware of the action required since the 1990s (cf. Schindler, 1997: 154).[42]

At the same time, the lack of financial resources for the return performances means that cultural exchange "in the 'opposite direction' lies almost completely in the personal initiative of the individual institution managers" (*ibid.*: 156). In 2012, the MMB justified this lack of reciprocity in that "location-specific projects" are not able "to be brought to Germany" (I_60: 1-2). A German musician engaged in intercultural exchanges in Asia, Africa and South America for several decades proposes: "Europe is a completely hermetic space. Everybody here is enough for themselves." (I_28: 82) A German dance choreographer opines:

> Bringing out productions in Germany [is difficult], because productions need to be seen in advance, but they can only be seen abroad, and often because these productions often do not have the same quality as solely German productions. (I_20: 59)[43]

Many artists view these return performances as an essential part of the cooperation process that is at present lacking. First of all, the clichés regarding the opposite partner, which continue to be manifest, need to be dealt with: "The reality of India needs to be brought to Germany" (I_77: 1) Among other benefits, the varying reactions of audiences in Germany and

---

41 See also I_72: 22, Ch. 5.5.1, 6.3, 6.4, 6.6.

42 Despite the age of his publications, Schindler's work is interesting for this study because of the light it casts on the role of the Goethe-Institut in German-Indian relations.

43 For more on the discussions regarding artistic quality, see Ch. 5.5.2.

India are valuable for informing future work (cf. I_25: 58). The reception it is afforded in both locations changes the cooperation project and its result (cf. I_9/I_10: 135-136). One German theatre director is convinced that his cooperative work has been continuously improved by its sixty or so performances in India and Germany (cf. I_25: 10). This opinion was supported by many of the other interviewed experts (cf. I_26: 18, 22, I_20: 35).[44]

Not least, these return performances would be of great benefit to Germany's cultural diversity: Shuddhabrata Sengupta is a member of RAQS who was surprised to discover in the course of his work visits to Germany – for example, for his exhibition at the *Documenta* in Kassel – that the diversity of German society is not reflected in its culture, leading him to remark: "I believe it would do Germany a great deal of good if its various cultures were to be receive more space." (Sengupta quoted in: Kusch/Beckmann, 2011: n.p., see also Hoffmann, 1999: 189)

5.4.2 Time Limits: Too Short for a Challenging Cooperation

> When we come together as two theatres from differing cultures, there is a great potential for us to develop something together, but much more has to come together than simply 'I'll come over for four weeks and quickly put something on under awful conditions'. (I_25: 4)

Alongside money, limited time is one of the most significant factors in cooperation. As the quotation above makes clear, many actors in German-Indian cooperative projects see the limited time that such projects usually have available as a challenge (see also I_54: 62, I_45: 122).[45] The question of what the additional time requested will be used for was answered by one German cooperation partner:

> I thought that was very good in [name of a cooperative project – author] and that it also is a part of its [...] success that we were able to profit from the project [...], that we had so much time [...], that we were able to travel here and there, and really get to know one another, that we could think about things in peace [...]. This is the sort of thing [...] that is really necessary [...] in improving intercultural awareness. (I_25: 80)[46]

---

44 Also Schäffler/Mittelstädt (2008: 46 f.), Majumdar (2012: n.p.).

45 Also I_32: 18, I_37: 83-84, I_25: 80, I_72: 9, I_20: 22, I_70: 20. Only two actors spoke of time pressure being a push factor (cf. I_20: 41-42, I_43: 16).

46 See also I_7: 386-388, 400, I_70: 60. For intercultural exchange requiring an extended timeframe, see the website of the *Heinrich-Böll Stiftung* at http://tinyurl.com/p9ujczj (Accessed: 26.07.2013).

Time is essential for the complex preparations required by a cooperative project. Partners need to be able to meet and get to know one another in their individual forms of artistic practice and spheres of life (cf. I_21: 19, I_70: 103-107).[47] The partners need to be able to build trust – a form of social capital (cf. Herbert Quandt-Stiftung, 2010: 16 ff., Ch. 2.3) – with one another in order to fulfil the preconditions for a successful cooperation, as most of those interviewed confirm (cf. I_32: 16-28, I_72: 6-7).[48] Meanwhile, this trust is essential in overcoming the differences and tensions that arise during the course of the cooperation process (cf. I_15: 151, 205). In addition, the preparatory phase is the time for identifying shared and individual goals (cf. I_37: 17-20, 83-84 and Ch. 6.2), researching and discussing the themes of the cooperation (cf. I_54: 175, I_72: 10, 28-29)[49] as well as creating the basic conditions needed for the shared creative process.[50]

Within the cooperation process, this time is required for communication between the partners. Cooperative work is communicative work (cf. I_62: 23, I_75: 21).[51] In order to allow the partners to approach one another, they must be able to discuss their artistic differences and conflicts in order to negotiate an agreement: "After much debate and deliberation we came to the consensus." (Majumdar, 2012: n.p.)[52]

The length of time required for a cooperative project depends on the type of cooperation. As a rule, just a few days need to be planned for a guest performance.[53] Meanwhile, cooperative projects in the sense

---

47 Also I_72: 10-11, 22, 28-29, I_45: 122, I_10: 51, I_32: 119, I_37: 17-20, I_7: 386-388, 412, I_75: 19, I_20: 11, I_11: 56-57, I_67: 41, I_70: 60. Because Indian culture is based on personal relationships, time for intensive relationship building is highly significant.

48 Also I_13: 5, 15, 22, I_65: 9-12, I_63: 47, I_31: 4, I_28: 36, I_75: 2, 18-19, I_9/I_10: 29, 53-55, 122, 126, 148, I_25: 14-16, 24, I_6: 7, I_70: 50, 91-92, I_7: 419-425, I_62: 13, I_58: 3, I_49: 35, I_26: 6, I_67: 34, Ganesh (2011: n.p.), Stepf (2011b: 1). Trust was described as an essential lubricant for cooperation by the American economist and Nobel Prize winner Kenneth Arrow as far back as 1974 (see Frings, 2010: 16, cf. also Putnam/Gross, 2001: 21). For a deeper insight into intercultural trust in international cooperation, see Carlos F. Vittar's dissertation at the University of Lüneburg in which he provides an instrument for the practical creation of trusting relationships (cf. Vittar, 2008).

49 See also I_25: 74, I_26: 4, I_32: 90-93, I_49: 35, I_20: 11, I_11: 56-57, I_67: 41.

50 With regard to time, financial frameworks, location, responsibilities, etc.

51 Also I_54: 195, I_37: 87, I_9/I_10: 36, I_49: 19, 35, 45, I_43: 4, Hoyle (2012b: 37 ff.). The specific type of communication is often called 'dialogue', cf. Ch. 2.1.

52 Also I_72: 10, I_75: 19, I_26: 39-40, I_15: 205, I_32: 71, I_62: 23, I_7: 392-394. See also Sehouli (2012: 66): "There can be no fair compromise, or robust and lasting solution found in haste and without enough time."

53 A guest performance in the sense of an invitation for artists to prevent their work in a city and return home directly afterwards (cf. I_73: 26).

used in this study, with the intention of working together to develop something new (cf. Ch. 2.1 and 6.9), depend on artistic processes and interpersonal interactions. The subjects interviewed for this study provided a wide variety of estimates of the length of time required for this kind of cooperative project ranging from between two months to three years (cf. I_67: 76, I_32: 83-85).[54] In reality, the time required for the realisation of cooperative projects ranged from two weeks, one or two months, or one to three years (cf. I_9/I_10: 140, I_25: 4).[55] When the goal of the cooperation is structural development, as a rule the partners work together for between four and five years (cf. I_50: 60, I_21: 20).[56] In the cooperative project "India goes 3D", intended to contribute toward the development of an electronic music scene in India, the partnership between the artists was based on six years of cooperative work (cf. I_54: 5, I_15: 211). The subprojects contained within the program of structural development generally have a much shorter time frame ranging from a few weeks, as was the case for the tours to Mumbai, Bangalore, and Delhi for the presentation of the concept of "India goes 3D".

The amount of time required is also to an extent dependent on the branch of culture in which the cooperative project is taking place. In comparison to projects in the fields of dance and theatre, those in music and visual art seem to have a tendency to be more frugal with time. One Indian musician reports on his style of cooperation with his European partners in the following terms:

> [W]e just meet on the night of the gig, maybe meet at the club, figure it out, and do the performance. [...] [T]hat happens a lot in the electronic music scene with projects, and people just quickly collaborate, quickly move on [...]. (I_15: 83, 87, see also I_31: 5, 26)

In the visual arts, cooperation abroad is generally limited to a maximum of around one week. Here, a cooperative project *per se* in the sense of this study does not generally take place. Instead, exhibitions are realised with the already completed works of a variety of artists (cf. I_32: 24-25).

Many cooperation projects feel the pinch of their time limit. In a retrospective of its sponsorship program for cooperation, IFAB has acknowledged[57] that time limited sponsorship provokes forced working

54 Also I_45: 122, I_20: 65, IFAB (2001: 20).

55 See also I_72: 13, I_75: 7, I_43: 11-12, I_70: 54.

56 Also I_66: 153, I_73: 48, I_54: 66, 170-171, I_5: 4.

57 The IFAB began its Arts Collaboration Program for the support of interdisciplinary cooperative projects within India in 1997. The program was modified in the following years to take into account the experiences gathered from the various projects that had been implemented.

processes, which results in a focus on an immediate result instead of artistic practice in the cooperation (cf. Mitra, 2004: n.p.):

> It has become increasingly clear to us [IFAB staff – author] that many collaborative ideas cannot be contained within a restricted time frame and that partnerships between artists are often most productive when they are not focused exclusively on tangible outcomes. (IFAB, 2004a: 13 f.)

Because of the limited time available for the initiation and implementation of a cooperative project, projects are undertaken precipitously with unknown partners (cf. I_67: 40, I_37: 8), ignoring points of contention and the process of cooperation, and instead focusing on the rushed production of a showable result (cf. I_7: 408-410, 416).[58] The result is a superficial dialogue between the cooperating partners (cf. I_20: 41-42) in which conflicts, intensified by the compressed timeframe, continue to exist beneath the surface – bringing with them the risk of an early end or non-repetition of the cooperation (cf. I_32: 54-59).[59] A cooperative project completely free of time constraints is not realistic, however it seems obvious that serious consideration needs to be given to the role played by the time factor in the planning of cooperations in the future.

The time available for the cooperative work is finally also limited on the artists' side. Because of the low status of artists in India, Indian cultural actors often have to earn their living alongside their artistic practice (cf. Ch. 3.2.5). While they are paid for their engagement in international cooperative projects, this pay is time-limited and is not capable of providing a regular livelihood (cf. Ch. 5.4.3). With the end of the project, the Indian partners are once again forced to rely on their alternative sources of income outside of the arts. As a consequence, they are unable to put aside the work that guarantees their livelihood in order to take part in a time-limited cooperation. As a consequence, they are often not able to devote their full attentions to the cooperative work, as one German partner describes:

> [The Indian partner] unfortunately had a lot of other work to do. If it had been two full months, where we had been able to take on a couple of other things, it would have been exactly right. But really [...] the person who comes on board with a cooperation like that really has to be there for it. And [the Indian partner] really was not. He had his work, he had his classes, and he had his boss – who could call him day and night [...]. He was under a huge amount of pressure. (I_32: 83-85)[60]

---

58 See also I_70: 20.

59 See also Stepf (2011a: n.p.), *ibid.* (2011b: n.p.), Ch. 5.7.

60 Also I_32: 95, 107, I_62: 19, I_15: 87, I_20: 41-42.

Obligations at home which limit the time available for cooperative projects also exist on the German side: "I can't just jump around for weeks [in India], and leave [the theatre in Germany – author] closed [...]. That just can't happen." (I_25: 10, see also I_70: 18, I_45: 107)

When the time available for the cooperation also has to be shared with other obligations, an inequality between the actors arises. Those who have the time bring more to the shared project than those who have less time. The consequence is that the work that arises from the cooperation bears the influence the partner who had time available more strongly. This creates differences and dissatisfaction, and can even lead to the failure of the whole project (cf. I_32: 95).[61]

In sum, cooperation projects require a high degree of effort in terms of coordination and organisation in order to ensure the availability of all the partners.[62] This means that the time made available to the participants in the project also needs to be appropriately remunerated (cf. I_75: 17, I_43: 16, 22, I_9/I_10: 46). This point, raised by a number of the experts interviewed, indicates the connection between the time and money factors, and leads us to consideration of the next parameter of artistic cooperation.

5.4.3 Financing: Short term and Short sighted

The financial factor is an elementary part of every cooperative project. The funds available to the participants range from a few thousand euros (cf. I_70: 87-88) to more than 50,000 (cf. I_54: 117, I_50: 75), 100,000 (cf. I_43: 11-12) or even to several hundreds of thousands (cf. I_70: 22-24, 79-85).[63] As a rule, the budget is heavily limited and can only cover a part of the working requirements of the project (cf. I_50: 77).[64]

As with time, the question needs to be asked here – what do the artists need more funding for? The answers here are similar. The limited budget,

---

61 See Ch. 5.9.

62 The more partners involved, the more effort is required to coordinate the group (cf. Rautenstrauch *et al.*, 2003: 85 and Holzberg, 2009: 55). "However, the higher the intensity of the relationships between the [participants], the more important it becomes to coordinate them." (Rautenstrauch *et al.*, 2003: 67)

63 These so-called prestige projects therefore have sums of millions available for their use. The main role of these large-scale campaigns is to undertake representation (cf. Ch. 2.2 and 4). A good example of a project of this type is sending the hundred or so musicians of the Berlin Philharmonic, as well as their instruments, abroad (cf. I_28: 68, Schäffler/Mittelstädt, 2008: 48).

64 Also I_50: 51, 69, 79-84, I_31: 33, I_45: 311-316, 377, I_54: 211-212, I_28: 68, I_43: 11-12, Schneider (2008b: 18 ff.), Dickersbach (2013: n.p.). These sums of money always need to be set in relation to the number of persons involved in order to be significant.

like the limited timeframe, forces the artists to neglect the preparation and post production processes: "Funding coming from Germany in general starts with jumping into the project and ends with the premiere performance or exhibition", according to one Indian cultural actor, who has observed and accompanied national and international cooperative projects with Indian artists (I_67: 34).

Sponsorship for cooperative projects is often project-based: "Max Mueller Bhavan, they support you financially […] one by one." (I_49: 76-78)[65] This short-sighted form of funding has the consequence that the process of creative cooperation within the partnership is cut short (cf. I_37: 46-47, I_29: 1).[66] Instead of being able to engage with the differing cultural realities and artistic practices of their partners in the international cooperation, the partners need to work to secure the next financing package for their artistic work or cultural institution (cf. I_9/I_10: 46-49, I_29: 6). This also means that long-term planning cannot take place because of the short term nature of the funding cycle, as the manager of one Indian cultural institution explains:

> [T]here is no guaranteed funding every year after. So then what happen[ed] is you cannot plan ahead and we have now more than forty employees, 23 dancers and doorman and there are lot of the management staff and technicians and 40 plus […] staff. […] So planning ahead is really difficult because you don't know where you have, whether you have that fund to do that project. So that's the biggest challenge we have. (I_45: 37)

Current forms of cultural sponsorship focus on supporting international cooperations. The artists interviewed spoke of a "trend" or even an "imperative" towards cooperation, in order to receive funding for their art, or to be eligible for funding awards (I_39: 6, I_78: 3-7, I_72: 29-30). International cooperation in the arts is booming and there are very few funding awards and funds that do not focus on international partnerships in their awarding criteria. Cooperative work means being worthy of funding. If no cooperation is in place, it is often constructed simply in order to comply with the demands of funding criteria. This leads to the creation of cooperations on a purely financial basis: "Collaborations are just collaborations for the sake of funding." (I_39: 6) According to the expert interviewees, however, these financially motivated cooperations are not capable of functioning (cf. I_37: 32, 54-59, I_29: 2). These experts are unanimous in their opinion that cooperation can only be successful and

---

65 See also the confirmation of this statement by the Goethe-Institut (cf. I_54: 135). Faschingeder speaks of a "project culture" in the sponsorship of cultural activity (Faschingeder, 2001: 117).

66 For more on this problem see also Ch. 5.5.2.

lead to the establishment of a sustainable partnership when it is based on genuine interest in the partner, their expertise, and their artistic practice (cf. I_72: 28-29, 49, I_62: 31).[67] But instead of allowing cooperations "based on genuine interest" to arise "naturally", current forms of sponsorship "fabricate" them (I_67: 3, 38). The actors are required to work like machines. One of the consequences of this 'synthetic creation' of cooperations are partnerships that collapse because of the disparity of the interests involved (cf. I_28: 32, 44, Kämpchen, 2013a: 67).

As a rule, sponsorship for cooperation is awarded according to criteria based on regional or national, thematic, or branch requirements (cf. I_72: 27-29, 54-55, I_25: 4).[68] Anmol Vellani speaks of a form of "donor driven" sponsorship for cooperative projects, in which it is the donor and not the artist who is now able to determine what art is, or what it should become (Vellani, 2009c: 195).[69] This state of affairs becomes even more sensitive when the donors are European and the artists come from the 'Global South' (cf. Dickersbach, 2013: n.p., Fischer-Lichte/Bharucha, 2011: 5).

International cooperation as a rule usually has the goal of overcoming the hurdles raised by the division of the world into national communities (cf. Steinkamp, 2013: 12). Accordingly, the awarding of funding on a regional basis stands in stark contradiction to the basic interest at the heart of international cooperation: to free oneself from regional limitations and construct a continuous cultural relationship network with the rest of the world.

Overseas partners who are selected for sponsorship on the basis of their geographical region often feel exploited (cf. I_67: 3, I_68: 14, I_78: 17). They are aware that their selection has taken place due to the regional allocation of sponsorship funds. Instead of being partners whose interests and needs are acknowledged on an equal footing, there are statistics at the service of their supposed 'partners' in order to enable the fulfilment of their goals (cf. I_67: 40, I_39: 6).[70] The mutual ownership[71] of the shared project – a key criteria for equality (cf. I_78: 11 and Ch. 6.13) – is obsolete: "We could not take ownership for the proposals as we had no part

67 See also I_15: 13 and Ch. 6.1.

68 Also I_9/I_10: 121, I_61: 37, I_63: 107, I_43: 7-8, I_69: 46, I_37: 72-74, I_32: 1, 23, 111.

69 This type of cultural politics is against the principle of artistic freedom in Article 5, Paragraph 3 of the German Basic Law (cf. Ch. 2.2).

70 Also I_37: 8, I_72: 54-55, Hardie (2011: 22 ff.), Vellani quoted in: *ifa* (2013: 15 f.).

71 That is the ability to possess, determine development (cf. e.g. Thermann, 2005: 7) and take responsibility for projects, programs, and initiatives. Ownership is an element of social capital (cf. Steinkamp, 2013: 16 and Ch. 2.3) and a goal for participative processes (cf. Thermann, 2005: 32).

in developing. The projects were not connected with our mandate." (I_78: 7, see also I_67: 40, Vellani quoted in: ifa, 2013: 12) As a consequence, these 'supporters' have been dubbed "India's new patrons" (I_61: 37, I_72: 50, see also Ch. 5.9.1). This makes the determinative power of the sponsor and the structures of dependence within international cooperation clear. Artists feel forced to accommodate their practice, both in terms of its content as well as personally, to the demands of the donor: "And I know many of us go to find German collaborators because we know we get funding for a project." (I_49: 165, see also I_55: 8, I_72: 29-30)

When cooperation is supported by more than one sponsor, there is a high probability that the requirements of these two donors will be different. In the best case, these varying conditions will be confusing for the artists. In the worst case, they will be irreconcilable and impossible to fulfil (cf. I_67: 7-12, I_43: 12-13, I_39: 27). The following question seems to offer a meaningful basis for future discussion: "Who are the funding agencies accountable to?" (Bandyopadhyay, 2009: 199)[72] An answer to this would allow for a much higher degree of transparency with regard to the selection criteria for sponsorship, the current lack of which is felt deeply by many cultural actors.

5.5 Context, Process, Result: The Levels of Cooperative Work

The process of artistic work in a cooperation has three levels, according to one participant at the 'Artistic Coproduction' (*Künstlerisches Koproduzieren*) workshop at the 57th Loccum Cultural Policy Colloquium in 2012. These are namely the context, the process, and the result. International cooperative projects invite their participants to engage with the world of others on these three levels (cf. Burke, 2005: 172 ff.). The following chapter is dedicated to an analysis of these three levels, before we engage in a detailed discussion of the challenges that arise in the encounter between partners from highly different social and cultural backgrounds.

5.5.1 The Lack of Contextual Knowledge

"Well-founded knowledge of the geographical, political, social, and cultural conditions are the basis of every employment abroad." (Balla, 2008: 144, see also Lepenies, 1995: n.p.) International cooperation in the

72 See also here Dickersbach (2013), who engages critically with the KSB's 'TURN' sponsorship program for artistic cooperation between Germany and African countries.

arts does not take place in a "vacuum" (I_14: 27), but in a context. Here, there is a gap between German actors and their knowledge about India, and Indian actors and their knowledge of Germany:

> While the Indian partners usually speak very good English and are extensively informed about Germany, their German guests often have mediocre to poor English [knowledge of an Indian language can generally by excluded completely – author] and have very little knowledge about India. (Schmid, 1997: 85, see also Kämpchen, 2013a: 66)[73]

Despite their mobility, German creative as a rule know much less about India's cultural achievements than the Indian artists do about German history, art, and culture (cf. e.g. I_11: 39, I_16: 7-8, Surana, 2009: 24 ff.).[74] This betrays the Eurocentric tendency of the German actors, who treat the European way of living and thinking as a universal standard. A representative of the MMB explains the situation as follows:

> Indian artists and intellectuals are often markedly more broadly informed and orientated than Europeans [...] because a large portion of their education [...] has taken place overseas. This means they understand quite precisely how [...] the cultural landscape and the academic discourse in England or the USA, or Holland, Germany [...] works. (I_42: 14, 46, see also I_62: 3, I_47: 27-29)

Kämpchen sees the foundations of the ignorance regarding India in German scholarship and education: "Academic life in Germany is still broadly Eurocentric [...]." (Kämpchen, 2013b: n.p.)[75]

This lack of knowledge on the part of the German actors regarding the context in which they are moving is not just limited to the artists themselves. It can be clearly seen in the European cultural organisations working with partners in India, as Anmol Vellani, founder and former director of IFAB made clear at the conference "European external cultural relations – Expectations from the outside" on 12th December 2012 in Brussels.[76] This is despite the fact that a limited knowledge of the artistic

73 According to Singh, the Indian personality knows the teaching of Buddha, Ghandi, and Tagore, as well as the works of Shakespeare, Beethoven, Bach, and Tolstoy (2009: 132).

74 Hans-Georg Wieck here stresses a lack of Indian knowledge about Germany. This study has seen no evidence of this (cf. Wieck, 2006: 2 f.).

75 There are however scholars of historiography who defend themselves against this Eurocentric perspective. One of these is the Bengali scientist and historian Dipesh Chakrabarty. In his monograph "Provincializing Europe: Postcolonial Thought and Historical Difference" he seeks to counter the prevailing point of view that makes European history a universal model for development (cf. Chakrabarty, 2010).

76 For more detail on the conference including its program, see http://tinyurl.com/qbpfjkg. Its proceedings are available in English at http://tinyurl.com/p2h3kan (Both accessed: 30.07.2013).

and cultural landscape of the partner leads to mistakes and losses in the cooperation process. Western cultural institutes fail to recommend, for example, in a cultural landscape like India, where infrastructure is often inexistent, established forms of financing such as co-financing (cf. Ch. 3). Furthermore, well-known Indian artists who are experts in their genre, and therefore 'ideal' cooperation partners, are often not identified by Europeans, who are completely unaware of the goals and structures of the Indian actors (cf. I_47: 19-20). Cooperative projects often remain ineffective in their context (cf. I_50: 97). This results in projects doomed to fail from their beginning, leading to frustration and a lack of understanding on both sides.

The asymmetry in the dialogue between the German and Indian partners conditioned by their differing level of awareness of their partner's culture reflects the power relationship evident in India during the period of British colonial rule between 1858 and 1947 (cf. I_62: 4, I_16: 7-8).[77]

5.5.2 The Orientation of the Cooperation: Process, Result, or both?

The current system of cultural sponsorship supports cooperative projects on the basis of their processes and results. On the one hand, cooperative work should result in a high-quality artistic result that serves as evidence of "the value of the cultural product created through the cooperation" (Schneider, 2011d: 21). At the same time, the essence of the cooperation is the shared process of engagement between the partners (cf. I_72: 24).[78] Both of these orientations seem to exclude the other (cf. I_38: 2-6). The focus on results, however, dominates in donor driven projects, with their limited time and funding (cf. I_11: 57).[79] This is despite the great significance of the content of the cooperation processes (cf. I_11: 9-10, I_43: 18)[80] – not least for the outcome of the project, as the following presentation of the results of the study will show.

The cooperation process is characterised by the activities of transferral and translation (cf. I_31: 12, I_68: 12). These processes of understanding require the partners to communicate extensively with one another

---

77 See also Voll (2006: 1026 f.), Knopp (2013: n.p.) and Ch. 5.9.1.

78 Added to this is the changeability of culture in itself, which is not static but develops and changes itself constantly.

79 A focus on results in the form of quantitative and concrete things such as "media reports, artistic creations, statistics on exchange program participants" (Knopp, 2006: 120).

80 Also I_75: 11, I_9/I_10: 133.

(cf. I_63: 104-108).[81] This communication includes conflicts of an artistic and cultural nature (cf. I_25: 12, I_32: 24-28). These crises and conflicts are productive, because solutions to them strengthen the partnership and allow it to develop further (cf. I_37: 79-81, I_26: 39-40).[82]

Meanwhile, sponsors demand the rapid delivery of a high quality result (cf. I_25: 44, I_32: 107),[83] so that the recipients of their funding can prove themselves worthy of the money (cf. I_11: 58, I_20: 38-40). This means that creative differences and conflicts in the process are avoided, and differences are overlooked: "As the collaboration became targeted only towards the grand final performance […] the problems and tensions emerging out of the process were conveniently glossed over." (Mitra, 1998b: 2, see also I_32: 7) The result of this is that the cooperation is liable to collapse under the weight of these unresolved tensions (cf. I_32: 9-17, 49, 93-95) and that the product-orientated exchange contributes solely to Huntington's prophesied 'clash of the cultures' (cf. Knopp, 2006: 121).

The process presents an opportunity for the cultural actors to learn from and with one another (cf. I_49: 185, I_50: 36),[84] and thereby to broaden and deepen their artistic abilities: "People want to collaborate to learn from each other, skills, things that different cultures and different artists have as their knowledge base." (I_67: 50-53, see also I_67: 36) When artists discuss their experiences and exchange the knowledge that they have gained, pass on their knowledge, encourage the mutual development of skills, and confront and engage with the reality of each other's work and life, the person and their art are able to grow. In the sense of the 2005 UNESCO Convention, they are contributing to diversity. This diversity then exercises an influence on their broader practice: "Personally, the project opened up completely new areas in clay for me and has provided me a completely new direction in which to work." (Mitra, 2004: 2 f.) This diversity is presented, amongst others, to the artists' audience:

> What is it about the piece that moves people so much, or that affects them so directly? What did we actually do there? And one of my answers is actually; perhaps it is the group itself, and how it acts together on the stage. That is to say the element that is not explicitly in the story or in any of its statements. These seven people on the stage with different skin colours, with different

81 Also I_70: 50-52, I_43: 4, I_62: 26, I_72: 52-53, I_75: 11, I_19: 33, I_68: 5, I_73: 32. See also Ch. 6.8 and 6.10.

82 See also Srivatsan (2002: 7), Sennett (2012: 156 ff., 227 f.), Holzberg (2009: 75) and Ch. 5.6.

83 See also I_37: 31-32, I_11: 56-57. This result is in turn based on a project proposal and an idea that also needs to be rapidly developed by cultural actors (cf. I_25: 74, I_20: 37-38).

84 Also I_72: 24, I_73: 32, I_9/I_10: 130-131.

> accents […] they are there together and look at each other and you can see the friendship in this group, which is in itself a beautiful utopia […]. I just want [the audience] to see that between cultures, that intercultural understanding and community, that this idea of a hybrid culture that grows together and enriches itself through the community of its members, that becomes a broader, richer, more beautiful culture […]. (I_25: 12)

Finally, this focus on the process serves the willingness to allow a country and its characteristics to unfold itself, or to give it the necessary space to do so (cf. I_20: 42).

At the international theatre festival *Theaterformen 2013* in Hannover, a representative of a theatre in Switzerland described his own institute's approach to the sponsorship of international cooperation projects: "Inviting artists, letting them look and see – just allowing them to be there without the obligation to cooperate."[85] This freedom seems almost ideal, but it does not reflect the current state of sponsorship for cooperation. As a rule, sponsors demand an equal focus on process and results. On the one hand, representatives of the MMB stress the role of the process as a yard stick for the cooperative work (cf. I_73: 26, I_69: 95-96, I_63: 97), apparently because as experts in cultural sponsorship and mediation they are essentially aware that a focus on results stands against the 'nature' of artistic activity:

> Art cannot be understood as something that needs to be solved, or brought to an end. It is the beginning of something new that leads somewhere where one never expected to go, and to things that it is impossible to think and see in advance, but which can only first develop in the process of confrontation with the self […]. (Eva Sturm quoted in: Trunk, 2011: 15)

On the other hand, according to artists, the MMB in reality does await a result in parallel: "[T]hey [the MMB] are very interested to see what comes out of it either as a presentation or an exhibition or workshop, whatever model […]" (I_63: 88). Here it should be remarked that even platforms such as workshops, festivals, and conferences – that is to say locations where cooperation can only really be initiated – are also expected to deliver results.

The question of why sponsors demand rapid results from short live cooperation projects instead of processes, which cannot guarantee a

85 This statement is taken from a podium discussion with cultural workers from Europe, Asia, and Africa. The discussion entitles 'Opportunities and Obstacles in Cultural Cooperations' took place amidst the colloquium 'Sinn und Unsinn internationaler Kulturkooperationen' (Meaning and Nonsense of International Cultural Cooperations), alongside the *Theaterformen 2013* festival in Hannover (see http://tinyurl.com/m39x5hs, Accessed: 03.12.2013).

result, but which can be much more beneficial, needs to be pursued. Georg Lechner is of the opinion that this is a result of the limited funding and human resources available to the cultural institutions (cf. Lechner, 2004: 262 f.). It is probably the case that the institutes require their activities to have a certain visibility to both their target audience overseas as well as in Germany in order to justify the funding that they receive (cf. I_73: 32, I_20: 43).[86] In addition, there is the question of personal acknowledgement for the manager of the institute (cf. I_72: 52-53). An orientation towards process also seems to raise fears amongst donors that the beneficiaries will simply vanish with the money, instead of putting it towards the intended artistic activity.

> I do hope for something to come out of it, I'm not specific on what should come out of it, I obvious believe that if they are good people and they are talented and intelligent and smart and come from the right place, something naturally and organically will form and I don't like to force it too much. But at the same time I don't want it to become that: 'Oh I've been to Bangalore and it was a vacation [...].' (I_63: 102)[87]

The standard of quality demanded by sponsoring institutions in holding the results of a cooperation to the level of professional quality seen amongst German artists also leads to a risk-aversion on the part of the participants, who seek to limit the amount of risky experimentation in the process of cultural exchange (cf. I_20: 32). This is because the foreign partners are generally not confident of their ability to measure up to European standards of artistic quality (cf. I_6: 4-5, I_20: 38-40).[88] As a consequence, the cooperation becomes minimalized, as a German *dramaturg* explains:

> How much risk do you take on when you engage in this kind of presentation [...] project? And how much risk do you not allow? [...] Do we really want to take risks in terms of content or aesthetics when the whole project is a risk in itself? Shouldn't we say: 'We're going to go along a proven way and find ourselves a good solid piece, and let [German dramatist – author] put it on so that we at least know that two parts of it – the piece and the director – are going to work and the rest can go to pieces. With the actors [...] and so [...].' So it was calculated [...] what comes out at the end. That was not a risk. (I_70: 33-36)[89]

86 Also Goethe-Institut e. V. (2012b: 7).

87 This quotation makes clear that donors' focus on results is not unique to any one culture, although Indian culture is viewed as having a process focus according to its high context, and the German as having a results focus due to its low context.

88 Knüsel speaks on this subject of a "delayed imperialism" (Knüsel, 2011: 71, cf. Ch. 5.9.1).

89 Also I_70: 38, 92, I_20: 38-40. On the risks of cooperative projects see Ch. 6.9, 6.10.

By taking an already existent, rather than a newly developed piece, directed by a German dramatist whose standards are known to the donor because he is already successful in his practice, guarantees a high-value artistic result. The remaining risk, that the Indian partners do not 'play along' or produce a less-valuable result is pushed aside (cf. I_73: 32). International cooperation, which should predominantly consist of a participative process, and be "open from the beginning [...] to the needs, questions, and interests of the participants to ensure the highest possible level of engagement and polyphony" (Trunk, 2011: 55), is damaged by this type of cooperation. What made this cooperation successful – including the presentation of a high quality result (cf. I_25: 12) – was the previously organised and implemented two-year process of coming together (cf. I_70: 20).

The process and the result have a measurable influence on one another. A successful product is based on an intensive process of engagement between the partners (cf. I_63: 103).[90]

5.5.3 The Practice of Adaptation and Reproduction

Germany's cultural infrastructure and arts scene are unique, as is the Indian cultural landscape. In comparison, they are very different (cf. I_50: 17, 45, 69, I_76: 8),[91] even though some of the local challenges they face may be similar (cf. I_28: 76, I_11: 34). These variant realities condition cooperative projects (cf. I_11: 15 and Ch. 5.5.1):

> Cultural cooperations have a certain problem in facing intercultural projects implementation which is always context specific including local environment, difficulties, and sensitivities. (I_14: 14)

This fact allows us to conclude that artistic and cultural management practices, as well as the resources available, need to be adapted to the needs of the local context in which the cooperative project is taking place (cf. I_66: 29). This context orientation – which can be understood as the use and recognition of existing systems and structures, connection with local knowledge and local networks, strengthening local processes and activities, and identifying local needs (cf. I_20: 47) – was recognised

[90] Monika Gintersdorfer, the German director, supports this thesis. She describes her cooperation with actors and dancers from the Congo and Ivory Coast as a shared choreography, or shared authorship, which she directs (cf. Monika Gintersdorfer's words on 15.12.2013 at the public discussion following the performance of *Mobutu choreografiert* at the *Theater Bremen*; a segment of the discussion has been archived by the author).

[91] Also I_20: 28, I_11: 28, I_28: 24.

as important by the cultural actors interviewed for this study (cf. I_37: 56, I_14: 13).[92] However, in practice, this adaptation takes place in the form of a "copy and paste" transfer from 'West' to 'East' (I_21: 7) or from 'North' to 'South' without regard to context orientation, although it is commonly known that direct copying without making adaptations for local conditions cannot produce a functioning result, and can only reproduce ignorance and unequal power relationships (cf. I_54: 6, 63-64, I_76: 9, Ch. 5.9.1).[93]

The Cultural Management Program of the Goethe Institute in South Asia provides an example: Cultural actors from South Asia receive training as cultural management through programs including seminars on the subject. These seminars are led by scholars from the West (cf. I_7: 132-141), who teach the young Asian cultural actors how artistic concepts are methodically, financially, and politically implemented with success in Europe (cf. I_66: 153). However, this knowledge transfer in the sense of a simple adaption is a fallacy. If it is not adapted to the needs of the concrete reality in which it is to be applied through a process of context-oriented transfer it is useless.[94]

An Indian participant in the Cultural Management Program between 2012-13 makes clear that knowledge from the West needs to be 'translated' for the Indian reality:

> She [an Indian cultural actor] [c]omes from that background [India] and she was the first person who was talking to us in our context. Because everybody else [the Western seminar leaders – author] was giving us examples from their country. And so they bring a very different approach, [...] I felt that it was nice to have [the Indian cultural actor that provided 'translation'– author] in the room because she kept bringing us back [...] to India, and if there was a point which we didn't relate to, she [...] kept giving us examples of [...] work happening in India [...]. So if we didn't have [the Indian cultural actor] doing that and behaving as an anchor, we might be a little lost. (I_7: 150-160)

Alongside participation in seminars, the course participants undertook a stint at a German cultural institution. On the one hand, this foreign studentship provides a form of inspiration, on the other, however, it might be asked whether a domestic studentship in cultural work in a specifically Indian context may not have been of greater practical value, as one Indian cultural worker presents:

92 Also Vellani (2006: n.p.).

93 Also I_72: 44-45, I_7: 66-68.

94 Cf. here also the perspective of international development – for example, in Nuscheler (2006: 468).

> [E]ven though I know that I can't replicate a model which is in practice in Germany, I can come back inspired and hopeful of being able to do that in my country. [...] I know some of my fellows [...] would love to probably be able to intern somewhere in India itself, and not Germany, because [...] that is what will help them with their project. (I_7: 225-226, 272)

Indian cultural experts see the participants as well as the hosts of the program as responsible. While the course participants learn some skills, they are not able to engage critically with the content of the course. Instead, they are limited to reproducing this content without questioning if and how it might be appropriate and useful for them and their context. They have the mistaken expectation that the European actors were familiar with their own context and its operation. In this respect, those responsible for the program create the false impression amongst the participants that this transfer of European or Western ideas, strategies, and concepts can be applied in a different context without adaptation (cf. I_61: 34-37, I_78: 14, 21, 30). The result of this export of knowledge without an effort to make the transfer effective can be illustrated in the career of an Indian drama teacher, who had learned the 'German' method of theatre teaching: "I can't do anything here [in India] to do with what we [Indian theatre teachers] learned from you [Germans] [...]." (I_70: 4-5)

For the Indian cultural experts interviewed in the course of this study, the cause for this adaptation and reproduction is the behaviour of the European cultural institutions, which found cooperation programs with partners from the 'Global South' characterised by a one-sided pattern of thinking and action. They consider what knowledge and expertise they are able to offer their partners (cf. I_78: 27, I_72: 19-20). From their perspective, the processes of learning and development are primarily something that the foreign partner needs to engage in.[95]

The current structure of cooperative projects is accordingly not designed as a two-way street, described by Bode as "a systematic weakness of the one-sided export-oriented Goethe-Institut" (Bode, 2002: 153). The one-way principle strengthens the existing pattern of teacher-student or donor-recipient relationship between the actors from the 'Global South' like India, and those from the 'Global North' like Germany (cf. Ch. 5.9.1). The politically trumpeted learning from one another (cf. Ch. 2.2) – in the sense of a mutual influence and sensitisation for other forms of thinking and acting – seems to recede into the far distance. Indian cultural actors see here the foundations of a new form of imperialism or cultural colonialism (cf. I_11: 74, I_61: 37).

---

95 The term 'capacity building' is often used in this context, meaning the development of competences and structures.

Examples of this form of adaptation can be found in German-Indian partnership in every branch of the arts. The Indian theatre, for example, stands in the tradition of Brecht and other great German dramatists (cf. I_72: 53-54, Kumar, 2001: 33). The young Indian children's and youth theatre scene follows the Berlin 'GRIPS' Theatre (cf. I_39: 37, Spiess, 2009: 60). However the adaptation of topics and styles without connection to Indian culture is not successful (cf. Schäffler/Mittelstädt, 2008: 47):

> Then they simply did a copycat production [...] with Indian actors there [in India], [...] and it was so cut off from this German context that the piece didn't work at all, and didn't work with the actors. (I_25: 4)[96]

Currently, Indian cultural actors are increasingly pushing for a separation from the Western 'template' used in the development of Indian contemporary art for the following reason:

> We have spent three hundred years listening to Western pieces, we cannot spend the next two hundred letting the West decide and determine what we [...] are going to talk about in our own structures. (I_72: 32-34)[97]

German partners that seek to avoid adaptation in their cooperation projects are necessary for this disengagement from the West:

> [Name of a German theatre producer] wants [...] that people [in India] like it. And that it is Indian enough, and that they do not have the feeling again 'here come the Germans'. (I_70: 50)

5.5.4 Experimentation and Failure as Valuable Moments of Cooperation

Cooperative projects are risky work (cf. I_73: 36-38, I_70: 38).[98] It is not usually possible to foresee what happens in the course of a cooperation, and what the end result of the partners' work will be (cf. I_25: 12, I_69: 28):[99] "The combination of the thoughts and imaginations of others makes the creative process much more complex and unpredictable." (Fowler, 2012: 18) Indeed, this leads inevitably to failures:

---

96 On the adaptation of Western contemporary dance in India see Sharma (2000: 13), on the same phenomenon in the visual arts see I_22: 6.

97 Also I_72: 24, 56, I_59: 5, Lisbonne-de Vergeron (2006: 34) and Huntington (2002: 674): "For four hundred years 'intercultural relations' meant adapting other societies to Western culture."

98 Also I_68: 15-16, I_67: 3, I_78: 24 and Sennett (2012: x).

99 See also I_9/I_10: 123, Ch. 5.5.2, 6.9 and 6.10.

> When [...] artists [...] come together it is always implicit that it will misfire. Either because there is no production together, which is sometimes the better decision, or because something gets developed that turns out as being not very high quality. That can always happen. (I_73: 32)[100]

The reasons and opportunities for failure are varied: "poorly defined goals, mistaken expectation of success, a lack of communication, [...] a lack of trust, or cultural differences" (Holzberg, 2009: 7). Indeed, this study confirms that failure can also be the result of an overly hasty choice of partner, aesthetic differences, or disconnected hierarchical structures (cf. Ch. 5.2 and 5.9.1).

It is worth remarking, that failure has up till now been a taboo in the discourse of international cooperative projects in the arts. Unease and gaps in the cooperation are not articulated. One German cultural actor explains this problem using the final report of a project, which was orally discussed with the Indian partner in the presence of the German donor:

> Everything that we said was correct, we did not invent anything, we simply left a few things out. That is all. We did not say anything that was untrue. That is, he didn't say anything that was wrong, but honestly, we left out part of the truth [i.e. the failure – author]. (I_32: 1)[101]

This is despite the fact that failures and their mistakes offer a unique chance to learn and to improve cooperative work in the future by exposing the critical points within cooperative projects (cf. I_19: 28-30, I_78: 2, 25-26).[102] The cultural actors interviewed for this study viewed failure as a valuable experience within the cooperation process: "Mistakes [can be] a very important part of artistic development [...]." (I_73: 36-38)[103]

When failure is not openly discussed, or when it cannot be openly discussed, important knowledge about potential failures and how to deal with them is lost. Why then is this a taboo? Cultural actors hide their experiences of failure because of a fear of losing current or future

---

[100] Also I_73: 36-38, I_69: 95-96, I_78: 25-26. Rautenstrauch *et al.* speak of an "empirically proved increased risk of the cooperation failing" (Rautenstrauch *et al.*, 2003: 110 f.).

[101] See also I_32: 9, I_49: 181 and the research diary of this study (Entry on 09.12.2012): "There must be failed cooperation projects [...] but I don't see them or I can't see them because nobody is telling me about them." Extracts from the research diary can be found in Annex 1 to this study in its form as a doctoral dissertation. See the Note on the Translation. The full diary is archived with the author.

[102] See also Sennett (2012: 154 ff.). Failure is also an opportunity in a scientific sense, which allow the mechanics of normal functions to be assessed relative to those dedicated to dealing with failures (cf. Meuser/Nagel, 2009: 54).

[103] Also I_32: 22, I_19: 28-30, 42.

donors and supporters. This has the consequence that cooperative projects continue to be idealised, because their failure is not allowed to be seen:

> Everybody always talks about how great his or her partnership was. Of course, it is natural to want to do a bit of […] advertising at conferences. I have to present myself, I have to sell myself. (I_73: 33)[104]

It is not just the fear of losing potential donors, but an existential fear, which leads actors to carry on even when they are no longer convinced of the profitability of cooperation themselves (cf. I_30: 3, I_78: 25-26, I_20: 13):

> I thought: 'Shit, how are we going to get through this?' I wanted to leave and I had to consider – how do I do it, do I do it, do it, do it. But I have to honestly admit, if I had dropped the project, that would have been my income for the first half of 2012. […] I would not have been able to fly back. I didn't have anything. I only did it because of the money and, for me, money is not the main consideration when it comes to art. But in this case I would have been faced with such a big loss. (I_32: 111, see also I_32: 21)

Cultural institutes like the MMB see failure as a natural process in the establishment of the program. One representative of the institute explains:

> And obviously, exactly according to this dialectical principle, where we are not dealing with a finished program, but where we are first working to establish the topics and areas of work, this naturally means that one considers a lot of things. It can then be the case that a piece goes relatively far, and then in the middle of the thing you realise that in fact it is perhaps not going to work, or that perhaps this is the wrong partner, or that this isn't the right time. Then you drop it and perhaps pick it up again later, or it stays dropped. This is all totally normal. (I_42: 48, see also I_49: 188-189)

At the same time, failure amongst cooperation partners financed by the institute is only tolerated by the MMB up to a certain point in time within the cooperation process:

> There are of course cases like this, and I think everybody has experienced one. The question, though, is always how far it goes. There are different ways of reacting. One of these is that when there is a process of getting to know one another, using this as the best point to see if it should go ahead or not. And the situation where cooperation takes place and then breaks off does happen,

104 See also I_70: 90, I_32: 99, I_73: 36-38, Lambert Mousseka and Stefanie Oberhoff quoted in: Trunk (2011: 37 f.).

> but is perhaps not the [...] ideal factor, instead you say during the encounter phase: 'It makes sense [...] or it doesn't.' (73: 34, see also I_69: 30-34)

When the discourse on failure is finally opened, it will also require a clarification of what it actually means to "fail" and at what point this failure enriches the process, and when it might be more productive to break off a process that threatens to fail.

5.6 The Challenges of International Partnerships: Intercultural Differences

> Sometimes collaborations can create more problems than they contribute to the production of art and art education, especially when it comes to intercultural collaborations. (I_67: 3, see also Roberts, 2012: 33)

The following section will discuss the problems referred to here, which can lead to the failure of intercultural cooperation between partners from the 'Global North' and the 'Global South'. It should be remarked that it is the thesis of one Indian creative, that the level of the cooperation can be recognised according to the number and intensity of the challenges that it involves (cf. I_16: 14-15).[105]

The language of a cooperative project consists of verbal and aesthetic, or cultural, types of speech (cf. Srivatsan, 2002: 5). Both of these languages are important in the development of the artistic product of the cooperation. The different languages of the partners themselves are often a source of misunderstanding:

> Misunderstanding seems to be pre-programmed into encounters between different cultures first of all. This has to be the case because the partners are not even able to understand one another linguistically, without even considering the special challenges of artistic language. First of all they have to learn one another's language, backgrounds, conventions, and forms and to understand one another in the most basic sense. All of that is of course only approximately possible. (I_42: 46, see also I_50: 132, I_22: 14-23, I_20: 20)

It can be remarked that in German-Indian cooperation, as is most likely the case in most international cooperative projects around the world, English is the predominant spoken language. This means that

---

105 According to this thesis, the greater the challenges, the higher the engagement required from the participants in the cooperation, and thereby the grade of the cooperation (cf. I_16: 14-15, see also Fowler, 2012: 18). If these are too great, however, cooperations can also fail.

both of the partners – the Indian as well as the German – are therefore communicating in a foreign language. The observations made in the course of this study showed a broad level of competence in this regard on the part of the German partners. These are as a rule able to speak English at levels varying from the most rudimentary to the highly professional according to their education and use of the language in a professional context. Because of the status of English as an official language in their country, the Indian partners on the other hand are often in possession of a highly differentiated vocabulary, which they put to use in cooperative projects. The differing level of ability in the shared language of the project often leads to misunderstandings. Added to this is the problem that every country has its own variety of English. For Germans, Indian English is often difficult to understand. One Indian actor confirms this situation from the opposite direction: "They have a […] slightly different language even though we all speak English. The way we speak it is a little different, the humour is different you know." (I_63: 59) Although it often leads to deep division between cultural actors, this language difference receives no attention in the arts (cf. Srivatsan, 2002: 6 f.).[106]

When the partnership cannot be based on a shared aesthetic language, which makes cooperation easer (cf. I_75: 16, I_28: 6), the differing artistic languages used by the partners can lead to conflicts, as the following quotation illustrates:

> But the Indian dramatist said, […] he played this Raga there and made us all very emotional, and you don't understand that and that's why you simply cut it, and it was perfect at that point [in the piece]. And I have no idea if he was right or not. Of course it is a fact that I did not recognise this particular Raga, and therefore didn't value it as such […]. (I_25: 72)[107]

For the German partners, the roots of this different understanding of cultural practice and the connected differences in artistic language lie in the different level of professionalism between the partners:

> Theatre in India is a 'theatre of passion', and in Germany it is a 'theatre of profession'. And that is the first big difference that you have to overcome. […] On a small scale, this means that the actors complain that they have to rehearse eight hours a day. Because this precision, and this again and again suddenly presenting something exactly, is something that they do not have,

---

106 On differences in language and humour as a challenge in intercultural encounter, see also Hofstede (2001b: 299 ff.).

107 Also I_70: 20, 50, I_9/I_10: 145, I_68: 7, I_75: 8, 24, I_1: 5, I_63: 63. See also Wartemann (2002: 94). Ragas represent the basic melodic structure of Indian music, and determine which tones are appropriate in a piece of music.

> and they find it boring. [...] Because the theatres do, somehow, because the content of a piece interests them, they do it, then they go to rehearsal, they rehearse a bit, and then it goes on stage. Just somehow. But it is more about keeping the head busy and making theatre, and theatre is more than just a social communications platform, it is a hugely aesthetic form of expression – I see this again and again. And we are of course marked by our professional German theatre, which pays a lot of attention to aesthetics. And I find these are just the kind of moments where two different understandings of what theatre is clash together. (I_70: 50)[108]

It is questionable whether these confrontations can be exclusively put down to the differing professional basis of the partners. However, through their formal training, and comprehensive engagement with their art, German actors possess a social and cultural capital in the sense articulated by Bourdieu, which enables them to act and communicate in the mode of professional cultural practice, in contrast to their Indian partners (cf. Ch. 2.3). This ability provides an advantage when seeking to make the partnership speak with one's own aesthetic language (cf. Ch. 5.9.1).

Communication is a central component of the cooperative project, as the presentation of the results has already made clear (see Ch. 5.4.2, 5.5.2, 6.5, 6.9).[109] However different cultures have different styles of communication, which can lead to failures in communication (cf. I_28: 38, I_39: 20). There are two broad types of communication: the direct and indirect, as well as a high and low relation to context. Direct communication is typical of the German culture, and means that instructions and information can be passed on clearly and directly. The Indian style of indirect communication, on the other hand, passes of information encoded and implicitly (cf. I_32: 41, 45). The potential for conflict that these differing styles of communication inherently contain is highlighted by the documentary of the German-Indian theatre partnership 'Do I know U?'. The different approach to criticism in both cultures leads to further tensions:

> That means at that moment I did something that made [the Indian partner] lose face. But I didn't know that. Because I had the feeling we were on the same level and we could say when we were discouraged. [...] Somehow I just had to say that, as you might do in Germany. But I did not know that that would make him lose face. And after that he was very closed, very grumpy, and first of all didn't say

---

[108] See also I_70: 28-30, I_68: 23-24, Ch. 3.2.2 and 3.2.5.

[109] This is in addition to the fact that art, the basis of every cultural cooperation, is a means of communicating social realities (cf. I_75: 33, I_21: 23).

> anything […]. Two days later he explained it in a way that I could understand. I noticed there was something there, but not exactly what it was. (I_32: 81)[110]

India is a culture with a high context relation – that is, communication takes place "over the context of the interacting persons" and is therefore nonverbal (Schmid, 1997: 47).[111] Social networks with a continual exchange of information are important for this type of communication. On the other hand, Germany is a culture with low context relation. Important communications are mediated through language (cf. Schmid, 1997: 47), and require a low level of previous knowledge on the part of the recipient. This study confirmed this lack of contextual knowledge on the part of the German partner in Chapter 5.5.1.

When the actors interviewed were asked to report on the challenges in their cooperative projects, they first of all narrated the large number of cultural differences that influence international cooperation at length (cf. I_63: 59, 63, I_22: 14-23, I_23: 16-17). The cultural difference that dominates cooperative work significantly is, according to both the German and Indian actors, the specific cultural relation with time (cf. I_32: 81, I_62: 14).[112] German punctuality stands opposed to the Indian flexibility regarding the keeping of appointments: "When the [Indian partner] said we will rehearse at five, and still weren't there at eight." (I_32: 71, see also I_9/I_10: 95-97) This flexibility takes many forms of commitment in India, as the following statement from a German dramatist shows:

> That gets done very, very often in India. It is completely forgivable and normal, and it took a lot of effort to get used to the fact that when somebody is engaged in something and gets a better offer just before, then they're gone. That's why I didn't know until the end whether the actors would stay with us for the whole time. (I_32: 19, see also I_22: 14-23, I_70: 28)

This differing understanding of time can lead to further affronts in German-Indian partnerships. Short-term Indian planning often comes across as chaotic and uncontrolled to German actors.[113] Because of the Indian reality, which demands a high degree of flexibility and improvisation, however, this seems to be a realistic behavioural strategy:

---

110 Also I_68: 10-16, I_62: 22, 28, I_6: 8, I_32: 107; against this is the perspective of a German cultural worker, that the Indian partners possess a definite culture of criticism (cf. I_25: 10). This quotation makes clear the hierarchy that exists clearly for the Indian partner, but that the German partners do not seem to appreciate.

111 For more on non-verbal communication see Bennett (2001: 5 f.). Circa eighty per cent of human communication takes place non verbally. See http://tinyurl.com/q8sb5xm (Accessed: 04.08.2013).

112 See also I_22: 14-23, I_31: 30, I_6: 4-5, I_9/I_10: 85.

113 Also I_28: 118, I_32: 35, I_15: 47.

> I get on [the Indians] nerves with my crazy punctuality, my organisation, my anxiety, my tension, my stress, my need to be in control, and suddenly what is normal [in Germany was there in India] really a completely out of place way of behaving […]. (I_25: 38)

The differing work ethics and approaches between German and Indian actors are rooted in the structural differences between the countries, which have created differing conditions and frameworks for working (cf. I_75: 8, I_63: 59).[114]

The social hierarchy that forms an inescapable part of life in India and exercises an influence in almost all areas of life presents an additional significant cultural difference for the German actors. These hierarchies, on which Indian culture is based, also have an influence on cultural cooperation (cf. I_32: 13, I_68: 8). The consequence is a degree of confusion on both sides, which can even lead to conflict (cf. I_32: 7, 45, 107). A German creative reports:

> This also makes it difficult, […] because [India] is still an extremely hierarchical society. [As a German dramatist], I am used to working in a team with a very flat hierarchy, and I am not at all used to letting the big boss hang out, or they get a shock when my actors shout at me and I […] say 'calm down and control yourself' […] instead of shouting back at them. […] And then they are totally shocked because of the lack of respect towards me even though I am the big boss and the great guru and artist, and then I say: 'No, I'm not. I often don't know what to do.' And that is quite confusing. (I_25: 20)

5.7 The Short Life of Artistic Cooperations

The great weakness of international cooperation in the arts at the moment is their impermanence and fleetingness (cf. Steinkamp, 2013: 2). Although the ideal goal is for stable and long-term partnerships (cf. I_75: 10), this study found few examples of pairs or teams of artists that have worked with one another or will work with one another a second or a third time, even though they were satisfied with the process and result of their cooperation with one another.[115] This phenomenon is ascribed to the difficulty of achieving a follow-up or long-term financing on the basis of a single project:

> Why they always stop and […] don't go so deep, and break that point where you can say 'now you've really got it, and got to know one another'? Why

---

[114] See also I_30: 8-9, I_31: 29-30, I_70: 54, I_22: 14-23, Nag in: Nambiar (2012: 6), Gronemeyer in: Kumar (2012: n.p.).

[115] This demands reflection on the experiences of the cooperative project. See Ch. 6.12.

> they always stop and start again from the beginning with new teams [...]? You know what it is like in the arts – short lived. The people fly from here to there. Maintaining that kind of alliance [...] is not easy. Especially over the years. The answer to those questions is easy: air fares [...]. (I_70: 62-67, see also I_65: 4)

In this way, cooperation projects become short-lived affairs that pop up in the cultural landscape and then disappear (cf. Ch. 4). Indeed, in its reflection on its cooperation program, IFAB discovered that the conclusion of the cooperative artistic work in most cases brought about a complete end to the exchange, interaction, and dialogue between the artists (cf. IFAB, 2001: 20).

On the other hand, cooperation projects between Indian artists and the MMB were often repeated. That is to say that Indian artists worked together with the MMB repeatedly over years or even decades (cf. I_50: 10-12, 26, 64, I_63: 6-8, 18, 53):[116]

> [A]ctually we've been working with the Max Mueller Bhavan for about three years. [...] [I]t's always two ways, I mean it's not only where they [the MMB] call us [Indian artists] and ask us [...] whether we want to be a part of it. If we have an interesting idea we go back to them and ask them if they would like to support it. (I_50: 10, 66-67)[117]

This regularity is increased when the Indian artists represent or lead an Indian institution (cf. I_45: 26, I_49: 89).[118] This is an indicator for the recognition that the institutionalisation, or the institutional formalisation of stability, continuity, structure, and long-term cooperation in German-Indian partnerships is able to bring (cf. Ch. 6.6). It is, however, also important to remember that the binding element in the repeated partnership between the MMB and Indian actors is the funding that the MMB is able to provide over several years before it departs from the project (cf. I_50: 59, I_54: 7, I_42: 42). In this way, however, the medium-term investment of financial resources allow the institution to build up sustainable partnerships with Indian actors in keeping with the focus of the regional institutes.[119] This enables the institutions to create a stimulating space for action which would not otherwise exist.

---

116 See also I_45: 1, 26, I_47: 8, 26-27, I_49: 89, I_59: 6, I_39: 45. The fact that proposals for cultural projects in the context of the Year of Germany in India were submitted to the Goethe-Institut exclusively by existing contacts of the institute confirms this result.

117 See also I_42: 14, I_9/I_10: 14, I_29: 18, I_32: 17.

118 Also I_47: 8-9, I_63: 18.

119 By 'medium term' the experts interviewed as a rule meant three to five years.

Another example of stable cooperation between artists can also be found in those who have had the opportunity to develop their first cooperative project over a number of years, which has the effect of cementing their relationship. This is the case in the cooperative project 'Do I know U?':

> That is also interesting, because now we have created a whole different relationship out of that project [...]. I am already on my third project with [name of the Indian partner], what else has happened? I don't know if [Indian partner] and [German partner] are doing something together. But of course in this project, over this long period [...] we developed alliances and friendships where everybody involved is still doing his own projects on a smaller scale. (I_70: 61)

Artists report that they continue to work together either with former partners or with new partners that they have got to know via past partnerships. There continues to be continuity, even though those involved separate in the first instance after their intensive cooperation:

> We worked together for three years [...]. I think that then necessary. In any case I had to get out of the connection [...]. At that point, it was good that it was over. (I_70: 70-71)[120]

A shared artistic interest is an important condition for continued cooperation:

> This shared passion has encouraged us to look for other stories that could bring us together again. We continue to discuss ideas and actively plan for our next endeavour to devise theatre collectively. (Majumdar, 2012: n.p., cf. Ch. 6.1)

5.8 The Loss of Experience

A discussion of the quality of cooperative projects in the sense of the quality of their processes, their results, and the effectiveness of their product on the partners (cf. I_67: 21-24) and their contexts has yet to be undertaken (cf. I_54: 8, 100). Donors and institutes demand evaluation from their funding recipients in the form of project reports,[121] however these evaluations are simply bureaucratic, which do not seriously confront the work (cf. I_33: 1-9). Furthermore, this form of brief formal evaluation

---

120 See also I_28: 110.

121 Additional partners in the cooperation that were not sponsored by the institute were not included in these evaluations (cf. I_32: 10).

on the part of the institutes does not allow for an objective reflection (cf. I_49: 185, 193, I_32: 103). A representative of the MMB states:

> The reports are just an instrument. One has to decide how to use them. That is also a question of time, of course. Like in every organisation there is a time plan with financial years and budgets and project evaluations. However these financial time plans are not optimal for a project. For example, if I had today as my deadline for the jamboree, I would have to write a project report today, which would look very different now than it would in a year. If you say [name of a German artist] met with some people and had an interesting conversation, you wouldn't be able to tell what happened straight away. That's why these formal and pre-formulated reports often have little to say. (I_73: 46)

An exchange between the partners or with donors on the cooperative project only takes place superficially. This damages the chances for a deep understanding of the process of cooperation and the partnership itself:

> I wonder whether […] I would really like to know honestly, very critically […] a response to my work or to the organisation's work. And this honest feedback, […] I don't know if I get it enough from my funders or sponsors […]. And I'm not sure […] whether yet there's a space for that […] we've created in this partnership. Very honest critical feedback. […] We never talked about our partnership. […] Sometimes in fact we've had to be reminded that: 'Hello, this is a partnership.' […] I don't think I've ever had critical feedback. And even when I say that: 'This is not really working, I don't think we've done a good job here.' I always get encouragement. And sometimes I just want to say: 'No, let's nail this one!' Because we want to know what's happening or why it's going wrong. So I don't know if we get enough of that as partners from each other. (I_49: 107, 111, see also I_32: 57)

With the fact that experiences are not exchanged within a cooperation or with other outside actors, the participants' valuable knowledge about their work together is lost. Cooperative projects undertaken without assessment give up their chance to change dynamics and to recognise and act on problems early in the cooperation process (cf. Rautenstrauch *et al.*, 2003: 90, 125).

5.9 The Definition of Cooperation: Ideal and Reality

There is no uniform understanding of what cooperation is and has to offer: "Each member of the team […] naturally understood the spirit of collaboration differently." (Mitra, 2004: 2 f.) But a commonly shared understanding of the phenomenon is of two or more artists bringing together their ideas and concepts in order to allow something new to arise, which would not have been possible if they had remained alone (cf. Ch. 2.1):[122]

> We are not doing something German or Indian now, we are developing something that will be sometimes German and sometimes Indian, as well as both at the same time […], so that something really new will come out of this encounter, and the part of themselves that all of those involved put in. (I_25: 10)[123]

Ideally, all of the partners are or can be equally involved in the creation of this collective product (cf. I_7: 548, I_67: 15), by contributing their resources, their expertise, and their creativity (cf. I_47: 30-31, I_13: 32).[124] This means that all of those involved have ownership of the result (cf. I_67: 15). Ideally, each partner in the cooperation should profit from their participation (cf. I_7: 548, I_25: 4, 82, I_43: 24-25), especially as the actors learn from one another, and thereby develop and broaden their repertoire and scope for expression (cf. I_67: 17-18, 36, I_45: 533).[125] Cooperation should be free and arise in a natural way: "That's collaboration! You know, it's not been forced on me, it's not imposed, I don't have to, I'm not creating something that's artificial, and I'm interested genuinely in something […]." (I_13: 25)[126]

This is a highly idealised understanding of cooperation (cf. I_67: 3, I_19: 26-27), which depends on the principle that the partners are equal and outside of hierarchical conditions (cf. I_67: 15). As a rule, cooperations primarily exist instead according to the classic model of a co-production, where German cultural actors lead the production and their partners, the Indian artists, participate in the project (cf. I_25: 4, 44-50, 72).[127] The German partners are here responsible for the definition, conception, and planning of the project in advance of the co-production that they want to undertake with their Indian partners. The result is often unsatisfactory – and looks more 'German' than 'Indian'. The cultural export model is maintained.

The root of this model lies in the inequality of the participants. The Indian and German partners begin and undertake their cooperation under fundamentally different conditions that lead to clear hierarchies, which

122 Anna Steinkamp speaks here of the effectiveness of networks and cooperations (cf. Steinkamp, 2013: 10).

123 Also I_73: 26, I_45: 533-535, I_67: 14-16, I_15: 205, I_50: 157, I_9/I_10: 128, I_28: 6, I_69: 28, 34.

124 Also I_50: 157, I_56: 3, I_75: 15, I_7: 534-540.

125 Also I_22: 28, I_54: 195, I_15: 47, I_58: 10, I_43: 3, Garcia dos Santos (2011: 55).

126 See also I_75: 14, I_49: 87, Ch. 5.1, 5.2, 6.1 and 6.2.

127 See also I_37: 30-31, I_62: 11, I_20: 60.

as a rule make cooperation more difficult (cf. I_32: 18, I_70: 50).[128] The next step is therefore to clarify what these unequal starting points are that limit equality and lead to hierarchy.

5.9.1 The Structure of Cooperation: Inequality leads to Hierarchy

"Different levels of contributions to the collaborations lead to problems and tensions." (I_67: 3) A donor-beneficiary relationship is not compatible with a partnership of equal (cf. I_20: 57, I_18: 28, I_56: 11). Because of their ability to contribute a different type and amount of resources, inequality and therefore hierarchies of power and control arise between the partners in a cooperative project (cf. I_20: 51-52, Seubert, 2009: 89). This is particularly the case with regard to financial resources, which are often contributed entirely by the Western partner (cf. I_75: 5, I_70: 18, 26-28, 86).[129] German-Indian cooperation projects are often 100 per cent financed by institutions like the MMB (cf. I_69: 84, I_66: 71), or the German partner applies for grants from German donors, without the Indian partner having the chance to see or contribute to the content of the application (cf. I_75: 5, I_70: 26-28). Indeed, the Indian partner is not allowed to submit an application on their own (cf. Dickersbach, 2013: n.p.): "There is a complete inequality from the very beginning that can only be got rid of with great difficulty if at all." (I_70: 26) This asymmetry of give and take is also made clear in the fact that other resources are unable to balance out this financial dominance: "You know the West has the money and we have the so-called resources [sarcastic laugh – author] the kind of 'intellectual resources'." (I_61: 32-33, see also Dickersbach, 2013: n.p.)[130]

The party receiving funds feels beholden to the giver, while the giver feels superior to the receiver (cf. I_32: 32-33). This leads to a certain dominance on the part of the actors that contribute the financial resources to the cooperation project (cf. I_26: 35, Rautenstrauch *et al.*, 2003: 83). They are the ones who decide what, how, and with whom action is undertaken because of their financial superiority (cf. I_25:

---

128 Only one German artist was of the opinion that hierarchies could make cooperation in the partnership easier, because they provide a clear structure for activities and responsibilities meaning that the partners no longer need to distribute tasks and responsibilities.

129 Also I_11: 69-70, I_50: 157, I_48: 3, I_20: 14, 46, I_30: 4, I_1: 18-19, I_25: 20, I_32: 61, I_43: 24-25, I_31: 27, I_18: 2, I_72: 19-20, I_69: 106, Lechner (2004: 290). Cf. here also Ch. 5.4.3 and 2.3: Social capital provides access to economic resources.

130 The manner of spoken speech is not usually commented on. Here it makes the meaning of the sentence clearer.

50, 58, I_1: 18-19). Their economic capital allows them to realise their own intentions, and to override or silence the voice of their partner (cf. Dickersbach, 2013: n.p.):

> And that meant we had it double, that we always sat down afterwards and exercised financial control. And in that way I didn't and do not let the power go out of my hands, for my own interests – that is my own artistic interest. I decided what happened with the money [...]. I have a budget in my hand and I decide who gets more money, who gets less [...]. I dominated that quite strongly. (I_25: 58)

At the same time, the German or Western partner that contributes the funding also bears the sole responsibility for proving its correct use for the purposes of the cooperation to the donor (cf. Dickersbach, 2013: n.p.). This increases the inequality of the actors even further:

> We had the money and we also had to have a whip in the hand to get hold of the receipts. We always asked: 'What did you spend that on? What is this expense here?' So actually it was a huge difference in position. (I_25: 63-64)[131]

Partners from the 'Global South', like those from India, therefore feel themselves of lesser value because of this financial inequality (cf. I_25: 26, I_32: 2-4). This is confirmed by the fact that they are furthermore not trusted as being worthy of finance (cf. Dickersbach, 2013: n.p.). As a consequence, they are not motivated to take over responsibility for the financial interests of the joint project (cf. I_70: 26-28).

As an artist from the 'Global South' commented at the *Theaterformen 2013* festival in Hannover: The existence of the money is not the problem, it is the way it is used that determines hierarchy. No partnership can be founded on the asymmetry that results from these financial conditions (cf. I_7: 540-546), because the content of the work and the goals of the partners cannot be discussed on the same level.

A further unequal precondition between the German and the Indian partners is presented by the actors' different level of professionalism – falling under Bourdieu's theory of cultural capital (cf. Ch. 2.3). While the Indian partners are often amateurs – artists who work because of their love for art, with mostly self-taught skills, who practice art along with the career that provides their livelihood – those from the West are often professional trained, and able to devote their lives to and earn a living from their art (cf. I_25: 18-20, I_62: 18-20):

131 Also I_25: 50, 58, I_20: 46, I_72: 4, 16, I_47: 31-35, I_70: 26-28, 86.

> It starts with the training. Of course we [the Germans] have been doing nothing other than theatre for [...] 15, 20, 25 years [...]. And then of course you don't find partners who you can speak to on the same dramatalogical level [...]. (I_70: 26-28)

This often leads to the establishment of a student-teacher relationship (cf. I_72: 19-20, I_75: 6),[132] where the German partner instructs, trains, and encourages his Indian 'students'. An Indian theatre producer explains:

> We still look up to the whites. It is a colonial remnant. In Bangladesh we say: 'The sahib has come.' That means 'master' [as teacher], [...] it is deeply rooted. (I_72: 32-34)[133]

On the one hand, the existence of this student-teacher relationship is a source of regret for the Germans (cf. I_68: 3, I_20: 57, I_68: 4),[134] on the other they confirm and strengthen this relationship in two ways. First of all, they think that it secures their professional and artistic quality (cf. Ch. 5.5.2), as the following quotation makes clear:

> Because I was the boss, there was a chance that there was an alright boss, and an orderly, sensible, artistically focused production, and that you could have an orderly product come out of it. (I_25: 50)

This manner of thinking is reflected in the Germans' action: "But when they wanted to do something with us, then they needed to understand that I didn't want to have any dance theatre scenes in my piece." (I_25: 72)

Secondly, famous German or Western artists are often invited to work with young undiscovered artists abroad. This leads to disparities in every cooperation – even entirely German ones:

> There is a German artist coming now who [...] will create an imbalance, because it is a name like Helena Waldmann. That means that there will already be an imbalance there because it is young Indian artists and an established German artist. Where this kind of thing happens, the Indian artist [...] completely withdraws. (I_69: 81, see also I_37: 82-83)

The rich experience and professional expertise of the German partner, based on decades of cultural practice (cf. I_25: 68), should not be

132 Also I_44: 35-36, I_39: 21, I_37: 14. It should be mentioned here that a student-teacher relationship is usual between Indians in the classical arts in the form of the guru-student relationship (cf. I_15: 207-209, I_73: 54).

133 See also here the statements of the German partner: I_25: 18.

134 The student-teacher relationship was also in evidence at the FACETS residence in the course of the Attakkalari dance Biennale. The mentors for the South East Asian residency participants were exclusively artists invited from the West.

diminished. However the question remains – how can the asymmetry be overcome? This poses a profound problem for the relation between the actors since the Indian partner is barely able to acknowledge their own abilities because of their profound feeling of inadequacy (cf. Liederer, 2013: 6), meaning that their experience and expertise cannot flow into the cooperative project.

As in the case of the student-teacher relationship, India's colonial history has a damaging effect on contemporary German-Indian relations, even though Germany had no role in the colonisation of the country (cf. Ch. 4.2). The aim of achieving an equal partnership between the former European colonial powers and their Indian colleagues seems incredible from the point of view of an Indian cultural actor:

> When people come to India from the West today, they have this idea that they want to be equal or on the same level. That is a very new thing. If we think back to when Westerners came to India fifty years ago to save India or to occupy India. The Westerners did not think about equality then! (I_72: 18)

India's colonial past continues to make itself felt, and produces an imbalance between the partners (cf. I_20: 51-52, I_32: 18),[135] particularly since the contemporary behaviour of the Western partners is so reminiscent of the actions of the colonial masters (cf. I_72: 55).[136] Indian artists are often selected to participate in German-Indian co-productions in order to embody the 'exotic': "And it was a little bit of brown skin, […] a little bit of Indian presence in the […] work which […] I don't remember enjoying it at all." (I_49: 155) In these circumstances, a hierarchy arises because of the overwhelming number of Indians artists in comparison to the German in a joint project (cf. I_49: 153): "Initially it was difficult, we felt overpowered by the number of Germans that came." (I_62: 16)

Finally, the infrastructural differences between Germany and India are decisive to the power relation between the participants in the cooperation (cf. I_37: 14, I_16: 12-13, I_39: 19). While institutional structures are barely existent in India, Germany has access to a global institutional network. As a consequence, individual Indian artists are placed in front of globally active German organisations:

> And this also comes in the virtue of Max Mueller being a much larger organisation or spread over multiple countries, we're two people living in

135 Also I_26: 38, I_25: 18; cf. also Sen (2007: 100 ff.).

136 Cf., for example, Ch. 3.2.4.

> New Delhi in India. So it's unfair to even think of it as an equal partnership […]. (I_50: 163)[137]

This leads to the consequence that the German institutions abroad generally do not have any Indian equivalent, but are only faced with individual artists. This provides imbalance from the very beginning of a relationship.

It can be summarised, that the influence of the participants on the function and product of a cooperation depends on the capital, resources, and abilities that they contribute, or are able to contribute to a partnership. The partners who are resource rich are able to exercise control. The partner who is unable to contribute – above all material – resources to a collaboration, is forced to obey:

> One party knows, the other doesn't. One gives orders, the other obeys. To bring it to a point: One has the first and last word, and the other is not allowed to think. (Garcia dos Santos, 2011: 55 f.)

5.9.2 "Equal Partnership"[138] and "Equality of the Partners":[139] Principle, Goal, or Utopia?

Many of those interviewed held that the inequality of the conditions between the partners in cooperative projects described here, which leads to the hierarchisation of cooperative structures, put paid to political claims of equal partnership, or dialogue between equals (cf. e.g. I_25: 18, 54, I_50: 157):[140]

> The much wished for equality […], that is always trumpeted in Germany is of course barely to be translated into the reality […]. (I_70: 26)

This means that there is a significant divergence between the political claims and the practical reality.

However, the representatives of the Indian cultural institutes and Indian stars provide one exception. Through their unique institutional power, connected to their level of fame and recognition, they are able to

137 See also I_47: 15-16, 29, I_44: 35-39.

138 Quoted from Lehmann (2008b: n.p.).

139 In German: Augenhöhe; literally, "eye-level". This term is often used with regard to intercultural cooperation, for example, on the website of the German Foreign Office: http://tinyurl.com/o86pa3o (Accessed: 12.11.2013).

140 See also I_63: 90-91, I_70: 50, I_26: 26-27, I_20: 54, I_1: 18-19.

represent themselves as entirely the equal of their foreign partners – above all the Goethe-Institut (cf. I_66: 85, 89, 151, 165, I_48: 2).[141]

According to the experts interviewed, an equality of position cannot exist alongside the pre-existing conditions of advantage and disadvantage created by the distribution of roles and positions amongst the members of the cooperation team on the basis of ability and experience (cf. I_50: 160, I_22: 28).[142] The position occupied by a particular actor allows him to be alone and completely responsible for the relevant area of competence. While their partners are able to express their opinion, they ultimately need to place their trust in the decision of the responsible person (cf. I_15: 205, I_9/I_10: 148, I_20: 53). According to the participants of the workshop *'Beispiele gelingender Kooperation (1) – Künstlerische Praxis und Improvisation'* (Examples of Successful Cooperation (1) – Artistic Practice and Improvisation) held from 21st-25th August 2012 at the *Ruhrtriennale* 2012-14, the trick here is 'delivering' in their own area of responsibility while taking into account those of their partners. According to this model, cooperation has the form of a "moving pyramid", according to which areas in require decisions to be taken (I_9/I_10: 149-151, see also I_20: 49).

This understanding of cooperation is accompanied by the following idea detailing how unequal power relationships can be avoided within a cooperating team (cf. Ch. 6.13): The production process and presentation of the artistic product of the cooperation project should be divided up in order to allow each partner to shape and bring out their own part of it independently. In this way, each of the partners is able to practice 'their own' art (cf. I_48: 22-23), while at the same time presenting a cooperative piece to the public through their appearance together (cf. I_15: 205, I_32: 17), one German artist describes this in the following terms:

> We [would] each be responsible for one part of the program on the evening. The sequences should be presented in turn. Each of the partners should at most be able to give their advice to the other, and then only if it is asked for.[143]

How far this form of collaboration can legitimately be called a partnership is questionable: "It seems like there's no partnership but actually for me that's an amazing partnership because we don't question each other. I trust him [...], he trusts me." (I_15: 205) This type of cooperation requires that the partners understand the art of their

141 Also I_39: 40-42, I_15: 213, I_13: 20-21, 27-28, I_47: 35, I_49: 21-28, 70-71, I_11: 15, I_54: 70, I_43: 2, I_20: 29, I_50: 62.

142 This excludes positions that are shared, meaning that at least two actors are required to work together in the same area of responsibility (cf. I_70: 50, I_25: 50, 56).

143 Quoted from an email from a German artist to the author. A copy of the email is archived by the author.

colleague, and are able to give his artistic practice their trust and estimation (cf. I_9/I_10: 150-151, Ch. 6.3, 6.4, 6.5).

One cooperating German-Indian team describes dialogue on equal terms as a "guiding light" (I_9/I_10: 151). Like the cooperative project itself, this form of dialogue is an idea that can often be aimed at but only seldom realised – and often then only after years of collaboration with a partner in the alien context of their reality (cf. I_32: 97). Bringing about this equality is therefore a long-term process involving years of work that requires sufficient time and funding to be possible (cf. I_73: 54, I_9/I_10: 151).

This is why the MMB views creating this kind of equality as being essential to its cultural program in India (cf. Ch. 2.2.1 and 2.2.2) and thereby a matter of course in its work with Indian artists, as a representative of the institute makes clear:

> In practical terms, [this kind of dialogue] can't work any other way. Either you have a dialogue on an equal footing or you don't have one at all. Otherwise you are teaching or presenting or imposing your views on somebody or whatever. [...] You have to be prepared to [have that kind of dialogue] as an institution, and you have to employ people who are also ready to do so. (I_42: 41-44)[144]

If in practical terms dialogue between partners on an equal footing is a given, then why do cultural institutions like the Goethe-Institut still have to explicitly specify the form as such. The explicit invocation of equality instead seems to draw attention to the fact that it remains elusive in a number of ways: "Discussion of dialogue at an equal level points to a lack of equality where it takes place. If it was indeed the case, there would be no need to place so much emphasis on the idea." (Gross, 2012: 22 f.) The same principle goes for the "partnership of equals" which is also often invoked but seldom implemented (Lehmann, 2008b: n.p.). Existing hierarchies of power – above all between European and non-European partners – cannot be levelled out, relativized, or veiled simply by expressions of a willingness to engage on an equal footing.

[144] Also I_69: 84, I_54: 13, 187-201.

Criteria for a Culture of Cooperation

Prospective Cultural Policy Measures

> I believe […], that it should come to an encounter between two artists. And that depends in a large part […] on how intensively one prepares that. That is actually the most important thing. […] That is […] to prepare as carefully as possible for an encounter on both sides. (I_42: 30)

The goal of this qualitative investigation is to present a portfolio of cultural policy tools for the management of the prerequisites, processes and structures of the individual phases, areas and aspects of international cooperation work. The prospective measures presented here comprise options and alternatives for the successful conception of future artistic cooperations in the international sphere and for planning the fulfilment of their many requirements. They are presented in conjunction with the answer to the question: Which cultural policy framework conditions are necessary for cultural creators in order to actually bring one of the "foundational motives of the FCP" – the "principle of dialogue" (Schwencke *et al.*, 2009: 38, cf. also Ch. 2.2) – as well as that of a dialogue of equals into practical reality? In other words – how is it possible to more closely approach the ideal of cooperation work? The results confirm that dialogue on an equal footing and a partnership-based cooperation cannot exist because, to date, the required cultural policy environment is lacking, so that cultural exchanges can only take place on a limited basis.

From the analysis of the expert interviews, there arise thirteen considerations for a new culture of cooperation in the international arts. The criteria for the proposed cultural policy measures which will be presented is their applicability and their feasibility. The goal of the recommended measures is a fair culture of cooperation in the FCP. This is essential in order to be able to realise partnership-based cooperations on the international scene (cf. Ch. 6.13).

The experiences which arise from the analysis of the interviews with the German and Indian cooperative project participants are valid in the first instance within the context of German-Indian cooperations from which they are drawn. Nevertheless, the following structural options for the initiation and conduct of international partnerships could be foundational for an international culture of cooperation – in particular between heterogeneous partners from the 'Global North' and the 'Global South.'[1] The conditions applicable to such a transfer of application are that the implications of the local conditions are not neglected and that the proposed cultural measures presented here are orientated to their context – that is, adapted to the characteristics, demands and resources available in the local situation to which they are to be applied (cf. Ch. 6.7). The Indian author, director, playwright and cultural scholar Rustom Bharucha emphasises: "The national context was far less important than the different regional and local contexts." (Fischer-Lichte/Bharucha, 2011: 7)

6.1 The "Development" of Partnership

Cooperations cannot be politically or bureaucratically 'prescribed', 'dictated' or 'announced' (cf. I_67: 35, 41, 50-53, I_30: 1).[2] Artists by themselves are capable of finding one another better than when they are brought together with a deliberate intention (cf. Sennett, 2012: 277). A meaningful mode of cultural sponsorship is to motivate actors who actually want to work together, as their shared aesthetic and artistic ideas and interests form the foundations for successful and long-lasting partnerships (cf. I_47: 22-23, I_49: 27, 170).[3] In order to identify such creative connections, artists must be able to contact and engage one another as part of a step-by-step encounter. As a representative of the IFAB (India Foundation for the Arts in Bangalore) explains:

> If you start a proper collaboration program the first thing you have to do is to provide people with money to go, see, talk, do a little bit of work, find the people with whom you feel you have some kind of connection, kind of ideas you are interested in, the nature of your practice, and then something clicks, a collaboration project might develop out of that [...]. It has to be a multi stage process. Artists get to know, understand each other. (I_67: 41, cf. also Vellani quoted in: ifa, 2013: 12)

In the future, a guiding concern must be to establish the means of contact described here. Cultural institutions such as the Goethe-Institut

---

1 This transferability will be made clear in the presentation of the results and prospects, when a possible form of partnership between the 'Global North' and the 'Global South' will be described arising from the experiences of German-Indian cooperation.

2 Also Hoffmann (1994: 17), Kämpchen (2013a: 67).

3 Also I_63: 39, 47, I_25: 44, I_72: 34, I_39: 33, I_62: 10, 30, I_37: 32, I_15: 13, Knüsel (2011: 71), Seubert (2009: 101 f.).

could take over this task (cf. Ch. 6.6).[4] The optimal structuring of these opportunities for encounter is crucial.

It is significant that platforms of exchange should be regularly and continually presented, in order that the artists should meet one another repeatedly and get to know each other extensively (cf. I_28: 112, I_32: 119).[5] In order to free participation in exchanges and cooperations from their exclusivity and ensure as wide as possible a participation (see Ch. 5.2, 5.3, 6.1), it is recommended that access to these platforms – which international cooperations arise from – should be opened to a multiplicity of actors (cf. I_58: 14). This is possible through supporting the mobility of potential co-operators in order to break the limited circle of artists supported by cultural institutes so far (cf. Ch. 6.6) and allowing the development of new locations – for example, outside of major cities (cf. I_35: 24-25, Ch. 2.2). A widened group of participants could also signify a break from the Western measuring stick which has been applied to the arts and, until now, has dominated them.

A platform of exchange cannot have as its aim the expected delivery of results (cf. Stepf, 2011b: n.p.). Ideally, it instead provides the conditions for partnerships – in that it offers cultural creators the space to begin to understand how they can work together (cf. I_67: 33-34, I_73: 34): "[I]t's a workshop, it's not such a complex thing but from that is the idea of something much larger and that's actually maybe a small part of something bigger later […]." (I_63: 108, cf. also I_15: 13, 99, 105, 121)

Within the conditions described above, such platforms would be an investment for the building of successful cooperations and networks (cf. I_54: 85-86, I_75: 26-30, I_39: 2) – in the sense of a "two-way structure of exchange" (Schönfeld, 2012: 16, cf. also Ch. 2.2).

---

4 In order to give an example here, the 'TURN' program from the 'Federal Cultural Foundation' (KSB – Kulturstiftung des Bundes) takes into account the requirements of the platform and provides a diverse array of opportunities for "gatherings" in their programs. The program description states: "In order to encourage thematic and artistic exchange between the partners, the Federal Cultural Foundation will organise a series of meetings for directors, curators, choreographers, writers, publishers, musicians, designers and filmmakers from the funded projects along with other experts in Germany and the participating African countries." (Quoted from http://tinyurl.com/mhreylu, Accessed: 24.10.2013)

5 Cf. here also I_63: 55, I_70: 54, 60, Ch. 6.8 and 2.1 as well as Staines (1996: 7). Repeated personal encounters – in order to learn to understand the partner and establish a position on the basis of mutual agreement. Repetition serves as an elementary component of cultural cooperation (cf. Sennett, 2012: n.p., Steinkamp, 2013: 13 and Ch. 2.1).

6.2 The Definition of the Basis of Cooperation: Who wants What, Why, and How?

The interests of cultural creators exert an influence on the shape of their cooperation work. Exchanges of views in relation to the aims and objectives of the participants – including a reflection and review of such expectations – do not take place. A German creative artist described the lack of such exchanges in the following terms:

> There were big mistakes made even in the development of the cooperation. There are questions that have to be clarified, openly and clearly, such as: What does [name of the Indian partner – author] want from [name of the German partner – author], what does [name of the German partner – author] want from [name of the Indian partner – author] and what do both of them want from the project? (I_70: 98-100)[6]

It is therefore in the first place to be recommended that the interests, goals and expectations are identified along with the partners at the beginning of the cooperation (cf. I_72: 30, I_70: 100). Along with the goals, it is also important that the roles and responsibilities, as well as the tasks and contributions are made clear (cf. I_37: 23), as partners are prone to understand and interpret the cooperation differently (cf. Mitra, 2004: 2 f. and Ch. 5.1). When the partners are aware of the expectations, the likelihood that they will be disappointed in the cooperation process is diminished.

> [N]ecessary for the collaborators [is] to […] clarify mutual expectations before the project gets underway, so that neither collaborator is unpleasantly surprised by the other's understanding of roles and responsibilities at a later stage. (Mitra, 1998a: 2)[7]

The statement and exchange of interests is the first step towards founding a partnership. This communication – where appropriate supported by an independent or external moderator (cf. Ch. 6.6) – fosters a trust (cf. I_19: 26-27) and a "transparency on both sides" (cf. I_20: 47),[8] which are prerequisite for a cooperation to take place on a mutual footing.

6 Cf. also Stepf (2011b: 1) and *id.* (2011a: n.p.). On the clarification of goals in cooperation work, see Rautenstrauch *et al.* (2003: 107, 116).

7 See also I_20: 47, Vellani quoted in: ifa (2013: 12), Rautenstrauch *et al.* (2003: 107), Holzberg (2009: 176).

8 On the fact that communication builds trust within a cooperation, see also Vittar (2008: 47), Holzberg (2009: 19, 80 ff.), Seubert (2009: 96) and Ch. 2.3. "Openness, transparency as well as reliability in terms of a timely information policy between the partners" are all proper to trustworthiness in communication (Holzberg, 2009: 84).

This approach, however, relies on the actors having undertaken a certain amount of reflection on their goals, as a German *dramaturg* notes:

> That should be something that comes at the beginning of a cooperation like this as well. What does everyone want with it? What does he expect for himself from it? How can I, how can my public, how [can] my team, and for that, that we had so clearly defined, that we just wanted to get our intercultural competence, we were concerned with that. That's also why a piece about intercultural conflicts. That was clear, that we also wanted to do that with the theme. Then, when you have that defined, you also work on it and then you also reap the benefits. (I_25: 82)

Open exchanges about one's own and others' goals are also important in order to learn to understand and acknowledge differing objectives (cf. I_70: 98-100), as well as to overcome mistrust between the partners as the following quotation illustrates:

> That there were indeed differences and that the [name of the Indian partner] maybe also had another, different interest, […] I [could] remember very well, that I [had] always tried with every project, so that I could set aside as much money as I could for my basic finances. Because I couldn't survive any other way […]. Then, suddenly, I could understand it. […] To take the perspective of the other person and just have a look, what could also be legitimate for them […] to have other interests in such a project than my own […], I am in a crisis of trust with you [Indian partner – author] and I want to say to you honestly why […]. Actually that isn't so bad, when you want something else and have other interests, but I think that we should talk about it openly. […] So that with the project we can also […] somehow improve other pieces for your theatre […] and when you say, […] we can bring in a project leader with that, then he can also at the same time do this and this for us, that's totally OK for me […], and that was sort of like a breakthrough. (I_25: 24-26)

As a second step, it is to be recommended that, the common goals and interests for the cooperation project are defined realistically and clearly alongside those of the individual participants (cf. I_25: 4, 26, I_32: 54-59).[9] This encompasses the development of a common artistic understanding (cf. Ch. 6.5). In the case of a conflict situation, these common goals, interests and understanding can – as the "lowest common denominator" (I_70: 98-100) – relieve some of the burden on the relationship and help to solve the problem:

---

9 See also I_14: 15, I_75: 25, I_49: 29, I_39: 35-36, I_9/I_10: 46, I_47: 29, Srivatsan (2002: 1), Wartemann (2002: 105).

> Finding the right balance between collective and individual expression [...]. This approach of allowing their individual concerns [...] while framing it within a complex collaborative process, enabled them to resolve intense moments of conflict around ideas and methodologies, without feeling a sense of loss. (Mitra, 2004: 3)

When goals – both individual and collective – are communicated transparently, it becomes possible for all partners to react to them by, for example, discussing the goals themselves, negotiating with one another and allowing them to be tailored to fit their mutual requirements (cf. I_67: 10, I_75: 25, I_70: 98-100). Alternatively, the participants may discover that they are unable to undertake a cooperative project due to insurmountable differences: for example, because they would have to sacrifice or place at risk their 'individuality'[10] in favour of the common partnership (cf. I_55: 7, I_9/I_10: 122-126, I_16: 15-16).

An advantage of this discussion of goals at the beginning of the cooperation is that the meaningfulness (or, respectively, 'pointlessness') of a partnership can be discerned at an early stage. A reflection on and assessment of the goals and expectations during the cooperation enables the modification and renegotiation of the interests involved (cf. Holzberg, 2009: 143 f.). Apart from this, an ongoing dialogue with regard to goals is also a means through which power relations can be brought into balance (cf. Rautenstrauch *et al.*, 2003: 85).

6.3 Understanding Cultural Contexts through Research

A cooperative project will be shaped by the reality in which it is anchored (cf. I_11: 15). It is therefore necessary for the participants to be aware of this reality. As research shows, German creatives generally have a limited knowledge of the cultural and political history of India, as well as of its artistic and cultural landscapes – including the locally active cultural institutions and actors.

Anmol Vellani, founder of the IFAB, explained the expectations that Indian cultural creators have of German artists and cultural institutions in the context of the Brussels Conference of European external cultural relations – 'Expectations from the outside' on the 12th December 2012:

> We expect European artists [and European institutions – author] to be thoroughly orientated in the context they will work in [...], to educate themselves about the regions where they wish to develop cultural relations.

10 Here, amongst other things, their values, aesthetic views, etc.

> Do your homework! [...] Seek information, leverage knowledge, networks and insights of [...] cultural institutions, not just government, [...] before deciding which European artists, expert or institutions should engage [...], be well prepared in terms of infrastructure. (Vellani quoted in: ifa, 2013: 12)[11]

On the basis of this unmistakable challenge, finding an answer to the following question moves to the centre: How can the European ignorance that leads to asymmetrical cultural relations and limits the possibilities of exchanges be overcome?

According to the statements of the interviewees, it is with an investigation of the literature or a search on the internet that they take their first steps towards orientating themselves in foreign contexts (cf. I_20: 23-24).[12] An introduction to the art and culture scene of the city of Bangalore, for example, is offered by the online journal 'Art and the City'.[13] It is doubtful, however, if such a prospect is sufficient to prepare German cultural workers to take part in cooperations with their Indian colleagues in an Indian context (cf. I_72: 22). Added to this is the problem that many Indian cultural actors are unable to present themselves and their work over the internet, since access to the web is limited and, therefore, exclusive (cf. I_68: 19-20).[14] This exclusivity with regard to the digital world is often the deciding factor in the question of who takes part in international partnerships and who does not (cf. Frieling, 2000: 36, Knopp, 2006: 118, Sennett, 2012: 145). Additionally, this exclusivity creates limitations with regard to content (cf. Hoffmann, 1998: 23). Digitisation has revolutionised and simplified cooperative work worldwide (cf. I_63: 60-61, Holzberg, 2009: 3). New communities of participants have been created (cf. I_9/I_10: 68, I_45: 73, I_28: 36), but this is "no guarantee of democratic, equal participation" (Frieling, 2000: 36, cf. Ch. 2.3).

It would seem that research taking place at the location in question would be a more effective and meaningful way "to encounter the art and

11 The speech makes it understood that Anmol Vellani has both the artists and cultural institutions of Europe in mind. See also I_63: 14.

12 Sometimes they take their first steps through consultations with colleagues and friends with knowledge of the host country, or with expatriates from the host country living in Germany with whom they may not be previously acquainted (cf. I_20, Stepf, 2011b: n.p.).

13 The online journal is accessible at: www.goethe.de/artandthecity (Accessed: 13.10.2013).

14 Amongst the reasons for the limited access are: Internet connections often exist only in large conurbations, the prohibitive expense of internet connections, a difficulty in becoming proficient with new technologies, a limitation by official censors on which websites can be visited, etc. (cf. CSCS/Centre for the Study of Culture and Society in Bangalore, 2012: 10, Answer to Question 8).

the living environment of the partner at the beginning of cooperative work" (Stepf, 2011b: 1 f.). Cultural institutions, such as the Goethe-Institut would be able to support creatives in their contextual orientation, as an Indian cultural worker explains:

> [O]ne simple straight forward point is that if they [the MMB, Max Mueller Bhavan – the Goethe-Institut in India – author] want to invite artists from there [Germany – author] to here [India – author] it's a good first step to understand the landscape. (I_63: 14)

Research trips enable artists to explore and establish connections for themselves within local structures, as a statement from this German cultural worker shows:

> In the meantime, I've got to know many personalities of the Indian theatre scene […]. I deal with the reality of my colleagues' lives: how they live, how they think, how they make theatre in India, what the conditions are that they are working in. (I_70: 92)

If it were possible to repeat these research trips, so that several encounters might take place between the partners, a relationship based on trust could be built up between the partners in order to create the conditions for a cooperative project, as the *dramaturg* describes:

> My Indian colleagues began to trust me – to trust that I understand Indian themes and that I can bring Indian reality on to the stage – that I can write pieces with them that will be understood in India, and move people, move an Indian audience. (I_70: 92, see also I_72: 3)

Even a merely rudimentary understanding of a foreign context demands exhaustive research, along with the expenditure in time and money which that requires. Such searches for contextual orientation can only succeed, therefore, when their time and finances are carefully accounted for (cf. Stepf, 2011b: 1 f.). Cooperation sponsors such as the Goethe-Institut, are aware, however, that the time set aside for the project and the money which is placed at the disposal of cultural workers do not allow them the freedom to undertake preliminary research into either their partners or the artistic and cultural landscape in which they operate (cf. I_54: 4, I_20: 23-24).[15] Understanding the contexts in which one's partner is operating,

---

15 It should be pointed out here that the TURN program of the KSB which promotes artistic partnerships between Germany and African states does so while taking into account a research period. It states in the program description: "In the first round of applications, the Foundation awarded one-time funding to project-preparatory research projects […]." (Quoted from the website: http://tinyurl.com/mhreylu,

is a significant factor in the success of partnerships. It is time for sponsors to acknowledge and support the acquisition of such contextual knowledge commensurately with its high importance (cf. Dickersbach, 2013: n.p.). This approach would also ensure that, in accordance with the principle of the 2005 UNESCO Convention, knowledge of cultural diversity would continue to grow (cf. Ch. 2.2).[16]

6.4 Intercultural Competence through Intercultural Training

As the results of this investigation show, the inability to understand the artistic and cultural mores of the other party leads them to go unobserved in some cases – providing a source of conflict and misunderstanding which essentially arises from an ignorance and lack of knowledge. Alongside open conflict, inner conflict can also often arise in the forms, for example, of the feelings of shame, guilt and anger (cf. I_32: 41, 45, 71, 81). Both forms of conflict lead to relationship problems (cf. I_70: 8). This begs the question: How can this potential for conflict be minimised?

> The translation of partners' interactions and communication due to different cultural backgrounds is the tremendous achievement of every partnership in order that the collaborative work with each other can be continued. (I_68: 15-16, cf. also I_16: 1-2, I_32: 24-28)

The "translation" of interaction and communication between the partners mentioned in this quotation requires – alongside the appropriate contextual orientation previously discussed (cf. Ch. 6.3) – knowledge of other cultures, languages, and artistic practices. However, knowledge alone is not sufficient. A competent engagement with the cultural and aesthetic practices of the partner land is significant. Currently, both knowledge and engagement from the parties is assumed, but are only actually present in the rarest of cases. The case studies presented in this dissertation, and the discussion above of the challenges presented by differences in cultures document a lack of intercultural and linguistic preparation (cf. also I_16: 20-21, I_70: 44-45). At the "Artistic Co-production" workshop of the 57th Loccum Cultural Policy Colloquium in 2012, a German cultural

---

Accessed: 24.10.2013) Though Dickersbach has made the criticism that ten research projects costing 9000 EUR each would make most budgets laughably low if these "fact-finding missions" are to be considered prerequisites of a successful cooperation (Dickersbach, 2013: n.p.).

16 Chapter 3 of this dissertation also makes it clear how important contextual knowledge is, regardless of the type of activity in question.

worker posed the question: "Why should we be considered intercultural competent simply by virtue of our special gifts as 'culture people'?" Cultural creators are not themselves per se culturally sensitive. It would be an unrealistic presumption to proceed on the understanding that they are able to work in any given intercultural situation without preparation (cf. also I_22: 25-26).

The cultural sector is currently trying various methods of improving or compensating the lack of intercultural training within its ranks:

One possibility is to 'play off' differences and arguments about cultural and artistic peculiarities against one another thematically as part of the cooperative piece:

> Our theatre selves, with our doubts about the play, our doubts about each other, and even the many cultural jokes we cracked about each other in rehearsals, found their way into the play. (Majumdar, 2012: n.p.)[17]

A second option is to use an intermediary to accompany the process of working together who will play the role of a verbal and aesthetic translator:

> On the other hand, I only realised for the first time that I was utterly full of prejudice and fear – and that it is so helpful. It wasn't just that he [the intermediary – author] said to me once, for example: look at it from the other perspective, but rather also to simply take on that perspective one time. (I_25: 38)[18]

A prerequisite for the role of intermediary is "to be at home in both worlds" (I_20: 21) and to enjoy the acceptance of all of the participants in the cooperation. Along with the option of verbal translation also comes the danger that things may not be represented as they are intended and that non-verbal aspects of communication – such as the tone and intention – can get lost: as was reported in the case of a creative artist who was interviewed with regard to his experience of working with translators in European-Indian partnerships in the visual arts (cf. I_68: 3).

A third possibility is the provision of intercultural training sessions for all participants in the cooperation, in order to enable an understanding of the other partner within the context of their cultural difference, and so that the encounter does not fail at the outset due to cultural misunderstandings, as the following quotation from an interview makes clear:

17 Also I_26: 3, I_25: 58, 72, I_70: 50, I_14: 15, Wartemann (2002: 106).

18 See also I_22: 25-26, I_63: 61, I_70: 52, I_16: 22, Rautenstrauch *et al.* (2003: 120).

> When I first started working in India twelve years ago [...] I fell into almost all of the intercultural traps myself [...]. And I did a project that ended up going wrong in a really big way. (I_70: 44)

When the participants know and understand their intercultural differences, as well as why and how their partners react because they can view things from the perspective of the other party, it becomes possible for them to deal with the culturally specific interactions of their partners. They become capable of reacting in a culturally sensitive manner (cf. Stepf, 2011b: 1), for example, to the culturally-specific organisational structure in which the partner operates, or their unfamiliar style of communication. The aim of intercultural training is not to perpetuate stereotypes (cf. I_32: 5, I_26: 7-9, I_22: 14-23, I_72: 20) but to work as a cooperative team to identify and deconstruct assumptions with relation to the partners (cf. I_25: 10, 38, Wartemann, 2002: 95, 100).

However, in practice, intercultural training has its limits. Behind the acts of the cultural subject are individuals who act and communicate subjectively (cf. I_70: 28, 50) and therefore in a manner which defies 'typical' cultural norms:

> So, in the Indian style we would have started half an hour later. That would have been no problem. And he wanted to set an example that we were going to be starting absolutely [...] punctually [...] with this thing. Almost as if he was trying to push back and say: 'I do not want to be an Indian'. (I_32: 51)

Conflict can also arise from these individual postures. However, they can be more often traced back to an impoverished understanding of cultural differences, as a creative artist who dealt in depth with the concept of intercultural competence in the course of his international partnerships comments:

> If I hadn't been extremely concerned with why things go wrong, and how they work and why they work like that, I wouldn't have recognised at that time then why everything went wrong. [...] A lot of artists just say: "Yeah, it was kind of [...] strange." And [...] then you can see [...] they simply haven't thought about it on that kind of level, why something has gone wrong. Then you say: "There are interpersonal problems". (I_70: 44-45)

When cultural workers reflect together on the problems which they have with one another – rooted in linguistic, cultural and artistic differences, they open up room to manoeuvre (cf. I_22: 24), and it becomes possible for the team working on the cooperation to "find a common way forward" (I_20: 50) and to be "successful" together (I_25: 44).[19]

---

19 Also I_9/I_10: 6, 95-99, I_26: 6-9, I_15: 47, 207, I_32: 49, I_16: 6-7.

The strategy described here for dealing constructively with cultural diversity, however, in itself requires a certain degree of intercultural competence – which can be imparted by intercultural training. It seems sensible, therefore that the participants are prepared both 'here' as well as 'there' with this training on cultural encounters. A German *dramaturg* illustrates this approach as follows:

> Even before we concerned ourselves with the theatre, or with the theme of the piece, we dealt with the different cultural backgrounds on both sides. We went to a lot of Indian theatre. We [...] went to a lot of Opera, we showed them our castles [...], we ate their food, and they ate our food. (I_25: 38)[20]

Intercultural differences remain present throughout the cooperation process. Alongside the many requirements for preparing cooperations in the sense of an engagement with the culture of the partner, process-oriented intercultural training could also be taken into consideration.

As with the process of becoming familiar with the cultural context, the task of understanding cultural differences can be made easier through repeated – and therefore ever deeper – work and life experiences in foreign contexts (cf. I_70: 44-45, 90-94, I_32: 49, 103). Ongoing exchanges over years, or even decades, allows the understanding of the other culture and its artistic traditions to grow (cf. I_70: 54, I_25: 44, I_32: 41).[21] This can lead to the success of even the most challenging of cooperative projects (cf. I_69: 34, I_30: 7). The experts interviewed indicate that foreign cultures are easier and more quickly 'read' when the participants in intercultural encounters have the opportunity for repeated practice in doing so (cf. I_70: 97-98, I_9/I_10: 31, 143, I_20: 16).

6.5 Developing a Common Language

As English is, as a rule, the favoured worldwide language for international cooperation, it would be useful for a participant whose grasp of English was not sufficiently fluent to undergo a preparatory language course. Even a basic attempt to learn the language of the host country, such as Hindi, seems worthwhile, in order to pay tribute to its cultural value: "Even the attempt to speak a few phrases in the local language opens people's hearts." (Thomas Lennertz, quoted in: Stiller-

20 See also I_15: 65 and Stepf (2011b: 1): "Affording Hospitality" [Original title: Gastfreundschaft leisten können]. Hospitality is "essential to the success of intercultural dialogue" (Deutsche UNESCO-Kommission e. V., 2010: 9 f.).

21 See also the Indian perspective, which reaches similar conclusions (I_63: 59), and Ch. 4.

Kern, 2013: 47)[22] When the borders of linguistic communication have been reached, nonverbal communication can be tried out. The artistic participants can find a common language through the use of alternative forms of dialogue, such as visual, audial and tactile interactions (cf. Trunk, 2011: 61, Schneider, 2011e: 34). A German artist reports on a successful production "where nobody was at home in the language of the others – everything worked by trying out music and facial expressions" (I_77: 2, on this, see Ch. 5.6., 6.5 and 6.10). Aesthetic language, therefore, is not just about separation, but also about unification. On the artistic level, the artists can understand one another, even though the differences of culture and spoken language prevail between them. Artistic cooperations, therefore, encompass the chance to bring together separate cultures and languages through artistic expression.

Communication between all participants should ideally take place throughout the whole course of the cooperation process in a transparent manner (cf. I_49: 36, 45). Within the context of an ongoing understanding, conflicts can be pre-emptively discussed, and an ongoing process of adjustment can be guaranteed – for example, with regard to the overall objectives of the project (cf. Holzberg, 2009: 19, 137, Ch. 6.2). Above all, this approach builds trust between the partners and secures the dialogue between them (cf. Mitra, 1998a: 2).

The understanding of another culture – as a condition for a meaningful and successful cooperation – takes time, as one German artist remarks:

> So things like that I had to learn step by step. So I thought that I'm over the years now. Now we are in 2012 that I'm prepared to do differences. And I was partly prepared but not fully. (I_9/I_10: 89-91)[23]

In the future, the specific contextual and cultural features and characteristics of a cooperation should be accounted for in planning the finances and timetable of a project in order that the participants may, for example, have the chance to live together for at least a few weeks, during which they can eat, sleep and work together (cf. I_68: 10-11, I_58: 8, I_16: 14-16).[24] This close coexistence naturally brings conflict, but it also enables the conscious construction of a partnership (cf. I_32: 71, I_72: 21):

- the partners get to know one another[25]

---

22 Also Wieck (2006a: 3), Stepf (2011b: 1), Lechner (2004: 291), Knopp (2006: 120).

23 Also I_42: 46, I_32: 45, 103, I_70: 50-54, I_31: 29-30.

24 Cf. also Kämpchen (2013a: 67): "The ideal kind of exchange is living together in an enclosed space."

25 Cf. I_45: 94, I_70: 103-104. See also Ch. 6.1.

- the partners get to know each other's work and life situations[26]
- they become (more) intercultural competent[27]
- they absorb one anothers' aesthetic understanding[28]
- they are able to communicate extensively[29]
- they are able to develop the cooperation project[30]
- they are able to experiment together[31]

6.6 External Guidance: Context-sensitive Cultural Institutes and Sponsors

This section clarifies the ideal roles and functions which institutions for international cooperation projects are able to take up. Rather than initiating partnerships themselves, it would be of value if they were to establish regular platform events, in order to offer creatives the possibility to encounter one another on a regular basis and find partners independently (cf. I_67: 48, I_39: 2).[32] In doing so, cultural institutions like the Goethe-Institut would become established as "forums for dialogue", as they were originally conceived by the cultural policy makers of the 1970s (Kathe, 2005: 59, see also Ch. 2.2). Institutionally-based encounter programs "are based on the so-called contact hypothesis: that the consequence of intensifying interaction is increased and differentiated knowledge of both sides, an experienced similarity, and an intensification of feelings of sympathy from both sides which leads ultimately to the deconstruction of prejudices […]." (Nestvogel, 2010: 133 f.)

These platforms additionally offer the opportunity for participants to reflect on and exchange their experiences of cooperation projects (cf. Ch. 6.12). Serving as observer allows the institutions the possibility of understanding cooperation work in its various contexts – something which is indispensable in their primary role as sponsors (cf. Dickersbach, 2013: n.p.).

Locally acting cultural institutions such as the Goethe-Institut have the great advantage that they understand the cultural activities of both the German as well as the Indian partners within their respective cultural

26 Cf. I_28: 36, I_72: 22-23 and Ch. 6.3; mutual experience of life and work situations is only possible when the home life of those on both sides of the partnership is experienced by the other (see Ch. 6.8).

27 See I_72: 12 and Ch. 6.4.

28 Cf. IFAB (2000: 18), Stepf (2011b: n.p.).

29 See I_32: 67, 71, I_75: 4, I_31: 10.

30 Cf. I_37: 26-28, I_31: 10, I_28: 36, 82, I_72: 17, Majumdar (2012: n.p.) and Ch. 6.8.

31 See I_45: 122-124, 130, I_15: 13 and Ch. 6.10.

32 Cf. also I_66: 27 and Ch. 6.1.

context. They are therefore able to act as intermediary and translator within the cooperation project (cf. I_16: 3-5, I_54: 195, I_28: 68). In the case of conflicts or crises in the partnership, they can also play a useful role as moderator and mediator who is well informed about, and sensitive towards, cultural differences:

> Some of the projects [i.e. cooperations – author] [...] were troubled by contention over issues of leadership, cultural difference, ownership and equity, and programme staff [employees of the IFAB – author] were called upon to function in various capacities – as motivators, intermediaries, arbitrators, crisis managers and sympathetic critics [...] in order to ease the stresses and strains of the partnerships, help settle differences and explore a viable way forward. (IFAB, 1998: 3)[33]

Were the cultural institutes to take over the role of intermediary discussed in this quotation, a balance of influence with regard to the various relevant interests within the cooperation would be ensured. A basic condition of a partnership on equal terms could thereby be guaranteed. Cultural institutions have a stabilising – rather than a dominating – effect when acting as mentor to a cooperation, and continuity within such partnerships can be expected.

It is an essential condition of the external guidance role discussed here that the institutions fulfil their task in a manner which is sensitive to the context and cultures which are involved (cf. I_49: 113-115, I_78: 13).[34] The relevant institutional agents can gain this essential cultural sensitivity and contextual orientation in the field by conducting an ongoing dialogue with the cultural workers concerned (cf. I_49: 6, I_54: 149, I_42: 50). For many of those consulted, the benchmark of contextual orientation for an institution is the financing of projects which have no relation to its 'origins', but which are in the first place intended to meet a requirement of the local scene:

> [I]t's really good to have people like the Goethe who don't push an agenda of their own. But rather just watch what's happening and [...] provide a supportive layer. You know and they're very sensitive in that. (I_63: 24)[35]

---

33 Also I_62: 21, I_67: 25-30, I_32: 21, 107, I_37: 29, 74, I_54: 195, Rautenstrauch *et al.* (2003: 120), Sennett (2012: 228).

34 See also I_62: 6-7, I_42: 40, I_70: 95-96, I_1: 8, I_32: 17, I_28: 32, 128, I_66: 88-89, I_13: 7-9, I_45: 26, 101, 165, I_75: 26-30, I_54: 135, 147, 205, 207, I_33: 14, I_5: 7, Holzberg (2009: 80), Ch. 6.3 and 6.4.

35 Also I_39: 3-4, 7, I_29: 2, I_30: 5, I_49: 2-8, 87, 113-115, I_62: 6-7, I_75: 26-30, I_11: 3, 15, I_5: 5, I_13: 7-9, 23-24, I_54: 169, I_66: 7, I_45: 311-316, Wittek (2006: 234) und Bloch (2010: 16).

Instead of fulfilling essentially the role of a finance institution by providing grants on the basis of funding applications (I_42: 41-44), the creatives surveyed call on the institutes to "get involved in the local cultural scene" (I_42: 41-44) and to independently widen the range of people who they work with. In this regard, an Indian creative artist singles out the attitude of the IFAB as an example of best practice:

> They [IFAB – author] go hunting. And I think it's such an intelligent way of doing it, because you don't wait for people who thought of coming to you. You also go looking for people who haven't thought of coming to you, […] but who are still doing very good work. (I_49: 73)[36]

This direct and continuous contact with the scene is time intensive and demands engagement from those involved (cf. I_42: 50). This stands in contrast to the usual institutional practices of keeping personnel to a minimum and rotating staff (cf. I_30: 11, I_70: 96-97).[37] Employees of the Goethe-Institut in India stand out in this regard, in that they are highly connected to their host country and often engaged by the institute on a long-term, or repeated basis in India. It is by virtue of this that they obtain their in-depth knowledge of both culture and context. They are specialists in their region and can be effective facilitators for cooperations in that they are aware of local potential and how to support it.

6.7 Context-oriented Transfer

The context within which culture is produced and consumed is recognised as having meaning (cf. Ch. 5.5.1 and 6.3). This recognition has a determinative effect on further actions and exchanges.

An expert is able to serve as a medium via which the experience and knowledge which he has gained in his field can be accessed by a partner. It must be left to the partner, however, to accept it or not. As put forward by Dahrendorf and Lepenies in the 1970s and 1990s (cf. Ch. 2.2), this knowledge ought not to be transferred mechanically, but actively. When an expert shares his knowledge and his experience, he must allow his counterpart the space to adapt that knowledge and so apply it to the situation where it will be put to use – as an Indian cultural worker explains:

> Expose them to your experiences of finding answer to your challenges in your conditions and leave it to them what to adapt and adopt in their own

36 Also I_42: 41-44, I_68: 20, I_66: 157-159, I_69: 148.

37 See also Ch. 2.2.2 and 4.1.

> environment. (I_78: 29-31, see also Vellani quoted in: ifa, 2013: 15 f., Gieler, 2010: 44)[38]

This means, on the other hand, that those who are exposed to such knowledge ought to critically examine what they are learning from the experts and make it appropriate to their reality (cf. I_72: 45-46, I_61: 34-37). Context-orientation is, therefore, one condition for not falling into neo-colonial structures. As Roberto Ciulli, founder and artistic leader of the *Theater an der Ruhr* points out with regard to the international work of his house:

> We must be careful that we do not operate a new kind of colonialism with our work with the international course, and just exploit these artists from Iran, Asia and Africa. That can happen very quickly if we don't take the time to enter into long-term relations with these artists and confront their cultural and political contexts over an extended period. (Ciulli quoted in: Raddatz, 2013: 16)

As illustrated in the results section, the transfer of knowledge and experience can only be successful when a transfer, or translation, into their context takes place – for example, through an informed actor from the local scene (cf. I_21: 6, I_14: 16).[39] Another possibility would be to engage local, rather than expatriate trainers (cf. I_21: 6), who would be able to convey their context-specific experiences and locally-acquired knowledge. Prerequisite to this, however, is that there are experts in the local cultural landscape present in the first place. Because of the limited possibilities for training and the difficulty of practicing art professionally, the number of such experts is very low (cf. Ch. 3.2.2).

A further step towards placing the partnership on an equal foundation is to pose the question to the Western partner – or, as it may be, the partner from the 'Global North' – "What do you think we have to offer you? What do you want to learn from us?" (I_78: 28) Furthermore, the 'Global South' partners must be able to confidently ask what they are able to give to their Western partners – because both sides have expertise and knowledge to offer (cf. I_72: 26, I_20: 47). Martin Kämpchen stresses, for example, the things that Germans are able to learn from their Indian

---

38 The 'learning community' called for by Lepenies ought to be remembered here (cf. Ch. 2.2).

39 Also Gieler (2010: 44). A key role is played here, for example, by the local and regional staff from the Goethe-Institut (cf. I_66: 157), in order to secure a contextual reference, since they are often intermediaries between the director of the institute and local artists (cf. Kämpchen, 2004: 33). Although the project on the ground is particularly dependent on the social, cultural and structural relationships with local staff, they are often incorporated in the decision-making structures of the institute in a limited way.

partners: "high flexibility, adaptability, spontaneity and the willingness to live in the moment" (Kämpchen, 2013a: 66, cf. also Vellani quoted in: ifa, 2013: 15 f.).

Rather than continuing to allocate money and time to the useless and ineffective transfer of European or Western strategies and concepts, it seems advisable that partners in future cooperative projects between the 'Global North' and the 'Global South' develop new approaches and strategies oriented towards their individual experiences of life and work. This approach enables the participants to create their own local and regional solutions, and would do justice to the FCP's claim to offer "cultures help to help themselves" (cf. Schneider, 2011d: 21, see also Ch. 2.2).

6.8 Reciprocal Hosting, Project Phasing, Process-oriented Support

The location of the cooperation must – according to the various goals of the partners – be discussed before the beginning of the project (cf. I_15: 211). This also implies a conclusion as to the definition of the target group. It would be helpful here if the habits of institutions in addressing their target groups – with regard to the locations for receptions and productions – could be changed (cf. Ch. 2.2 and 6.1). Discovering new and alternative locations, however, costs time (cf. I_20: 17).

If an approach towards a process of mutual exchange is desired, then the entire development process of the cooperative work should take place in both Germany and India – in order that both partners have the chance to discover the environment of the other. A mutual exchange also means that the result of the cooperation project should be presented in India as well as Germany. Or is what is learned, experienced and created 'there' of too little worth 'here' – amongst the diverse and comprehensive infrastructure of Germany – to be shown, shared and reflected upon? The promise of a cultural policy of dialogue (cf. Ch. 2.2) must be practically implemented – in particular to pay the artists the appropriate respect (cf. Schmid, 1997: 59 ff.) – and to make foreign cultural work fit for the future (cf. Lechner, 2004: 292). Both locations – Germany and India must be integrated in the cooperation process and that of the presentation of its result, so that there can be an "equality of give-and-take", and that the German FCP can have an effect in German society (Bauer, 2010: 96 f.).[40] It will be necessary to increase the financial resources for cooperations in

[40] The discussion with regard to the connection 'of the internal and external' through 'feedback' is not a central concern of this work. On this, see Schneider (2008a: 8), Kettner (2009: 243) and Schneider (2011d: 22), cf. also Ch. 2.2 and 7.

order to reach this "reciprocity of cultural relations" (Hamm-Brücher/ Auswärtiges Amt, 1982: 191 f., cf. also Ch. 2.2).

The cooperative artistic piece arises out of several phases. It is accordingly logical that a timeframe is devised which takes the requirements of these individual phases into account. In particular, the many requirements of preparation demand time – to allow the members of the cooperation to understand the form, goal and potential of their work. In many partnerships, however, this preparation has, up till now, been allocated no time. As the results show, the time required for a cooperation project is dependent on various factors:

- Goal(s) of the cooperation[41]
- Orientation of the cooperation: process or result?[42]
- Cooperation experience of the participating actors[43]
- Experience of the partners in joint projects
- Contextual and intercultural competence of the participating actors[44]
- The genre in which the cooperation is taking place

It would be ideal where these individual factors to be taken into account for the sponsorship of a project, rather than a rigid time frame for cooperative work being specified. This is, however, conditional on the understanding that time is allowed for as a meaningful resource of the cooperation process when it comes to financing the project. The time factor is immediately connected to the money factor: "And the money from [name of a foundation which sponsors international cooperation work in the arts – author] was just so super, because we had three years' time to really develop it piece by piece." (I_70: 20-21, cf. also I_45: 445)

With respect to the further and parallel obligations which the creative artists have alongside the production of the cooperative piece, the separation of the cooperation project into several distinct phases ought to be a consideration. The separation of the common project into phases with intervals in between allows breaks in which the participants are able to have time for alternative activities – ensuring that the participants retain their independence (cf. Ch. 2.1). Apart from this, the participating artists

41 If the goal is to build long-term structures, the time allowed must stand in relation to the desired change of outlook in the partner countries.

42 Time resources are spared, when it is decided from the beginning of the cooperation if the goal of the cooperation is the process itself or the result it produces (cf. Ch. 5.5.2 and 6.9).

43 Cf. Ch. 6.3.

44 See I_63: 15, I_25: 80, I_30: 10, Ch. 6.3 and 6.4.

use this free space to reflect on their projects and shared processes, and allow them to come to maturity (cf. I_45: 122): "[L]ifes of partnerships need that space and time [...] to expand, to stop and to take a pause to grow." (I_49: 37)[45]

This way of organising the process of cooperation has its price, however. It would require an increased number of journeys, which would overwhelm the current system of financial support: which is already barely able to provide one personal encounter (cf. I_45: 105, 111, I_70: 103-104). The process and experience of the *Schnawwl* and *Ranga Shankara* case studies, however, speak definitively in favour of the phased time-interval model (cf. Ch. 5.4.2).

In order to allow a cooperation to unfold, it would be ideal if the financial conditions of nationality, genres and themes could be replaced by a system of open sponsorship (cf. I_25: 4), in order to offer artists the freedom to decide for themselves what, with whom and how ought to be negotiated and undertaken.[46] An appropriate credo could be 'as few criteria as necessary, as much free space as possible'. A meaningful criteria for sponsorship could be the extent to which the applicants have dealt with the process of cooperation as preconditioned work (cf. Hasan, 2000: 5). A further possible criteria would be the context-orientation of the cooperation – as the IFAB has already employed in their cooperation program:

> Primarily, the question is [...] whether they are able to convincingly situate collaboration in the context of their current needs as artists and the way these needs relate to the field. (Hasan, 2000: 1 f., see also I_78: 21)

This framework of criteria brings sponsoring institutions with contextual orientation to the fore (cf. I_20: 47, I_29: 2).[47]

It would be meaningful to support cooperations generously according to their requirements (cf. I_78: 8-11) rather than handing out a fixed subsidy

45 Also I_70: 103-107, I_72: 10, IFAB (1999: 9 f.). During the breaks in their cooperative projects, most partners are able to use the internet to continue to work with one another (cf. I_45: 122). As an example of international cooperation undertaken in phases or intervals, mention could be made here of the work of the stage director Monika Gintersdorfer and the visual artist Knut Klaßen with the Ivoirian choreographer Franck Edmond Yao, also known as Gadoukou la Star. In 2005, they founded a multinational ensemble for the development of theatre and video projects in Germany and Cote d'Ivoire. Since 2012, they have been participants in the TURN program initiated by the KSB. See http://www.gintersdorferklassen.org/ and http://tinyurl.com/mhreylu (Both sites accessed: 24.10.2013).

46 In accordance with the artistic freedom described in Article 5, Paragraph 3 of the German Basic Law (cf. Ch. 2.2).

47 Cf. also Vellani (2009c: 194) and Ch. 6.6.

of predetermined size. This financial requirement is for the participants in the cooperation to determine, by sketching their planned working process – including the time it is expected to require. This move from a project to a process-oriented – and therefore long(er) term – mode of sponsorship[48] is one towards enabling an effective and sustainable partnership, by placing the cooperating parties in a situation of mutual responsibility for the professional use of the project's time, money and resources (cf. Steinkamp, 2013: 11). Furthermore, the cooperating partners can use this approach to influence their respective contexts on an ongoing basis (cf. I_50: 62, I_25: 24, 63-64, I_45: 320-321).

The desolate budgetary situation of the FCP[49] stands in contrast to its claim to long-term effectiveness. It follows that trends in the sponsorship of cooperative projects must be followed as the available funds are not set to grow in the future. Rather than the further sponsorship of many project-oriented co-productions, it is important that, in the future, generous and ongoing support should be given to fewer process-oriented partnerships. The character of these process-oriented projects renders them profitable, as the following chapter illustrates.

6.9 The Process as Result

The 'Arts' department of the British Council[50] in New Delhi has overcome the dichotomy between the orientation of cooperations towards either process or results and discontinued its support for Anglo-Indian cooperation in the arts (cf. I_38: 2-6). This 'no alternative' strategy, however, cannot be the solution to the problem.

Similarly to the interests of the parties involved in a cooperation, the orientation of the project must be identified and negotiated from the outset – particularly with the sponsors (cf. I_6: 12): "[I]t's a little bit of how do you structure it so that the expectations on both sides are clear." (I_63: 103, cf. Ch. 6.2) The key difference is between the two aspects of 'product' and 'process' (cf. I_73: 32): "So either I am making an artistic project or somehow a social or intercultural one, which doesn't [depend] on the artistic goal." (I_25: 44, cf. also I_38: 2-6) The likelihood that the

48 A period of several years are meant with the expression 'long-term' (cf. I_49: 76-79, I_45: 37, 54-62, 253, 320-321).

49 "The Foreign Office financed the programmes of cultural intermediary organisations with 284.5 million euros in 2012." Quoted from http://tinyurl.com/nsh76kn (Accessed: 16.03.2014) For the detailed finances of the FCP, see the 17th report of the Federal Government's Foreign Cultural and Educational Policy (cf. Federal Government, 2014: 10 ff.).

50 For a description of the British Council, see Ch. 3.2.2.

sponsor will demand a product orientation and define what that product ought to be is high, as the following statement of an Indian sponsor makes clear:

> [S]tep two that it's made very clear even before they [the artists from overseas – author] come here [India] that there is this very specific thing that we [the Indian cultural sponsors – author] want to achieve and are you [the overseas artists – author] interested to do that? (I_63: 103)

If the product, – or result – orientation moves decisively in the direction of a cooperation, those taking part must define and coordinate their interests with one another (cf. Ch. 6.2).

Some of those interviewed gave the opinion that the process of working together needed to be sacrificed to the quality of the cultural product; or that the quality was the focus, over the requirements of producing a meaningful cooperative piece (cf. I_38: 2-6, I_73: 32). In presenting the results, however, it becomes clear that good processes, which are founded on dialogue between the partners, are essential requirements of successful cultural products or productions. Therefore, the cooperative work which takes place during the development process is at least as important, if not in fact more important, than the product of the cooperation (cf. I_38: 8, Hoyle, 2012: 2).[51] Because the process is an element of a successful product – or result, it ought to be valued accordingly: for example, in that the process, which does not form part of a specific, self-contained work in the traditional sense, can and may be presented to the public and sponsors (cf. I_63: 100, 88, I_9/I_10: 40-44). However, an Indian theatre producer warns:

> The problem with Goethe and all of these institutes is that they [...] do not understand that showing the process is already a very good result, and that out of that, a meaningful partnership arises. (I_72: 52-53)[52]

Process orientation – like cooperation work in general – from the outset takes courage and the willingness to take risks on the part of both the sponsor and the sponsored, who must be prepared to exhibit a work in progress, rather than an end result (cf. I_73: 32, I_75: 12-13).[53] Trunk comments: "The possibility to initiate processes 'for art's sake', without anticipating a result, is traditionally in no way to be expected." (Trunk,

---

51 Also Schneider (2011d: 21), *ibid.* (2011a: 5), IFAB (1999: 9 f.).

52 It should be noted that some of those interviewed were of the opinion that the MMB created no obligation to deliver results (cf. I_49: 35, I_15: 13).

53 See also Schneider (2011d: 21), *ibid.* (2011a: 5).

2011: 15) Knopp believes that Europeans rarely possess the ability to tolerate incomplete processes (cf. Knopp, 2006: 119).

It cannot be denied that process-orientation comes with its price with regard to resources in terms of time and money, and stands in opposition to 'short-sighted' cultural policy (cf. Lechner, 2004: 240, Ch. 5.4, 5.5). In order for process-orientation to survive, it must be accounted for in the timetabling and financial planning of cooperations, otherwise it will always fall back behind the focus on results. A long term outlook in the temporal and financial planning of cooperations does not automatically guarantee success. It does, however, allow the actors to place the character of the process on a solid basis, upon which they can be given the time and space to build their result.[54]

6.10 A Culture of Experimentation and Failure

Success and failure are two sides of the same coin. Risking failure is the way to success. In order to allow successful cooperation work to take place in the future, it therefore needs to become possible to address failure, to reflect on it and to discuss it (cf. I_32: 22, 57, I_73: 33, Ch. 6.12). This discussion also invites the debate: What does failure actually entail for artists and their sponsors, and how can various types of failure be dealt with (cf. I_32: 95)? In seeking a new culture of cooperation in the arts, it would be meaningful to allow failure as an inevitable part of the risky process of cooperation. The cycle of experiment and failure can open out exclusively success and result focused structures of sponsorship (cf. I_10: 121, Schneider, 2011a: 5, *ibid.*, 2011d: 20, Sennett, 2012: 13).[55]

Lechner describes his idea in terms of the establishment of a 'culture of failure' as follows:

> A place which would take on exclusively good failed projects, which would deal with the reasons and circumstances of their failures, and finally bring the best of them to the success which they deserve. (Lechner, 2004: 155, cf. also Brauer, 2010: 62)

While Lechner suggests this approach solely for Goethe-Institut projects, it would be meaningful to create an independent, scientific,

---

54 A future concern must be the identification of qualitative criteria for international collaborations in the arts.

55 Laymert Garcia dos Santos, curator and Professor of Sociology and Philosophy at the University of Campinas in Sao Paulo comments: "The cooperation has to be the real driving force of the experiment" (Garcia dos Santos, 2011: 56).

testing and recording body for failed partnerships, in order to identify opportunities for development in their areas of difficulty.

The development of a culture of experiment and failure is practically possible through a step-by-step approach to sponsorship. Participants would be granted a 'small'[56] financial contribution at the beginning of their cooperation (cf. I_62: 29), in order to try their cooperation ideas for a few weeks or months:

> [A] seed grant is intended to provide collaborators with an opportunity to test assumptions, confront potential sources of disagreement, and better appreciate one another's concerns and expectations [...]. (IFAB, 2004: 13)[57]

Following this phase, the cooperating partners would decide, ideally with their sponsors, if it would be meaningful or not to take the partnership further (cf. I_73: 32, I_32: 54-59, IFAB, 2002b: n.p.). If not, then only a small sum has been lost. If the tried cooperation idea is realised with a full-scale sponsorship, the likelihood of a successful collaboration can be increased by the mutual knowledge and trust which the partners have gained in the course of the trial period (cf. I_78: 24, IFAB, 2004a: 10).[58] As Thomas Rautenstrauch, Lars Generotzky and Tim Bigalke in their fundamental research on cooperation point out:

> Cooperations often begin with relatively insignificant transactions which are associated with only a low risk, in order to test and develop trustworthiness on both sides. It is only later that more complex relationships develop. (Rautenstrauch *et al.*, 2003: 66)

A cooperation process which is divided into at least two, and possibly more phases (cf. I_73: 32), further allows a pause after each stage in order for reflection on the project to take place: "[A] number of smaller performances stretched out over the collaboration period, ruled out the much-needed space for sustained self-critique on the part of the collaborators." (Mitra, 1998b: 2)[59] Where there are multiple phases, it does not necessarily follow that a single process must immediately deliver a result of high cultural value (cf. I_70: 38, I_63: 108).[60] Cultural creators are free to experiment, and fail:

---

56 As a rule, a sum in the order of some thousands of euros.

57 Also I_73: 34, I_70: 89, IFAB (2001: 19), *ibid.* (2002a: 18), *ibid.* (2002b: n.p.), Vellani quoted in: ifa (2013: 12).

58 Cf. also IFAB (2002a: 7) and *ibid.* (2000a: 19).

59 See also I_78: 24 and Ch. 6.12.

60 Compare also IFAB (2004a: 4) and Ch. 6.9.

> When you work in small systems, [...] where you muck in and nobody observes you, then you can try anything possible. That is much simpler than to take on bigger risks – because you can fail and that's fine. You just failed. (I_70: 38)

6.11 Ongoing Cooperative Work

> So I think that's an ideal way of looking at the collaboration, if it's leading to more collaboration in the future [...]. (I_15: 211)

In cooperative work, artistic production is undertaken together. From this follows the presentation of the results: for example, a concert, a theatre piece, or a dance exhibition in India (cf. Ch. 5.5.2)[61] – or the processes as the case may be (cf. Ch. 6.9). But how is the cooperation to be carried on when the partners separate from one another and, to take an example, the role taken by an Indian actor can no longer be filled in Germany? How can Indian musicians in India continue to make music without their German colleagues? As a rule, partnerships come to an end with the first presentation of the cooperative artistic piece (cf. I_20: 60, I_25: 82-84). This runs against the grain of the FCP's claims, which stress that the continuity, sustainability and long-term nature of international relationships is important (cf. Bauer, 2010: 96 f. and Ch. 2.2).

In order to allow joint work to become more sustainable in the future, it is therefore necessary to ensure that the partners are able to continue and carry forward development in their respective local contexts:

> I had suggested to them that we could now also continue to play the same piece if we could fill the German roles with Indian actors, which we could have done just as well. It didn't need an international cast. That has a special charm, but it would work just as well. And they wanted that. (I_25: 82)

This context-oriented transfer of the cooperative piece as a fundamental element of working together requires additional resources in terms of time and money, if the cooperative pieces are not to continue to go up in smoke. With adequate resourcing, the transformation of these cooperative pieces into independent and autonomous pieces which can then live on would be a practical proposition. In doing so, the cooperative pieces could be integrated within the Indian cultural landscape and also 'played back' to Germany (cf. Ch. 6.8).

---

61 It should be noted here, that the presented results of cooperation work are for the most part not material objects. The survival and afterlife of the results of such cooperations therefore poses an additional challenge.

A result of this wider presentation would be that the cooperative pieces would be able to have their effect on both of the cultural contexts which contributed to their creation, and could eventually form part of a network. This way of following up cooperations would strengthen their continuity and sustainability. Of course, on the basis of financial limitations, it would not be possible to transfer all such cooperative pieces. Therefore, it would be necessary to reach a selection. Accurately identifying the criteria for this selection would be decisive and essential. An alternative would be to promote fewer partnerships from the outset, but provide those few with all the necessary resources to fully carry out meaningful preparation and follow-up processes for the cooperation (cf. Ch. 6.8).

It would be commendable to ensure the long-term planning of cooperation work, in order to build a network of cooperations. A sustainable approach would begin to show its effect in the medium term, when networks have been created to lead artists from one cooperation to the next and offer them potential partnerships which were previously unattainable. Furthermore, the institutional stakeholders – above all on the Indian side – who mediate cooperative work stand to gain.

6.12 The Exchange of Experiences: "We were trying to make sense..."[62]

A continuous process of reflection regarding the process of cooperation enables the participating actors to ensure the quality of the cooperation on an ongoing basis, and gives them the whole duration of the creative work as space for development (cf. Garcia dos Santos, 2011: 56). Thus, the performance of the partnership will be strengthened – the basis for a successful cooperation (cf. Steinkamp, 2013: 19).[63]

The documentary on the cooperation between *Ranga Shankara* and *Schnawwl* illustrates one possibility of undertaking such reflection. In this case, one of the German partners filmed the cooperation and interviewed all of the participants throughout the course of the project – critically discussing their process of working together. The result is a documentary which clearly depicts the difficulties of the cooperation – both for themselves and for others. The complexity of cooperating in the face of a diverse multitude of challenges and misunderstandings is known to the partners and visible to colleagues and viewers.[64]

---

62 The title of a reflective documentary on international cooperation in the arts (cf. Fabianczyk/Hoyle, 2012).

63 On the positive effects of an ongoing process of reflection and exchange of experiences, cf. Rautenstrauch *et al.* (2003: 90, 125), Holzberg (2009: 86).

64 On the complexity of networks and cooperations, see also Steinkamp (2013: 11).

The experiences which arise from international cooperations – including their failures and mistakes – can be of use for the future planning and realisation of worldwide partnerships (cf. Lechner, 2004: 296). Therefore, the collection of these valuable insights is an important task (cf. Rautenstrauch *et al.*, 2003: 107). A platform which would bring together artists, cultural mediators and sponsors, as well as policy makers, to share and exchange their experiences of intercultural partnerships, as well as to analyse and discuss their cooperations would be a most welcome institution. These experiences could then provide the relevant perspectives for the future development of a culture of cooperation as applied to individual structures and contexts (cf. I_49: 193, I_14: 13-18). Such critical reflection on shared projects demands, however, that sponsored actors should have no fear of sanctions in the form of the denial of future funding.

Cultural institutes which act as intermediaries for cooperations could support such exchanges of experience – in that they would moderate and organise the platforms, such as conferences and symposia at which they would take place (cf. Ch. 6.6). This knowledge, as well as experiences from the partnerships could be documented and made publicly available. This documentation would be undertaken with the intention of providing comprehensive information on the partnerships and to secure publicity for the potential of international partnerships in the arts, as well as their reputation amongst experts. Ideally, such documentation could be presented on a website, which would offer an 'at a glance' view of cooperative concepts around the globe, as well as a virtual platform of exchange for artists.[65] Along with the challenges and limitations of cooperative work, examples of best practice could also be presented, and distinguished as appropriate (cf. Ch. 6.13).

As partners in reflection and in the evaluation of artistic partnerships, the cultural institutes and sponsors would have the unique chance to get to understand the challenges and opportunities presented by cooperations, and to respond appropriately to these with regard to their support and sponsorship and, as the IFAB describes:

> [...] facilitate grantees to forge links with one another, and help IFAB [as supporter and mediator of the cooperation – author] to expand its understanding of the broader implications of this programme [the IFAB cooperation programme – author] [...], to reflect on the challenges of

---

65 Similarly, the website http://www.labforculture.org/de# (Accessed: 15.11.2013); "an information and knowledge platform for the support of cultural cooperation" (Schwencke *et al.*, 2009: 63).

collaboration in the arts and air the doubts and concerns about the projects before they were activated. (IFAB, 2003: 9, see also *ibid.*, 2002: 19)[66]

6.13 "Fair Cooperation": The Path to a "Cooperation based on Partnership"[67]

There is no cultural dialogue between the rich and poor – instead, they contend for the balance of concrete political and economic power. A dialogue between cultures requires justice, or just conduct; at a minimum, the desire and capacity to pursue it. (Johannes Rau, President of Germany from 1999 to 2004)[68]

The existing power relationships allow partnerships on equal terms (or what Hamm-Brücher described thirty years ago as the "equal value of cultures", Hamm-Brücher/Foreign Office, 1982: 191 f., cf. also Ch. 2.2) can only take place within limits. They remain, for example, a challenge to the German-Indian cultural dialogue (cf. I_22: 14-23), and in the relationships between partners from nations in the 'Global North' and 'Global South'. Framing the actors and their cultures within hierarchies can lead to conflicts which place the joint project in jeopardy (cf. Nestvogel, 2010: 140). What, however, are the requirements, structures and structural conditions which must be in place to minimise the European dominance over their partners from the 'Global South' and allow a partnership in the form of a relationship between equals – which the Federal Government has claimed "must play a central role in the Foreign Cultural and Educational Policy"[69] – to arise? Because the equality of the partners is a prerequisite of intercultural cooperation and encounter (cf. Wartemann, 2002: 99), particularly with regard to relationships with states from the developing world. This approach was brought to the fore by the UNESCO Convention of 2005 (cf. Ch. 2.2).

First of all, respect for one another must be recognised as a meaningful factor in allowing two cultures to encounter one another as equals:

Dialogue on an equal footing at its best means bringing the greatest possible respect to encounters with others to try and understand them as deeply and

66 Alongside a so-called 'Grantee Orientation Meeting', where those who have been sponsored by the cooperation program of the IFAB can exchange their experiences, the IFAB also places the documents of previously supported programs at the disposal of new applicants (cf. IFAB, 2004b: n.p.).

67 With regard to a cooperation of equals, see Ch. 1, 2.1 and 2.2.

68 Quoted from Rau (2002b: n.p.).

69 Quoted from http://tinyurl.com/oug2kox (Accessed: 16.03.2014).

as accurately as possible, and also to respect those things in people which have not been revealed or cannot be understood. (Kämpchen, 2013a: 67)[70]

In this quotation, respect is a consequence of trying to understand others, and accept them in their difference (cf. I_25: 10, I_57: 10, I_26: 39-40).[71] For the interviewees, respect as well as trust were seen as prerequisites for cooperation on a meaningful basis (cf. I_15: 95-99, I_26: 39-40).[72] This respect for one's partner and this type of artistic practice needs to be learned: "[W]e had to learn to accept them the way they were and they had to learn to see the beauty in how we were, so this was the real struggle." (I_26: 7-9) As with dialogue, "listening […] is essential" (Sehouli, 2012: 48, cf. Ch. 2) in showing that respect.

When this respect is lacking – or is too great, as in the case of a 'pupil-teacher' relationship – dialogue on an equal footing is not possible. The balancing act between these extremes required in order to obtain and maintain this equal footing is difficult (cf. I_75: 8). It is questionable, therefore, whether respect is able to bypass the hierarchies which prevail within cooperating teams, or whether it can only be given "when there are no longer any unresolved dependencies in place" (I_62: 9).

The unequal allocation of resources, especially of a financial nature is the greatest hindrance for a partnership of equals. As a rule, it is the Western or European partner who brings the monetary basis for the artistic cooperation. This fact gives rise to a power relationship (see Lechner, 2004: 294 f.). This unequal allocation of resources would only be resolved were cooperations without material means to take place (cf. I_70: 92-93). With that, the hierarchisation of the cooperation actors would be resolved (cf. I_16: 5-6, I_70: 62). That is, however, unrealistic.

An alternate possibility would otherwise be to prevent partnerships between actors from wealthy countries – such as those of the 'Global North' – and poor – such as found in the 'Global South'. This is a defensive, and furthermore destructive, solution which would allow Western Countries to evade their responsibilities.[73] International cooperation is anchored

---

70 Also I_25: 54, Garcia dos Santos (2011: 56), Dickersbach (2013: n.p.), Varma (2007: 1141).

71 Nikolaus Schneider speaks of "respect-tolerance", allowing other positions "when the human value and rights of all are protected in them" (Schneider, 2013: n.p.). This respect-tolerance requires: "Conscious confidence in one's own convictions, humility towards one's knowledge of the truth and respect for the beliefs and experiences of others – provided that they do not place human dignity in question." (*ibid.*)

72 See also I_39: 35-36, I_9/I_10: 148, I_48: 4, I_50: 168, I_67: 54-57 as well as Arzoglou (2006: 982) and Singh (2009: 38 ff.).

73 See the UNESCO Convention of 2005 on this topic, which states that industrialised countries ought to cooperate with so-called 'developing countries' in a special way in order to protect cultural diversity (see Ch. 2.2).

within the German FCP (cf. Ch. 2.2) and should therefore form a practical element in the realisation of this policy.

Lechner suggests a strict reciprocity between the Indian and German partners in order to reach a "maximum equality of the parties" (Lechner, 2004: 291). Key to this is that a fund is established and financed together by the partners "from which bilaterally, or later multilaterally, developed projects can be funded and carried out following suitable consultation and division of roles." (*ibid.*: 294 f.) The extent to which this reciprocity has worked so far can be seen during the course of this work (cf. Ch. 3.2.4 and 4). Indian cultural workers are, however, united in their opinion that an equal level of investment in the financing of cooperations would be a step towards equality between the partners (cf. I_26: 29, I_11: 65-66, I_37: 75-76).

A first step could consist of the partners recalling the "historical baggage" of their relationships (Tibi, 2001: 29, 37) and broaching their unequal playing fields – above all in the material sphere (cf. I_25: 18, I_19: 26-27).[74] As a member of staff from the Goethe-Institut explains:

> OK, we [the MMB – author] have the money, he [the Indian cultural worker – author] doesn't. That is always disproportionate. But I think with [name of the Indian cultural worker] one can talk about it frankly – and I would call that a dialogue on an equal level. (I_69: 106)

This should also involve a discussion about the source of the money, and the goals which the sponsorship is intended to achieve (cf. I_37: 65-70, 75-81, I_9/I_10: 134-135). As with the process of defining and dealing with the interests of the parties (cf. Ch. 6.2), it is recommended that the participants discuss their understanding of the meaning of partnership (cf. Mitra, 1998a: 2).

Ultimately, however, these discussions cannot overcome the serious inequalities within the cooperation due to the financial dominance of the West.

Some of the respondents represent the opinion that equality is in fact able to arise because the monetary contribution of the German partner can be compensated for (cf. I_15: 219, I_26: 31-35).[75] The contribution of a different kind of resources by the Indian partner – such as creativity, or intellectual ability, for example – can be a solution. This, however, seems questionable, as it is the financial contribution which each partner brings

74 Cf. also I_32: 37, I_20: 51-52. Rather than forcing equality, the recognition of diversity. This attitude is one which can generate justice, and therefore fairness (cf. Faschingeder, 2001: 147 f.).

75 Also I_54: 201, I_37: 20-21, I_45: 372-391.

which creates the equality or inequality within a partnership (cf. I_20: 38 and Ch. 5.9.1). The non-monetary contributions which can be made are mostly of a non-material nature, and therefore not able to be readily compared in terms of their value. Indeed, they are seen as having a lower value than a monetary contribution (cf. I_15: 219).

An effective possibility to reduce this dominance is: distribute financial control and money which has been placed at the disposal of the cooperation equally between the parties as recommended by a German *dramaturg*:

> […] the [name of a German sponsoring institution – author] are just right to give them [the Indian partners – author] a sum directly, and gave us [the German partners – author] another one […] as equal partners. […] and everybody has their money. (I_25: 62, cf. also I_29: 9-10, I_37: 62)

Mutual financial responsibility makes the creation of a cooperation of equal partners possible. Since no single party is responsible for the whole of the financial management, the partners are obliged to consult with one another with respect to the use of the funds. Consequently, decisions with regard to content, organisation and material need to become democratic – or at least more democratic (cf. I_72: 14-15, I_37: 63-65). However, this requires the Indian partner – that is, the partner from the 'Global South' – to fulfil the conditions of the German – or Western – sponsor, which were developed within a Western context and seldom function in the reality of India or other nations of the 'Global South':

> Of course nobody in India understands what kind of accounting the [name of a German sponsoring institution – author] wants. […] It is also quite complicated to explain why things ought to be exactly as they are supposed to. […] Sometimes, of course, things work completely differently and it is just difficult for the Indian theatre to get to grips with these procedures, because they have a completely different reality. When you have to produce some kinds of bills […]. Completely ridiculous. You can't ask a rickshaw driver for a bill. (I_70: 26-28, cf. also I_25: 58)

It could be recommended to cultural sponsors in light of this quotation, that the distribution of money to all of those participating, rather than a single actor in the cooperation who takes responsibility for the funds on behalf of all of the partners, would be beneficial to the equality of those within the partnership. This would also have the effect of reducing the bureaucratic hurdles for all of those involved in the cooperation to a realistic height (cf. I_37: 74, Vellani quoted in: ifa, 2013: 15 f.).

All cooperation partners ought to have a share in financing the cooperations, so that the actors have a financial investment in their artistic cooperation and give one another mutual support. This requires from the European partner that the foreign partners are granted a share in the financial interest of the cooperation. A cultural worker from Germany describes his approach thus:

> Whatever happens, I always try and include local partners financially, even if it has to be with contributions in kind, so that they don't have the feeling that it's the Europeans who come and pay for everything. (I_20: 54-55)

Dealing with the resources is, therefore, not just the job of the Indian or non-European partner, but also that of the German or European. Identifying and winning the support of sources of finance in the 'Global South' such as sponsoring cultural institutions, businesses and private persons could allow the development of a long-term material structure allowing a level of equality in this regard (cf. I_15: 219).

In parallel to this, financial opportunities for art and culture in India, and all of the structurally disadvantaged partner countries of the 'Global South' need to be established. The long term effort to reshape frameworks which develop the cultural landscape to the point at which it is able to finance itself independently is something which needs to be strongly pushed by both partners.

These far reaching structural changes in partner countries would entail the recognition of the current basis which so-called 'partnerships' have been based on up till now. If Western partners are in actuality merely sources of finance, they could be rendered obsolete in the future through the development of alternative methods of financing projects in the 'Global South'. Independent financial opportunities offer the chance to put to rest relationships grounded in the roles of patron and client. Put differently: To dissolve the power relationship and renew the roles (cf. I_22: 29) as a partnership of equals in accordance with the stated aim of the FCP since the 1980s, a reciprocal process of giving and receiving has to be established (cf. Hamm-Brücher/Auswärtiges Amt, 1982: 191 and Ch. 2.2).

The central question is whether the donors are willing or able to give up their role – which has legitimized their existence up to this point. For them, it would mean changing, and placing their own powerful and controlling position and way of functioning into question (cf. I_37: 10, Schneider/Gad, 2011: 15, Hoffmann, 2008: 175). This requires the willingness to give up, or to share, power.

That a change or structural reform – requiring effort on both sides for its realisation – is necessary was clear at the *Theaterformen* festival 2013 in Hannover. A Belgian artist defined the future of international cooperation as being about the ability to decide together what is needed for what, and where the money will come from. His colleagues from Asian, African and Latin American countries were in agreement. To date, cooperation projects between countries from the 'Global North' and the 'Global South' still largely proceed according to the paradigm that decisions on the allocation and usage of funds lies in the hands of the European partner. An Indian artist comments on this fact with a proverb:

> 'Up until the lion tells the story, the story will be told by the hunter.' […] [S]o similarly up until the time we [the Indians – author] start directing our projects the story will be told by somebody else [the Europeans – author]. (I_26: 24, cf. also I_69: 84)

To summarise, it should be noted: Fairness and equality are ideals which are, and can only be reached in certain few cases, following many years of discussion and approaches by the partners. Cooperations between the 'Global North' and the 'Global South', therefore, remain ambivalent relations (cf. Ch. 4.2). Rather than seeing to reach a full equality in all things, it seems more realistic to aim for a fair partnership. The definition what is 'fair' can be clarified as follows.

The word 'fairness' expresses justice: an "ideal state of social interaction […], in which there is a reasonable, impartial and reliable balance of interests and the distribution of goods and chances between the groups or persons taking part" (Lackner, 2010: 138).[76] 'Fairness' means paying attention to equal opportunities and conditions – not taking them for granted, as has been made normative by the FCP in claiming equality and partnerships on equal terms (cf. Ch. 2.2). As Chapter 5 of this dissertation illustrates, international cooperation in the arts is a field of unsimilar conditions and requirements.

In the case of the notion of 'fair play', fairness is an attitude of sportsmanship: in thought as well as action, which consists of applying the greatest possible respect and dignity to one's fellow players. 'Fair play' is defined by the foundation of the same name in the following terms:

> Fair play means people learning to…
>
> … think in alternatives and try out other models.
>
> … respect the goals and needs of others.
>
> … make their counterparts successful.
>
> … develop an awareness of their own motives.
>
> … be flexible and behave as the situation demands.[77]

Art is not a sport and cultural encounters are "no game" (Lehmann, 2010: n.p.), but both contribute to international understanding. The rules

---

[76] For a detailed definition of fairness, see, for example, http://tinyurl.com/pz9opc3 (Accessed: 03.01.2014).

[77] Quoted from http://tinyurl.com/p8j5sey (Accessed: 12.01.2014).

of a game of sport, to which all of the players must adhere (cf. Petersen, 2010: 21) – in accordance with the understanding of fair play – seem to be a helpful guideline for the realisation of artistic cooperations because they represent the combination of cultural and political perspectives illustrated in this chapter. Fair play invites the sportsman, or the artist, to experiment (cf. Ch. 5.5, 6.9, 6.10), to identify his own goals and the goals of others – respecting their diversity and their contradictions (cf. Ch. 5.6, 6.2), acting in accordance with the requirements of the context (cf. Ch. 5.5, 6.3, 6.4, 6.5, 6.6 and 6.7) and, finally, to make his fellow players, or cooperation partners, "successful"[78] in their own reality (cf. Ch. 6.11 and 6.12). The referee, who has the job of guaranteeing fair play, is in the case of 'Fair Cooperation', the institutions which are acting as cooperation mentors in their role as mediator, intermediary and moderator (cf. Ch. 6.6, 7). When parameters such as the location, timing and funding of the cooperation can be negotiated equally (cf. Ch. 6.8), fair cooperation in the sense of fair play can be established.

The expression 'fair play' leads one to the expression 'fair trade'. This term refers to a generally equitable mode of behaviour in commodity exchanges on the local, regional, national and international levels – resting on dialogue, transparency and respect within the economic partnership.[79] This fair trade also naturally embraces the "economic relationship in the cultural sphere" (Gad, 2012b: 73). The goal of fair trade is an increase of participation, ownership and responsibility on the part of the manufacturer – in particular those from the countries of the 'Global South'. This leads to a variety of actors and a diversified array of products, recalling – to return to the topic of this dissertation – the cultural and political perspectives of unfolding partnerships in the arts (cf. Ch. 6.1). Fair trade makes a meaningful contribution to development and sustainably improves the life of the people who are involved in the production process by providing better trading conditions for producers – with the support of social capital, amongst other measures.[80] Through the cultural and political perspectives with regard to fair cooperation identified here, this research project aims to sustainably develop the practice of global cooperation for creative work in the arts.

Taking into account the success of the term 'fair trade' – and above all, the model of the Fair Trade Logo[81] – this investigation would like

---

78 *Ibid.*

79 For a definition and explanation of the principles of fair trade, see http://tinyurl.com/opsczpx (Accessed: 19.09.2013).

80 On the effectiveness of fair trade, see http://tinyurl.com/ptsekks and http://tinyurl.com/nbo35bn (Both accessed: 14.09.2013). On the term 'social capital', cf. Ch. 2.3.

81 See http://www.fairtrade-deutschland.de/ (Accessed: 18.11.2013).

to suggest the development of a similar method for the certification of fair cooperations – consisting of a recognised brand or label. The criteria upon which this label would be awarded must be defined – ideally as part of a dialogue with directly participating stakeholders. The results of this research project could form the basis of such a discussion.

Analogously to the fair trade movement, the concept of 'fair cooperation' which has been proposed here above all concentrates on relationships between countries of the 'Global South' and the 'Global North'. In conclusion to this section, it might be proposed that the cultural-political perspectives presented here regarding the initiation and implementation of international cooperations could form the basis for an international culture of cooperation between heterogeneous partners from countries of the 'Global North' and the 'Global South' if their full potential, for example, in the area of context-oriented transfer, were to be realised (cf. Ch. 6.7).

Art, Cooperation, and Cultural Policy

Conclusions and Outlook

With regard to the cultural policy prospects presented in Chapter 6, it "could be argued against them that a great number of projects have in the past arrived at a similar condition or are doing so at present." (Lechner, 2004: 295)[1] Lechner's position is seemingly strengthened by Lehmann's description of the program work of the Goethe-Institut in the following terms:

> Cultural exporters are like space ships. They fly to a country, open the doors, show off the culture, and then close the doors and fly away again. In contrast, we know the local conditions, how to take the pulse on the ground, and we are also able to bring in the inspiration of the German cultural scene. We work in the long term. That is the only way to gain people's confidence. The network that arises from that has its own quality. (Lehmann in: Breukelchen, 2010: 51 ff.)

Against this description, this thesis on artistic cooperations in the FCP illustrates that fair cooperation work can be further developed – from being the stated goal to the operative principle of the German FCP. Each cooperation project with its individual actors is unique (cf. Lehmann, 2010: n.p.), and there can be no panacea for reshaping global cooperation. The personal encounters which take place within each cooperation require a sensitive and individual approach.

However, the cultural policy perspectives which are presented in this dissertation with regard to the process of cooperation can, and should, encourage reflection and discussion on the current and future culture of cooperation in the international arts: not in a piecemeal fashion, but on a continual basis. What is needed is a scholarly investigation of cooperative work in the age of globalisation, a playful exploration of its conditions, structures and processes, as well as a recognition that cooperation itself is an experiment.

1 According to Kathe, the Goethe-Institut responded well to Dahrendorf's theses in 1970, and their content has long been carried over into reality (cf. Kathe, 2005: 59, 293).

In its own way, the world from which the cooperation partners from the 'Global North' come is unique, and not subject to comparison. This is also true for their partners from the 'Global South'. The inequality of conditions means that the participants in each cooperation bring different capital to their own project. Their ideas about and expectations of cooperation work are also different. International cooperation as "the encounter of different cultures" is characterised by "collectively shared assumptions and individual requirements" (Nünning, 2005: 81 f.). These need to be revealed, analysed and understood to allow the participants to engage in the cooperation on a more or less equal level.

Figure 1*: The ideal of a cooperation process (author)*

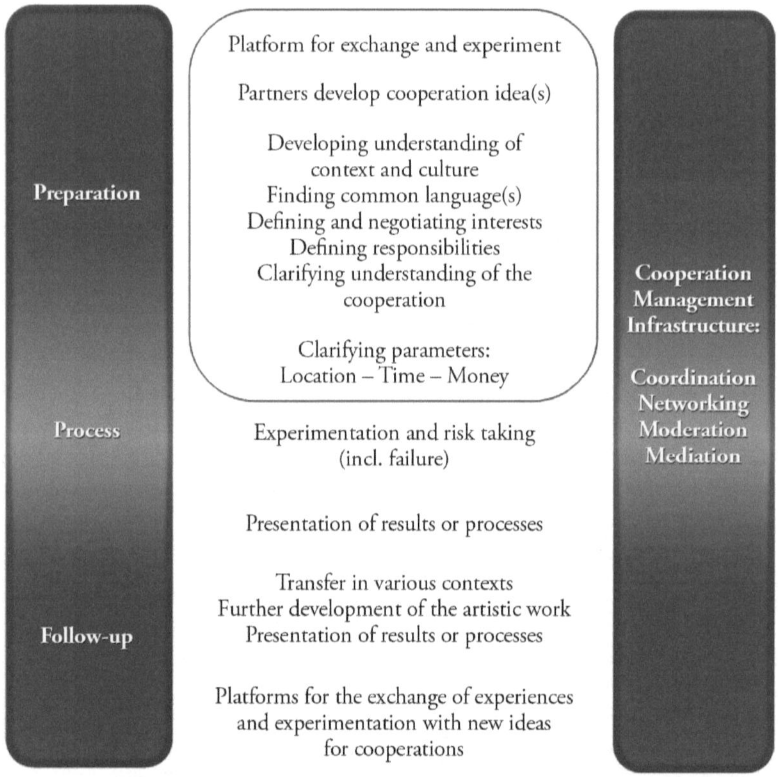

Attempting to level in the obvious difference between 'North' and 'South' cannot be the solution. It is also not possible, as the results of the research presented here illustrate. Rather, existing partnerships and relationship models must be made more sensible with regard to their conditions and terms. Structures and processes need to be the subject of discussion and reflection. This activity requires much more attention and resources in terms of time and money than are at present devoted to it. Follow up processes, for example, offer a jumping off point for the preparation of the next cooperative project with the same or other partners. In this sense, they represent the end of new beginnings.

The results of the investigation and the cultural policy frameworks for cooperation work in the FCP which arise out of it are summarised in the diagram of a potential ideal cooperation process. Cultural institutions, networks and agencies can serve as intermediaries to moderate the cooperation: mediating with regard to the various cultures, contexts and cultural practices involved and smoothing the way in the course of conflicts.

Central to this ideal is the prospect of developing long-term, effective and fairer structures for the implementation of a cooperation of partners between the 'North' and 'South', which also allow for the acknowledgement of failure, and the recognition of limits in the case of differences between the actors.[2] Every failure also contains a new way forward: "When we recognise and make use of the chances offered by crises, we can grow and develop further".[3] Accordingly, the gamble – and the great chance – of working in international cooperation is that the multitude of cultures and forms of cultural expression on which cooperation work is based remain and continue to be fruitful, despite the possibility of failure and manifold challenges – particularly of an intercultural nature. If this cultural diversity is respected in all of its contrasts, and does not attempt to artificially create or reduce these contrasts to uniformity in the course of the cooperation process, it is something which enriches all of those who take part – the public as well as those who work in the creative field:

> Sudden irritation, dissonances, culture shocks, experiences of alienation [...], they can be taken up as a challenging, fascinating, and frustrating space for learning and gaining experience, and used for a deepened understanding of yourself and other people. (Nestvogel, 2010: 140, cf. also Kämpchen, 2013a: 66 f.)

The cultural freedom which prevails in pluralistic societies is grounded on the principle of the same clear appreciation of cultural diversity which is acknowledged in this quotation.

The discourse on global cooperation concerning the recognition, preservation and advancement of this cultural diversity offers scope for

2 On this point see also Terres des hommes (2003: n.p.).

3 Quoted from http://tinyurl.com/qjjtg7g (Accessed: 09.11.2013).

action with regard to the unrealised potential of artistic cooperations. This thesis, therefore, is a contribution to securing the quality and sustainability of the conduct of actors in the FCP. The concept of a new culture of cooperation is at the disposal of policy and practice in every sector of society – both internal and external – as advice, exhortation and food for thought. As Chapter 1.2 makes clear, cooperations in the arts are also best-practice examples in economic partnerships. The results of the research presented here with regard to the FCP, therefore, are also relevant for all actors who cooperate in an international context. It is important that experiences are open to cooperating actors within other sectors.

Why the topic of international cultural cooperations has up to now not been examined and reflected on in the context of domestic cultural policy is questionable (cf. Schneider, 2011d: 21, Knüsel, 2011: 72), since "foreign cultural policy is the other side of the coin to domestic cultural policy" (Lepenies, 1996c: 200). The findings of this thesis are, therefore, relevant not just for cultural foreign policy in Germany, but for its cultural domestic policy. Germany is a destination country for immigration (cf., for example, Wieck, 2006: 5, Schwencke *et al.*, 2009: 74). One of the primary effects of globalisation is a society which is internationalised and made increasingly heterogeneous by migration. Lehmann observes: "At home and abroad, the effects of globalisation and migration are becoming increasingly inseparable from one another." (Lehmann, 2011c: n.p., see also Schreiner, 2011: 114 f., Gross, 2012: 23)[4] In German domestic social policy, intercultural cooperation is being assigned an ever more central role (cf. Knüsel, 2011: 72). The development of Germany's society requires a working coexistence of culturally diverse actors on an equal footing.

While "our own cultural substance is rooted [internally], it is only from this root that our external cultural policy can grow" (Hamm-Brücher, 1980: 113 f.). The propagation and sponsorship of equal partnerships externally will only be legitimate when partnerships on an equal footing are a functioning reality internally. Otherwise, they are of a dubious nature and their legitimacy will be open to question: "Europe must practice what it preaches in order to be taken seriously." (*ifa*, 2013: 18, see also Sen, 2007: 123, Hamm-Brücher, 1980: 15)

International cooperations in the arts are only beginning to be explored. Intercultural cooperation requires structures and frameworks which need to be provided by political and other institutions. With this in mind, the following points for potential – and necessary – future research arise.

4 For a detailed debate on the connections and disconnects of internal and external cultural policy, see Bauer (2010: 98 f.).

Reflection on practice is an important component of this thesis. The experiences and insights of cooperating parties have been key to forming criteria for the concept of international cooperation in the arts. Many actors, however – for example, from other countries – have not yet been taken into account, so that there remains a future task in systematically incorporating these perspectives into the research on the FCP. Further studies aimed at a "cultural policy for artists" are necessary (Schneider, 2013c: 14). It is only in this way that cultural and social diversity can be recognised and secured for the long term.

A systematic recording of experiences is the first step towards the research of effectiveness. Research work which demonstrates the value and sustainability of international artistic cooperations is necessary. Artistic and cooperative processes which have established themselves and evolved over years or decades are favourable subjects for the analysis of effectiveness in this regard.

The insights presented here should find application in cooperative 'North'-'South' relationships in order to be further differentiated. It would be ideal to accompany partnerships from the beginning to the end of their work and research them in a process-orientated manner. This would allow the peculiarities of the phases of establishment, development and completion to be grasped. Longitudinal analysis of these issues can give a sense of the long-term success of cooperations and the reasons for their stability or instability which go beyond the time period covered by the observation (cf. *ibid.*). "In this context, the analysis of negative examples offers the potential to avoid mistakes in future cooperations and produce a corresponding 'learning effect'." (Holzberg 2009: 172)

The work of cooperations is very specific, because it is dependent on the structures and contexts on the ground, as well as the various personalities which are involved. This thesis on German-Indian cooperations is based on further research on artistic cooperation in the international context. On this basis, analysis which investigate the bilateral relationships between German creatives and other actors in Africa and Asia would be significant insofar as they incorporate the specific cultural landscapes and politics of their respective countries (cf. Ch. 3). Also important would be research into multilateral relationships, which as well as being a contemporary theme, are also a matter of necessity, and therefore increasingly being utilised.

Finance is one of the greatest challenges for cooperations. It makes inequality and imbalance essential elements of cooperations (cf. Ch. 5.9.1) and influences their success and sustainability. In particular, the effectiveness of cultural sponsorship programs and institutes on the local cultural landscape, as well as in partner countries, needs to be more deeply illuminated. The result of this process will be a responsibility, of which some cultural sponsors at the moment seem to be entirely unaware.

In the course of this thesis, relevant research topics and fields were identified, for example, the concept of the 'Year of Germany' as an instrument of the FCP, and specific forms of cooperation, such as residencies. Scientific discussions are also important with regard to the development of 'South-South' cooperations: that is, the cooperation of 'developing countries' with one another, as put forward in the UNESCO Final Declaration from Mexico City in 1982 (cf. Ch. 2.2), the establishment of local finance strategies and self-supporting structures for the arts in countries of the 'Global South', as well as the realisation of the 'return' or 'feedback' of overseas cultural work to Germany.

Beginning from the fact that artistic cooperation serves as a model for other sectors (cf. Ch. 1), the question poses itself: How can a specific culture of artistic cooperation be fruitful for non-artistic partnerships on a national and global level? The study of interdisciplinary and cross-boundary intercultural cooperation is a meaningful topic for further research.

Sources and Bibliography

Abels, Gabriele, Behrens, Maria (2009): *ExpertInnen-Interviews in der Politikwissenschaft. Eine sekundäranalytische Reflexion über geschlechtertheoretische und politikfeldanalytische Effekte.* In: Bogner/Littig/Menz (Ed.) (2009): 159-180.

Albers, Sönke (Ed.) (2009): *Methodik der empirischen Forschung.* 3. Edition. Wiesbaden.

Alrutz, Megan, Kovac, Kim Peter (2011): *Cultural Translation in International Collaborations. US Artists 'Dance' with Theatermakers from Abroad.* In: ASSITEJ International (Ed.) (2011): 4-12.

Arbeitsgruppe *Kultur und Entwicklung (2011): Konferenz Kunst. Kultur. Konflikt. 17.-18.05.2011. Dokumentation.* München.

Arickal, George (2012): *Partner und Konkurrenten zugleich. Wichtige Dimensionen deutsch-indischer Beziehungen.* In: Diözesan-Caritasverband für das Erzbistum Köln e. V. (Ed.) (2012): 9-12.

Arwind, Deepika (2012): *The Bangalore Lysistrata Project | Indo-British Theatre Collaboration*, s.l.

Arzoglou, Eleni (2006): *Interning in India: A Personal Account of Lessons Learnt.* In: Voll/Skoda (Ed.) (2006): 981-985.

ASSITEJ International (Ed.) (2011): *The Annual Magazine of ASSITEJ International 2011*, s.l.

Atteslander, Peter (2000): *Methoden der empirischen Sozialforschung.* 9. Edition. Berlin.

Auswärtiges Amt (1969): *Kulturabkommen zwischen der Bundesrepublik Deutschland und Indien.* Bundesgesetzblatt, Teil II No. 60, 1969 – P. 1713-1723. Bonn. See: http://tinyurl.com/q7xamdm (Accessed: 09.11.2013).

Auswärtiges Amt (1970): *Leitsätze für die auswärtige Kulturpolitik.* Bonn. In: Schneider (Ed.) (2008a): 184-190.

Auswärtiges Amt (2000): *Agenda für die deutsch-indische Partnerschaft im 21. Jahrhundert.* New Delhi. 18.05.2000. See: http://tinyurl.com/mgwyz47 (Accessed: 09.11.2013).

Auswärtiges Amt (2002): *Aufgaben der deutschen Außenpolitik. Südasien am Beginn des 21. Jahrhunderts.* Berlin. See: http://tinyurl.com/lxbmjde (Accessed: 09.11.2013).

Auswärtiges Amt (2003): *Auswärtige Kultur- und Bildungspolitik.* Berlin. See: http://tinyurl.com/olnxxam (Accessed: 09.11.2013).

Auswärtiges Amt (2006): *Gemeinsame deutsch-indische Erklärung anlässlich des Besuchs des indischen Premierministers in Deutschland.* 23.04.2006. Berlin. See: http://tinyurl.com/qyeoodu (Accessed: 09.11.2013).

Auswärtiges Amt (2007): *Gemeinsame Erklärung zur Weiterentwicklung der strategischen und globalen Partnerschaft zwischen Deutschland und Indien.* New Delhi. 30.10.2007. See: http://tinyurl.com/pweecel (Accessed: 09.11.2013).

Auswärtiges Amt (2009): *Menschen bewegen – Kulturpolitik im Zeitalter der Globalisierung. Dokumentation der Konferenz, des Kulturabends und der Tage der Auswärtigen Kulturpolitik.* Berlin. See: http://tinyurl.com/jwms5dd (Accessed: 09.05.2012).

Auswärtiges Amt (2011): *Auswärtige Kultur- und Bildungspolitik in Zeiten der Globalisierung. Partner gewinnen, Werte vermitteln, Interessen vertreten.* Berlin. See: http://tinyurl.com/nhyuwys (Accessed: 09.11.2013).

Auswärtiges Amt (2012a): *Beziehungen zwischen Indien und Deutschland.* Berlin. See: http://tinyurl.com/p5bzdsx (Accessed: 09.11.2013).

Auswärtiges Amt (2012b): *Globalisierung gestalten – Partnerschaften ausbauen – Verantwortung teilen. Konzept der Bundesregierung.* Berlin. See: http://tinyurl.com/lqefrq3 (Accessed: 09.11.2013).

Auswärtiges Amt (2012c): *Grußwort von Staatsministerin Cornelia Pieper zur Eröffnung der 'Days of India' am 11.05.2012.* Hamburg. See: http://tinyurl.com/n2tflmk (Accessed: 09.11.2013).

Auswärtiges Amt (2012d): *Rede von Außenminister Guido Westerwelle anlässlich des CDU/CSU-Kongresses "Asiens neue Gestaltungsmächte" am 13.06.2012.* Berlin. See: http://tinyurl.com/o4kz77k (Accessed: 09.11.2013).

Auswärtiges Amt (2013): *Gemeinsame Erklärung zur Weiterentwicklung der strategischen und globalen Partnerschaft zwischen Deutschland und Indien. Gemeinsam die Zukunft gestalten.* 11.04.2013 in Berlin. See: http://tinyurl.com/kw8mtyk (Accessed: 09.11.2013).

Auswärtiges Amt (s.a._a): *Dialog zwischen den Kulturen.* Berlin. See: http://tinyurl.com/mcqk3c5 (Accessed: 14.09.2013).

Auswärtiges Amt (s.a._b): *Wo die Musik spielt. Kultur und Kommunikation in der deutschen Außenpolitik.* Berlin. See: http://tinyurl.com/mxxdha6 (Accessed: 09.05.2012).

Auswärtiges Amt/Goethe-Institut e. V. (2004): *Rahmenvertrag.* München/Berlin. See: http://tinyurl.com/p887pqy (Accessed: 09.11.2013).

Auswärtiges Amt/Kulturabteilung (2000): *Auswärtige Kulturpolitik – Konzeption 2000.* Bonn/Berlin. See: http://tinyurl.com/osygdku (Accessed: 09.11.2013).

Axelrod, Robert (1987): *Die Evolution der Kooperation.* München.

Balla, Tina (2008): *Krisen ohne Grenzen. Auswärtige Kulturpolitik als Krisenprävention.* In: Schneider (Ed.) (2008a): 142-152.

Bandyopadhyay, Samik (2009): *Respondents.* In: Deshpande/K.V./Iyengar (Ed.) (2009): 197-200.

Barthel, Karoline (2010): *Ethisches Verhalten in der zwischenmenschlichen Kooperation in Organisationen – eine Betrachtung auf der Basis spieltheoretischer Überlegungen.* In: Beschorner/Schmidt/Verbohle/Schank (Ed.) (2010): 45-56.

Bartmann, Christoph (2011): *Vom Dialog zum Gespräch. Ein Gastbeitrag zum Kulturaustausch.* In: Institut für Kulturpolitik/Universität Hildesheim (2011): 45-49.

Batra, Satish K. (2001): *German-Indian Relations. Some Reflections.* In: Jain (Ed.) (2001): 159-162.

Bauer, Gerd Ulrich (2009a): *Viel Praxis, wenig Theorie – Kulturelle Programmarbeit: Kunst, Musik, Literatur, Film, Architektur.* In: Maaß (Ed.) (2009a): 127-148.

Bauer, Gerd Ulrich (2009b): *Kein Stiefkind mehr – Die Auswärtige Kulturpolitik in Forschung und Lehre.* In: Maaß (Ed.) (2009a): 423-427.

Bauer, Gerd Ulrich (2010): *Auswärtige Kulturpolitik als Handlungsfeld und "Lebenselixier": Expertentum in der deutschen Auswärtigen Kulturpolitik und der Kulturdiplomatie.* München.

Bauersachs, Hannah (2012): *Kooperation von Kultur und Wirtschaft im Rahmen der Deutschlandjahre. Über die Notwendigkeit und Herausforderung der Erschließung einer Forschungslücke.* Stuttgart. See: http://tinyurl.com/mmcgx4o (Accessed: 09.11.2013).

Baus, Sriparna (2008): *A Summary of the Conference.* In: Wälde (Ed.) (2008a): 231-243.

Ben J. Riepe Kompanie e. V. (2012): *Don't Ask, Don't Tell. Eine Produktion von Ben J. Riepe Kompanie and Navtej Johar/Studio Abhyas.* Sachbericht an das Goethe-Institut. Düsseldorf.

Bennett, Milton J. (2001): *Intercultural Competence for Global Leadership.* Milan. See: http://tinyurl.com/nnpjzvp (Accessed: 19.09.2013).

Bergold, Jarg, Thomas, Stefan (2010): *Partizipative Forschung.* In: Mey/Mruck (Ed.) (2010): 333-344.

Berkemer, Georg/Frasch, Tilman (Ed.) (1997): *Die deutsche Zusammenarbeit mit Südasien.* Beiträge zur Südasienforschung. Band 176. Stuttgart.

Bertelsmann Stiftung (Ed.) (2006a): *Cultures in globalisation: a Europe-India dialogue on global challenges and cultural visions; proceedings of the International Cultural Forum New Delhi,* held in November 2005/Malte C. Boecker. Gütersloh.

Bertelsmann Stiftung (Ed.) (2006b): *Interkulturelle Kompetenz – Schlüsselkompetenz des 21. Jahrhunderts? Thesenpapier der Bertelsmann Stiftung auf Basis der Interkulturellen-Kompetenz-Modelle von Dr. Darla K. Deardorff.* Gütersloh.

Bertelsmann Stiftung (Ed.) (2010): change. Das Magazin der Bertelsmann Stiftung, Ausgabe 1/2010. Schwerpunkt: *Globalisierung. Eine Welt ohne Grenzen. Chancen einer vernetzten Gesellschaft.* Gütersloh. See: http://tinyurl.com/mfz475t (Accessed: 15.09.2013).

Bertram, Christoph, Däuble, Friedrich (Ed.) (2002): *Wem dient der Auswärtige Dienst? Erfahrungen von Politik, Wirtschaft, Gesellschaft.* Opladen.

Beschorner, Thomas, Schmidt, Matthias (2010): *Kooperation und Ethik – Zur Einführung.* In: Beschorner/Schmidt/Verbohle/Schank (Ed.) (2010): 9-16.

Beschorner, Thomas/Schmidt, Matthias/Verbohle, Kristin/Schank, Christoph (Ed.) (2010): *Kooperation und Ethik.* München.

Betz, Joachim/Hein, Wolfgang (Ed.) (2005): *Neues Jahrbuch – Dritte Welt – Zivilgesellschaft.* Wiesbaden.

Beyme, Klaus von (1998): *Kulturpolitik und Nationale Identität. Studien zur Kulturpolitik zwischen staatlicher Steuerung und gesellschaftlicher Autonomie.* Wiesbaden.

Bhabha, Homi (2000a): *Die Verortung der Kultur.* Tübingen.

Bhabha, Homi (2000b): *Die Frage des Anderen: Stereotyp, Diskriminierung und der Diskurs des Kolonialismus.* In: Bhabha (2000a): 97-124.

Bhagat, Chetan (2012): *What young India wants. Selected essays and columns.* New Delhi.

Bliss, Frank (2010): *Sozio-kulturelle Aspekte in der entwicklungspolitischen Theorie und Praxis.* In: Wilhelm (Ed.) (2010): 202-216.

Bloch, Werner (2010): *Zwischen Kabul und Kalkutta: Kunst bei 48 Grad. Das Goethe-Institut in Delhi hält in der Zukunftsregion Südasien viele Fäden in der Hand.* In: Deutscher Kulturrat e. V. (Ed.) (2010a): 16.

B.L.O.T. (Ed.) (2012): *Posteventreport. India Goes 3D. 19-29 April 2012.* Delhi. Mumbai. Bangalore, s.l.

Blume, Georg (2011): *Der neue deutsche Wanderzirkus.* Stuttgart. See: http://tinyurl.com/kfopub7 (Accessed: 09.11.2013).

Bode, Christian (2002): *Die kulturellen Mittlerorganisationen.* In: Bertram/Däuble (Ed.) (2002): 149-162.

Bogner, Alexander/Littig, Beate/Menz, Wolfgang (Ed.) (2002): *Das Experteninterview. Theorie, Methoden, Anwendung.* Wiesbaden.

Bogner, Alexander/Littig, Beate/Menz, Wolfgang (Ed.) (2009): *Experteninterviews. Theorien, Methoden, Anwendungsfelder.* 3. Edition. Wiesbaden.

Bogner, Alexander/Menz, Wolfgang (2002): *Das theoriegenerierende Experteninterview. Erkenntnisinteresse, Wissensformen, Interaktion.* In: Bogner/Littig/Menz (Ed.) (2002): 33-70.

Bogner, Alexander/Menz, Wolfgang (2009a): *Experteninterviews in der qualitativen Sozialforschung. Zur Einführung in eine sich intensivierende Methodendebatte.* In: Bogner/Littig/Menz (Ed.) (2009): 7-31.

Bogner, Alexander/Menz, Wolfgang (2009b): *Das theoriegenerierende Experteninterview. Erkenntnisinteresse, Wissensformen, Interaktion.* In: Bogner/Littig/Menz (Ed.) (2009): 61-98.

Böhm, Andreas (2010): *Theoretisches Codieren: Textanalyse in der Grounded Theory.* In: Flick/Kardorff/Steinke (Ed.) (2010): 475-485.

Böhm, Birgit (2005): *Vertrauensvolle Verständigung herstellen: Ein Modell interdisziplinärer Projektarbeit.* Freie Universität Berlin.

Borchardt, Andreas/Göthlich, Stephan E. (2009): *Erkenntnisgewinnung durch Fallstudien.* In: Albers (Ed.) (2009): 33-48.

Bourdieu, Pierre (1982): *Die feinen Unterschiede. Kritik der gesellschaftlichen Urteilskraft.* Frankfurt a. M.

Brauer, Cletus (2010): *Interdisziplinäre Kooperation als Schlüssel zu ethischem Wirtschaften.* In: Beschorner/Schmidt/Verbohle/Schank (Ed.) (2010): 57-76.

Braun, Christina von/Kleinke, Henry/Präsidium des Goethe-Instituts (Ed.) (2010): *Unser Goethe-Institut. Dem Präsidenten zu Ehren. Klaus-Dieter Lehmann zum 70. Geburtstag.* München.

Braun, Eckhard (2012): *Außenkulturpolitik. Bericht vom 57. Loccumer Kulturpolitischen Kolloquium.* In: Kulturpolitische Gesellschaft e. V. (Ed.) (2012): 66-67.

Breuer, Franz/Lettau, Antje (s.a.): *Kurze Einführung in den qualitativ-sozialwissenschaftlichen Forschungsstil.* Münster. See: http://tinyurl.com/kyoyg42 (Accessed: 09.11.2013).

Breukelchen, Tanja (2010): *Kultur wird immer eigenständig sein. Prof. Dr. Klaus-Dieter Lehmann, Präsident des Goethe-Instituts und Kuratoriumsmitglied der Bertelsmann Stiftung, über das Verhältnis von Kultur und Globalisierung.* In: Bertelsmann Stiftung (Ed.) (2010): 51-53.

Broder, Henryk M. (2006): *Kulturdebatte: Dialog? Nein, danke!.* See: http://tinyurl.com/mxd3vn8 (Accessed: 13.09.2013).

Bronger, Dirk (1995): *Städte und Metropolen – Konfrontation der Kulturen.* In: Rothermund (Ed.) (1995a): 48-58.

Bundesregierung (1977): *Stellungnahme der Bundesregierung zu dem Bericht der Enquete-Kommission "Auswärtige Kulturpolitik" des Deutschen Bundestages* – Drucksache 7/4121/Drucksache 8/927. Bonn. See: http://tinyurl.com/k237qvb (Accessed: 09.11.2013).

Bundesregierung (2008a): *Aktionsplan Zivile Konfliktprävention, Konfliktlösung und Friedenskonsolidierung.* Berlin. See: http://tinyurl.com/kr8ndnz (Accessed: 09.11.2013).

Bundesregierung (2008b): *Krisenprävention als gemeinsame Aufgabe. 2. Bericht der Bundesregierung über die Umsetzung des Aktionsplans 'Zivile Konfliktprävention, Konfliktlösung und Friedenskonsolidierung'.* Berichtszeitraum Mai 2006 bis April 2008. Berlin. See: http://tinyurl.com/mgjzba4 (Accessed: 07.07.2013).

Bundesregierung (2010): *3. Bericht der Bundesregierung über die Umsetzung des Aktionsplans 'Zivile Konfliktprävention, Konfliktlösung und Friedenskonsolidierung'.* Berichtszeitraum Mai 2008 bis April 2010. Berlin. See: http://tinyurl.com/kfm9s7v (Accessed: 09.11.2013).

Bundesregierung (2014): *17. Bericht der Bundesregierung Auswärtige Kultur- und Bildungspolitik 2012-2013.* Berlin. See: http://tinyurl.com/nvequ7p (Accessed: 16.03.2014).

Bundesverband Deutscher Stiftungen (Ed.) (2013): *Aus Fehlern lernen – Potenziale für die Stiftungsarbeit.* Berlin. See: http://tinyurl.com/mm2n79f (Accessed: 09.11.2013).

Bundeszentrale für politische Bildung (Ed.) (2004): *Pocket global. Globalisierung in Stichworten.* Bonn. See: http://tinyurl.com/obawhdp (Accessed: 09.11.2013).

Bundeszentrale für politische Bildung (Ed.) (2006): Aus Politik und Zeitgeschehen. No. 28-29. *Dialog der Kulturen.* Bonn. See: http://tinyurl.com/lec5wzu (Accessed: 09.11.2013).

Bundeszentrale für politische Bildung (Ed.) (2007): Informationen zur politischen Bildung. No. 296/3. Quartal 2007. *Indien.* Bonn. See: http://tinyurl.com/l4e4t6m (Accessed: 09.11.2013).

Bundeszentrale für politische Bildung (Ed.) (2008): Aus Politik und Zeitgeschichte. No. 22/2008. 26.05.2008. *Indien.* Bonn. See: http://tinyurl.com/l6scqhm (Accessed: 09.11.2013).

Bundeszentrale für politische Bildung (Ed.) (2012): Aus Politik und Zeitgeschichte. No. 44-45/2012. 29.10.2012. *Kolonialismus.* Bonn. See: http://tinyurl.com/m2pvz7b (Accessed: 03.01.2014).

Burke, Peter (2005): *Was ist Kulturgeschichte?* Frankfurt a. M.

Centrum für Evaluation Universität des Saarlandes (Ed.) (2010): *Evaluation der Initiative "Kultur und Entwicklung".* Saarbrücken.

Chakrabarty, Dipesh (2010): *"Europa als Provinz". Perspektiven postkolonialer Geschichtsschreibung.* Frankfurt a. M.

Chakraborty, Abhishek (2012): *Ignite the Dancer.* In: The Asian Age, New Delhi, 01.11.2012, p. 15. See: http://tinyurl.com/o6vsgxr (Accessed: 09.11.2013).

Chakraborty, Kishore (Ed.) (2013): *Cultural Diplomacy Dictionary.* Berlin. See: http://tinyurl.com/om6kss4 (Accessed: 09.112013).

Chaterjee, Madhusree (2012): *Indian cities should merge the old and new: German urban designer.* See: http://tinyurl.com/l8nefc7 (Accessed: 09.11.2013).

Christoph, Ralph H. (2012): *Sachbericht der cologne on pop GmbH. Projekt: India goes 3D vom 19.-29.04.2012 in Mumbai, Bangalore und Delhi.* Köln.

Commission on Global Governance (1995): *Our Global Neighbourhood. The Report of the Commission on Global Governance.* Oxford.

CSCS (Centre for the Study of Culture and Society) (Ed.) (2012): No title (Questions and Answers to India's Cultural Policy). Bangalore.

Czerwanski, Anette (Ed.) (2003): *Schulentwicklung durch Netzwerkarbeit. Erfahrungen aus den Lernnetzwerken im 'Netzwerk innovativer Schulen in Deutschland'.* Gütersloh.

Dalal, Sayatan (2012): *Disco, on silent mode.* In: DNA – After Hrs., Mumbai, 14.04.2012, p. 7. See: http://tinyurl.com/nyb8jt9 (Accessed: 09.11.2013).

Debiel, Tobias/Wulf, Herbert (2013): *Indiens BRICS-Politik: Unentschlossen im Club.* See: http://tinyurl.com/mwqhz2v (Accessed: 25.12.2013).

Deindl, Christian (2005): *Soziale Netzwerke und soziales Kapital. Einfluss auf Lebenszufriedenheit und Vertrauen.* Diskussions-Papier der Forschungsgruppe Arbeit, Generation, Sozialstruktur (AGES) der Universität Zürich. See: http://tinyurl.com/qc26j3g (Accessed: 04.01.2014).

Denscheilmann, Heike (2013): *Deutschlandbilder. Ausstellungen im Auftrag Auswärtiger Kulturpolitik.* Reihe: Auswärtige Kulturpolitik. Wiesbaden.

Department of Culture/Ministry of Human Resource Development/Government of India (1990): *Report of the High-Powered Committee appointed to review the performance of the National Akademis and the National School of Drama.* New Delhi.

Deppermann, Arnulf (2001): *Gespräche analysieren. Eine Einführung.* Opladen.

Deshpande, Sudhanva/K.V., Akshara/Iyengar, Sameera (Ed.) (2009): *Our Stage: Pleasures and Perils of Theatre Practice in India.* New Delhi.

Deutsche Gesellschaft für Auswärtige Politik (1996): *Internationale Politik.* No. 51. Bonn.

Deutsche Gesellschaft für Technische Zusammenarbeit (2006): *Mainstreaming Participation. Kulturelle Aspekte von Partizipation. Dialog auf Augenhöhe.* Aus der Reihe Förderung partizipativer Entwicklung in der deutschen Entwicklungszusammenarbeit. Eschborn. See: http://tinyurl.com/mm8bf5h (Accessed: 09.11.2013).

Deutsche Gesellschaft für Technische Zusammenarbeit (2008): *Capacity WORKS. Das Managementmodell für Nachhaltige Entwicklung.* Eschborn. See: http://tinyurl.com/nop5d99 (Accessed: 23.02.2014).

Deutsche Gesellschaft für Technische Zusammenarbeit (2010): *Kultur und Entwicklung.* Eschborn.

Deutsche Gesellschaft für Technische Zusammenarbeit/Direktion für Entwicklung und Zusammenarbeit/Schönhuth, Michael (2005): *Glossar Kultur und Entwicklung. Ein Vademecum durch den Kulturdschungel.* Eschborn. See: www.kulturglossar.de (Accessed: 13.06.2013).

Deutsche UNESCO-Kommission e. V. (1995): *Unsere kreative Vielfalt: Bericht der Weltkommission "Kultur und Entwicklung".* Kurzfassung. Bonn. See: http://tinyurl.com/ohm35fe (Accessed: 09.11.2013).

Deutsche UNESCO-Kommission e. V. (1998): *The Power of Culture – Aktionsplan über Kulturpolitik für Entwicklung.* Verabschiedet von der UNESCO-Weltkonferenz "Kulturpolitik für Entwicklung", 30. März bis 2. April 1998 in Stockholm/Schweden. Bonn. See: http://www.unesco.de/458.html (Accessed: 09.11.2013).

Deutsche UNESCO-Kommission e. V. (2005): *Übereinkommen über Schutz und Förderung der Vielfalt kultureller Ausdrucksformen. Magna Charta der internationalen Kulturpolitik.* Bonn. See: http://tinyurl.com/nnpc98x (Accessed: 09.11.2013).

Deutsche UNESCO-Kommission e. V. (2008): *Kulturelle Bildung für Alle. Von Lissabon 2006 nach Seoul 2010.* Bonn: See: http://www.unesco.de/2559.html (Accessed: 07.07.2013).

Deutsche UNESCO-Kommission e. V. (2009): *Kulturelle Vielfalt gestalten. Handlungsempfehlungen aus der Zivilgesellschaft zur Umsetzung des UNESCO-Übereinkommens zur Vielfalt kultureller Ausdrucksformen (2005) in und durch Deutschland. Weißbuch.* Bonn.

Deutsche UNESCO-Kommission e. V. (2010): *UNESCO-Weltbericht. In kulturelle Vielfalt und interkulturellen Dialog investieren. Deutsche Kurzfassung des UNESCO-Weltberichts: Investing in cultural diversity and intercultural dialogue (2010).* Bonn.

Deutsche UNESCO-Kommission e. V. (2011): *Nachhaltige Entwicklung.* UNESCO heute. Magazin der Deutschen UNESCO-Kommission. No. 2/2011. Bonn.

Deutsche UNESCO-Kommission e. V. (2013): *Vielfalt. Kooperation. Aktion. Aktionspunkteplan 2013 bis 2016. Handlungsempfehlungen aus der Zivilgesellschaft zur Umsetzung der UNESCO-Konvention zum Schutz und zur Förderung der Vielfalt kultureller Ausdrucksformen in und durch Deutschland.* Bonn.

Deutscher Akademischer Austauschdienst (Ed.) (2009): *Dialog durch Kooperationen.* Potsdam.

Deutscher Bundestag (1975): *Bericht der Enquete-Kommission Auswärtige Kulturpolitik gemäß Beschluss des Deutschen Bundestages vom 23. Februar 1973* – Drucksache 7/215 (neu) (Verhandlungen des Deutschen Bundestages: Drucksachen 7/4121). Bonn. See: http://tinyurl.com/oxqv34c (Accessed: 09.11.2013).

Deutscher Bundestag (2007a): *Neujustierung der Auswärtigen Kulturpolitik.* Drucksache 16/6604. Berlin. See: http://tinyurl.com/o7deuhr (Accessed: 09.11.2013).

Deutscher Bundestag (2007b): *Schlussbericht der Enquete-Kommission "Kultur in Deutschland" vom 11.12.2007* – Drucksache 16/7000. Berlin. See: http://tinyurl.com/6o9g9e (Accessed: 03.03.2014).

Deutscher Bundestag (2009): *Antwort der Bundesregierung auf die Große Anfrage der Abgeordneten Jürgen Trittin, Volker Beck (Köln), Marieluise Beck (Bremen), weiterer Abgeordneter und der Fraktion BÜNDNIS 90/DIE GRÜNEN* – Drucksache 16/11485: Zur Indienpolitik der Bundesregierung. Berlin. See: http://tinyurl.com/kswppjf (Accessed: 09.11.2013).

Deutscher Bundestag (2011): *Bericht der Bundesregierung zur Auswärtigen Kultur- und Bildungspolitik 2010/2011.* Berlin. See: http://tinyurl.com/ox6gm26 (Accessed: 18.01.2014).

Deutscher Bundestag (2012): *Unterrichtung durch die Bundesregierung. Globalisierung gestalten – Partnerschaften ausbauen – Verantwortung teilen.* Drucksache 17/8600. Berlin. See: http://tinyurl.com/nbynjf8 (Accessed: 09.11.2013).

Deutscher Kulturrat e. V. (Ed.) (1999): *Kulturpolitik für das 21. Jahrhundert – Anforderungen an die Informationsgesellschaft.* Bonn.

Deutscher Kulturrat e. V. (Ed.) (2009): *politik und kultur – Zeitung des Deutschen Kulturrates.* Ausgabe 6/09. Berlin. See: http://tinyurl.com/ya679oj (Accessed: 09.11.2013).

Deutscher Kulturrat e. V. (Ed.) (2010a): *politik und kultur – Zeitung des Deutschen Kulturrates.* Ausgabe 5/10. Berlin. See: http://tinyurl.com/mxkbd7r (Accessed: 09.11.2013).

Deutscher Kulturrat e. V. (Ed.) (2010b): *politik und kultur – Zeitung des Deutschen Kulturrates.* Ausgabe 6/10. Berlin. See: http://tinyurl.com/qel8qs9 (Accessed: 09.05.2012).

Deutscher Kulturrat e. V. (Ed.) (2012): *politik und kultur – Zeitung des Deutschen Kulturrates.* Ausgabe 3/12. Berlin. See: http://tinyurl.com/qyp3ncz (Accessed: 20.02.2014).

Deutscher Kulturrat e. V. (Ed.) (2013b): *politik und kultur – Zeitung des Deutschen Kulturrates.* Ausgabe 5/13. Berlin. See: http://tinyurl.com/qg8f39v (Accessed: 20.02.2014).

Deutsches Übersee-Institut (2002): *Kompendium der deutsch-indischen Beziehungen.* Hamburg.

Deutsch-Indische Gesellschaft e. V. (Ed.) (1998): *INDO-ASIA. Politik, Kultur, Wirtschaft in Indien – Südasien – Ostasien.* 40. Jahrgang. Stuttgart.

Deutsch-Indische Gesellschaft e. V. (Ed.) (2003): *Festschrift zum 50-jährigen Bestehen der Deutsch-Indischen Gesellschaft: 1953 – 2003.* Stuttgart. See: http://tinyurl.com/pnmqhd6 (Accessed: 30.06.2013).

Devidayal, Anjali (2010): *India: arts education conference.* See: http://tinyurl.com/l9ccer5 (Accessed: 09.11.2013).

DeWalt, Kathleen Musante/DeWalt, Billie R. (2002): *Participant observation: a guide for fieldworkers.* Walnut Creek u. a.

Dhanwani, Rashmi (2012): *Challenges for cultural managers on global stage. About creating a potential nerve system of ideas.* In: Arts Management Newsletter, Bi-monthly Magazine for the global Perspective in Arts and Business. Ausgabe No. 112. Dezember 2012. P. 4-7. See: http://tinyurl.com/l2g4loc (Accessed: 12.09.2013).

Dickersbach, Safia (2013): *An Open Letter To The Federal Republic Of Germany: Africa Is Not A Country.* See: http://tinyurl.com/onwkzcj (Accessed: 07.01.2014).

Dingels, Hans-Eberhard/Voll, Klaus (2006): *Relationship without Impact? India and Germany Facing the Turbulent World of the 21st Century.* In: Voll/Skoda (Ed.) (2006): 1186-1191.

Diözesan-Caritasverband für das Erzbistum Köln e. V. (Ed.) (1999): *Meine Welt. Zeitschrift des Deutsch-Indischen Dialogs.* Heft 1. Jahrgang: 16. Juli 1999. Bad Honnef.

Diözesan-Caritasverband für das Erzbistum Köln e. V. (Ed.) (2000a): *Meine Welt. Zeitschrift des Deutsch-Indischen Dialogs.* Heft 1. Jahrgang: 17. Juli 2000. Bad Honnef.

Diözesan-Caritasverband für das Erzbistum Köln e. V. (Ed.) (2000b): *Meine Welt. Zeitschrift des Deutsch-Indischen Dialogs.* Heft 2. Jahrgang: 17. Dezember 2000. Bad Honnef.

Diözesan-Caritasverband für das Erzbistum Köln e. V. (Ed.) (2001): *Meine Welt. Zeitschrift des Deutsch-Indischen Dialogs.* Heft 1. Jahrgang: 18. Juli 2001. Bad Honnef.

Diözesan-Caritasverband für das Erzbistum Köln e. V. (Ed.) (2002): *Meine Welt. Zeitschrift des Deutsch-Indischen Dialogs.* Heft 1. Jahrgang: 19. Juli 2002. Bad Honnef.

Diözesan-Caritasverband für das Erzbistum Köln e. V. (Ed.) (2012): *Meine Welt. Zeitschrift des Deutsch-Indischen Dialogs.* Heft 2. Jahrgang: 29. Bad Honnef.

Diözesan-Caritasverband für das Erzbistum Köln e. V. (Ed.) (2012/13): *Meine Welt. Zeitschrift des Deutsch-Indischen Dialogs.* Heft 3. Jahrgang: 29. Bad Honnef.

Diözesan-Caritasverband für das Erzbistum Köln e. V. (Ed.) (2013a): *Meine Welt. Zeitschrift des Deutsch-Indischen Dialogs.* Heft 1. Jahrgang: 30. Bad Honnef.

Diözesan-Caritasverband für das Erzbistum Köln e. V. (Ed.) (2013b): *Meine Welt. Zeitschrift des Deutsch-Indischen Dialogs.* Heft 2. Jahrgang: 30. Bad Honnef.

Dizdar, Christian (2008): *Machtbalance als Erfolgsfaktor von interorganisationalen Beziehungen.* In: Hülsmann (Ed.) (2008): 13-158.

Drews, Albert (Ed.) (2012): *Außenkulturpolitik. Aktuelle Herausforderungen in einer Welt im Umbruch. 57. Loccumer Kulturpolitisches Kolloquium.* Rehburg-Loccum.

Düwell, Kurt (2009): *Zwischen Propaganda und Friedensarbeit – 100 Jahre Geschichte der deutschen Auswärtigen Kulturpolitik.* In: Maaß (Ed.) (2009a): 61-111.

Eikels, Kai van (2013): *Die Kunst des Kollektiven. Performance zwischen Theater, Politik und Sozio-Ökonomie.* München.

Eisfeld, Katrin (2004): *Vom Geben und Nehmen. Die Goethe-Institut und deutsche Kulturpolitik im Ausland (unter besonderer Berücksichtigung des Goethe-Instituts Dakar).* Magisterarbeit. Universität des Saarlandes.

Emge, Richard Martinus (1967): *Auswärtige Kulturpolitik. Eine soziologische Analyse einiger ihrer Funktionen, Bedingungen und Formen.* Habilitation. Universität Bonn.

Emmrich, Jennifer (2012): *Chancen und Grenzen von Evaluationen in der Auswärtigen Kultur- und Bildungspolitik.* In: Drews (Ed.) (2012): 107-120.

Enzensberger, Hans Magnus (1996): *Auswärts im Rückwärtsgang. Hans Magnus Enzensberger über die Blamage der deutschen Kulturpolitik im Ausland.* In: Sartorius (Ed.) (1996): 36-43.

Erffa, Wolfgang von (1996): *Deutsch-indische kulturelle Beziehungen an der Schwelle zum 21. Jahrhundert.* Vortrag vor der Asiatic Society, Durbar Hall, Bombay, 09. Oktober 1996. In: Indian Council for Cultural Relations (Ed.) (1996): 95-112.

Ermert, Karl (2011): *'Anything goes' geht nicht mehr. Über Medien, Jugend, Werte und kulturelle Bildung.* In: Kulturpolitische Gesellschaft e. V. (Ed.) (2011a): 54.

Ernst, Sonja (2013): *Leben in den Slums von Mumbai. Katherine Boo: "Annawadi und der Traum von einem anderen Leben".* 21.01.2013. See: http://tinyurl.com/nppahbl (Accessed: 09.11.2013).

Fabianczyk, Magda/Hoyle, Sophia (Ed.) (2012): *'We were trying to make sense …' Exploring Artist and Non-Artist Collaborations.* London.

Fangerau, Heiner/Halling, Thorsten (2009): *Netzwerke. Allgemeine Theorie oder Universalmetapher in den Wissenschaften? Ein transdisziplinärer Überblick.* Bielefeld.

Faschingeder, Gerald (2001): *Kultur und Entwicklung. Zur Relevanz soziokultureller Faktoren in hundert Jahren Entwicklungstheorie. Geschichte, Entwicklung, Globalisierung.* Band 1. Frankfurt a. M.

Faschingeder, Gerald (2010): *Auf widersprüchlichem Terrain. Kultur und Entwicklung greifbar machen.* In: Wilhelm (Ed.) (2010): 27-37.

Feilcke, Adelheid/Körber, Sebastian/Wedel, Heidi/Wetzel, Enzio/Wilhelm, Jürgen (2012): *Kunst. Kultur. Konflikt. Impulse für die Kulturarbeit in Krisenregionen.* Berlin.

Fietz, Yvonne (2009): *Partizipation durch Kultur.* Bonn. See: http://tinyurl.com/m6qepfo (Accessed: 09.11.2013).

Fischer, Martina (2009): *Kultur vor neuen Aufgaben – Konflikttransformation und Friedenskonsolidierung.* In: Maaß (Ed.) (2009a): 195-217.

Fischer, Walter Boris (2004): *Kunst vor Management. Führung und Förderung von Kulturinstitutionen.* Zürich/Chur.

Fischer-Lichte, Erika/Bharucha, Rustom (2011): *Dialogue: Erika Fischer-Lichte and Rustom Bharucha.* See: http://tinyurl.com/o2zshmt (Accessed: 27.01.2014).

Flick, Uwe (2007): *Qualitative Sozialforschung. Eine Einführung.* Reinbek bei Hamburg.

Flick, Uwe (2009): *Qualitative Sozialforschung. Eine Einführung.* 2. Edition. Reinbek bei Hamburg.

Flick, Uwe/Kardorff, Ernst von/Steinke, Ines (Ed.) (2000a): *Qualitative Forschung. Ein Handbuch.* Reinbek bei Hamburg.

Flick, Uwe/Kardorff, Ernst von/Steinke, Ines (Ed.) (2000b): *Was ist Qualitative Forschung? Einleitung und Überblick.* In: Flick/Kardorff/Steinke (Ed.) (2000a): 13-29.

Flick, Uwe/Kardorff, Ernst von/Steinke, Ines (Ed.) (2009): *Qualitative Forschung. Ein Handbuch.* 6. Edition. Reinbek bei Hamburg.

Flick, Uwe/Kardorff, Ernst von/Steinke, Ines (Ed.) (2010): *Qualitative Forschung. Ein Handbuch.* 7. Edition. Reinbek bei Hamburg.

Flick, Uwe/Kardorff, Ernst von/Steinke, Ines (Ed.) (2012): *Qualitative Forschung. Ein Handbuch.* 8. Edition. Reinbek bei Hamburg.

Fowler, Tilly (2012): *A Million Minutes: A highly subjective glossary of important, problematic and contested terms.* In: Fabianczyk/Hoyle (Ed.) (2012): 17-23.

Frahm, Annika (2009): *"Wir können ja kein Museum einfliegen".* Medieninfo des Goethe-Instituts Dezember 2009/Januar 2010. München. See: http://tinyurl.com/klcfmse (Accessed: 09.11.2013).

Franke, Barthold (2001): *Die Verachtung der Kulturpolitik.* In: Goethe-Institut Inter Nationes e. V. (2001): 61-71.

Fraunberger, Friederike/Sommer, Anette (1993): *Die Umsetzung des erweiterten Kulturbegriffs in der Programmarbeit des Goethe-Instituts.* In: Wierlacher (Ed.) (1993): 402-415.

Friebertshäuser, Barbara/Prengel, Annedore (Ed.) (2003): *Handbuch Qualitative Forschungsmethoden in der Erziehungswissenschaft.* Weinheim.

Frieling, Ralph (2000): *Zwischen "Bollywood" und Internet.* Eine Tagung an der Ev. Akademie Iserlohn, 28.-30.4.2000. In: Diözesan-Caritasverband für das Erzbistum Köln e. V. (Ed.) (2000a): 34-36.

Frings, Cornelia (2010): *Soziales Vertrauen. Eine Integration der soziologischen und der ökonomischen Vertrauenstheorie.* Wiesbaden.

Fuchs, Max (2007): *Kulturpolitik.* Wiesbaden.

Fuchs, Max (2008): *Kultur Macht Sinn.* Wiesbaden.

Fuchs-Heinritz, Werner/König, Alexandra (Ed.) (2005): *Pierre Bourdieu.* Konstanz.

Fücks, Ralf (2012): *Kunst als politische Intervention. Einleitung zum Vortrag von Prof. Dr. Hans-Thies Lehmann: "Ästhetik des Aufstands? Grenzgänge zwischen Politik und Kunst in den neuen sozialen Bewegungen".* Eine Veranstaltung im Rahmen der neuen Berliner Reihe "Foreign Affairs". Berlin. See: http://tinyurl.com/kppvguh (Accessed: 09.11.2013).

Gad, Daniel (2008): *Kultur und Entwicklung. Eine Übersichtsstudie zu Schnittfeldern deutscher Akteure der Auswärtigen Kultur- und Bildungspolitik und der Entwicklungszusammenarbeit.* Stuttgart. See: http://tinyurl.com/lf77uvl (Accessed: 09.11.2013).

Gad, Daniel (2009): *Geberländer und Akteure.* Stuttgart. See: http://tinyurl.com/oz9wggh (Accessed: 09.11.2013).

Gad, Daniel (2010): *Mit kultureller Vielfalt gestalten. Ein Plädoyer für eine kulturpolitisch durchdachte Entwicklungstheorie.* In: Wilhelm (Ed.) (2010): 94-113.

Gad, Daniel (2011): *Kulturelle Bildung als Ziel und Methode in der Entwicklungszusammenarbeit.* Bonn. See: http://tinyurl.com/nbouhyq (Accessed: 09.11.2013).

Gad, Daniel (2012a): *Kulturförderung in und von Entwicklungsländern als Handlungsfeld der Auswärtigen Kulturpolitik.* In: Drews (Ed.) (2012): 83-90.

Gad, Daniel (2012b): *Die Kunst der Entwicklungszusammenarbeit. Konzeptionen und Programme einer auswärtigen Kulturpolitik nordischer Staaten.* Dissertation. Universität Hildesheim.

Gandhi, Leela (1998): *Postcolonial Theory: A Critical Introduction.* New York.

Ganesh, Deepa (2011): *Stories from everywhere.* See: http://tinyurl.com/plchuxr (Accessed: 09.11.2013).

Ganguly, Sumit (2008): *Der indisch-pakistanische Konflikt.* In: Bundeszentrale für politische Bildung (Ed.) (2008): 32-38.

Garcia dos Santos, Laymert (2011): *Die Welt besteht aus vielen Welten.* In: Goethe-Institut e. V. (2011d): 54-56.

Gati Dance Forum (2012): *W.R.A.P.: Working in Research, Advocacy and Policy for Dance. Phase II. December 2013-January 2014. A progress Report & Future Steps.* New Delhi.

Geertz, Clifford (1973): *The Interpretation of Cultures: Selected Essays.* New York.

Geertz, Clifford (2007): *Welt in Stücken. Kultur und Politik am Ende des 20. Jahrhunderts.* 2. Edition. Wien.

Geertz, Clifford (2008): *Dichte Beschreibung. Bemerkungen zu einer bedeutenden Theorie von Kultur.* In: Wirth (Ed.) (2008): 453-487.

Gerhardter, Gabriele (2001): *Netzwerkorientierung in der Sozialarbeit. Eine überblicksartige Zusammenstellung zu "soziale Netzwerke" und "Organisationsnetzwerke".* See: http://tinyurl.com/lq3lszf (Accessed: 09.11.2013).

Ghosh, Arundhati (2013): *Arts funding in India: Hard times require furious dancing.* Bangalore. See: http://tinyurl.com/ac3xrdz (Accessed: 09.11.2013).

Gieler, Wolfgang (2010): *Entwicklungspolitisches Verständnis und die Bedeutung von Kultur im globalen Kontext.* In: Wilhelm (Ed.) (2010): 38-48.

Girtler, Roland (2001): *Methoden der Feldforschung.* Wien *et al.*

Girtler, Roland (2008): *Die 10 Gebote der Feldforschung.* Berlin. See: http://tinyurl.com/y93x92q (Accessed: 09.11.2013).

Glaser, Barney G. (2002): *Constructivist Grounded Theory?* In: Forum Qualitative Sozialforschung/Forum Qualitative Social Research. Vol. 3. No. 3. Berlin. See: http://tinyurl.com/qbnorh4 (Accessed: 09.11.2013).

Glaser, Barney G. (Ed.) (2007a): *The Grounded Theory Review: An international journal.* Vol. 6, No. 2, March 2007. Mill Valley. See: http://tinyurl.com/lru6gn9 (Accessed: 09.11.2013).

Glaser, Barney G. (2007b): *All is Data.* In: Glaser (Ed.) (2007a): 1-15.

Glaser, Barney G./Strauss, Anselm L. (2005): *Grounded Theory. Strategien qualitativer Forschung.* 2. Edition. Bern.

Gläser, Jochen/Laudel, Grit (2004): *Experteninterviews und qualitative Inhaltsanalyse als Instrumente rekonstruierender Untersuchungen.* Wiesbaden.

Gläser, Jochen/Laudel, Grit (2009): *Wenn zwei das Gleiche sagen... Qualitätsunterschiede zwischen Experten.* In: Bogner/Littig/Menz (Ed.) (2009): 137-158.

Goel, Balbir (Ed.) (2010): *Karlsruhe meets India.* Karlsruhe.

Goethe-Institut e. V. (1971): *Jahrbuch 1971.* München.

Goethe-Institut e. V. (1995): *Leitlinien für die Arbeit des Goethe-Instituts im Ausland.* München.

Goethe-Institut e. V. (1996a): *Das Goethe-Institut.* München.

Goethe-Institut e. V. (1996b): *Jahrbuch 1995/1996.* München.

Goethe-Institut e. V. (1998): *Grundsätze für die zukünftige Arbeit. Aufgaben und Ziele des Goethe-Instituts.* München. In: Schneider (Ed.) (2008a): 206-218.

Goethe-Institut e. V. (1999): *Durchblick. Zehn Thesen zur Rolle des Goethe-Instituts.* München. In: Schneider (Ed.) (2008a): 219-221.

Goethe-Institut e. V. (2008): *Kultur und Entwicklung.* München.

Goethe-Institut e. V. (2009): *Satzung vom 20. November 2009 auf Basis der Satzung vom 21. September 2000.* München. See: http://tinyurl.com/q3dljqo (Accessed: 09.11.2013).

Goethe-Institut e. V. (2010a): *Jahrbuch 2009/2010.* München. See: http://tinyurl.com/lufeypq (Accessed: 19.09.2013).

Goethe-Institut e. V. (2010b): *Magazin 1.10 Reportagen Bilder Gespräche.* München. See: http://tinyurl.com/lpyr22m (Accessed: 13.06.2013).

Goethe-Institut e. V. (2010c): *Magazin 2.10 Reportagen Bilder Gespräche.* München. See: http://tinyurl.com/l44yka8 (Accessed: 13.06.2013).

Goethe-Institut e. V. (2010d): *Magazin 3.10 Reportagen Bilder Gespräche.* München. See: http://tinyurl.com/mgxv7ny (Accessed: 13.06.2013).

Goethe-Institut e. V. (2011a): *Jahrbuch 2010/2011.* München. See: http://tinyurl.com/mw2zvl6 (Accessed: 19.09.2013).

Goethe-Institut e. V. (2011b): *Pressemappe. Jahrespressekonferenz 2011.* München. See: http://tinyurl.com/pw39u5s (Accessed: 09.11.2013).

Goethe-Institut e. V. (2011c): *Der Bildungsauftrag des Goethe-Instituts.* München. See: http://tinyurl.com/par8emq (Accessed: 12.09.2013).

Goethe-Institut e. V. (2011d): *Magazin 2.11 Reportagen Bilder Gespräche.* München. See: http://tinyurl.com/n2xcvwx (Accessed: 18.09.2013).

Goethe-Institut e. V. (2012a): *Perspektiv – Wechsel. Residenzprogramme des Goethe-Instituts.* Berlin.

Goethe-Institut e. V. (2012b): *Rechenschaftsbericht 2011/2012.* München. See: http://tinyurl.com/npaddfy (Accessed: 19.09.2013).

Goethe-Institut e. V. (2012c): *Pressemappe. Jahrespressekonferenz 2012.* München. See: http://tinyurl.com/nfnskh6 (Accessed: 09.11.2013).

Goethe-Institut e. V. (2012d): *Jahrbuch 2011/2012.* München. See: http://tinyurl.com/kkyzk8t (Accessed: 25.12.2013)

Goethe-Institut e. V. (2013): *Reportage Bilder Gespräche. Das Magazin des Goethe-Instituts.* No. 04/13. München. See: http://tinyurl.com/qf3mgge (Accessed: 09.11.2013).

Goethe-Institut e. V. Bangalore (2000): *40th anniversary – Max Mueller Bhavan Bangalore: 1960-2000.* Bangalore.

Goethe-Institut e. V. New Delhi (2011): *Contract Between Goethe Institute, New Delhi and The Just Environment Charitable Trust,* New Delhi. August 25, 2011.

Goethe-Institut e. V. New Delhi (2012a): *Abschlussbericht zur Indien-Tournee der Indisch-Deutschen Koproduktion "Boy with a suitcase/Der Junge mit dem Koffer" im Rahmen von "Deutschland und Indien" 2011-12.* New Delhi.

Goethe-Institut e. V. New Delhi (2012b): *ATSA 2013-14 Information Mailer.* New Delhi.

Goethe-Institut e. V. New Delhi (s.a._a): *India goes 3D! (interne Projektbeschreibung).* New Delhi.

Goethe-Institut e. V. New Delhi (s.a._b): *DO I KNOW YOU? "Indien-Tournee der dt.-indischen Produktion: Boy with a Suitcase/Der Junge mit dem Koffer". Projekt-Kurzvorstellung.* New Delhi.

Goethe-Institut Inter Nationes e. V. (2001): *50 Jahre Goethe-Institut. Murnau – Manila – Minsk.* München.

Goethe-Institut Portugal (s.a.): *Lisboa – Maputo – Berlin. Eine Film-Dokumentation eines internationalen Musikprojekts.* Lissabon.

Gould, Helen G./Marsh, Mary (2004): *Culture: Hidden Development. Creative exchange. Network for culture and development,* s.l.

Government of India/Planning Commission (2011): *Faster, Sustainable and More Inclusive Growth. An Approach to the Twelfth Five Year Plan.* New Delhi. See: http://tinyurl.com/q8blmcx (Accessed: 09.11.2013).

Government of India/Planning Commission (2013): *Twelth Five Year Plan (2012-2017).* Social Sectors. Vol. III. New Delhi. See: http://tinyurl.com/krulhe3 (Accessed: 08.11.2013).

Graf, Gunter (2011): *Der Fähigkeitsansatz im Kontext von Informationsbasen sozialethischer Theorien.* In: Sedmak/Babic/Bauer/Posch (Ed.) (2011a): 11-28.

Grätz, Ronald (2012a): *Die Zukunft Europas aus der Kultur gewinnen.* In: Drews (Ed.) (2012): 45-50.

Grätz, Ronald (2012b): *Lisboa – Maputo – Berlin. Ein transkulturelles Musikprojekt am Goethe-Institut in Lissabon 2006-2008.* In: Kimmich/Schahadat (Ed.) (2012): 219-233.

Groll, Tina (2011): *Die Stadt der offenen Funknetzwerke.* See: http://tinyurl.com/qjvl4xv (Accessed: 15.09.2013).

Gross, Bruno (2012): *Außenkulturpolitik in einer sich verändernden Welt. Welchen Herausforderungen müssen wir uns stellen?* In: Drews (Ed.) (2012): 19-24.

Günsche, Karl-Ludwig (1997): *Die Auswärtige Kulturpolitik als Hilfe der Wirtschaft.* In: Die Welt vom 24.03.1997.

Günther, Hans Otto (Ed.) (1956): *Indien und Deutschland. Ein Sammelband.* VIII. Frankfurt a. M.

Günther, Lothar (1993): *40 Jahre Deutsch-Indische Gesellschaft (e. V.). Ein Rückblick.* Stuttgart.

Gupta, Amaresh (2012): *Indische Erfahrungen in Deutschland. Festrede anlässlich der Kölner Indien-Woche am 9. Juni 2012.* In: Diözesan-Caritasverband für das Erzbistum Köln e. V. (Ed.) (2012): 17-19.

Hall, Edward Twitchell (1959): *The Silent Language.* New York.

Hall, Edward Twitchell (1976): *Beyond Culture.* New York.

Hall, Edward Twitchell/Hall, Mildred R. (1984): *Les différences caches.* Hamburg.

Hall, Edward Twitchell/Hall, Mildred R. (1990): *Understanding cultural differences.* Yarmouth/Maine.

Hall, Stuart (2000a): *Rassismus und kulturelle Identität.* Hamburg.

Hall, Stuart (2000b): *Der Westen und der Rest: Diskurse und Macht.* In: Hall (2000a): 137-179.

Hamm-Brücher, Hildegard (1980): *Kulturbeziehungen weltweit. Ein Werkstattbericht zur auswärtigen Kulturpolitik.* München/Wien.

Hamm-Brücher, Hildegard/Auswärtiges Amt (1982): *Zehn Thesen zur kulturellen Begegnung und Zusammenarbeit mit Ländern der Dritten Welt.* In: Schneider (Ed.) (2008a): 191-196.

Hampel, Annika (2012): *'Partnerschaftliche Zusammenarbeit' Auswärtiger Kulturpolitik: Einzuforderndes Ideal in einer herausfordernden Praxis.* In: Drews (Ed.) (2012): 97-106.

Hanika, Karin/Wagner, Bernd (Ed.) (2004): *Kulturelle Globalisierung und regionale Identität. Beiträge zum kulturpolitischen Diskurs.* Bonn.

Hardie, Yvette (2011): *To Act Individually and Collectively with Confidence. Arterial Network as an African Model of Artistic Collaborations.* In: ASSITEJ International (Ed.) (2011): 20-24.

Harnischfeger, Horst (2000): *Die auswärtige Kulturpolitik vor einem Wendepunkt.* Bonn. See: http://tinyurl.com/pjqme3n (Accessed: 09.11.2013).

Hartman, Souza de (1996): *Navjot Altaf.* Final Evaluation. Grant Number: 1996-0-006, s.l.

Hasan, Anjum (1998): *Geeta Ramanujam.* Final Evaluation. Grant Number: 1998-0-002, s.l.

Hasan, Anjum (2000): *Harish Nagrecha.* Final Evaluation. Grant Number: 2000-0-007, s.l.

Häußling, Roger (Ed.) (2009): *Grenzen von Netzwerken.* Wiesbaden.

Havenga, Michele/Locke, Natania (2010): *Corporations and Partnerships in South Africa.* Alphen aan den Rijn.

Heinrichs, Harald/Kuhn, Katina/Newig, Jens (Ed.) (2011): *Nachhaltige Gesellschaft. Welche Rolle für Partizipation und Kooperation?* Wiesbaden.

Hempfer, Klaus W./Traninger, Anja (Ed.) (2010): *Der Dialog im Diskursfeld seiner Zeit. Von der Antike bis zur Aufklärung.* Stuttgart.

Hemrajani, Nikhil (2012): *German brew in Mumbai for you.* In: Hindustan Times, Mumbai, 12.04.2012, p. 1 and 5. See: http://tinyurl.com/oab8xpm (Accessed: 09.11.2013).

Herbert Quandt-Stiftung (2010): *Vertrauen. Die Bedeutung von Vertrauensformen für das soziale Kapital unserer Gesellschaft.* Bad Homburg v. d. Höhe.

Hessische Vereinigung für Volkskunde (Ed.) (2011): *Kultur & Politik: Aspekte kulturwissenschaftlicher und kulturpolitischer Spannungsfelder.* Schriftenreihe Hessische Blätter für Volks- und Kulturforschung, 47, 07.11.2011. Marburg.

Hillger, Doris (2007): *Chancen für alle? Bildung zwischen Analphabetismus und Eliten-Förderung.* Bonn. See: http://tinyurl.com/ozoswx6 (Accessed: 09.11.2013).

Höfer, Renate/Keupp, Heiner/Straus, Florian (2006): *Prozesse sozialer Verortung in Szenen und Organisationen – Ein netzwerkorientierter Blick auf traditionale und reflexiv moderne Engagementformen.* In: Hollstein/Straus (Ed.) (2006): 267-293.

Hoffmann, Hilmar (1981): *Kultur für alle.* Frankfurt a. M.

Hoffmann, Hilmar (1994): *Eine neue Offensive ist erforderlich.* In: Hoffmann/ Maaß (Ed.) (1994): 13-21.

Hoffmann, Hilmar (1996a): *"Dritte Säule" der Außenpolitik. Zur aktuellen Diskussion um die auswärtige Kulturpolitik.* In: Internationale Politik, März 1996, p. 15-20.

Hoffmann, Hilmar (1996b): *Globalisierung als Herausforderung.* In: Sartorius (Ed.) (1996): 275-284.

Hoffmann, Hilmar (1998): *Gedanken zum Dialog der Kulturen.* In: Deutsch-Indische Gesellschaft e. V. (Ed.) (1998): 24.

Hoffmann, Hilmar (1999): *Das Goethe-Institut als Netzwerk für den Kulturdialog.* In: Deutscher Kulturrat e. V. (Ed.) (1999): 185-209.

Hoffmann, Hilmar (2008): *Kultur für alle.* In: Schneider (Ed.) (2008a): 168-180.

Hoffmann, Hilmar/Maaß, Kurt-Jürgen (1994): *Freund oder Fratze? Das Bild von Deutschland in der Welt und die Aufgaben der Kulturpolitik.* Frankfurt a. M./ New York.

Hofstede, Geert (1980): *Culture's Consequences – International Differences in Work Related Values.* London/New Delhi.

Hofstede, Geert (1991): *Cultures and Organizations. Software of the Mind.* New York.

Hofstede, Geert (1993): *Interkulturelle Zusammenarbeit. Kulturen – Organisationen – Management.* Wiesbaden.

Hofstede, Geert (1997): *Lokales Denken, globales Handeln. Kulturen, Zusammenarbeit und Management.* München.

Hofstede, Geert (2001a): *Culture's Consequences – Comparing Values, Behaviors, Institutions and Organizations Across Nations.* 2. Edition. London/New Delhi.

Hofstede, Geert (2001b): *Lokales Denken, globales Handeln. Interkulturelle Zusammenarbeit und globales Management.* 2. Edition. München.

Hofstede, Geert (2006): *Lokales Denken, globales Handeln. Interkulturelle Zusammenarbeit und globales Management.* 3. Edition. München.

Hofstede, Geert/Hofstede, Gert Jan (2005): *Cultures and Organizations. Software of the Mind: Intercultural Cooperation and Its Importance for Survival.* New York.

Hofstede, Geert/Hofstede, Gert Jan/Minkov, Michael (Ed.) (2010): *Cultures and Organization. Software of the Mind: Intercultural Cooperation and Its Importance for Survival.* 3. Edition. New York.

Hollstein, Betina/Straus, Florian (Ed.) (2006): *Qualitative Netzwerkanalyse. Konzepte, Methoden, Anwendungen.* Wiesbaden.

Holtz, Uwe (2009): *Entwicklungspolitisches Glossar.* Universität Bonn. See: http://tinyurl.com/p3tu6x7 (Accessed: 13.09.2013).

Holzberg, Martin (2009): *Erfolgsfaktoren sektorübergreifender Kooperationen. Ein empirischer Beitrag zur Kooperationsforschung unter besonderer Berücksichtigung von Stiftungen.* Wiesbaden.

Höpel, Thomas (2007): *Von der Kunst- zur Kulturpolitik.* Stuttgart.

Hoyle, Sophia (2012a): *'We were trying to make sense …': Introduction.* In: Fabianczyk/Hoyle (Ed.) (2012): 2-5.

Hoyle, Sophia (2012b): *'We were trying to make sense …' Artist and non-artist participation and collaboration: Conclusion.* In: Fabianczyk/Hoyle (Ed.) (2012): 37-39.

Hülsmann, Michael (Ed.) (2008): *Kontinuitätsorientierte Koordination dynamischer Kooperationen.* Wiesbaden.

Huntington, Samuel P. (2002): *Kampf der Kulturen: Die Neugestaltung der Weltpolitik im 21. Jahrhundert.* 7. Edition. München.

ICUnet AG (s.a.): *Die Kulturdimensionen. Ein erprobtes Modell zum weltweiten Kulturvergleich.* Passau. See: http://tinyurl.com/k4kl4jc (Accessed: 09.11.2013).

ifa (Institut für Auslandsbeziehungen e. V.) (Ed.) (1994): *Interkulturelle Kommunikation und Interkulturelles Training.* Stuttgart.

ifa (Institut für Auslandsbeziehungen e. V.) (Ed.) (1995a): *Kultur für Europa – Europäische Kulturpolitik.* Kulturaustausch. Zeitschrift für internationale Perspektiven. Ausgabe III/1995. Stuttgart.

ifa (Institut für Auslandsbeziehungen e. V.) (Ed.) (1995b): *Migration und Kultureller Wandel.* Kulturaustausch. Zeitschrift für internationale Perspektiven. 45. Jahrgang. 1. Vierteljahr. Stuttgart.

ifa (Institut für Auslandsbeziehungen e. V.) (Ed.) (2006): *Die deutsch-indischen Kulturbeziehungen seit 1990. Literaturauswahl.* Reihe Literaturrecherchen. Heft 18. Stuttgart. See: http://tinyurl.com/muqml74 (Accessed: 09.11.2013).

ifa (Institut für Auslandsbeziehungen e. V.) (Ed.) (2009): *Tradition und Aufbruch. Die deutsch-indischen Kulturbeziehungen. Bestandsaufnahme und Empfehlungen.* Stuttgart. See: http://tinyurl.com/lno3znk (Accessed: 09.11.2013).

ifa (Institut für Auslandsbeziehungen e. V.) (Ed.) (2010a): *Dossier Kultur und Entwicklung.* Stuttgart. See: http://tinyurl.com/kdurgj7 (Accessed: 09.11.2013).

ifa (Institut für Auslandsbeziehungen e. V.) (Ed.) (2010b): *Das Deutsche in der Welt.* Kulturaustausch. Zeitschrift für internationale Perspektiven. Ausgabe IV/2010. Stuttgart.

ifa (Institut für Auslandsbeziehungen e. V.) (Ed.) (2011a): *Weniger ist mehr.* Kulturaustausch. Zeitschrift für internationale Perspektiven. Ausgabe I/2011. Stuttgart.

ifa (Institut für Auslandsbeziehungen e. V.) (Ed.) (2011b): *Zweifeln ist menschlich. Aufklärung im 21. Jahrhundert.* Kulturaustausch. Zeitschrift für internationale Perspektiven. Ausgabe IV/2011. Stuttgart.

ifa (Institut für Auslandsbeziehungen e. V.) (Ed.) (2013): *European external cultural relations – Expectations from the outside.* Conference Report. Brussels, 12 December 2012. ifa-Edition Culture and Foreign Policy. Stuttgart. See: http://tinyurl.com/p2h3kan (Accessed: 09.11.2013).

ifa (Institut für Auslandsbeziehungen e. V.)/Robert Bosch Stiftung (Ed.) (2007): *Kulturreport Fortschritt Europa*, 1. Stuttgart. See: http://tinyurl.com/n8pyd3r (Accessed: 09.11.2013).

IFAB (India Foundation for the Arts Bangalore) (1998): *Annual Report April 1997 – March 1998.* Bangalore.

IFAB (India Foundation for the Arts Bangalore) (1999): *Annual Report April 1998 – March 1999.* Bangalore.

IFAB (India Foundation for the Arts Bangalore) (2000a): *Annual Report April 1999 – March 2000.* Bangalore.

IFAB (India Foundation for the Arts Bangalore) (2000b): *Anschreiben und Ausschreibung Arts Collaboration Programme 2000.* Bangalore.

IFAB (India Foundation for the Arts Bangalore) (2001): *Annual Report April 2000 – March 2001.* Bangalore.

IFAB (India Foundation for the Arts Bangalore) (2002a): *Annual Report April 2001 – March 2002.* Bangalore.

IFAB (India Foundation for the Arts Bangalore) (2002b): *Anschreiben und Ausschreibung Arts Collaboration Programme 2002.* Bangalore.

IFAB (India Foundation for the Arts Bangalore) (2003): *Annual Report April 2002 – March 2003.* Bangalore.

IFAB (India Foundation for the Arts Bangalore) (2004a): *Annual Report April 2003 – March 2004.* Bangalore.

IFAB (India Foundation for the Arts Bangalore) (2004b): *Anschreiben und Ausschreibung Arts Collaboration Programme 2004.* Bangalore.

IFAB (India Foundation for the Arts Bangalore) (2012): *Annual Report April 2011 – March 2012.* Bangalore.

IFAB (India Foundation for the Arts Bangalore) (s.a.): *You arrive not expecting more wealth than the riches you gained along the way.* Bangalore.

Ihlau, Olaf (2008): *Indien auf dem Sprung zur Weltmacht – Essay.* Bonn. See: http://tinyurl.com/ntbjc6w (Accessed: 09.11.2013).

Ihne, Wilhelm (2006): *Einführung in die Entwicklungspolitik.* Hamburg.

Imhasly, Bernard (2008): *Ein reiches Land mit armen Menschen.* Bonn. See: http://tinyurl.com/p4eg37v (Accessed: 09.11.2013).

India Theatre Forum (2010): *Copyright Kotwal.* Chennai.

Indian Centre for Philanthropy (1999): *Directory of Indian Donor Organisations.* New Delhi.

Indian Council f. Cultural Relations (Ed.) (1996): *Indien in der Gegenwart.* 1 (1996) 3-4. New Delhi.

Indian Council f. Cultural Relations (Ed.) (1997): *Indien in der Gegenwart.* 2 (1997) 1-2. New Delhi.

Indian Council f. Cultural Relations (Ed.) (1998): *Indien in der Gegenwart.* 3 (1998) 1-2. New Delhi.

Indien-Institut (München) (Ed.) (2004): *75. Gründungs-Jubiläum des Indien-Instituts: Chronik 1929-2004.* München.

Institut für Kulturpolitik der Kulturpolitischen Gesellschaft e. V. (Ed.) (2007): *Jahrbuch Kulturpolitik. Europäische Kulturpolitik.* Band 7. Essen.

Institut für Kulturpolitik/Universität Hildesheim (2011): *Kultur. Politik. Diskurs. Aus Lehre und Forschung des Instituts für Kulturpolitik der Universität Hildesheim.* Heft 12/2011. Hildesheim.

Ischreyt, Hans (1964): *Deutsche Kulturpolitik: Information über die pluralistischen und totalitären Formen. Ein Leitfaden.* Bremen.

ITI (Internationales Theaterinstitut) (Ed.) (2013): *Jahrbuch 2013: Was bleibt.* Berlin.

Ittstein, Daniel Jan (2002): *Dialog der Kulturen.* Diplomarbeit. Universität Passau.

Ittstein, Daniel Jan (2009): *Potenziale der Musik als strategisches Instrument Auswärtiger Kultur- und Bildungspolitik am Beispiel der deutsch-indischen Beziehungen.* Dissertation. Universität Passau.

Iyer, Sanjay (2010): *Kali-Kalisu: An Arts Education Teacher Initiative. Teacher Training for Arts Pedagogies: The Kali-Kalisu Case'.* Bangalore.

Jain, Rajendra Kumar (Ed.) (2001): *India and Germany in a changing world.* New Delhi.

Jain, Rajendra Kumar (2007): *Der blasse Kontinent.* In: ifa/Robert Bosch Stiftung (Ed.) (2007): 38-41.

Jütte, Wolfgang (2006): *Netzwerkvisualisierung als Triangulationsverfahren bei der Analyse lokaler Weiterbildungslandschaften.* In: Hollstein/Straus (2006): 199-221.

Kakar, Sudhir (2006): *Cultural Encounters in the Era of Globalisation.* In: Bertelsmann Stiftung (Ed.) (2006a): 122-125.

Kämpchen, Martin (2004): *Bengalischer Leuchtturm, praktische Wege aus der Armut – das Goethe-Institut in Kalkutta.* In: Frankfurter Allgemeine Zeitung, 22. Juli 2004, No. 168, p. 33.

Kämpchen, Martin (2012): *Indien und Deutschland im kulturellen Dialog. Erfahrungen und Reflexionen.* In: Diözesan-Caritasverband für das Erzbistum Köln e. V. (Ed.) (2012): 13-14.

Kämpchen, Martin (2013a): *Deutsch-indische Kulturbeziehungen wohin? Martin Kämpchen antwortet auf die Fragen von Annika Hampel.* In: Diözesan-Caritasverband für das Erzbistum Köln e. V. (Ed.) (2013a): 65-67.

Kämpchen, Martin (2013b): *Indische Literatur in Deutschland.* See: http://tinyurl.com/kbuuqz5 (Accessed: 20.02.2014).

Kapoor, Sanjna (2009): *A Catalyst for Theatre.* In: Deshpande/K.V./Iyengar (Ed.) (2009): 185-190.

Kathe, Steffen R. (2005): *Kulturpolitik um jeden Preis: Die Geschichte des Goethe-Instituts von 1951 bis 1990.* München.

Kempf, Wilhelm/Kiefer, Marcus (Ed.) (2009): *Forschungsmethoden der Psychologie. Zwischen naturwissenschaftlichem Experiment und sozialwissenschaftlicher Hermeneutik. Band 3: Psychologie als Natur- und Kulturwissenschaft. Die soziale Konstruktion der Wirklichkeit.* Berlin.

Kettner, Peter (2009): *Menschen bewegen – Das Auswärtige Amt in der Außenkulturpolitik.* In: Maaß (Ed.) (2009a): 239-248.

Khokar, Ashish (2001): *New directions, old ways.* Bangalore. See: http://tinyurl.com/lq5q2g4 (Accessed: 09.11.2013).

Kimmich, Dorothee/Schahadat, Schamma (Ed.) (2012): *Kulturen in Bewegung. Beiträge zur Theorie und Praxis der Transkulturalität.* Bielefeld.

Klaic, Dragan (2009): *Bangalore: Asian cultural actors connect,* s.l.

Klein, Armin (2009): *Kulturpolitik: Eine Einführung.* 3. Edition. Wiesbaden.

Klein, Simone/Siegmund, Karin (2010): *Partnerschaften von NGOs und Unternehmen. Chancen und Herausforderungen.* Wiesbaden.

Klinge, Katharina (2007): *Interkulturelles Training mit synthetischen Kulturen. Konzeption und Evaluation einer multimedialen Lernsoftware zur interkulturellen Sensibilisierung. Dissertation.* Westfälische Wilhelms-Universität Münster (Westfalen).

Kneidinger, Bernadette (2013): *Geopolitische Identitätskonstruktionen in der Netzwerkgesellschaft. Mediale Vermittlung und Wirkung regionaler, nationaler und transnationaler Identitätskonzepte.* Wiesbaden.

Knopp, Hans-Georg (2006): *Intercultural Competence Between India and Germany.* In: Bertelsmann Stiftung (Ed.) (2006a): 116-121.

Knopp, Hans-Georg (2008): *Kultur: Die vierte Säule nachhaltiger Entwicklung.* In: Goethe-Institut e. V. (2008): n.p.

Knopp, Hans-Georg (2010a): *Zwischen Kulturförderung und Kulturentwicklung: Die Auswärtige Kulturpolitik und die Entwicklungspolitik.* In: Wilhelm (Ed.) (2010): 140-147.

Knopp, Hans-Georg (2010b): *Verantwortung in der auswärtigen Kultur- und Bildungspolitik.* In: Braun/Kleinke/Präsidium des Goethe-Instituts (Ed.) (2010): 14-21.

Knopp, Hans-Georg (2013): *Gastvortrag von Prof. Dr. Hans-Georg Knopp am Institut für Kulturpolitik der Universität Hildesheim in der Veranstaltung 'Kultur in Transformation. Innenansicht zur Außenpolitik des Goethe-Instituts' am 09.07.2013.* Mitschrift.

Knüsel, Pius (2010): *Kultur für alle – Illusion oder konkrete Utopie? Soziale Kulturarbeit ist nicht Populismus.* In: Kulturpolitische Gesellschaft e. V. (Ed.) (2010c): 47-50.

Knüsel, Pius (2011): *Was soll das? Die staatlich geförderte internationale Kulturarbeit glaubt an die Planbarkeit kultureller Prozesse. Die Wirklichkeit sieht anders aus.* In: ifa (Ed.) (2011a): 70-72.

Koivunen, Hannele/Marsio, Leena (2006): *Fair Culture? Ethical dimension of cultural policy and cultural rights.* Helsinki. See: http://tinyurl.com/p3sjbjr (Accessed: 18.11.2013).

Köppel, Petra (2008): *Konflikte und Synergien in multikulturellen Teams.* Wiesbaden.

Körber, Hans-Joachim (2006): *Economic Globalisation and Cultural Exchange: Chances and Challenges from a Retail Company's Point of View.* In: Bertelsmann Stiftung (Ed.) (2006a): 80-85.

Körber, Sebastian (2009): *Image, Marke, Branding – Die veränderte Arbeit am Deutschlandbild.* In: Maaß (Ed.) (2009a): 185-193.

Kramer, Dieter (2011): *Europäische Ethnologie und die Enquete-Kommission Kultur in Deutschland des Deutschen Bundestages.* In: Hessische Vereinigung für Volkskunde (Ed.) (2011): 35-47.

Krause-Nehring, Catherine (2007): *Die Airbus-Kultur. Eine kulturelle und politische Analyse des Flugzeugbaus bei Airbus unter besonderer Berücksichtigung der deutsch-französischen Beziehungen.* Dissertation. Universität Passau.

Krewer, Bernd (1996): *Kulturstandards als Mittel der Selbst- und Fremdreflexion in interkulturellen Begegnungen.* In: Thomas (Ed.) (1996): 147-164.

Kruse, Jan (2010): *Reader "Einführung qualitative Interviewforschung".* Freiburg.

Kuckartz, Udo (1999): *Computergestützte Analyse qualitativer Daten. Eine Einführung in die Methoden und Arbeitstechniken.* Opladen.

Kuckartz, Udo (2003): *Qualitative Daten computergestützt auswerten: Methoden, Techniken, Software.* In: Friebertshäuser/Prengel (Ed.) (2003): 584-595.

Kuckartz, Udo (2005): *Einführung in die computergestützte Analyse qualitativer Daten.* Wiesbaden.

Kuckartz, Udo/Grunenberg, Heiko/Dresing, Thorsten (Ed.) (2007): *Qualitative Datenanalyse: computergestützt. Methodische Hintergründe und Beispiele aus der Forschungspraxis.* 2. Edition. Wiesbaden.

Kuhn, Berthold (2006): *The Growing Importance of Civil Society in India.* In: Voll/Skoda (Ed.) (2006): 1069-1070.

Kulturpolitische Gesellschaft e. V. (Ed.) (2010a): *Kulturpolitische Mitteilungen.* Zeitschrift für Kulturpolitik der Kulturpolitischen Gesellschaft. No. 128, I/2010. Bonn.

Kulturpolitische Gesellschaft e. V. (Ed.) (2010b): *Kulturpolitische Mitteilungen.* Zeitschrift für Kulturpolitik der Kulturpolitischen Gesellschaft. No. 129, II/2010. Bonn.

Kulturpolitische Gesellschaft e. V. (Ed.) (2010c): *Kulturpolitische Mitteilungen.* Zeitschrift für Kulturpolitik der Kulturpolitischen Gesellschaft. No. 130, III/2010. Bonn.

Kulturpolitische Gesellschaft e. V. (Ed.) (2010d): *Kulturpolitische Mitteilungen.* Zeitschrift für Kulturpolitik der Kulturpolitischen Gesellschaft. No. 131, IV/2010. Bonn.

Kulturpolitische Gesellschaft e. V. (Ed.) (2011a): *Kulturpolitische Mitteilungen.* Zeitschrift für Kulturpolitik der Kulturpolitischen Gesellschaft. No. 132, I/2011. Bonn.

Kulturpolitische Gesellschaft e. V. (Ed.) (2011b): *Kulturpolitische Mitteilungen.* Zeitschrift für Kulturpolitik der Kulturpolitischen Gesellschaft. No. 133, II/2011. Bonn.

Kulturpolitische Gesellschaft e. V. (Ed.) (2012): *Kulturpolitische Mitteilungen.* Zeitschrift für Kulturpolitik der Kulturpolitischen Gesellschaft. No. 136, I/2012. Bonn.

Kulturpolitische Gesellschaft e. V. (Ed.) (2013): *Kulturpolitische Mitteilungen.* Zeitschrift für Kulturpolitik der Kulturpolitischen Gesellschaft. No. 140, I/2013. Bonn.

Kulturpolitische Gesellschaft e. V./Deutscher Kulturrat e. V. (Ed.) (2002): *Europa fördert Kultur. Ein Handbuch zur Kulturförderung der Europäischen Union.* Essen.

Kumar, Kuldeep (2001): *Deutschland-Festival in Indien.* In: Diözesan-Caritasverband für das Erzbistum Köln e. V. (Ed.) (2001): 33.

Kumar, Rinky (2012): *Fancy some culture curry? The Indo-German production, Boy with A Suitcase, returns with a four-city tour across India and will be staged in Mumbai for the first time*, s.l.

Kumbier, Dagmar/Schulz von Thun, Friedemann (Ed.) (2006): *Interkulturelle Kommunikation: Methoden, Modelle, Beispiele.* Hamburg.

Kusch, Regina/Beckmann, Andreas (2011): *Achten Sie auf die Umlaute! In Goethes Namen: 60 Jahre deutsche Kulturarbeit im Ausland.* See: http://tinyurl.com/m2u6b8l (Accessed: 09.11.2013).

Lackner, Robert (2010): *Wie viel Verrücktheit geht noch? Warum die Welt so ist, wie sie ist.* 2. Edition, s.l.

Lambah, Satinder Kumar (1997): *Marksteine der indisch-deutschen Beziehungen der vergangenen fünfzig Jahre.* In: Indian Council for Cultural Relations (Ed.) (1997): 6-17.

Lamnek, Siegfried (1995): *Qualitative Sozialforschung.* Band 1: Methodologie. 3. Edition. Weinheim.

Lamnek, Siegfried (2005): *Qualitative Sozialforschung.* 4. Edition. Weinheim.

Lau, Jörg (2001): *Bildungsroman Bundesrepublik: Das Goethe-Institut und die Entwicklung der BRD.* In: Goethe-Institut Inter Nationes e. V. (2001): 39-48.

Lechner, Georg (1995): *Stand der deutsch-indischen Kulturbeziehungen – Aspekte aus der Arbeit des Goethe-Instituts.* Vortrag im Rahmen des deutsch-indischen Symposiums. Badenweiler.

Lechner, Georg (2004): *Auf der Suche nach Kultur. Vierzig auswärtige Jahre in Goethes Namen. Ein Werkstattbericht aus drei Kontinenten.* Berlin.

Lechner, Georg (2012): *Indien bleibt ein Heimwehland. Über deutsch-indische Kulturbeziehungen.* In: Diözesan-Caritasverband für das Erzbistum Köln e. V. (Ed.) (2012): 4-8.

Lederer, Michael (2005): *Gemeinsam oder Einsam? Von der Funktion und Wirkung von Sozialkapital bei unterschiedlichen Theoretikern.* Bregenz.

Lee, John (2010): *Unrealised Potential: India's 'Soft Power' Ambition in Asia. St Leonards/Australien.* In: Foreign Policy Analysis, No. 4, 30.06.2010. See: http://tinyurl.com/owk3o5o (Accessed: 09.11.2013).

Lehmann, Klaus-Dieter (2008a): *Die Kulturinitiative des Goethe-Instituts.* In: Goethe-Institut e. V. (2008): n.p.

Lehmann, Klaus-Dieter (2008b): *Kulturelles Selbstverständnis. "Nicht als Missionare auftreten".* See: http://tinyurl.com/phnwjoo (Accessed: 28.10.2013).

Lehmann, Klaus-Dieter (2010): *Künftige Rolle der Auswärtigen Kulturpolitik. Auf die Wege kommt es an.* See: http://tinyurl.com/lbeb9mc (Accessed: 09.11.2013).

Lehmann, Klaus-Dieter (2011a): *Kulturaustausch ist kein Nationbranding.* In einem Interview mit dem digitalen Fernsehsender der ARD EinsExtra spricht Präsident Klaus-Dieter Lehmann anlässlich des 60. Geburtstags des Goethe-Instituts über Geschichte, Organisation, Aufgaben und aktuelle Arbeitsschwerpunkte. See: http://tinyurl.com/k9nec5p (Accessed: 13.06.2013).

Lehmann, Klaus-Dieter (2011b): *60 Jahre Goethe-Institut – Rede von Präsident Klaus-Dieter Lehmann.* 07.07.2011. München. See: http://tinyurl.com/nzh48pl (Accessed: 25.11.2013).

Lehmann, Klaus-Dieter (2011c): *60 Jahre Goethe-Institut. München.* See: http://tinyurl.com/nwzuygc (Accessed: 11.07.2013).

Lehmann, Klaus-Dieter (2013): *Präsident Lehmann im Interview: "Es sind kleine Tropfen, die das Glas füllen". Klaus-Dieter Lehmann über Goethe und die Politik.* München. See: http://tinyurl.com/p7eobg3 (Accessed: 21.10.2013).

Lehmann, Klaus-Dieter/Zimmermann, Olaf (2013): *Die Welt lesbarer machen. Goethe-Institut im Porträt.* Berlin/München.

Lepenies, Wolf (1995): *Das Ende der Überheblichkeit. Wir brauchen eine neue auswärtige Kulturpolitik: Statt fremde Gesellschaften zu belehren, müssen wir bereit sein, von ihnen zu lernen.* See: http://tinyurl.com/oewyce3 (Accessed: 07.07.2013).

Lepenies, Wolf (1996a): *Wozu deutsche Auswärtige Kulturpolitik?* In: Sartorius (Ed.) (1996): 44-56.

Lepenies, Wolf (1996b): *Selbstkritische Moderne. Neue Leitbilder im Kontakt der Kulturen.* In: Deutsche Gesellschaft für Auswärtige Politik (1996): 3-14.

Lepenies, Wolf (1996c): *Wozu deutsche Auswärtige Kulturpolitik?* In: Schneider (Ed.) (2008a): 197-205.

Lepenies, Wolf (2012a): *Als Vorbild ausgedient.* See: http://tinyurl.com/q97j2t8 (Accessed: 19.09.2013).

Lepenies, Wolf (2012b): *Demokratie ist keineswegs das Monopol Europas.* See: http://tinyurl.com/pkx6lzz (Accessed: 24.11.2013).

Leßmann, Ortrud (2011): *Verwirklichungschancen und Entscheidungskompetenz.* In: Sedmak/Babic/Bauer/Posch (Ed.) (2011a): 53-74.

Liechti, Peter (s.a.): *Namibia Crossings. Spirits & Limits. Eine Film-Dokumentation einer schweizerisch-namibischen Musikkooperation*, s.l.

Liederer, Katherine (2013): *Performing "Indian": Postcolonial Theatre and Identity Politics for the Whole Family.* Art Meets Research Konferenz 2013/Universität Hildesheim. Conference Paper 04/13/13, s.l.

Lisbonne-de Vergeron, Karine (2006): *Contemporary Indian views of Europe.* London.

Lohmann, Jessica (2008): *Interorganisationales Lernen: Ein Ansatz für die Verstetigung von Kooperationen.* In: Hülsmann (Ed.) (2008): 287-396.

Lonner, Walter J./Malpass, Roy S. (Ed.) (1994): *Psychology and Culture.* Boston/ London.

Lotz, Rainer (2001): *Germany's Cultural Relations with India on the Eve of the 21st Century.* In: Jain (Ed.) (2001): 133-146.

Ludwig, Volker (2001): *Goethe mit GRIPS: A winning team.* In: Goethe-Institut Inter Nationes e. V. (2001): 137-138.

Lüsebrink, Hans-Jürgen/Walter, Klaus Peter/Fendler, Ute/Stefani-Meyer, Georgette/ Vatter, Christoph (Ed.) (2004): *Französische Kultur- und Medienwissenschaft. Eine Einführung.* Tübingen.

Maaß, Kurt-Jürgen (Ed.) (2009a): *Kultur und Außenpolitik.* 2. Edition. Baden-Baden.

Maaß, Kurt-Jürgen (2009b): *Überblick: Ziele und Instrumente der Auswärtigen Kulturpolitik.* In: Maaß (Ed.) (2009a): 25-32.

Maaß, Kurt-Jürgen (2009c): *Das deutsche Modell – Die Mittlerorganisationen.* In: Maaß (Ed.) (2009a): 269-280.

Magdowski, Iris (2012): *Auslandskulturpolitik im Kontext von Wertevermittlung: Das Verhältnis Deutschland-China als Beispiel.* In: Drews (Ed.) (2012): 69-74.

Maier, Felicia (2008): *Der kulturpolitische Auftrag des Goethe-Instituts.* In: Schneider (Ed.) (2008a): 32-44.

Majumdar, Abhishek (2012): *A Small, Small World: Living with Difference in Intercultural Theatre.* Bangalore.

Makowka, Vivian (2012): *Das Goethe-Institut als Kulturvermittler – eine empirische Untersuchung zum Kulturnutzungsverhalten der Teilnehmer von Deutschkursen am Standort Istanbul.* Bachelorarbeit. Universität Hildesheim.

Malavarapu, Siddarth (2013): *BRICS: Hoffnung auf eine gerechte Weltordnung.* Bonn. See: http://tinyurl.com/melyold (Accessed: 25.12.2013).

Maletzke, Gerhard (1996): *Interkulturelle Kommunikation: Zur Interaktion zwischen Menschen verschiedener Kulturen.* Opladen.

Malik Vatsyayan, Kapila (1972): *Some aspects of cultural policies in India.* Paris.

Mataga, Jesmael (2013): *Good Governance and Cultural Diversity: The Aspect of Cultural Mobility in International Cooperation*, s.l.

Mattelart, Armand (2006): *Kultur und Globalisierung.* Zürich.

Mattl, Ulla-Alexandra (2011): *Art is a catalyst for change. In conversation with Anmol Vellani*, s.l.

Max Mueller Bhavan (1995): *Proceedings of the Symposium "Towards an Agenda for Cultural Exchange"*, held by the Goethe-Institut/Max Mueller Bhavans in South Asia at Lonavla/India from March 21-24, 1994. New Delhi.

Mayring, Philipp (2010): *Qualitative Inhaltsanalyse. Grundlagen und Techniken.* 11. Edition. Weinheim.

Medjedovic, Irena (2007): *Sekundäranalyse qualitativer Interviewdaten – Problemkreise und offene Fragen einer neuen Forschungsstrategie.* Bremen. In: Journal für Psychologie, Jg. 15 (2007), Ausgabe 3. See: http://tinyurl.com/ppd65o2 (Accessed: 03.10.2013).

Meitzner, Andreas (2012): *Zum Konzept Auswärtiger Kulturpolitik des Auswärtigen Amtes.* In: Drews (Ed.) (2012): 121-130.

Melchers, Konrad/Meyns, Peter (2010): *Entwicklungszusammenarbeit.* In: Meyns (Ed.) (2010a): 51-59.

Mentschel, Stefan (2007a): *Indiens Außenpolitik. Einführung und Überblick.* Bonn. See: http://tinyurl.com/no2tnof (Accessed: 04.11.2013).

Mentschel, Stefan (2007b): *Nonie und Noorie. Herkunft und soziales Umfeld beeinflussen die Bildungschancen – auch in Indien.* Bonn. See: http://tinyurl.com/ozmdtn3 (Accessed: 06.06.2013).

Merkel, Christine M. (2010): *Kulturelle Vielfalt. Das UNESCO-Abkommen als Grundlage für internationale Zusammenarbeit auf Augenhöhe.* In: Wilhelm (Ed.) (2010): 68-87.

Merkel, Christine M. (2013): *Towards a better governance of culture for development. Mobilising tacit knowledge in and through UNESCO.* Bonn.

Messner, Dirk (2010): *Globalisierung und Globaler Wandel.* In: Meyns (Ed.) (2010a): 103-112.

Metzendorf, Maria-Inti (2011): *Cultural Planning and Cultural Mapping. Kartierung und Analyse von Kultur als Grundlage für Stadtentwicklungsprozesse.* In: Kulturpolitische Gesellschaft e. V. (Ed.) (2011a): 56-57.

Meuser, Michael/Nagel, Ulrike (2009): *Experteninterviews und der Wandel der Wissensproduktion.* In: Bogner/Littig/Menz (Ed.) (2009): 35-60.

Mey, Günter/Mruck, Katja (2009). *Methodologie und Methodik der Grounded Theory.* In: Kempf/Kiefer (Ed.) (2009): 100-152.

Mey, Günter/Mruck, Katja (Ed.) (2010): *Handbuch Qualitative Forschung in der Psychologie.* Wiesbaden.

Mey, Günter/Mruck, Katja (Ed.) (2011a): *Grounded Theory Reader.* 2. Edition. Wiesbaden.

Mey, Günter/Mruck, Katja (2011b): *Grounded-Theory-Methodologie: Entwicklung, Stand, Perspektiven.* In: Mey/Mruck (Ed.) (2011a): 11-50.

Meyers, Reinhard (s.a.): *Theorien internationaler Kooperation und Verflechtung. Ein Überblick über Integrationstheorien und ihre Bezugsrahmen.* Westfälische Wilhelms-Universität Münster (Westfalen). See: http://tinyurl.com/o6ovk7k (Accessed: 30.08.2013).

Meyns, Peter (Ed.) (2010a): *Handbuch Eine Welt. Entwicklung im globalen Wandel.* 2. Edition. Wuppertal.

Meyns, Peter (2010b): *Entwicklungstheorien.* In: Meyns (Ed.) (2010a): 43-50.

Michael, Antje (2008): *Kulturelle Kinder- und Jugendarbeit in Krisenregionen.* In: Schneider (Ed.) (2008a): 153-168.

Michaelis, Rolf (1995): *Krach bei Goethe.* In: Die Zeit, No. 33/1995. See: http://tinyurl.com/lph6n97 (Accessed: 21.06.2013).

Michels, Eckard (2001): *Keine "Stunde null": Vorgeschichte und Anfänge des Goethe-Instituts.* In: Goethe-Institut Inter Nationes e. V. (2001): 13-24.

Millan, Janika (2011): *Eine 'Kultur des Lesens' für die Stärkung der Zivilgesellschaft. Netzwerke in dem Projekt "Informations- und Bildungskompetenz für sozial Benachteiligte" in Bolivien, Peru und Brasilien. Eine Untersuchung über Kultur und Entwicklung, einem neuen Akzent in der Vermittlungsarbeit am Goethe-Institut.* Diplomarbeit. Universität Hildesheim.

Millan, Janika (2012): *Kultur und Entwicklung – oder: Kann Außenkulturpolitik Armut bekämpfen?* In: Drews (Ed.) (2012): 91-96.

Ministry of Culture/Government of India (2012-2013): *Results-Framework Document (RFD).* New Delhi. See: http://tinyurl.com/p9roafm (Accessed: 13.06.2013).

Ministry of Culture/Government of India (2013-2014): *Outcome Budget 2013-14.* New Delhi. See: http://tinyurl.com/nz52nfe (Accessed: 13.06.2013).

Mitra, Madhuban (1998a): *Attakkalari Public Charitable Trust of Contemporary Performing Arts. Development of concepts and treatment for a proposed dance video.* Final Evaluation. Grant Number: 1998-1-008, s.l.

Mitra, Madhuban (1998b): *Janapadam.* Final Evaluation. Grant Number: 1998-1-006, s.l.

Mitra, Madhuban (2004): *Anjani Khanna.* Final Evaluation. Grant Number: 2000-0-009 and 2002-0-010, s.l.

Mittelstädt, Eckhard/Fechner, Meike (Ed.) (2008): *Grimm & Grips. Jahrbuch für Kinder- und Jugendtheater: 2008/2009.* Band 22. Berlin.

Moll, Sebastian (2009): *Von der Kulturrepräsentanz zum kulturellen Dienstleister.* In: Deutscher Kulturrat e. V. (Ed.) (2009): 36.

Morr, Markus (2011): *Einführung in das Themenfeld Kultur und Politik.* In: Hessische Vereinigung für Volkskunde (Ed.) (2011): 7-10.

Mörtenböck, Peter/Mooshammer, Helge (2010): *Netzwerk Kultur. Die Kunst der Verbindung in einer globalisierten Welt.* Bielefeld.

Müller, Harald/Rauch, Carsten (2008): *Indiens Weg zur Wirtschaftsmacht.* Bonn. See: http://tinyurl.com/nhgdru6 (Accessed: 09.11.2013).

Mumme, Martin (2006): *Strategien Auswärtiger Bewusstseinspolitik. Von der Macht der Ideen in der Politik. Eine kritische Analyse der deutschen auswärtigen Kulturpolitik und Vorschläge zu einer neuen Strategie.* Würzburg.

Munshi, Surendra (2005/2008): *Foreword.* In: Wälde (Ed.) (2008a): vii-x.

Nambiar, Shruti (2012): *A Story from a Suitcase. The play, Boy with A Suitcase, is the result of a three-year-long Indo-German collaboration between two theatres.* In: The Indian Express-Talk, Mumbai, 06.04.2012, p. 6.

Nandakumar, Prathibha (2011): *Drama from Deutschland.* Bangalore.

Nandi, Jayashree (2012): *Indian textiles inspired German designer.* In: The Times of India, New Delhi, 29.10.2012, p. 8. See: http://tinyurl.com/q4tuevu (Accessed: 28.06.2013).

Narayan, Shoba (2013): *Why we don't value our arts enough. No arts institution in India pays enough attention to cultivating demand.* See: http://tinyurl.com/pvvvror (Accessed: 31.08.2013).

Nassehi, Armin (2006): *Dialog der Kulturen – wer spricht?* In: Bundeszentrale für politische Bildung (Ed.) (2006): 33-38. See: http://tinyurl.com/poa2t55 (Accessed: 19.09.2013).

National Colloquium on Culture Policy (1992): *Approach Paper On The National Policy On Culture & Observation, Comments, Recommendations Thereon.* New Delhi. See: http://tinyurl.com/pmbhsuv (Accessed: 27.06.2013).

Nestvogel, Renate (2006): *Intercultural Learning in a Globalizing World.* In: Voll/Skoda (Ed.) (2006): 1015-1021.

Nestvogel, Renate (2010): *Interkulturelle Begegnungen.* In: Meyns (Ed.) (2010a): 133-141.

Niklas, Daniel (2005): *Auswärtige Kulturpolitik als integraler Bestandteil bundesdeutscher Außenpolitik – Länderbeispiel Indien.* Magisterarbeit. Katholische Universität Eichstätt-Ingolstadt.

Nohlen, Dieter/Nuscheler, Franz (1992): *Handbuch der Dritten Welt. Grundprobleme, Theorien, Strategien.* Band 1. Bonn.

Nünning, Ansgar (Ed.) (2004): *Metzler Lexikon. Literatur- und Kulturtheorie. Ansätze – Personen – Grundbegriffe.* 3. Edition. Stuttgart/Weimar.

Nünning, Ansgar (Ed.) (2005): *Grundbegriffe der Kulturtheorie und Kulturwissenschaften.* Stuttgart/Weimar.

Nuscheler, Franz (2006): *Entwicklungspolitik.* Bonn.

Nye, Joseph (2004): *The Benefits of Soft Power.* See: http://tinyurl.com/y84c5z (Accessed: 04.01.2014).

No Author (1998): *Indisch-deutsche Kulturbeziehungen.* In: Indian Council for Cultural Relations (Ed.) (1998): 147-158.

No Author (2011): *Antworten auf urbane Zukunftsfragen. Medieninfo des Goethe-Instituts September 2011.* München. See: http://tinyurl.com/ofbtew7 (Accessed: 13.06.2013).

No Author (2012a): *A German extravaganza in Mumbai from Apr 13.* In: Hindustan Times, Mumbai, 11.04.2012, p. 2. See: http://tinyurl.com/os9vgss (Accessed: 28.06.2013).

No Author (2012b): *Bridging the gap.* The Economic Times, Mumbai, 24.04.2012, p. 4. See: http://tinyurl.com/qen6nsc (Accessed: 28.06.2013).

No Author (2012c): *Strengthening Indo-German relations.* In: Mint, New Delhi, 27.10.2012, p. 11. See: http://tinyurl.com/pwha9gn (Accessed: 09.11.2013).

No Author (2012d): *Bavaria and India.* In: Mint, New Delhi, 27.10.2012, p. 11. See: http://tinyurl.com/qgdbhnq (Accessed: 28.06.2013).

No Author (2012e): *Indo-German Urban Mela to showcase growth of sustainable city spaces.* See: http://tinyurl.com/qaqz9sf (Accessed: 28.06.2013).

No Author (2012 f.): *German expertise in infrastructure will benefit India: Planning Commission Member Arun Maira.* See: http://tinyurl.com/orzdqvp (Accessed: 13.06.2013).

No Author (2012g): *Peep into future: To improve quality of life, head to Indo-German Mela.* See: http://tinyurl.com/p4dvs7o (Accessed: 13.06.2013).

No Author (2012h): *State of Culture.* In: The Hindu. See: http://tinyurl.com/phz759j (Accessed: 13.10.2013).

No Author (2013): *Days of India in Germany – Abschlussveranstaltung. Zehn Vereinbarungen unterzeichnet.* In: Diözesan-Caritasverband für das Erzbistum Köln e. V. (Ed.) (2013a): 40-41.

Oranskaia, Tatiana (2006): *India as the Largest Country of South Asia.* In: Voll/Skoda (Ed.) (2006): 1093-1099.

Palazhy, Jayachandran (2009): *Contemporary Dance in India.* Art & the City – Arts in India – Performing Arts – Dance and Theatre. Bangalore. See: http://tinyurl.com/oojegs7 (Accessed: 30.11.2012).

Panke, Peter (2006): *Sänger müssen zweimal sterben. Eine Reise ins unerhörte Indien.* München.

Pätzold, Henning (2005): *Sekundäranalyse von Audiodaten. Technische Verfahren zur faktischen Anonymisierung und Verfremdung.* Forum Qualitative Sozialforschung/Forum: Qualitative Social Research, 6(1), Artikel 24. See: http://tinyurl.com/qclo23c (Accessed: 03.10.2013).

Paul, Rito (2012): *Pavilion showcases 60 yrs of Indo-German relations.* In: DNA (Daily News & Analysis), Mumbai, 21.03.2012, p. 6. See: http://tinyurl.com/pngvaxr (Accessed: 13.09.2013).

Perthes, Volker (2012): *Neue Weltordnungspolitik: Wenn Schwellenländer die Schwelle überschreiten.* See: http://tinyurl.com/phwqjqj (Accessed: 30.06.2013).

Pesch, Ludwig (2012): *Zur zeitgemäßen Vermittlung einer zeitlosen Musik.* In: Diözesan-Caritasverband für das Erzbistum Köln e. V. (Ed.) (2012): 52-54.

Petersen, Thomas (2010): *Individualethik und Kooperation im Spannungsfeld von Gesellschaft und Gemeinschaft.* In: Beschorner/Schmidt/Verbohle/Schank (Ed.) (2010): 17-32.

Pfadenhauer, Michaela (2009): *Auf gleicher Augenhöhe. Das Experteninterview – ein Gespräch zwischen Experte und Quasi-Experte.* In: Bogner/Littig/Menz (Ed.) (2009): 99-116.

Pfannkuche, Walter (2010): *Kulturelle Normen und interkulturelle Kooperation.* In: Beschorner/Schmidt/Verbohle/Schank (Ed.) (2010): 33-44.

Prabhu, Vidya (2012): *The German Connect.* In: Indian Express, Mumbai, 17.04.2012, p. 6. See: http://tinyurl.com/ngxkzwn (Accessed: 09.11.2013).

Prager, Dave (2011): *Delirious Delhi.* Noida.

Prakash, Anupama/Iyer, Sanjay/Krishnamurthy, Aruna/Kumar, C. Suresh (Ed.) (2011): *Arts Education Teacher Training: A Process Document. Based on 'Kali-Kalisu': A Pioneering Project of India Foundation for the Arts and Goethe-Institut/ Max Mueller Bhavan, Bangalore.* Bangalore. See: http://tinyurl.com/kkrh4jp (Accessed: 28.10.2013).

Przyborski, Aglaja/Wohlrab-Sahr, Monika (2010): *Qualitative Sozialforschung.* München.

Punj, Deepshikha (2012): *Inspired by Space and Nature.* In: The Sunday Standard Magazine, New Delhi, 29.10.2012, p. 3. See: http://tinyurl.com/pz7p6ns (Accessed: 28.06.2013).

Punnamparambil, Jose (1999): *Globalisierung und Indiens (Regional) Literatur.* In: Diözesan-Caritasverband für das Erzbistum Köln e. V. (Ed.) (1999): 28-30.

Punnamparambil, Jose (2002): *Indien: Zwischen Mythos und Mausklick. Literatur aus Indien auf der Münchner Frühjahrswoche.* In: Diözesan-Caritasverband für das Erzbistum Köln e. V. (Ed.) (2002): 30-31.

Punnamparambil, Jose (2012): *Eine "andere" Beziehung.* In: Diözesan-Caritasverband für das Erzbistum Köln e. V. (Ed.) (2012): 3.

Purkayastha, Prabir (2009): *Our Battles.* In: Deshpande/K.V./Iyengar (Ed.) (2009): 159-165.

Putnam, Robert D. (Ed.) (2001): *Gesellschaft und Gemeinsinn.* Gütersloh.

Putnam, Robert D./Goss, Kristin A. (2001): *Einleitung.* In: Putnam (Ed.) (2001): 15-44.

Raddatz, Frank (2013): *Wir bleiben Fremde unter Fremden.* In: ITI (Ed.) (2013): 13-19.

Radtke, Olaf-Frank (2011): *Kulturen sprechen nicht. Die Politik grenzüberschreitender Dialoge.* Hamburg.

Rana, Kishan S. (2002): *Indien und Deutschland im 21. Jahrhundert.* See: http:// tinyurl.com/oowufpe (Accessed: 19.09.2013).

Rau, Hertha (2001): *Wie aus Goethe-Institute Max-Müller-Bhavans wurden. Von Heimo Rau stammt die Idee, die Goethe-Institut in Indien Max-Müller-Bhavan zu nennen.* In: Diözesan-Caritasverband für das Erzbistum Köln e. V. (Ed.) (2001): 18.

Rau, Johannes (2002a): *Dialog der Kulturen – Kultur des Dialogs. Toleranz statt Beliebigkeit.* Freiburg im Breisgau.

Rau, Johannes (2002b): *Rede anlässlich der Eröffnung des Rundgesprächs zum Thema 'Religion, Kultur, Nation und Verfassung: Multiple Identitäten in modernen Gesellschaften' am 11. April 2002 im Schloss Bellevue.* Berlin. See: http://tinyurl.com/ku44nxr (Accessed: 23.02.2014).

Rautenstrauch, Thomas/Generotzky, Lars/Bigalke, Tim (2003): *Kooperationen und Netzwerke. Grundlagen und empirische Ergebnisse.* Lohmar/Köln.

Reding, Viviane (2006): *The Media, Globalisation and Culture.* In: Bertelsmann Stiftung (Ed.) (2006a): 86-91.

Richter, Heimo (2001): *Indo-German Relations.* In: Jain (Ed.) (2001): 3-10.

Riecker, Dorothea (2013): *Indiens großes Sprachenexperiment. An 1.000 Schulen wird Deutschunterricht eingeführt.* In: Goethe-Institut e. V. (2013): 19-21.

Riede, Nadine (Ed.) (2012): *Sachbericht der Berlin Music Commission EG für das Projekt "India goes 3D" vom 19.-29. April 2012. Im Rahmen von "Deutschland und Indien 2011-2012: Unendliche Möglichkeiten".* Berlin.

Rieger, Hans Christoph (1995): *Die Liberalisierung der Wirtschaft.* In: Rothermund (Ed.) (1995a): 524-536.

Roberts, David (2012): *From 'heroin' to heroines.* In: Fabianczyk/Hoyle (Ed.) (2012): 33-36.

Roßkopf, Claudia (2010): *"The Power of Culture" – Auswärtige Kulturarbeit zwischen Anspruch und Wirklichkeit.* Magisterarbeit. Johannes-Gutenberg-Universität Mainz.

Rothermund, Dietmar (Ed.) (1995a): *Indien. Kultur, Geschichte, Politik, Wirtschaft, Umwelt. Ein Handbuch.* München.

Rothermund, Dietmar (1995b): *Die deutsch-indischen Beziehungen: 6. Die Kulturbeziehungen.* In: Rothermund (Ed.) (1995a): 479-482.

Roy, Catherine Rhea (2011): *All for the stage.* See: http://tinyurl.com/nnrja4q (Accessed: 31.05.2012).

Sangmeister, Hartmut (Ed.) (2009): *Entwicklung und internationale Zusammenarbeit. Eine Einführung.* Reihe: Weltwirtschaft und internationale Zusammenarbeit. Band 5. Baden-Baden.

Sangmeister, Hartmut/Schönstedt, Alexa (Ed.) (2010): *Entwicklungszusammenarbeit im 21. Jahrhundert. Ein Überblick.* Reihe: Weltwirtschaft und internationale Zusammenarbeit. Band 8. Baden-Baden.

Sartorius, Joachim (Ed.) (1996): *In dieser Armut – welche Fülle! Reflexionen über 25 Jahre auswärtige Kulturarbeit des Goethe-Instituts.* Göttingen.

Sattler, Julia (2007): *Nationalkultur oder europäische Werte? Britische, deutsche und französische Auswärtige Kulturpolitik zwischen 1989 und 2003.* Wiesbaden.

Saure, Ina Kristin/Tillmanns, Annika (2006): *German-Indian Cooperation: What are the Cultural Differences? Training Germans for India.* In: Voll/Skoda (Ed.) (2006): 959-962.

Sausmikat, Nora (2012): *Kooperation braucht Vertrauen.* In: Stiftung Mercator (Ed.) (2012): 92-101.

Schäffler, Erik/Mittelstädt, Eckhard (2008): *Sternstunden des Kulturaustausches, Eckhard Mittelstädt im Gespräch mit Erik Schäffler über die indische Form des Geschichtenerzählens, das Staunen und die Alltagsprobleme im Theater.* In: Mittelstädt/Fechner (Ed.) (2008): 45-48.

Schindler, Klaus (1997): *Die Kulturbeziehungen Südasien-Deutschland. Die Rolle der Goethe-Institute.* In: Berkemer/Frasch (Ed.) (1997): 151-158.

Schmid, Antje (1997): *Der Kulturdialog des Goethe-Instituts aus ethnologischer Sicht dargestellt am Beispiel Indien.* Magisterarbeit. Universität Köln.

Schmidt, Ulla (2012): *Deutschland als Partner in Europa und der Welt – eine Kritik des AKBP-Konzepts 2011 des Auswärtigen Amtes.* In: Drews (Ed.) (2012): 131-138.

Schnawwl (Schnawwl Nationaltheater Mannheim) (s.a.): *Der Junge mit dem Koffer.* Programmheft Deutsch/Englisch. Mannheim.

Schneider, Axel (2000): *Die auswärtige Sprachpolitik der Bundesrepublik Deutschland.* Bamberg.

Schneider, Claudia (2008): *Die Gemeinschaft Europäischer Kulturinstitute in Berlin.* In: Schneider (Ed.) (2008a): 71-83.

Schneider, Nikolaus (2013): *Toleranz ist eine aktive Tugend. Warum der Respekt gegenüber anderen Religionen ein zentrales evangelisches Anliegen ist. Und immer wieder Kraft kostet.* See: http://tinyurl.com/nmn8rqj (Accessed: 24.11.2013).

Schneider, Wolfgang (Ed.) (2007): *Grundlagentexte zur Kulturpolitik.* Hildesheim.

Schneider, Wolfgang (Ed.) (2008a): *Auswärtige Kulturpolitik. Dialog als Auftrag – Partnerschaft als Prinzip.* Bonn.

Schneider, Wolfgang (2008b): *Vom Export zum Netzwerk, vom Event zur Intervention. Zum Wandel Auswärtiger Kulturpolitik.* In: Schneider (Ed.) (2008a): 13-31.

Schneider, Wolfgang (2010): *Cultural Diplomacy: Einbahnstraße, Sackgasse, Kreisverkehr, oder? Risiken und Nebenwirkungen einer Kulturentwicklungspolitik.* In: Wilhelm (Ed.) (2010): 86-93.

Schneider, Wolfgang (2011a): *Internationality needs cultural policy. International coproduction in theatre for young audiences.* In: Theater der Zeit (Ed.) (2011): 4-6.

Schneider, Wolfgang (2011b): *Empowering the Performing Arts. Cultural diversity made by Theatre for Young Audiences*, s.l.

Schneider, Wolfgang (2011c): *Building Bridges, Crossing Borders.* In: ASSITEJ International (Ed.) (2011): 2-3.

Schneider, Wolfgang (2011d): *Kultur plus Politik gleich Kulturpolitik? Lebenskunst als gesellschaftlicher Auftrag.* In: Hessische Vereinigung für Volkskunde (Ed.) (2011): 11-23.

Schneider, Wolfgang (2011e): *Warum wir kein Migranten-Theater brauchen. Aber eine Kulturpolitik, die in Personal, Produktion und Publikum der dramatischen*

Künste multiethnisch ist. In: Institut für Kulturpolitik/Universität Hildesheim (2011): 33-35.

Schneider, Wolfgang (2012): *Wider die Instrumentalisierung der Künste. Plädoyer für eine Kurskorrektur in der Auswärtigen Kulturpolitik.* In: Drews (Ed.) (2012): 35-44.

Schneider, Wolfgang (2013a): *Theatre is Education for Development. A challenge to cultural policies in the performing arts*, s.l.

Schneider, Wolfgang (Ed.) (2013b): *Künstler. Ein Report. Porträts und Gespräche zur Kulturpolitik.* Bielefeld.

Schneider, Wolfgang (2013c): *Künstler sein? Eine Frage der Kulturpolitik.* In: Schneider (Ed.) (2013b): 9-14.

Schneider, Wolfgang/Gad, Daniel (Ed.) (2011): *Abschlussbericht Kultur und Entwicklung. Ein neuer Akzent in der Vermittlungsarbeit am Goethe-Institut.* Hildesheim.

Schödel, Günther (1997): *Indische Festspiele in Deutschland. September 1991 bis Mai 1992.* In: Indian Council for Cultural Relations (Ed.) (1997): 176-183.

Schöfthaler, Traugott (2007): *Gleichberechtigte Nord-Süd-Partnerschaft. Von kultureller Vielfalt lernen.* See: http://tinyurl.com/py3wla8 (Accessed: 07.07.2013).

Schöfthaler, Traugott (2009): *Multilateral vernetzt – Die UNESCO.* In: Maaß (Ed.) (2009a): 315-326.

Scholl, Georg (2001): *Vom Stiefkind zu Mamis Liebling. Theoriedefizit der Auswärtigen Kulturpolitik.* Stuttgart. See: http://tinyurl.com/p4spjfg (Accessed: 15.09.2013).

Schönfeld, Franziska (2012): *Künstlerische Koproduktion statt "Nation Branding". Auswärtige Kulturpolitik als Gegenstand beim Kulturpolitischen Kolloquium in Loccum.* In: Drews (Ed.) (2012): 13-18.

Schönhuth, Michael (2002): *Entwicklung, Partizipation und Ethnologie.* Habilitation. Universität Trier.

Schönhuth, Michael (2006): *Kultur, Kulturpolitik und Entwicklungszusammenarbeit. Die politischen, wirtschaftlichen und kulturellen Beziehungen werden weltweit immer komplexer.* München.

Schönhuth, Michael (2010): *Kultur im Fokus der Entwicklungspolitik und Entwicklung im Fokus der Auswärtigen Kulturpolitik.* In: Wilhelm (Ed.) (2010): 182-189.

Schreiner, Patrick (2008): *Auswärtige Kulturarbeit zwischen Konzeption und Umsetzung. Steuerungsprobleme in einem schwierigen Politikfeld.* SWP-Studien. Berlin.

Schreiner, Patrick (2011): *Außenkulturpolitik. Internationale Beziehungen und kultureller Austausch.* Bielefeld.

Schuh, Günther/Friedli, Thomas/Kurr, Michael A. (2005): *Kooperationsmanagement.* München.

Schulte, Karl Sebastian (2000): *Auswärtige Kulturpolitik im politischen System der Bundesrepublik Deutschland: Konzeptionsgehalt, Organisationsprinzipien und Strukturneuralgien eines atypischen Politikfeldes am Ende der 13. Legislaturperiode.* Berlin.

Schumacher, Martin/Leonhard, Joachim-Felix (2001): *Was sich ändert, bleibt.* In: Goethe-Institut Inter Nationes e. V. (2001): 9-12.

Schütze, Anja (2010): *Kultur – eine Theorie* (Text aus der Publikation "Interkulturelles Training/Materialien und Übungen" Deutsche Sportjugend Dezember 2009), Berlin. See: http://tinyurl.com/okplu75 (Accessed: 18.09.2013).

Schwencke, Olaf/Bühler, Joachim/Wagner, Marie Katharina (2009): *Kulturpolitik von A-Z.* Berlin.

Sedmak, Clemens (2011): *Fähigkeiten und Fundamentalfähigkeiten.* In: Sedmak/ Babic/Bauer/Posch (Ed.) (2011a): 29-52.

Sedmak, Clemens/Babic, Bernhard/Bauer, Reinhold/Posch, Christian (Ed.) (2011a): *Der Capability-Approach in sozialwissenschaftlichen Kontexten. Überlegungen zur Anschlussfähigkeit eines entwicklungspolitischen Konzepts.* Wiesbaden.

Sedmak, Clemens/Babic, Bernhard/Bauer, Reinhold/Posch, Christian (2011b): *Vorwort.* In: Sedmak/Babic/Bauer/Posch (Ed.) (2011a): 7-10.

Sehouli, Jalid (2012): *Marrakesch.* Hamburg.

Sen, Amartya (2005): *The Argumentative Indian. Writings on Indian Culture, History and Identity.* London.

Sen, Amartya (2007): *Die Identitätsfalle. Warum es keinen Krieg der Kulturen gibt.* München.

Sen, Amartya (2010): *Die Idee der Gerechtigkeit.* München.

Sengupta, Anindita/Victor, Anish/Ghosh, Arundhati/Vellani, Anmol (s.a.): *The State of the Performing Arts in India.* Bangalore.

Sengupta, Shuddhabrata (2002): *IFA Arts Collaboration Programme Meet March 2002.* Review Report. Bangalore.

Sennett, Richard (2011): *Brutal Simplifiers.* Teil 1/5 bis 5/5 bei: BODYBITS OPENING, Haus der Kulturen der Welt Berlin, 28.03.2011. See: http:// tinyurl.com/oprpjft (Teil 1/5, hier automatische Weiterführung zu den Teilen 2-5; Accessed: 15.05.2013).

Sennett, Richard (2012): *Together: The Rituals, Pleasures and Politics of Cooperation.* London u. a.

Seubert, Sandra (2009): *Das Konzept des Sozialkapitals.* Frankfurt a. M./New York.

Sharma, Bharat (2000): *Dancing till/in/form Bangalore – point of view.* In: Goethe-Institut e. V. Bangalore (Ed.) (2000): 10-16.

Sidhardhan, Sanjith (2012): *Research is the best part of theatre: Abhishek Majumdar.* See: http://tinyurl.com/oobjz9r (Accessed: 16.09.2013).

Simson, Uwe (1971): *Zehn Thesen zur Kulturarbeit in Entwicklungsländern.* In: Goethe-Institut e. V. (1971): 9-11.

Sinah, Atish (Ed.) (2007): *Indian Foreign Policy.* New Delhi.

Singer, Otto (2003): *Auswärtige Kulturpolitik in der Bundesrepublik Deutschland: Konzeptionelle Grundlagen und institutionelle Entwicklung seit 1945.* Berlin. See: http://tinyurl.com/kfeav4m (Accessed: 05.01.2014).

Singh, Balmiki Prasad (2009): *India's Culture. The State, the Arts, and Beyond.* 2. Edition. New Delhi.

Singh, I. P. (2001): *Indo-German Relations: An Overview.* In: Jain (Ed.) (2001): 155-158.

Singh, Manmohan (Prime Minister of India) (2010): *Joint Declaration of the European Commission and India. 10.12.2010 in Brüssel.* See: http://tinyurl.com/pjceufh (Accessed: 06.07.2013).

Singh, Suhani (2012): *German choreographer Felix Bürkle and Indian dancer Hema Sundari Vellaluru pair up in starting point #3.* In: Time Out Mumbai, 28.09.2012. See: http://tinyurl.com/nn68cm6 (Accessed: 12.06.2013).

Skoda, Uwe (2007): *Kaste und Kastensystem in Indien. Eine Einführung.* Bonn. See: http://tinyurl.com/culzzm4 (Accessed: 09.11.2013).

Sonna, Birgit (2009): *Kunstszene Indien. Mumbai und New Delhi. Unverfroren, hintergründig, spirituell.* See: http://tinyurl.com/o7hp89a (Accessed: 20.06.2013).

Spiess, Clemens (2009): *Tradition und Aufbruch. Die deutsch-indischen Kulturbeziehungen. Bestandsaufnahme und Empfehlungen.* Stuttgart.

Spradley, James P. (1979): *The ethnographic interview.* Fort Worth u. a.

Srivatsan, R. (2002): *Reports from the evaluators on arts collaboration programme. IFA Arts Collaboration Programme Meet March 2002.* Review Report. Bangalore.

Staines, Judith (1996): *Network Solutions for Cultural Cooperation in Europe.* A document drafted for The European Forum for the Arts and Heritage. See: http://tinyurl.com/laty2ne (Accessed: 01.11.2013).

Staines, Judith (2012): *Germany + India 2011-2012.* See: http://tinyurl.com/opcku5g (Accessed: 13.06.2013).

Ständiger Ausschuss für Kulturelle Zusammenarbeit zwischen der Bundesrepublik Deutschland und der Republik Indien (Ed.) (2003): *Protokoll der 11. Tagung des Ständigen Ausschusses für Kulturelle Zusammenarbeit zwischen der Bundesrepublik Deutschland und der Republik Indien vom 16.-17. Juni 2003 in New Delhi.* See: http://tinyurl.com/q2eh7s6 (Accessed: 30.05.2013).

Stegbauer, Christian/Häußerling, Roger (Ed.) (2010a): *Handbuch Netzwerkforschung.* Wiesbaden.

Stegbauer, Christian/Häußerling, Roger (Ed.) (2010b): *Netzwerkanalyse und Netzwerktheorie. Ein neues Paradigma in den Sozialwissenschaften.* Wiesbaden.

Steinhilber, Jochen (2007): *Kompass 2020. Deutschland in den internationalen Beziehungen. Ziele, Instrumente, Perspektiven.* Berlin. See: http://tinyurl.com/o7xvszo (Accessed: 30.06.2013).

Steinkamp, Anna (2010): *Kultur als Motor für nachhaltige Entwicklung anerkannt. UN-Milleniumsgipfel zieht Zwischenbilanz.* In: Kulturpolitische Gesellschaft e. V. (Ed.) (2010d): 14-15.

Steinkamp, Anna (2013): *Network Governance. Governance Model for International Networks of Cultural Cooperation*, s.l.

Stepf, Sophia (2009): *Bollywood for Business. Mit Filmwissen kulturelle Gräben überbrücken.* See: http://tinyurl.com/pom2k7x (Accessed: 16.09.2013).

Stepf, Sophia (2011a): *Hans, Suresh and the Way They Do Things around Here. A Spotlight on Intercultural Competence.* See: http://tinyurl.com/oy6stvd (Accessed: 08.07.2013).

Stepf, Sophia (2011b): *Handlungsempfehlungen für interkulturelle Projekte mit institutioneller Zusammenarbeit.* Workshopergebnisse Wanderlust 11.4.2011, s.l.

Stiebitz, Antje (2013): *Das Land sitzt auf einem Pulverfass.* See: http://tinyurl.com/oqls5m6 (Accessed: 10.09.2013).

Stiftung Fair Play (2004): *Stiftungsziele.* See: http://tinyurl.com/p8j5sey (Accessed: 09.11.2013).

Stiftung Mercator (Ed.) (2012): *Wege der Verständigung. Wie Kulturdiplomatie mehr Vertrauen zwischen China und dem Westen schaffen kann.* Essen.

Stiftung Wissenschaft und Politik (Ed.) (2001): *Wie Indien Deutschland sieht. Indische Politiker über das Verhältnis zur Bundesrepublik.* Berlin. See: http://tinyurl.com/q662t9m (Accessed: 09.05.2012).

Stiller-Kern, Gabriele (Ed.) (2013): *Macht Mehrsprachigkeit glücklich?* In: Goethe-Institut e. V. (2013): 47.

Strauss, Anselm L. (1991): *Grundlagen qualitativer Sozialforschung: Datenanalyse und Theoriebildung in der empirischen und soziologischen Forschung.* München.

Strauss, Anselm L./Corbin, Juliet M. (1991): *Basis of qualitative Research. Grounded Theory procedures and techniques.* Newbury Park.

Strauss, Anselm L./Corbin, Juliet M. (1996): *Grundlagen Qualitativer Sozialforschung.* Weinheim.

Strauss, Dieter (2009): *Diesseits von Goethe. Deutsche Kulturbotschafter im Aus- und Inland.* St. Augustin.

Strohschneider, Peter (2010): *Dialogischer Agon.* In: Hempfer/Traninger (Ed.) (2010): 95-117.

Subramaniam, B. (2001): *India's Cultural Relations with Germany.* In: Jain (Ed.) (2001): 125-132.

Sunavala, Nergish (2012): *Mobile mela.* In: Time Out, Mumbai, 13.04.2012, p. 62. See: http://tinyurl.com/phqgn9g (Accessed: 28.06.2013).

Sunavala, Nergish/Arasu, Sibi (2012): *Mobile mela.* In: Time Out, New Delhi, 26.10.2012, p. 69. See: http://tinyurl.com/ojsngmx (Accessed: 28.06.2013).

Sundar, Pushpa (2006): *Promoting Social Integration: The Case for Community Foundations in India.* In: Bertelsmann Stiftung (Ed.) (2006a): 96-101.

Surana, Vibha (2009): *Die Europhonie der Kultur. Deutsch-indische Aha-Momente.* München.

Surekha, S. (2012): *Silently, they groove.* In: Mid Day, Mumbai, 19.04.2012, p. 34. See: http://tinyurl.com/pj2gm2e (Accessed: 28.06.2013).

Swoboda, Bernhard (2005): *Kooperation: Erklärungsperspektiven grundlegender Theorien, Ansätze und Konzepte im Überblick.* In: Zentes/Swoboda/Morschett (Ed.) (2005): 35-64.

Tan, Vu Nhat (2011): *Ein Gewinn für das ganze Land.* In: ifa (Ed.) (2011b): 71.

Team DNA (Daily News & Analysis) (2011): *How dancer Jayachandran Palazhy popularised Attakalari.* See: http://tinyurl.com/o23gcdu (Accessed: 08.12.2012).

Terkessidis, Mark (2010): *Interkultur.* Berlin.

Terre des hommes (Terre des hommes Deutschland e. V./Hilfe für Kinder in Not) (2003): *Institutionalisierte Partnerschaft zwischen Nord und Süd?*, s.l.

Theater der Zeit (Ed.) (2011): IXYPSILONZETT – Das Magazin für Kinder- und Jugendtheater. *Discovery, Venture, Risk.* No. 02/2011. Berlin.

Thermann, Andreas (2005): *Partizipation und Entwicklung. Die Bedeutung gesellschaftlicher Teilhabe an Entwicklungsprozessen und die Realität der neuen Poverty Reduction Strategy der Weltbank.* Marburg.

Thomas, Alexander (Ed.) (1991): *Kulturstandards in der internationalen Begegnung.* Saarbrücken.

Thomas, Alexander (Ed.) (1996): *Psychologie interkulturellen Handelns.* Göttingen.

Thomas, Alexander (2003): *Kultur und Kulturstandards.* In: Thomas/Kinast/Schroll-Machl (Ed.) (2003): 19-31.

Thomas, Alexander/Kinast, Eva-Ulrike/Schroll-Machl, Sylvia (Ed.) (2003): *Handbuch Interkulturelle Kommunikation und Kooperation.* Band 1: Grundlagen und Praxisfelder. Göttingen.

Throsby, David (2001): *Economics and culture.* Cambridge.

Tibi, Bassam (2001): *Kulturarbeit als Dialog zwischen den Zivilisationen. Das Goethe-Institut in einer sich entwestlichenden Welt.* In: Goethe-Institut Inter Nationes e. V. (2001): 25-38.

Tiriandis, Harry C. (1994): *Culture and Social Behaviour.* In: Lonner/Malpass (Ed.) (1994): 169-174.

Todorov, Tzvetan (2010): *Die Angst vor den Barbaren. Kulturelle Vielfalt versus Kampf der Kulturen.* Schriftenreihe bpb, Bd. 1.125. Bonn.

Triebel, Odila (2013): *Praxis, Reflexion und Rücktransfer. Das ifa-Forschungsprogramm Kultur und Außenpolitik.* In: Kulturpolitische Gesellschaft e. V. (Ed.) (2013): 64-65.

Trojanow, Ilija/Hoskoté, Ranjit (2007): *Kampfabsage. Kulturen bekämpfen sich nicht, sie fließen zusammen.* München.

Trompenaars, Fons/Hampden-Turner, Charles (2008): *Riding the Waves of Culture, Understanding Cultural Diversitiy in Business.* 2. Edition. London.

Trunk, Wiebke (2011): *Voneinander lernen – Kunstvermittlung im Kontext kultureller Diversität.* ifa-Edition Kultur und Außenpolitik. Stuttgart. See: http://tinyurl.com/kjbnyh9 (Accessed: 04.11.2013).

Tschernokoshewa, Elka (2009): *Interkultureller Dialog: Konzepte und praktische Schritte.* See: http://tinyurl.com/pd8d278 (Accessed: 23.02.2014).

Türkan, Anja (2012): *Digital Diplomacy – Der Wandel der Außenpolitik im digitalen Zeitalter. ifa-Edition Kultur und Außenpolitik.* Stuttgart. See: http://tinyurl.com/ltm9vbp (Accessed: 13.01.2014).

Ulmer, Brigitte (2008): *Gutes Karma für die Künstler Indiens. Im Schatten des China-Booms hat sich zeitgenössische indische Kunst einen der vorderen Plätze in der internationalen Kunstwelt erobert. Ein Augenschein in Delhi.* In: Neue Züricher Zeitung, 12.10.2008. See: http://tinyurl.com/marnquq (Accessed: 20.06.2013).

UNESCO (1970a): *Schlussdokument der zwischenstaatlichen Konferenz über institutionelle, administrative und finanzielle Aspekte der Kulturpolitiken.* Venedig.

UNESCO (1970b): *Key ideas from the resolutions adopted by the Intergovernmental Conference on Institutional, Administrative and Financial Aspects of Cultural Policies.* Venedig. See: http://tinyurl.com/kvag3aa (Accessed: 06.10.2013).

UNESCO (1972): *Zwischenstaatliche Konferenz über Kulturpolitik in Europa. Schlussbericht der von der UNESCO vom 19. bis 28. Juni 1972 in Helsinki veranstalteten internationalen Konferenz.* Pullach/München. See: http://tinyurl.com/lg8tfnk (Accessed: 06.10.2013).

UNESCO (1980): *Recommendation concerning the Status of the Artist.* Belgrad. See: http://tinyurl.com/ngkzbvd (Accessed: 10.11.2013).

UNESCO (1982): *Erklärung von Mexiko-City über Kulturpolitik. Weltkonferenz über Kulturpolitik. 26.07.-06.08.1982.* Mexiko. See: http://www.unesco.de/2577.html (Accessed: 09.10.2013).

UNESCO (2005): *Convention on the Protection and Promotion of the Diversity of Cultural Expressions.* See: http://tinyurl.com/mw72n77 (Accessed: 06.10.2013).

UNESCO (2006): *Leitfaden für kulturelle Bildung (Road Map for Arts Education). UNESCO-Weltkonferenz für kulturelle Bildung: Schaffung kreativer Kapazitäten für das 21. Jahrhundert.* Lissabon, 06.-09.03.2006. See: http://tinyurl.com/mrtoxjb (Accessed: 03.10.2013).

United Nations (2001): *Global agenda for dialogue among civilizations.* Resolution A/RES/56/6. See: http://tinyurl.com/kvq6xe3 (Accessed: 09.10.2013).

Unmüßig, Barbara (2008): *Kultur – keine Ware neben anderen. Über die UNESCO-Konvention zum Schutz von Kunst und Kultur.* Berlin. See: http://tinyurl.com/lcp9e6d (Accessed: 04.10.2013).

Vaid, Karan (2011): *Babelsberg trifft Bollywood. Deutschland und Indien feiern 2011 und 2012. 60 Jahre diplomatische Beziehungen.* Ein Interview mit Heiko Sievers vom Goethe-Institut/Max Mueller Bhavan New Delhi. 30.12.2011, s.l.

Varghese Mathews, Hans (2000): *My associations with the Institute.* In: Goethe-Institut e. V. Bangalore (Ed.) (2000): 8-9.

Varma, Pavan K. (2007): *Culture as an instrument of diplomacy.* In: Sinah (Ed.) (2007): 1135-1141.

Velayanikal, Malavika (2011): *The dancing life of Jayachandran Palazhy.* See: http://tinyurl.com/jw3yyok (Accessed: 08.12.2012).

Vellani, Anmol (2006): *Arts Entrepreneurship in the Age of Creative Industries.* Bangalore.

Vellani, Anmol (2009a): *Development without culture.* See: http://tinyurl.com/mcfswad (Accessed: 09.10.2013).

Vellani, Anmol (2009b): *Expanding the middle ground.* See: http://tinyurl.com/kco2ohy (Accessed: 09.05.2012).

Vellani, Anmol (2009c): *Respondents.* In: Deshpande/K.V./Iyengar (Ed.) (2009): 194-197.

Vellani, Anmol (s.a.): *The Changing Face of Contemporary Performance Festivals in India*, Bangalore.

Verbi (Verbi Software. Consult. Sozialforschung. GmbH) (2007): *MAXQDA Einführung 2007.* Marburg.

Vierhaus, Jirka (2010): *Kulturelle Vielfalt fördern und Kultur nutzen: Grenzen und Potentiale für die Entwicklungspolitik.* In: Wilhelm (Ed.) (2010): 160-181.

Vittar, Carlos F. (2008): *Interkulturelles Vertrauen im globalisierten beruflichen Kontext: Ein Erklärungsmodell.* Reihe: Strategisches Management. Band 64. Hamburg.

Volkert, Jürgen (Ed.) (2005): *Armut und Reichtum an Verwirklichungschancen: Amartya Sens Capability-Konzept als Grundlage der Armuts- und Reichtumsberichterstattung.* Wiesbaden.

Voll, Klaus Julian (2001): *Wie Indien Deutschland sieht. Indische Politiker über das Verhältnis zur Bundesrepublik.* SWP-Studie. Berlin. See: http://tinyurl.com/my44tsc (Accessed: 30.06.2012).

Voll, Klaus Julian (2006): *Intercultural Competence.* In: Voll/Skoda (Ed.) (2006): 1022-1034.

Voll, Klaus Julian/Skoda, Uwe (Ed.) (2006): *Rising India – Europe's Partner? Foreign and Security Policy, Politics, Economics, Human Rights and Social Issues, Media, Civil Society and Intercultural Dimensions.* Berlin.

Wagner, Bernd (2009): *Fürstenhof und Bürgergesellschaft. Zur Entstehung, Entwicklung und Legitimation von Kulturpolitik.* Essen.

Wagner, Britta (2003): *Arbeiten mit MAXqda. Kurze Einführung in die computergestützte Analyse qualitativer Daten. Bamberger Beiträge zur empirischen Sozialforschung.* No. 22. Bamberg.

Wagner, Christian (2005): *Indien in der deutschen Außenpolitik. Stand und Ausblick.* Berlin. See: http://tinyurl.com/mcjj5cb (Accessed: 12.06.2013).

Wagner, Christian (2011): *Die deutsch-indischen Beziehungen.* Paris/Brüssel.

Wälde, Martin (Ed.) (2008a): *Does culture make a difference? Progress and Development in India and its implications for international cooperation.* Kalkutta.

Wälde, Martin (2008b): *Preface.* In: Wälde (Ed.) (2008a): xi-xiv.

Wälde, Martin (2008c): *The Grammar of Progress and Development.* In: Wälde (Ed.) (2008a): 3-11.

Wallraff, Nadja (2011): *Eine 'Kultur des Lesens' zur Stärkung der Zivilgesellschaft. Kulturvermittlung im Projekt "Bildungs- und Informationskompetenz für sozial Benachteiligte" in Bolivien, Peru und Brasilien. Eine Untersuchung über Kultur und Entwicklung, einem neuen Akzent in der Vermittlungsarbeit am Goethe-Institut.* Diplomarbeit. Universität Hildesheim.

Wapnewski, Peter/Mücher, Christoph (Ed.) (2000): *Realitäten und Visionen. Hilmar Hoffmann zu ehren.* Köln.

Wartemann, Geesche (2002): *Theater der Erfahrung. Authentizität als Forderung und als Darstellungsform. Medien und Theater.* Band 10. Hildesheim.

Weber, Max (1972): *Wirtschaft und Gesellschaft.* 5. Edition. Tübingen.

Weigl, Aron (2012): *Das kooperative Modell der Konfuzius-Institute. Chinas Auswärtige Kulturpolitik in Deutschland.* In: Drews (Ed.) (2012): 75-82.

Welsch, Wolfgang (1995): *Transkulturalität.* In: ifa (Ed.) (1995b): n.p.

Welsch, Wolfgang (2012): *Was ist eigentlich Transkulturalität?* In: Kimmich/ Schahadat (Ed.) (2012): 25-40.

Wenzel, Bettina (2012): *Bericht über die Durchführung des Theater-Performance Projektes "An Actor Exits" (AAE) in New Delhi im Rahmen von "Deutschland und Indien 2011-2012: Unendliche Möglichkeiten".* Köln.

Wessler, Heinz Werner (2007a): *Indien – eine Einführung. Herausforderungen für die aufstrebende asiatische Großmacht im 21. Jahrhundert.* Bonn. See: http:// tinyurl.com/lvdruxa (Accessed: 06.06.2013).

Wessler, Heinz Werner (2007b): *Max Müller und der Postkolonialismus. Indologie und Südasienforschung in Deutschland.* Bonn. See: http://tinyurl.com/l8vtjqu (Accessed: 20.03.2012).

Wieck, Hans-Georg (1996): *Indien und Deutschland – eine Partnerschaft mit Zukunft.* In: Indian Council for Cultural Relations (Ed.) (1996): 74-81.

Wieck, Hans-Georg (2002): *Fünfzig Jahre Deutsch-Indische Gesellschaft, 1953 – 2003, Rückblick – Ausblick. Die Rolle der Mittler-Organisation und die Entwicklung der Deutsch-Indischen Gesellschaft.* See: http://tinyurl.com/ m3ekqvg (Accessed: 30.06.2013).

Wieck, Hans-Georg (2006a): *Die Deutsch-Indischen Kulturbeziehungen nach 1990. Kultureller Austausch – das älteste Beziehungsgeflecht zwischen den beiden Zivilisationsräumen.* Berlin. See: http://tinyurl.com/kd429qq (Accessed: 09.05.2012).

Wieck, Hans-Georg (2006b): *Germany and India – The Role of Civil Societies.* In: Voll/Skoda (Ed.) (2006): 1071-1082.

Wieck, Hans-Georg (2010): *Deutschland – Indien. Faszination und Transparenz.* In: Goel (Ed.) (2010): 29-41.

Wieck, Hans-Georg (2012): *Indien – Hegemonialmacht in Südasien?* Bremen. See: http://tinyurl.com/lomfjp6 (Accessed: 30.06.2013).

Wierlacher, Alois (Ed.) (1993): *Jahrbuch Deutsch als Fremdsprache.* Jahrgang 19. Grenzen und Grenzerfahrungen. München.

Wilhelm, Jürgen (Ed.) (2010): *Kultur und globale Entwicklung.* Berlin.

Wingert, Christine (2013): *Paradigmenwechsel in der Außenkulturpolitik?* Antwort der Bundesregierung auf die Große Anfrage der SPD-Fraktion. In: Kulturpolitische Gesellschaft e. V. (Ed.) (2013): 18-19.

Winter, Rainer (2011): *Ein Plädoyer für kritische Perspektiven in der qualitativen Forschung.* Forum Qualitative Sozialforschung 12(1). Berlin. See: http://tinyurl.com/karu5y7 (Accessed: 27.07.2012).

Winter, Stefanie (2000): *Quantitative vs. Qualitative Methoden.* Karlsruhe. See: http://tinyurl.com/7hgj3u6 (Accessed: 24.06.2013).

Wirth, Uwe (Ed.) (2008): *Kulturwissenschaften.* Frankfurt a. M.

Witte, Barthold C. (2001): *Praxis ohne Theorie? Auswärtige Kulturpolitik und die Wissenschaft.* Stuttgart. See: http://tinyurl.com/l5ptms2 (Accessed: 07.07.2013).

Wittek, Bernhard (2006): *Und das in Goethes Namen. Das Goethe-Institut von 1951 bis 1976.* Berlin.

Wöhrle-Chon, Roland (2006): *Intercultural Perceptions in a Globalising World.* In: Voll/Skoda (Ed.) (2006): 1173-1185.

Yin, Robert (2003): *Case Study Research. Design and Methods.* Applied Social Research Methods Series. Band 5. Thousand Oaks.

Zembylas, Tasos (2004): *Kulturbetriebslehre. Grundlagen einer Inter-Disziplin.* Wiesbaden.

Zentes, Joachim/Swoboda, Bernhard/Morschett, Dirk (Ed.) (2005): *Kooperationen, Allianzen und Netzwerke. Grundlagen – Ansätze – Perspektiven.* 2. Edition. Wiesbaden.

Zimmermann, Olaf/Geißler, Theo (Ed.) (2010): *Digitalisierung: Kunst und Kultur 2.0.* Berlin.

Cultural Management and Cultural Policy Education

The series exists to foster critical debate and to publish academic research in the field of cultural management and cultural policy as well as to open up a forum for discussions and debate on the topics of cultural management and cultural policy among researchers, educators, scholars, policy makers and cultural managers. It is also intended to provide reference tools for education and lifelong learning on cultural management and cultural policies.

It is becoming more and more evident that education in cultural management and cultural policy cannot and should not be separated from research being conducted in the field. Since its creation, ENCATC has recognised this need and has always been very active in pursuing, publishing, presenting, and disseminating research in cultural management and cultural policy to strengthen the understanding of cultural management and cultural policy issues.

Book Series Editor

ENCATC

European network on cultural management and policy

1, Avenue Maurice

B-1050 Brussels

Belgium

Tel: 0032.2.201.29.12

info@encatc.org; www.encatc.org

Book Series Director

Cristina Ortega Nuere, *3Walks, Spain*

This publication was evaluated by the ENCATC Research Award Jury:

Jury President

Annick Schramme, *ENCATC President, University of Antwerp / Antwerp Management School, Belgium*

Jury Members

Franco Bianchini, *University of Hull, United Kingdom*

Lluís Bonet, *University of Barcelona, Spain*

Jacques Bonniel, *University of Lyon II, France*

Anita Kangas, *University of Jyväskylä, Finland*

Jerry C Y Liu, *National Taiwan University of Arts, Taiwan*

Richard Maloney, *New York University, United States*

Jaime Alberto Ruiz Gutiérrez, *Universidad de los Andes at Bogota, Colombia*

ABOUT ENCATC

ENCATC is the leading European network on cultural management and policy. It is a membership NGO gathering over 100 higher education institutions and cultural organisations in over 40 countries. ENCATC was created in 1992 to encourage the exchange of knowledge, methodologies, experiences, comparative research and regular assessment of the sector's training needs in the broad field of cultural management from a European point of view through a wide range of working groups, projects, activities and events. ENCATC holds the status of an NGO in official partnership with UNESCO, of observer to the Steering Committee for Culture of the Council of Europe, and is co-funded by the Creative Europe programme of the European Union.

ABOUT THE ENCATC RESEARCH AWARD

The ENCATC Research Award on Cultural Policy and Cultural Management was launched in 2014 by the European network on cultural management and policy, ENCATC, to reward the best recently published PhD thesis presented by a young researcher.

This prestigious recognition aims to stimulate academic research in the field of cultural policy and cultural management with an emphasis on its applied implications. The ENCATC Award also has the ambition to contribute to the process of creating a network of scholars who are competent in doing comparative research projects in cultural policy and cultural management.

The ENCATC Research Award is granted each year to a recently published PhD thesis exploring, through comparative and cross-cultural research, issues at stake and taking a step from evaluative (descriptive) to comparative applied research. In addition, this Award is rewarded to a PhD thesis that can inform policymaking and benefit practitioners active in the broad field of culture.

Series titles

N° 4 – Elena BORIN, *Public-Private Partnership in the Cultural sector. A Comparative Analysis of European Models*, 2017.

N° 3 – Annika HAMPEL, *Fair Cooperation. A new Paradigm for Cultural Diplomacy and Arts Management*, 2017.

N° 2 – Alessia USAI, *The Creative City. Cultural Politics and Urban Regeneration between Conservation and Development*, 2016.

N° 1 – Elodie BORDAT-CHAUVIN, *When Cultural Policies Change. Comparing Mexico and Argentina*, 2015.

www.peterlang.com